L. L. Cummings
Peter J. Frost

Editors

Publishing in the Organizational Sciences

2nd Edition

Foundations for
Organizational
Science
A Sage Publications Series

SAGE Publications
International Educational and Professional Publisher
Thousand Oaks   London   New Delhi

For information address:

SAGE Publications, Inc.
2455 Teller Road
Thousand Oaks, California 91320

SAGE Publications Ltd.
6 Bonhill Street
London EC2A 4PU
United Kingdom

SAGE Publications India Pvt. Ltd.
M-32 Market
Greater Kailash I
New Delhi 110 048 India

Printed in the United States of America

Library of Congress Cataloging-in-Publication Data

Main entry under title:

Publishing in the organizational sciences / edited by L. L. Cummings,
    Peter J. Frost. — 2nd ed.
        p.   cm. — (Foundations for organizational science)
    Includes bibliographical references and index.
    ISBN 0-8039-7144-3. — ISBN 0-8039-7145-1 (pbk.)
    1. Management literature—Publishing.   2. Organization—Research—
Methodology.   3. Management literature—Authorship.   I. Cummings,
Larry L.   II. Frost, Peter J.   III. Series.
Z286.M29P82   1995
070.5'068—dc20   94-43876

This book is printed on acid-free paper.

95 96 97 98 99   10 9 8 7 6 5 4 3 2 1

Production Editor: Gillian Dickens   Typesetter: Christina Hill

Contents

Preface
to the 2nd Edition

O ver the past decade, several scholars have made use of the 1985 edition of our book, *Publishing in the Organizational Sciences*. While that version has been out of print for a few years now, we are pleased to present a new book. It is partly based on material included in the 1985 version and partly on new material.

Our motives in publishing this new version are not only to meet the continuing demand for the book but also to reflect several trends in the publishing side of our profession. We have witnessed the development of new journals and a wider diversity of types of outlets. We also think there now exist wider perspectives on reviewing than was the case a decade ago. We have tried to capture these trends and developments in this 1995 book.

We wish to thank Sage Publications for their willingness to work with us in a most encouraging manner. Just as the good graces and professionalism of the Richard D. Irwin Company made the 1985 version possible, so too has the excitement and professionalism of Sage contributed significantly to this version.

L. L. Cummings

Peter J. Frost

Preface
to the 1st Edition

The inspiration for this book came from many sources. The experience and insights from a three-year term as editor of the *Academy of Management Journal*, an early draft of a manuscript on the publishing process, a daytime walk in New York's Central Park prior to the 1982 Academy of Management national meetings, many discussions and meetings in Vancouver, British Columbia, and countless telephone calls between Vancouver and Evanston, Illinois, and several other North American cities—all these have shaped the final product.

We initiated this project because it was our view, from extensive reading of existing work on journal publishing, that no one had provided a true multiplicity of perspectives on the subject in the organizational sciences. No one had incorporated into one place a set of statements, ideas, research findings, and prescriptions that would provide readers with a real sense of the diversity and complexity of issues and approaches characteristic of this field. We believe we have produced a book presenting multiple, contradictory perspectives in publishing in the organizational sciences.

Our interest in a book on publishing stems from our conviction that publishing plays an important role in the field. Scientific journals provide the primary means for communicating and legitimating current ideas and research findings. Journals are also an important basis for establishing author visibility and authenticity in the field. Because journals are an important outlet for scholars' scientific work, they are a primary source for knowledge dissemination and are, in a sense, a calibrating device for the career progress of researchers. Journals also provide a vehicle for contributors to assess their efficacy and competence in their chosen discipline. As will become evident in this book, this instrumentality implies emotional issues for authors as well as for the substantive content of their discipline.

The field of organizational studies has witnessed significant, constructive controversies concerning paradigms, substance, and methodologies in the past decade. We believe a statement on publishing in this era ought to reflect that diversity. Therefore we invited scholars from a variety of backgrounds, both inside and outside the field, to collaborate with us on the project, to write about and, in some cases, to provide research reports on the publishing process in the organizational sciences. Most authors in this volume have considerable experience in the publishing process. We asked some scholars new to the field to provide particular perspectives on the publishing process. Authors wrote on the topics and issues we had identified in the framework of the book, but they were encouraged to follow their instincts in developing their ideas and arguments.

Looking at the finished product, we are very pleased with the outcome. We are impressed with the work of our collaborators. Authors have shared their experiences, expectations, feelings, and insights with us in a refreshingly candid and thoroughly professional manner. The book provides important glimpses of the human side of the enterprise as well as conveying a rich mix of information and ideas about publishing. We believe these perspectives will inform scholars in an interesting way, are sure to spark useful discussion and debate, and should provide themes that researchers will find fruitful for scientific investigation.

Writing this book with our colleagues has been a stimulating and enjoyable learning experience. We have contributed equally to the shaping and production of the book, and the alphabetical ordering of our names on the title page reflects this fact.

We think this is a timely book. We believe that editorial development, evaluation, and gatekeeping have played, are playing, and will continue to play important roles in the healthy development of the field. We hope that this volume contributes usefully to that outcome.

ACKNOWLEDGMENTS

Of course we acknowledge, with great gratitude and admiration, the courage and forthrightness of our contributors. Without them, this book would have been much less, if it had existed at all.

We thank Professors Ronald Taylor and David Cray.

The financial support of the Office of Naval Research and the J. L. Kellogg Research Professorship in Organizational Behavior and the Carlson Chair in Management at the University of Minnesota are gratefully acknowledged. We also thank the Social Sciences and Humanities Research Council of Canada and the Faculty of Commerce and Business Administration at the University of British Columbia.

No project of this magnitude could ever be successfully completed without the able assistance of high-quality secretarial support. We thank Ruth Dresen, Elaine Singer, Lori Thomas, Khim Seow, Rano Sihota, and Shari Altman for their high-quality, thoughtful care in facilitating the completion of this book.

Finally, we are most grateful to several colleagues who provided encouragement and professional support for the idea of such a book. As always, these are the unsung heroes/heroines who help authors to keep moving toward the successful completion of a project through their words and deeds of support and encouragement. Special thanks go to David Hickson, Linda Pike, Richard Side, and Karl Weick.

L. L. Cummings

Peter J. Frost

ONE

Perspectives on Publishing

Conceptual Perspectives
Introduction

L. L. CUMMINGS
PETER J. FROST

What is the publishing system in the organizational sciences? What purpose does it serve? Is it effective? Is it efficient? What should we focus on as important issues when we contemplate the publication system? These questions preoccupy the authors of the chapters in the opening section of the book. As we indicated in the Preface, one objective in producing this volume has been to try to capture the multiplicity of perspectives on publishing in the organizational sciences that we believe exists, and thereby to identify and examine the issues that pertain to this important aspect of scholarly life. A careful reading of the three chapters in this section will provide the reader with a rich and provocative set of ideas for thinking about the publishing process. The frameworks these authors develop and the interpretations they make of the publication system serve as a useful context for the material that follows in later sections of the book.

Professors Frost and Taylor ("Partisan Perspective: A Multiple Level Interpretation of the Manuscript Review Process in Social Science Journals") examine the publishing system in terms of decision-making processes. They focus primarily on the manuscript review decision and apply several different levels of analysis or lenses to explore what they believe is its multifaceted nature. They identify a variety of potential influences on the review decision including ideological and institutional effects that may define the fundamental " 'rules of the [publishing] game' " as well as shape choices of who decides who survives in the system. Other influences might be political effects that arise from pulling and mulling around a journal's review decisions by actors with different perceptions, interests, and amounts of power (and that may produce bargained decisions); organizational effects such as routines and standard operating procedures of a journal that may serve to enhance or to constrain the choices editors have for determining outcomes of manuscript reviews; and the effects that rational actors (e.g., editors or reviewers), through their preference functions, may bring to bear on the merits of manuscripts submitted for review to a given journal.

Frost and Taylor suggest a variety of research questions and applications that they believe will further our understanding and operation of the publication system. Their acknowledged bias is that of authors whose concern is, in large measure, with ways to create and maintain manuscript review decisions that are fair and open to innovation and variety.

Stanley Deetz ("The Social Production of Knowledge and the Commercial Artifact") argues that all knowledge, particularly in its published forms, is social and historical. Thus it is necessarily affected by prejudices of time, perspective, and space. However, Professor Deetz's analysis is *not* one of cynicism and despair. To quote him, "The presence of prejudice gives academic research and publication whatever life and relevance it has." He develops quite eloquently the argument that "to the extent that the commercial value of having a publication exceeds the social value of its knowledge claim, publication review processes may strive to be fair but the publication process as a whole becomes a strategic game lacking social responsibility, demeaning both its participants and the society that pays for it."

Deetz expands and defends these themes by analyzing knowledge production as a political process, a social process, and a communication process. He concludes his chapter with constructive suggestions as to directions we might take to make knowledge production and communication more democratic and worthwhile to society.

Professor Nord ("Looking at Ourselves as We Look at Others: An Exploration of the Publication System for Organization Research") treats the publication system as an organization, producing published research on organizations and organizational behavior. He turns the theories, models, and prescriptions of organizational theory and design, which we have developed for studying the organizations of others, to the analysis of our own publication system. He generates his analysis by constructing an imaginative and evocative MBA class session in which the publishing-system-as-organization is presented as a case to class members. They use as the reference point for their analyses a selection of major works in the field on organizational analysis, design, and power.

His approach to the publication system provides us with a variety of observations and insights. While some of these overlap with the other authors in this section, many are unique to his analysis. Nord suggests that the work of any field is to build theory, attract support from external constituents, and produce data that people inside and outside the field view as being of high quality. He attributes the low status of the organizational sciences to their failure to perform well on these criteria, but points to the potentially strong market for the products of these sciences, for the products of its publication system. He points to the centralized control structure of the publication system as a likely source of both a lack of innovation and a lack of replication of ideas. Journals have become too mechanistic, too much like palaces. They may be prisoners of their histories, the design fashions of the era of their origins, and the objectives and intentions of their founders and thus may be insensitive to current needs. They have become, perhaps, out of touch with their environments. Nord suggests the need for alternative organizational structures such as adhocracies and tenets to supplement and balance those in existence at present. Through the analyses and conversations of the members of his imaginary class, he traces out the dilemmas and offers solutions to the problems he identifies in the publication system.

ISSUES AND PERSPECTIVES

Several interesting issues emerge from the discussions the authors provide in their chapters. We highlight some of these here.

Communication Versus Control. Perhaps most pervasive of the themes addressed by the authors is that of the primary purpose of the publication system. The basic functions of the publication system, according to the authors, appear to be those of communication and control. These two functions are not necessarily independent of one another. The authors differ in the extent to which they emphasize one or the other of these functions and the implications of each function.

Journals provide a tried-and-true means to formally manage this flow, to communicate to readers manuscripts of high quality, screening out those of lesser value; to communicate recognition of good scholarship inside a field; and to communicate accomplishment of excellence so that decision makers, inside or outside the field, have a basis for determining allocation of resources for new research endeavors.

As a communication device, the system is flexible. Increased demand for a particular product denied access to existing journals can be met through establishing new journals. The market-sensitive, mediated exchange between authors and readers will determine the life span of ideas in journals. One source of inflexibility in the communication system stems from the role that libraries play in preserving journals and journal content well beyond the point that the readership would normally support.

Authors in this section devote attention to the publication process as a system of control. In each case the implication is that identification and management of the control aspects of publishing will improve the effectiveness of its communication function. Nord is perhaps most explicit about this trade-off. Professors Frost and Taylor, and Nord, all discuss the control function in journals as being a response to, a consequence of, scarce resources, particularly in the form of limited journal space. Differential access to resources among members of a scientific community and the institutionalizing forces of the publication system influence choices of gatekeepers and membership in the scholarly community. Frost and Taylor examine the dysfunctions of control in terms of gatekeepers (e.g., relative representation of males and females as editors and reviewers) and the effects of power differentials between actors in the review process, most notably between editors, reviewers, and authors. They include a discussion of the effects of powerlessness on the behavior of actors in the system and suggest that, particularly where such feelings exist among authors, one might expect alienation that drains the field of vitality. Control that leads to feelings of powerlessness may induce otherwise productive authors to leave the field or to switch to unimaginative, safe, game-playing research.

Nord points out that the publication system as a whole provides a wide variety of mechanisms for communication of scientific knowledge. Not all channels are equally powerful, however. "Those who control the most important channels exercise disproportionately more power than the others." Nord identifies benefits of control in the system. He includes in this context outcomes such as the screening out of low-quality work, protection of consumers from fraud, forcing of high standards among producers, and protection of the status of the profession. He identifies as costs of control publication lags, reviewer bias, and the screening out of new ideas in favor of routine material. He discusses also the high economic costs of production and the substantial time and opportunity costs of editing and reviewers that accompany the operation of the system.

He sees the conflict and struggles around manuscript review decisions in journals as potentially healthy. However, the centralized control structures of journals and the long periods of time during which they operate with a particular set of institutionalized patterns of relationships are likely to create conditions in which the leadership is out of touch with its environment. Such conflict and struggles as do exist are muted and unproductive. Furthermore, reward systems of most journals reward caution and punish risk taking, making it likely that editorial decisions are conservative. As a result, journals yield products that are standardized and predictable. Journals, then, are equipped to handle the routine rather than innovation and diversity.

Given that Frost and Taylor, and Nord, consider control in journals to be more or less dysfunctional, to inhibit open dialogue and discourse in the organizational sciences, what are their suggested remedies? Their prescriptions are wide ranging and the reader needs to consult the respective chapters for a full treatment of the subject.

Some recommendations are aimed at *restructuring journal organization.* These include Frost's and Taylor's suggestions for the formation of dual structure organizations—one to select and process the normal flow of manuscripts in the system; the other, operating through temporary project teams, to initiate and produce special issues devoted to current topics and knowledge areas. A second change suggested is that editors take steps to ensure that the composition of editorial boards be heterogeneous, to reflect the paradigm diversity of the field, and thus to increase the chances that journal output will reflect this diversity. A fourth organizational change, discussed in Nord's chapter, is for a reconceptualization of the role of journals from that of *archive* to that of *post office.* Journals, as post offices, could be reorganized to process a variety of types of messages: some long (papers), some short (notes), some in bundles (a volume/issue of journal articles), some as single, discrete items (single articles). The range of communication media in such a configuration could be broader than at present; it could include the use of computer technologies, an idea Nord discusses.

Some recommendations are aimed at *changing reward systems.* Nord suggests, for example, that journal editors signal, through their actions in the journals, rewards for both experimentation and replication. Creative failures should be tolerated and made visible in the hopes of spurring other, eventually more successful efforts in a research area. Replications of studies would be encouraged by making a specific amount of journal space (e.g., 10%) available in each journal issue for well-conducted studies of this nature.

Some recommendations are aimed at the *management of individual actions and attitudes.* Frost and Taylor suggest that editors manage the power differential between them and other actors in the process, most notably between themselves and authors. Such actions could come in a variety of ways that would serve to make the editor's relative power advantage work for the author's cause. For example, choice of reviewers to protect a manuscript that is interesting but controversial, or coaching authors to help them deal with seemingly contradictory feedback and advice from reviewers, reflect this idea.

Some recommendations are aimed at *changing the amount of resources in the system*. Nord discusses the possibilities of increasing journal space in prestigious journals by attaching property rights to the individuals who produce research in the field. He argues that, at the very least, attention be given to directing to journal publications some of the revenue that accrues to practitioners and organizations who use and profit from the research findings published by scholars in the field.

Professors Frost, Taylor, Deetz, and Nord have provided collectively a very comprehensive treatment of the communication versus control theme. While we are cognizant of Nord's caution that a few examples may not reflect a change in values, and we believe the pressures for distortion of communication and dysfunctional control exist in the system and need addressing, we would offer the following additional thoughts on the matter. Some of the issues raised by the authors are recognized by gatekeepers in the field and some of the change recommendations suggested by the authors have been implemented in recent years in one or another of the organizational science journals. Special issues on qualitative methodology and organizational culture in *ASQ*, appointments of women to editorial boards and to editorship of major journals such as the *Academy of Management Journal*, the *Academy of Management Review*, and the *Journal of Management Studies*, and controversial articles and debates published in the *Academy of Management Review*, *ASQ*, and the *Journal of Management* illustrate this point. Also, symposia on paradigm diversity, critical theory, and alternative research methodologies have all been presented at regional and national meetings of professional scholars in the field. This volume represents the same concern with diversity and a desire to open the dialogue and debate on important issues in the field.

Communication versus control in the publication system is not an either/or proposition. That is, it is not simply a matter of open communication or of control of its content and distribution. It involves a realization that, as long as we use journals as the major means of communication in our field, we will also be involved with controlling resources and outcomes. What is needed is a commitment to creating conditions that serve to keep communication open so as to advance knowledge, thereby resisting the press to uniformly routine and unnecessarily conservative publication decisions while at the same time preserving the *positive* aspects of control that serve to legitimate good scholarship and avoid publication of the work of frauds and charlatans. We are aware of the complexity of this task. To take seriously the concept of paradigm diversity and to be interested in fostering dialogue and debate is to realize that we work in a difficult terrain. Deciding what is false or even faked knowledge and distinguishing what is good scholarship from that which is the work of charlatans is not a simple matter. It turns on more than an examination of the facts, the academic merits of a case. It also involves an awareness of the political and historical underpinnings of the different perspectives involved.

We think that many of the changes in the formal publication system proposed by the authors in this section will promote an openness to fruitful dialogue in the field. As we pointed out above, we believe there is some anecdotal evidence of experimentation in journals along many of the lines they suggest. We consider further that the informal component of the publication system ought to be a target for change so that it becomes, in its various facets, more explicitly sensitive to needs, expressed in this section of the book, for forums for discourse across the various perspectives in the field. Symposia at professional meetings that bring together scholars of different persuasions and interests or deal with new, controversial, or unorthodox topics represent a grassroots response to the need for such communications. Such events help socialize researchers and sensitize them to the issues and arguments of a topic or field of study. Given that such events carry little weight in the legitimation of new knowledge because they are rarely published and are thus perishable, we believe, in addition, there is a need for more proactive and structured approaches to harness these existing informal channels. Options that we think are viable (and that we see in increasing evidence in the field) are organized conferences, some as single events, others that recur, that bring together scholars of diverse backgrounds to debate and discuss the interesting and important ideas of their fields. The product of such conferences can be captured in print, through monographs. These publications are frequently more flexible in their format and space availability than are journals and can thus capture many of the nuances and the complexity of the knowledge content produced.

In recent years, examples of these events include the annual conference on Interpretive Approaches to Organizational Communication at Alta, Utah, which brings together scholars from organizational behavior and speech communication; the conference on folklore and organization analysis at Santa Monica, California, in 1983, which featured organizational behaviorists, folklorists, and managers; the Organizational Culture Conference in Vancouver in 1984, which included scholars from anthropology, sociology, the humanities, speech communication, and organizational scientists of several different theoretical and philosophical persuasions as well as members of the business community. A final illustration is the newly instituted annual international conference on organization symbolism, held this year in Lund, Sweden. All these reflect, in our view, healthy responses to the need for open communication that may, over time, positively affect our journals, the formal publication system.

Careers and Careerism. All the authors in this section deal with the theme of careers and careerism. In each chapter is repeated a concern that the association between some aspects of publication in journals and membership and advancement in the field is dysfunctional to the field. All point to the gamesmanship it fosters and the stultification of good scholarship that results.

The connection is one that hinges in many cases on a numbers game. Progress in the field in such cases is measured in terms of number of publications, regardless of quality. Careerism frequently is the result. Frost and Taylor point out another variety of careerism, which involves engagement in research that does not necessarily interest the investigator, or advance the field, but is easy to do, is safe and acceptable. Nord identifies another variety in the form of research that focuses on fads and opportunism. They also point to investigators who break their research reports into several pieces for multiple publication. In many cases the report involved is essentially one integral contribution deserving of a single publication.

The interrelationship between careers and publishing is complex. The publishing system provides in one sense a basis on which the ladders for research careers are fashioned and this reflects not only formal steps such as gaining tenure and the right to teach and do research in the field, as well as receiving promotions up the hierarchy in university institutions, but also less formal ones that reflect increasing recognition and stature in the field. Career progression may or may not involve careerism. It depends upon the motives and actions of the individual.

Publication in academic journals may also be a rite of passage into the profession. This is especially so when the journal involved is deemed prestigious. While stages such as the receipt of a Ph.D. are also entry points into the field, acceptance on one's own terms as a scholar in a community wider than one's graduating university can come from initial publication in a major journal.

Journals also provide a forum for those whose careers are established, who continue to do work that is of potential interest to others in the research community. Publishing in journals provides scholars, at this stage in their careers, with an opportunity to test the strength of their ideas against the review system and to share them, if published, with a wider audience than would be available using any other publication medium in the field. It is a source of sustaining established scholars in the mainstream of a field, keeping them interested, sharp, and productive. Charles Perrow provides an insightful analysis of the career stages of a scholar in Chapter 12, "Journaling Careers."

Identifying these three aspects of the relationship between careers and publishing provides a way in which to approach the problems and possibilities inherent in the relationship. Operating the ladder that is inherent in the publication system so that it facilitates career progressions but not careerism requires the concerted attention of members of a scientific community. Senior members of that community serve as gatekeepers of journals, as members of committees that pass judgment on tenure and promotion cases, and as advisers on doctoral committees. In each case, as members of such bodies, they have opportunities to decouple to a large extent the link between playing publication games and being rewarded by career advancement and to influence the use of other, more constructive responses by their peers and those more junior in the field. Also, as many of the authors in this volume point out in their ideas and in their presentation of their ideas, an explicit attention to and pride in *craftsmanship* rather than gamesmanship needs to be nurtured in entering scholars and reinforced in those who are insiders.

While the insiders can have some influence, researchers in turn need to test the limits that others, especially gatekeepers, will allow rather than to assume those limits and adjust their actions accordingly. Applying Nord's notion of "seeing ourselves as we see others," we should "practice on ourselves what we prescribe for others." If we can recommend that our counterparts in other organizations take risks and stick their necks out so that they and their organizations succeed, we ought to be able to suggest the same for ourselves and to take steps to facilitate those actions. (We are grateful to Ms. Susan Koch, a graduate student at the University of Texas, for this insight.)

Viewing the publication process as a "rite of passage" for emerging scholars ought to sensitize us, particularly editors and reviewers, to the need to invoke criteria of care as well as competence in our handling of such cases. The chapters by Graham and Stablein (Chapter 6) and by Schoorman (Chapter 7) are thought-provoking and informative in this regard. They make clear too the trade-off that must be considered when we call for full disclosure of reviewer information to authors. Full communication of substance is desirable and frequently provided in the review process. Communication of tone (especially if negative) is a matter, in our view, for editorial judgment and discretion.

Legitimation. The final theme we discuss here is important and sometimes neglected in discussions of the publication system. We refer to the question of legitimation of the research enterprise in the organizational sciences. Nord points
out that one major roadblock to experimentation with our publication system is
the way publication systems of other disciplines work. It raises the question: Do
we have to look like they do, or at least appear sensible to them, especially given
our relatively low status, to be taken seriously, to survive?

We think it important that the world of other disciplines, of granting agencies
and other sources of legitimation, not be forgotten as we examine the publication
system. It serves multiple purposes, after all, and this is an important function of
the system whether intended or not. Nevertheless, we ought to be able to investigate the concerns about the effectiveness of the system raised by Frost and
Taylor, Deetz, and Nord, and to change it, where necessary, in ways that meet
standards of humanity and of science that *we,* as a community of organizational
scientists, consider important. We need ways to deal with the environment while
also being able to make changes inside the system, if this is necessary. We need
to look at ourselves and to look at others.

It is necessary that we manage the boundaries of the system effectively. Those
outside our publication system will inevitably judge our product by the rules
they understand. We need to identify, train, reward, and nurture those among us
who can educate such constituencies and effectively translate to them the validity of what is reflected in journals that do experiment with and promote diversity
in their publications. We need to protect innovation while at the same time promoting our interests externally.

Professors Frost, Taylor, Deetz, and Nord have identified, through their frameworks, many of the important issues that relate to the publication system. They
have confirmed and grounded the usefulness of some of the efforts that are currently made to make our journals more responsive to the field. They have pointed
up other aspects of the system where there is a need for investigation and change.
They stretch us in novel ways that should enhance our understanding of the system's operation, which serves to benefit both the individual scholar and the field
of organizational scientists. Their chapters follow.

1

Partisan Perspective
A Multiple-Level Interpretation of the Manuscript Review Process in Social Science Journals

PETER J. FROST

RONALD N. TAYLOR

One powerful source of influence on the direction of a scientific field is the academic journal. Knowledge in a field is disseminated in large measure through manuscripts published in journals; the careers of scholars, their visibility in a field, and their mobility in and across academic institutions are significantly influenced by the degree to which their work is published in the respected journals of their profession. At the same time, the potential for game playing in the review process is made explicit in prescriptions for manuscript publication given, somewhat tongue in cheek, by Chambers and Herzberg (1968) and by Mahoney (1978). Tactics they prescribe to authors for "winning" the refereeing game include use of obscure references, flattery, a barrage of submissions to an editor, footnotes acknowledging powerful friends, the highlighting of successful results, anticipating reviewer problems in the manuscript, and frequent citation of their own works.

Such influence and criticisms should be carefully studied to understand the nature of the influence and its relationship to the development of a scientific field. Despite numerous studies of how social science journals work (see Lindsey, 1978, for a comprehensive review of research), no conceptual or analytic framework exists for examining these phenomena. At the core of our publication systems is the manuscript publishability decision. Systematic studies of manuscript publishability decisions are needed to increase our awareness of what we say and what we do as scientists. Such reflexivity by social scientists has been called for by writers such as Gouldner (1976) and Habermas (1973) but is rarely attended to in practice.

We believe that academic journals and the publishability decisions that occur within them are organizational phenomena that are amenable to study through applications of organizational science knowledge. Despite the existence of theories and empirical research methodologies that organizational scientists have developed and applied enthusiastically to a wide variety of topics and situations, there has been little attempt to apply these same resources to look inward, critically, at our own institutions in an attempt to increase understanding of the very nature and development of a field itself (Nord, 1980). Application of organizational science knowledge to the academic journal represents a step in this direction.

In this chapter we analyze the manuscript review process in social science journals, and particularly the manuscript publishability decision, by applying a number of conceptual lenses or frameworks that have been developed in the organizational science field. The analysis is conducted at three levels: societal, organizational, and individual. First we apply an ideological influence perspective or model, which focuses on journal decision making in the broad context of scientific communities within which journal decision making takes place. Then, to the manuscript review process we apply perspectives derived from Allison's (1971) framework of decision making (the governmental politics, organizational processes, and rational actor models).

Based on our analysis of the journal decision-making process from the vantage points provided by these four models, we discuss possible avenues for further research on the publishability decisions of journals and possible improvements to the process.

Criticisms of journals and the decisions about what manuscripts to publish are discussed in several places in the relevant literature (e.g., Bedeian, Downey, Price, & Salancik, 1980; Frost, Taylor, & Cummings, 1981; Latané, 1979a, 1979b; Lindsey, 1978; Peters, 1976). Major sources of irritation and disaffection for dissatisfied readers tend to be the lack of quality in journal content, sterile journal material, and irrelevance of articles. Authors identify high rejection rates for their manuscripts (for example, four out of five submissions), excessive publication lags of accepted manuscripts, and unclear criteria used by editors and reviewers to accept or reject manuscripts. Journal editors sometimes express frustration with the poor quality of manuscripts and identify their own concerns as being high workloads, increasing production costs, publication deadlines, and authors' and institutions' demands for quick and/or favorable decisions to aid pending promotion and tenure decisions. Reviewers are often dissatisfied with high workloads and relatively low extrinsic rewards.

The central issues that underlie these and other concerns about the review process may relate to four major dimensions of decision making. The first dimension is *efficiency* of the decision process: that is, speed of decisions, rapidity of knowledge dissemination, cost control, and the editors', reviewers', and authors' use of time. A second dimension is *innovation:* openness to publishing material on new paradigms, new ideas, new methodologies, controversial issues, or material that excites, informs, or even challenges existing theories and practice. The third dimension concerns *quality,* which relates to the nature of knowledge produced: adequacy of arguments, methodology, and analysis contained in manuscripts (essentially a concern with preventing Type I or Type II decision errors). Quality also relates to decisions about the initial correctness of questions asked (a concern with preventing Type III errors). The fourth dimension deals with the *fairness* of decisions made: It is assumed that all scientists and their ideas have an equal chance to be published in journals. Fairness is the degree to which this ideal is fulfilled.

These dimensions are interrelated and interact so that improvements on one may involve improvements or declines on one or more of the other dimensions. Wade, for example, expresses the trade-off between the dimensions of innovation and quality as the "accept is to reject paradox" (Wade, 1979, p. 487). He explains that, while openness to manuscripts with variable content increases clutter and reduces overall quality, being closed to such material may cut off promising material. The unselective editor, on the other hand, may produce a journal containing too much worthless material. If too selective, however, the editor may create a sterile journal. Similarly, editors who increase efficiency through reducing decision turnaround time cause reviewers to rush to meet decision deadlines, thereby reducing the competence of reviews and review decisions.

Our analyses and our prescriptions for researching and operating the review process have an intended bias. Our approach is primarily that which represents the *author.* As such, the predominant emphasis of the research issues we identify and the prescriptions we propose has to do with innovation and fairness, although we do not ignore questions of efficiency and quality. Our perspective is likely to be different in some respects than those of other partisans—editors and reviewers, for example. We believe that discussion based upon the values, experiences, questions, and empirical answers that each partisan brings to the debate will greatly enhance our understanding and management of the publishing process, so that it serves well individual authors and the community of scholars in which they work.

TOWARD UNDERSTANDING
THE MANUSCRIPT REVIEW PROCESS

In this section we provide a conceptual framework for analysis of the manuscript review process, review some of the relevant research, discuss questions that need to be researched to better understand these processes, and identify appropriate research methodologies. We examine journal decision making in the larger context of society and then apply Allison's framework to the decision process. This framework integrates a diversity of research literatures that are not typically juxtaposed to examine a phenomenon in the field. Allison's governmental politics model emphasizes coalitions, power, and political behavior; his organizational processes model uses organizational theory, in particular that which deals with formal organizational structure and design; and his rational actor model harnesses decision theory literature. Each of the four models we use draws upon a particular set of assumptions, variables, and relationships. Each model brings into focus aspects and issues concerning the decision that are ignored by others but that appear to have a bearing on understanding decision making in journals.

Ideological Influence and the Manuscript Review Process

Ideology represents what a society defines as reality; it comprises beliefs about how the world operates, and articulates the values, expectations, standards, and so forth that are intended to inform and orient people's behavior (Berger & Luckmann, 1966; Wilson, 1973). Decision making, given this perspective, is influenced by the values, expectations, and standards of the society in which it is embedded (Clegg, 1975; Edelman, 1977; Gouldner, 1976; Habermas, 1973). This perspective brings into focus the ways a body of people—a profession, a school of thought, a community of scientists—sees, behaves, and acts.

The characteristics of an ideology are frequently "taken for granted" by most members of a society so that the ideology's impact on behavior is not immediately apparent unless made explicit in some way (Edelman, 1977). Nevertheless, an ideology is created, interpreted, maintained, and defended by the actions and attitudes of members of a society who have a vested interest in the ideology and its perpetuation. Such individuals constitute a dominant coalition within the society. The impact of ideology on decision making is assumed to be upon the very definition of social reality—including the "game" and "the rules of the game"— within which decisions are made (Legge, 1978). The ideological influence perspective on decision making is concerned with the societal values, expectations, and standards that surround the choice of a decision maker and what that choice reveals about what is legitimately included in the decision maker's domain (and about what is excluded from that domain).

Competing definitions of acceptable or legitimate scientific endeavor and notions of dominating ideologies, which shape the nature, focus, and content of scientific communication, are brought into focus when the manuscript review process is examined in terms of ideological influence (Clark, 1973; Edelman, 1977; Gouldner, 1976; Kuhn, 1970). Given this perspective, decisions to publish or reject manuscripts reflect editorial attention to a value system—frequently taken for granted—that governs the scientific research process. This value system may determine, in large measure, what is included in, or excluded from, the content of academic journals. Clark (1973), speaking as a black researcher and editor, articulated the ideological influence on scientific endeavors in his critique of psychology in which he argued psychology excluded discussion, research, and publication in areas of study such as exploitation, imperialism, and oppression—areas that are defined as important by black thinkers. Instead, Clark pointed out, psychology legitimated areas such as behavior control, deviance, criminality, and so forth. Editors, from Clark's perspective, are selected and then act to preserve the status quo of a dominant ideology of science. Editors attempting to legitimate knowledge that does not fit the prevailing social reality of the field in which the journal is published may not survive in the role. In the extreme case, the journal itself may not survive.

Ideologies are formulated or interpreted and are maintained by those in a group who have a vested interest in the values and practices inherent in particular ideologies. Given this assumption, selection of editors becomes an important choice for a dominant elite given that editorial choices of manuscripts for publication reflect and shape what is believed to be valid scientific knowledge. Selection of editors for journals as a reflection of ideological influence has been reported in the literature (e.g., Crane, 1967; Lewin & Duchan, 1971; Mitchell,

1951; Teghtsoonian, 1974; White, 1970; Yoels, 1971, 1974). Yoels (1971, 1974) studied the pattern of appointments of editor-in-chief to the *American Sociological Review* and other social science journals during the period 1948 to 1971. He reported that doctoral graduates of Columbia and Harvard who were editors-in-chief of social science journals were significantly more likely than other editors-in-chief to select their own university doctoral graduates for editorial appointments. Yoels suggested the existence of a relationship between the power structure of social science disciplines and the appointment of editors and the resultant dissemination of information (Yoels, 1974).

The virtual absence of women as editors of social science journals may also reflect a dominating value system. In APA journals during the period 1929 to 1949, Mitchell (1951) found that women accounted for only 1 journal editor year out of 187 journal editor years. During this same time period, 20% of APA Fellows were women. Teghtsoonian (1974) documents more recent evidence suggesting underrepresentation of women as editors of psychology journals. She used two samples of journals: (a) 11 journals in 1970-1972 and (b) APA journals in 1972. She observed that women were represented as published authors at a level consistent with their division membership in APA. However, in sample A, 5% of editors were women while 15% were authors. In sample B, 7% of editors were women, while 14% were authors. She examines several competing explanations for her findings, including lower publication rates and lower research quality for women researchers. Despite some sex-based differences in the sample, such as lower publication rates, the magnitude of the difference between women as editors and as authors suggests that editor selection in the journals studied was biased in favor of males. We suspect that this bias may be less marked in the present era, but we lack systematic empirical evidence to confirm this view.

Researching the Review Process. The ideological influence perspective on journal decision making suggests other issues that concern defining, maintaining, and communicating a social reality. Specifically, it appears useful to develop and test hypotheses about the mechanisms and dynamics through which the editors (and reviewers) of journals in a field are selected and monitored (including an examination of selection criteria), about the content that is included and excluded in journals as a result of the manuscripts that are accepted and rejected by editors (and reviewers), and about the likely roles that dominant coalitions might play in determining, interpreting, and maintaining ideology through their relationship to the manuscript review process. This perspective also directs us to a concern with the selection, training, and reward systems used to find, prepare, monitor, and motivate scholars in the various fields of science.

Focus on social class, on institutional, sex-structured, and other stratification patterns of scholars who research, edit, and publish in a field, is important. Equally important is an examination of the historical development of journals to attempt to understand the process of ideological influence on editorial decision making. If biased selection of editors occurs in journals, how does it occur? Are certain research groups excluded by virtue of inbreeding within research communities or covert networks of scholars? Lewin and Duchan (1971) and White (1970) suggest that bias against selection of women as journal editors may occur because men are reluctant to sponsor women in professions and are also reluctant to include them in informal networks of information and association that might serve to increase the visibility of women in the research communities from which editors are drawn. It is possible that influences such as social class may operate differentially in different subfields in a scientific community. For example, editorial boards of journals in some subfields of social science have a high representation of women and of minority groups, while this is not so in journals of other subfields.

One criticism of scholars in social science fields is that their research efforts are frequently opportunistic and entrepreneurial. Critics argue that topics chosen are faddish, research findings are published piecemeal, studies are rarely longitudinal, and systematic programs of research are rare (Dunnette, 1963; Nord, 1978, 1980). Examinations of the existence, extent, and effects of these practices in the context of the selection, training, and reward systems of a field may well prove fruitful.

The issues identified above are likely to be amenable to research techniques such as content analysis, interviewing, documentary analysis, and participant observation. Application of techniques and orientation from fields such as hermeneutics and literary criticism should also prove useful in seeking answers to questions about ideological influences and the publication of research (Burke, 1966; Edelman, 1971, 1977; Gusfield, 1976; Huff, 1983; Toulmin, 1958).

Ideological Influence Applications to the Manuscript Review Process

Our major concern when analyzing the manuscript review process from a societal perspective is with ideologies and with domination. Strategies intended to reduce the communicative distortion inherent in such domination (Habermas, 1973, 1975), and to encourage innovativeness of actors in the review process, ought to emphasize minimization of dominance—through actions on system-wide variables—linked to manuscript review decisions.

From this societal perspective, reducing power differentials may require voluntary or institutionalized action. Voluntary power sharing can be facilitated by the creation of a community of organizational scientists who can and will choose to encourage the development of diverse approaches to the assessment of knowledge. The content and intent of selection, training, and reward systems in the field ought to emphasize and support risk taking in decision making; tolerance for alternative interpretations of reality; ease and skill in use of power-sharing tactics; efforts to invent, rather than imitate, in developing and disseminating knowledge; and an orientation toward problems and situations that favor diversity rather than uniformity (Frost, 1980; Weick, 1979).

At this macro-societal level of influence, actors impinging on the review process include ruling elites and various publics, most notably the professional readership in the field. Providing structured avenues to shared power and thus greater flexibility and innovativeness in the process involves increasing the options and reducing the dependencies that actors have on other actors engaged in the decision process. Funding and other resources provided to authors, editors, and reviewers ought to be free from constraints intended to influence choices of topics, and recommendations and decisions on manuscript publication. Funding ought to allow actors the flexibility to go elsewhere for decisions and actions, to initiate new ideas, to start new journals, or to bypass the journal altogether through books or other media forms.

A different strategy for minimizing communicative distortion and for increasing innovativeness involves establishing or facilitating informal and formal avenues for the exercise of countervailing power in a scientific system. Formal countervailing power can be created by establishing boards of appeal to whom people can take grievances relating to the production and publication of scientific knowledge (Newman, 1966). An author who feels intimidated or wronged in the review process could appeal a review decision and have the manuscript subjected to independent assessment. Readers who perceive censorship of ideas and methodologies could have recourse to the same device. Another strategy for opening the journal system to new ideas involves representation of different paradigms to key decision-making committees in a field.

Informal countervailing power can be established through legitimation and encouragement of lobbying behavior by people who perceive inequalities and abuses of power in the review process of journals in their field. A norm for scientists that stresses collective action to press for change would likely stimulate diversity and awareness of alternatives in the process.

A more radical strategy with implications for avoiding dysfunctions in the field has been advocated by Nord (1978). He suggested that the manuscript review process in academic journals be eliminated. This has the obvious advantage of saving a number of the costs associated with the review process. The costs saved are reviewers' time, the opportunity costs incurred by rejecting valuable manuscripts, and the loss of manuscripts containing at least some sound original ideas. In addition to these cost savings, the "open gate" policy produces the benefits of deemphasizing the importance of publications in career development and professional status and, we hope, its adoption would lead to less gamesmanship and more emphasis upon publication quality rather than quantity. This is important where publications have become ends in themselves rather than means for reporting and advancing knowledge.

Nord's prescription has its costs, some of which he acknowledges. He speculated that in the short run the journals would be plagued by a glut of low-quality articles and that the number of pages would be costly to publish. However, he suggested that the use of a researcher's number of publications to evaluate his or her career progress would be less attractive and researchers might become more concerned with presenting a complete development of their work rather than rushing into print with its dissected parts. Nevertheless, abolition of editorial review as a basis for publication of manuscripts remains a high-risk venture, which is unlikely to be embraced by journals, in which editors perceive a need for control of costs, publication time, and quality. Nord's proposed strategy is intended as a jolt to scientists, to generate thought and discussion about extremes in the operation of academic journals on a field.

THE GOVERNMENTAL POLITICS
MODEL OF MANUSCRIPT REVIEW

The governmental politics perspective views decision making as the political result of bargaining among organizational actors. This model focuses attention on the perceptions, motivations, power, and maneuvers of players in a political game. Decisions are made by pulling and hauling among the organizational actors—the impact of these actors is depicted in terms of their access to the game and to the regularized channels of action in the organization, to their power and skill, and to their desire to use this power. Power is assumed to be influenced by variables such as position (in the game), expertise, control over information, ability to influence other players' objectives, access to others with information, and so forth. Actors take stands and act in the bargaining exchange in terms of their power, their perspectives on the problem, their stakes in the issue, and the deadlines that are attached to decisions.

Manuscript review decisions are seen as the outcomes of bargaining among key actors. Evidence of the political nature of the review process comes from several sources. Pfeffer, Leong, and Strehl (1977) have pointed out that the assessment of the worth of social science research output is far more subjective and more political than is the case with physical science research. They observed greater use of particularistic standards of evaluation (assessments influenced by nepotism, friendship, professional affiliation, and so forth) in social than in physical science fields. Mahoney (1977), in a controlled experiment, reported reviewer bias against manuscripts containing results contrary to reviewers' theoretical perspectives. Similarly, Abramowitz, Gomes, and Abramowitz (1975) observed that reviewers with leftist leanings provided more generous evaluations of manuscripts containing data supporting proactivism of students than those containing data supporting antiactivism students. Mahoney, Kazdin, and Kenigsberg (1978) found a correlation between self-citation by authors and reviewers' acceptance of manuscripts. In a study of editorial decisions in management and social science journals, Kerr, Tolliver, and Petree (1977) reported author reputation as being positively correlated with manuscript acceptance. Silverman (1976), drawing on his experience as an editor of the *Journal of Higher Education,* described the boundary spanning covert roles an editor plays as a means of accomplishing goals and of getting things done. The editor, in Silverman's experience, is sometimes a methodologist, sometimes a scholar. On occasions, he is an organizational man (Silverman's terms) and, at other times, a social being; each role is a response to different organizational actors and issues.

Frost et al. (1981), in a preliminary report of interviews with organizational science journal editors, observed that an important source of editors' perceived power resides in their conscious choice of reviewers. Publication of controversial or marginal manuscripts, in this sense, depends on the choice of potentially sympathetic or hostile reviewers.

Rodman and Mancini (1977) identify three areas of editorial decision making that are not open equally to all actors in the review system. These are submissions by authors who are sponsored by individuals of special status, inside track submissions that come from authors having a special relationship with editors, and background communications between some—but not all—parties to a review decision (e.g., confidential reviewer comments to editors or telephone, luncheon, and other informal discussions between editors and reviewers about an author's submission, and so on). Rodman and Mancini report that editors acknowledge a high incidence of each of these three events. While their findings do not reveal what editors do in response to such submissions, in combination with the research cited above, they do provide a sense of the political nature of at least some aspects of the review process.

Given the lack of agreement among social scientists as to what constitutes valuable research and what a given manuscript contributes to a field, and given the prevailing uncertainty as to causes and effects in prevailing models and theories in social science, it is perhaps reasonable to predict that the review decision outcome will involve judgment and/or compromise among the various actors in the process (Thompson, 1967).

Decision-making strategies involving judgment and compromise have been depicted and discussed within the context of organizational choice by several authors (Baldridge, 1971; Cyert & March, 1963; Frost & Hayes, 1979; Pettigrew, 1973; Pfeffer, 1981; Pfeffer & Salancik, 1978). Such strategies include an important role for power and political behavior as determinants of decision outcomes. The power available to actors in the decision process appears to reside in organizational and individual sources. Hickson, Hinings, Lee, Schneck, and Pennings (1971) and Pfeffer (1981) identify some organizational sources such as level of formal authority, degree of control over resources, accessibility to information, and ability to reduce uncertainty for other organizational members. French and Raven (1960) identify some individual sources (frequently linked to organizational sources) such as level of expertise and personal charisma.

Researching the Review Process. The manuscript review decision perceived as a political game or process brings into focus several actors, the most important ones being, perhaps, the editor, the reviewer, and the author. These three actors can be depicted as a triad as well as in various dyadic combinations (editor-author, editor-reviewer, author-reviewer). Each of these actors brings to such interactions various resources and personal characteristics that provide him or her with power bases from which to influence the manuscript review decision. The bases include formal authority or position power (perhaps most applicable to the editor), control over information (for example, ground rules for manuscript acceptability), access to audiences and legitimation of ideas (a gatekeeping role available to editors and reviewers), availability of alternative manuscripts and of outlets for manuscripts, as well as the actor's status (often institutionally linked), and technical expertise.

Research that examines power differences and relationships among these key actors should prove of considerable value in understanding how manuscript decisions are made. It should be possible to identify conditions in which actors are relatively equal in power in the triad or in a given dyad as well as those in which actors are relatively unequal in power. Different behaviors by respective actors and different outcomes would be expected under each of these two conditions. We should expect, under conditions of relatively equal power, for example, that behavior of the actors would approximate a negotiated or bargained outcome involving extensive dialogue between the actors.

We should expect, under conditions of unequal power, that the behavior of actors would be different. The high-power actor will perhaps attempt to define and impose a reality on the low-power actors. Actors with high power relative to other actors in an exchange relationship have considerable discretion to influence the outcomes of that exchange. What they do with this discretion will likely be a function of their values and intentions and of the consequences of their actions once implemented. Intentions and values apart, power has the capacity to corrupt the power holder, particularly in the sense that powerful actors may treat less powerful actors in demeaning ways, devaluing the worth of the latter's work and treating the low-power actor as an object—as a means to an end—rather than as another human being or as a colleague in the research enterprise (Nord, 1977). Under such conditions, low-power actors become alienated from the process (Israel, 1971).

Studies of married couples, employer-servant, and manager-subordinate relationships in which power differences between actors were either large or small lend support to this view (Kipnis, 1972; Kipnis, Castell, Gergen, & Mauch, 1976). Kipnis and his colleagues, in field and laboratory studies, observed that people with power frequently attempted to influence those without power. They believe that they control the less powerful person's behavior and performance and think poorly of the latter and of his or her original contribution to any outcomes in the relationship. They observed also that individuals with high power tend to distance themselves psychologically and socially from those with low power.

Research is necessary into the potential existence, level, and nature of alienation among editors, authors, and reviewers who have low power in a review relationship. Some possible scenarios for low-power actors in this process are sketched below.

The low-power actor, if alienated by a relationship with an actor of high power, may simply disengage, ending the process. Alienated editors, reviewers, or authors may withdraw from the process and may simply cease contributing to the production and assessment of scientific knowledge. (Latané, 1979b, ascribes a decline in manuscripts submitted to the *Journal of Personality and Social Psychology* during 1977 to the dissatisfaction that authors felt with editorial policies introduced at that time.)

Alternatively, authors can choose to withdraw from the spirit and intention of the scientific process while giving it lip service, contributing only in a mechanical sense. For example, an alienated author who desires visibility and recognition in his or her field may give up attempts to contribute original creative work, including the pursuit of interesting and researchable ideas, and attend to research that has already been defined and assessed as real and valuable by the more powerful editors or reviewers. Alienation in this case is reflected in a channeling of research efforts toward "playing the game"—to "making it"—in the system. Such alienated behavior among actors is likely to produce mindless, bureaucratic, uncreative research and to encourage unimaginative, conservative reviewing, and is likely to yield editorial actions on manuscripts that reinforce the status quo.

Powerful editors can also influence the content of a manuscript revision, perhaps unduly. For example, the terms an editor lays out for revision of a manuscript may be such that an author is faced with having to give up the essence of his or her style and substance to ensure that it is published in the journal.

Alienated behavior may include falsification of data to make it acceptable for publication, tapping more powerful individuals to influence the review process, accepting manuscripts to repay or incur favors or to keep material from competing journals, and self-interested recommendations of flawed manuscripts that support the recommender's own research. These are not easy behaviors to document empirically, yet researchers such as Snell (1973) and Ceci and Peters (Holden, 1980), who falsified previously published manuscripts by changing author names and some minor manuscript content, found that the falsifications went largely undetected in the review process. Ceci and Peters rewrote abstracts, altered the opening sentences and inserted fake names and institutional affiliations on 10 articles published in 10 widely read psychological journals. These papers were resubmitted to the journals in which they had previously been accepted. Only three of the journals detected the deception. Snell submitted previously published manuscripts containing minor modifications of content and his own, rather than the actual author's, name to five journals. None of the journals spotted the changes. Snell points out that more subtle plagiarisms and falsifications are likely to succeed if the author presents impressive, though false, evidence in a manuscript.

Wolins (1962) encountered the data falsification issue in a study in which he reanalyzed the data supplied to him by five authors. In seven reanalyses, he found errors of sufficient magnitude to change the results of the studies involved. Twenty-one other authors who replied to Wolins's request for data from their recently published works indicated that their data were either lost, misplaced, or accidentally destroyed.

Alienated actors may resist rather than withdraw from the review process. They may attempt to overthrow the existing system so as to redress the power imbalance, or they may attempt to create new journals that provide them with more power and a different outlet for their manuscripts. Examples of both actions are likely to be found among scientific journals and are amenable to research that would test these and other hypotheses.

Viewing manuscript decisions as a political process involving the use and perhaps the abuse of power by key actors in the process identifies aspects of decision making that are very different than those that emerge when the decision is looked at as a rational action or as the outcome of interacting organizational routines. It highlights negotiated as well as possibly covert manipulative aspects of the publishability decision.

Governmental Politics Applications to the Manuscript Review Process

Modifying the balance of power between and among actors in the review process can be accomplished by *intervention,* by altering the power differential in a specific review situation, in effect by managing power differentials, or by *design,* by institutionalizing power-sharing structures that are intended to apply to all review decisions. Power in each case may be given to, or taken from, others.

Managing Power Differentials—Cooperative Strategies. Actors in a power relationship have both latent and actual (used) power (Bachrach & Baratz, 1962; Heydebrand, 1978; Nord, 1976). Efforts to manage high power differentials require that actors with high power act to reduce the differential in a given situation by using less than their full power, or that they harness the differential in ways beneficial to other actors in the exchange (Deutsch, 1949, 1962). Laboratory studies of behavioral and attitudinal outcomes when power is used in cooperative rather than competitive contexts support the notion that actors with high power can work productively with low-power actors provided the context is congenial (Tjosvold, 1982; Tjosvold & Deemer, 1980). In Tjosvold's studies, high- and low-power actors in a competitive context were suspicious of each other, withheld resources, and developed negative attitudes toward one another. Low-power actors reported high insecurity about the relationship. Opposite outcomes were observed in a cooperative context. High- and low-power actors developed a liking and trust for each other and a willingness to work toward common goals.

Strategies that incorporate two-way communication between actors, integrative problem solving rather than competitive (win-lose) responses, and coaching rather than judgmental/critical behavior provide opportunities for minimizing existing power differentials (Blake & Mouton, 1961; Filley, 1975; Meyer, Kay, & French, 1965).

Actions by editors pertinent to manuscript review decisions include use of additional reviewers for controversial manuscripts, author selection of reviewer pools for editors to choose from, author-referee dialogues prior to editorial decisions on manuscripts (Glenn, 1976), choice of sympathetic rather than critical reviewers, editors acting as referees on manuscript assessment where the content requires special attention, and editor/referee coaching of authors for manuscript revision.

Strategies such as those outlined above emphasize greater power sharing between editor and author through greater participation on the part of the author in the decision process. However, participation is not a sufficient condition for equalizing power (Locke & Schweiger, 1979; Mulder & Wilke, 1970). The crucial action appears to be use of participation by the high-power actor to increase the expertise, the expert power base of other actors in the exchange. For example, the editor may provide, through communication of extensive feedback from reviewers and him- or herself, insights into the manuscript material that allow the author to improve the quality of the manuscript substantially (whether for resubmission to the journal or to be sent elsewhere). Editors of several organizational science journals do this with some or all author submissions.

Managing Power Differentials—Conflict Strategies. Actors with high power may intervene in particular situations to modify the power balance. Editors with high relative power may choose to overrule referees whose actions or recommendations (e.g., cursory reviews, personal attacks) contravene the spirit of fair assessment. Editors can threaten to reveal a reviewer's name to an author if a tardy review is not forthcoming. Rodman (1970) has reported success with this strategy. Reviewers with high relative power can threaten resignation if they perceive an editorial decision to be manipulative.

Conflict strategies also provide an opportunity for intervention attempts by actors with low relative power toward modifying the power balance. For example, referees with low relative power can petition or create a lobby of reviewers to confront editors or authors perceived to be abusing the decision process.

Authors with low relative power can move to multiple submissions of their manuscript to journals to gain leverage (Peters, 1976). Authors can also intervene by persisting, by reasserting the case for a paper with an editor/referee when it has been rejected (Kosinski, 1979).

Strategies such as coaching or intervention are not cost-free, of course. They involve considerable investments of time and effort by both high- and low-power actors and may extensively delay the decision time for a manuscript. Applied to many authors and manuscripts, the strategies may lead to serious publication delays. Cooperative, coaching strategies may also create conditions in which the author, if overly compliant and trusting, yields his or her ideas in the manuscript to the judgments and recommendations of the editor or the reviewer (the high-power actor). The resulting manuscript may be an improved product but it may cost the author's integrity. This is perhaps particularly a danger when manuscript acceptance is tied to institutional decisions in promotion or tenure affecting an author. The benefits of coaching low-power actors likely outweigh the costs, nevertheless.

Conflict strategies such as multiple submissions will probably overload journals already burdened with high submissions. It is not inevitable that an author will take the first manuscript acceptance he or she gets from a journal (Turner, 1976). However, given the orientation of minimizing power differences between actors such as editor and author, ground rules can no doubt be worked out. Authors could be asked to specify to which journals a manuscript has been sent and agree, in return for speedier reviews, to a deadline for accepting or rejecting a journal's acceptance of a manuscript (Turk, 1976).

Institutionalizing the Equalization of Power. Strategies discussed above reflect acceptance of existing power differentials between actors and emphasis is upon strategies for managing power imbalance in specific situations. Other strategies can be focused on designing systems to equalize power across situations in a journal. Research on communication and information networks suggests that power equalization and effective decision making for complex tasks is best accomplished by establishing all channel rather than star or chain networks (Bavelas, 1950). Review situations in which one actor has high formal power relative to other actors facilitate and sustain the differential when one actor receives all the inputs and controls the flow of information to each of the other actors. This is perhaps the pervasive structure for most review processes in prestigious scientific journals. The powerful editor is at the center of the process and is the only actor dealing directly with other actors in the process. The restricted communication network also facilitates increased power of reviewers relative to authors because the latter must proceed in relative ignorance of how the reviewer evaluates manuscripts. The power potential of the reviewer is particularly high in blind reviews. The reviewer can make recommendations with relative impunity because he or she does not have to confront the author. Glenn (1976) has suggested that critiques by reviewers be submitted to authors for response before the editor makes a decision on whether to accept or reject the papers. The author would be allowed to respond only to major points and factual errors made by the reviewer.

The network can be altered to equalize power among actors by opening channels, thereby increasing the chances of redistributing expertise and authority, which are the bases of expert and formal power (Mulder & Wilke, 1970). Multiple exchanges between editor, reviewer, and author are feasible in an era of conference call technology and professional association meetings, both national and international. In addition, viewing the review board or panel as part of the network suggests that editors, authors, and reviewers can call for activation of additional channels and interactions to further reduce power inequalities. Policy on all channel networks can include membership of panels as negotiated outcomes, that is, members are proposed and selected by editors, authors, and referees. The *Personality and Social Psychology Bulletin,* a journal perceived to be both innovative and efficient, requests as standard policy that authors nominate three potential reviewers of their manuscript at the time of submission. The journal also instituted a system for evaluating journal functioning on an ongoing basis but dismantled it due to lack of interest (Latané, 1979a).

The primary disadvantages or costs of structural changes are the potential for time delays in the review and publication decision outcomes and, perhaps more substantively, the protection of reviewer and author from biases that may be associated with removing the "blind" character of a review, which is intended to minimize recommendations and decisions linked to personal likes and dislikes between actors. Nevertheless, the identity of authors can frequently be detected in blind reviews—especially in very specialized research areas where the community of researchers is small. To ensure a truly blind review, the process should include the editor. Only administrative personnel really need to see the name of the author to correspond with the author. However, if the editor is not blind to the author's identity, then negotiated, shared communication channels may prove beneficial to author and journal.

Institutionalizing power equalization in journals may yield a new set of biasing factors. We anticipate that it would slow the review process. Given an emphasis on negotiation and on two-way communication, it is also possible that it would favor strong personalities with high interpersonal competence.

THE ORGANIZATIONAL
PROCESSES MODEL OF MANUSCRIPT REVIEW

This perspective depicts decisions as outcomes of organizations operating in regular, systematic ways, the unit of analysis being organizational action. The model assumes that organizations function according to established procedures, routines, and standard operating procedures (SOPs). It also assumes that these programmed organizational processes establish the context and, to a large degree, constrain the choices open to decision makers at the top of organizations and thus constrain organizational action. It also includes the condition in which the absence of programs and standard operating procedures for dealing with organizational events can constrain choice.

Most editors inherit a system of routines and procedures for selecting and rejecting manuscripts when they take on the job. In addition, there are SOPs and routines that originate outside the journal organization and are acquired by editors and reviewers from the training and indoctrination received during their "apprenticeship" and in subsequent years (Mintzberg, 1979). Thus it is possible to depict two sets of routines: the bureaucratic and the professional. Changing bureaucratic routines can be accomplished by altering the things organizations attend to; changing professional routines requires changes in the actors involved in the process.

The decision to accept or reject or request revision of a manuscript is an organizational action, the result of interacting between the routines and procedures practiced by governing bodies, editorial boards, reviewers, managing and copyediting departments, suppliers, printers, readers, and authors. The editor deciding on the publishability of a given manuscript is constrained by the nature of the journal's mandate (for example, to publish empirical versus conceptual material), by production deadlines, by space and cost limitations, by the quality focus, by the number of manuscript submissions, by the turnaround time of reviewers assessing manuscripts, as well as by the procedures and approaches that reviewers use to make and convey recommendations to the editor.

The existence of routines for processing a manuscript (for example, assessment guidelines to reviewers, deadlines for first decision notification to authors, decision rules for resolving reviewer disagreements, and so on) and the implementation of these routines impinge on and shape the editor's decision. They constrain what the editor can do with a manuscript, and this may be either functional or dysfunctional for dissemination of knowledge in a field. Absence of such routines may also affect the decision outcome. So the nature and speed of decision making varies because of the presence or absence of reviewer routines and procedures. Whitley (1970) observed that a highly institutionalized reviewer system involving a formal review board produced faster editorial decisions on manuscript publishability than did an informal arrangement involving an editor and his immediate colleagues. This suggests that a formal mechanism such as an editorial board may improve the efficiency of the review process.

McNamara and Woods (1977) surveyed published articles in four psychological journals and concluded that an absence of editorial policies and procedures in these and other journals has led to a failure of journal editors to detect and reject unethical studies in social science literature. Rodman (1970) identifies the absence of standardized procedures for reviewers as a prime cause of delays in editorial decisions about manuscripts.

Research into manuscript review as an organizational process has been limited largely to a concern with reviewer routines and procedures. The research has centered on the nature and extent of interreviewer agreement on manuscripts and prescriptions for improving the level of agreement through such approaches as standardized assessment forms, reviewer training, and so forth. Researchers disagree on the level of interreviewer agreement that occurs in the review process. For example, among pairs of reviewers who examined 193 manuscripts, Smigel and Ross (1970) report 72.5% agreement to accept or reject a manuscript. Scott (1974), on the other hand, using decision data from a two-year period as associate editor of the *Journal of Personality and Social Psychology,* reported a correlation of only $r = .26$ between reviewers on the crucial "recommended to accept" decision. McReynolds (1971) found an interreviewer reliability of $r = .45$ among reviewers of conference research papers. Based on a hypothetical model of editorial review as a probabilistic process, Stinchcombe and Ofshe (1969) argued that reviewer assessment of the true worth of manuscripts is highly error prone and that many good papers are likely to be rejected by the typical review process. But, generally, theory and research about organizational processes has not been applied to the manuscript review decision.

Researching the Review Process. Manuscript review decisions and the organizational procedures and routines that constrain them can also be studied in terms of the relative utility of alternative organizational structures and designs for effective decision making. For example, processing manuscripts from submission by authors to final editorial decision and publication or rejection can be examined in terms of structural variables such as centralization, standardization, coordination, and their interrelationships (Blau & Schoenherr, 1971; Mintzberg, 1979). Similarly, journal organizations can be studied as systems (Burns & Stalker, 1961), in terms of the nature of differentiation and integration mechanisms in organizations (Lawrence & Lorsch, 1967), in terms of information processing (Galbraith, 1973), interdependence of work units (Thompson, 1967), innovation management (Duncan, 1976), or requisite variety (Weick, 1979). Organizational research that deals with strategic choice (e.g., Child, 1972) should provide avenues for the systematic study of the interaction between editors and the organizational routines that they must deal with in review decisions.

Organizational Processes Applications to the Manuscript Review Process

Some researchers argue that editorial decision making would be improved if the reviewer procedures were better harnessed. Newman (1966), for example, recommends that editors publish standards and acceptance criteria that reviewers should adhere to (and that authors can attend to in preparing manuscripts). He also recommends the use of at least three reviewers for each article. Wolff (1973) urges development of objective checklists and training programs so that, ideally, manuscripts can be assessed by trained clerks. Bowen, Perloff, and Jacoby (1972) express similar sentiments. Scott (1974), however, argues that the editor's decision on suitability of a manuscript is inherently a judgment call based on reading reviewer comments and recommendations and the manuscript itself. Given the lack of paradigm development in the social sciences and the diversity of orientations in any given social science field, a low level of inter-reviewer agreement perhaps accurately reflects the facts of social science research. Scott stresses the need to develop procedures that will protect the author from arbitrary and narrowly based decisions on a submitted manuscript rather than developing schemes and routines that attempt to create a convergence of reviewer assessments.

Scott argues that, while an editor may have to make the final judgment on manuscripts, the application of some existing decision strategies involving the development of voting procedures and routines may prove to be useful ways of improving reviewer inputs to the editorial decision. For multiple-attribute decision making, the least demanding procedure for aggregating preferences regarding manuscript characteristics is, perhaps, for the reviewer or editor to set preference constraints (Coombes, 1964; Dawes, 1971), an approach commonly used in cognitive process studies. A number of such constraints can be set up to operate either conjunctively (all must be satisfied) or disjunctively (only one needs to be satisfied). The constraints may be set up sequentially and may depend on the results of preceding evaluations. The usual operating mode with these procedures is to search for an alternative that satisfies the constraints, without trying to determine whether a better alternative exists. This procedure could be applied appropriately to choice of manuscripts for publications given that manuscripts typically are judged at one time against criteria that exist in the minds of reviewers and editors. It also permits shifts in constraints to reflect experience of reviewers or editors with regard to quality of manuscripts available to the journal.

The procedures discussed above are useful for multiple-person situations because different reviewers can impose different constraints. Hence their preferences can be reflected without trying to aggregate them into a simple social choice function.

One group of voting strategies involves the SPAN technique proposed by MacKinnon and MacKinnon (1969). Each member of a reviewing panel, for example, would be given a fixed number of votes that he or she could allocate directly to manuscripts being reviewed or to other reviewers. The underlying rationale is that reviewers should allocate votes to other reviewers when the former feel they have less knowledge than do other reviewers and when they can identify other reviewers' greater expertise. This process is iterated in SPAN until all votes are distributed to alternatives. The major advantage of SPAN voting as an application to the manuscript review process is that more knowledgeable evaluations would result because the preferences of reviewers would be weighted according to their recognized expertise. A disadvantage may be the concentration of evaluation of manuscripts on certain topics in the hands of a relatively small number of recognized authorities who may tend to resist new ideas. Of course, the SPAN voting strategy would require that all reviewers be known to each other.

In applying the logrolling strategy to manuscript review processes, reviewers would be permitted to trade off votes on manuscripts that they consider relatively unimportant, but that other reviewers may consider very important, in exchange for future votes on manuscripts that they feel are very important (Buchanan & Tullock, 1962; Coleman, 1966). By use of this method, even a relatively non-influential single reviewer (not aligned with a coalition) can express some of his or her preferences. This process may operate in manuscript review procedures at present through reviewers informing the editor, for example, that, "after all, I have not accepted many of the manuscripts I have reviewed, therefore this one that I feel strongly about should be accepted." The advantage of formalizing the procedure is to ensure that many neutral votes will not mask the strong preferences that are expressed by a few reviewers. If no reviewer feels strongly about a manuscript, it will not be accepted.

Attention to design of the journal organization should improve the conditions under which the editor decides the fate of a manuscript. The review decision (the outcome of organizational processes) may be improved by the establishment of routines and systems that coordinate and sequence the movement of the manuscript through its various phases, while preserving flexibility to attract and assess content that is innovative and requires special treatment in some way. To attain optimum flexibility and consistency in organizations, Hedberg, Nystrom, and Starbuck (1976) invoke the metaphor of organizations as tents and prescribe minimum levels of organizational elements such as consensus, consistency, and rationality. Duncan (1976) suggests an ambidextrous organization to accomplish these objectives. Weick (1977) suggests the development of self-designing systems to increase efficiency and innovation in organizations.

Duncan's prescription of an ambidextrous organization is informative and illustrates the application of organizational processes ideas to journal design. The editor seeking to produce, in a timely fashion, manuscripts that contribute significantly to the field, needs an organization that processes innovative submissions efficiently. Organizational goals, rules, and procedures that clarify and distinguish what is needed by each organizational unit and actor (e.g., reviewers, managing editors, copy editors, authors, and so on) and that coordinate their activities ought to facilitate an efficient process of translating manuscripts into published acceptances or redirected rejections. On the other hand, handling and assessing the innovative content of manuscript submissions requires, in Duncan's terms, a more flexible organizational component and ways to harness the reviewing and editorial functions that allow for flexibility and creativity of operations. Editors may need to establish a pool of reviewers, with greater diversity of characteristics in terms of age, minority representation, area of expertise, professional training or orientation, and so on, who can be retained to operate as a task force or a team, reporting to the editor in ways independent of the editor's regular reviewing board. They may be given a special mandate to seek out and help authors develop challenging or stimulating aspects of manuscripts that might otherwise be rejected, or to act as devil's advocates by responding to the review recommendations of other individuals who have a different mandate in the process.

Editors may recruit a project team of reviewers, perhaps appoint a project manager editor, and charge that group to develop and shape a special issue devoted to a particular research theme. This might permit an infusion into the journal organization of new ideas about the substantive content of the journal as well as the processes whereby manuscripts are selected.

The Duncan organizational process model applied to academic journals would require development of a broad policy and organizational structuring to allow one phase and one set of organization actors to pursue the review decision with a minimum of formality and centralized decision making and a high degree of complexity (in the sense of diverse, highly professional occupational specialties) so as to diagnose and assess innovative submissions. It would require a second phase and set of organizational actors to process the manuscripts to completion in the journal. This second phase would emphasize formalized rules and procedures, centralized decision making, and a low level of complexity. Integration of the two phases would be in the hands of the editor or of a team of editors, depending upon the extent to which the journal has been, or needs to be, differentiated (Lawrence & Lorsch, 1967). Duncan's ambidextrous organization may serve to make the constraints on editorial decisions due to organizational processes more manageable. Considerations of cost and availability of reviewers may make it unwieldy for some journals, however.

Other prescriptions for managing organizational processes include development of computerized listings of experts in a variety of fields as is used in the *Human Organization* journal. This allows an easily retrievable, diverse pool of potential reviewers for an editor to use. The potential costs of such an approach include installation and maintenance of the system and the potential unevenness in reviewer reports to an editor relative to those from a smaller board of regular reviewers. Latané (1979a) describes routines introduced into the operation of the journal *Personality and Social Psychology Bulletin,* which, in only five years, emerged as a major journal in its field. Successful routines included limitation of articles to four pages whenever possible; assessment of submission fees to share quality control costs with authors (this fee was discontinued when a new publisher, Sage, absorbed the production cost of the journal); instructions to authors to provide camera-ready copy of their manuscripts to save time and money (also discontinued because of adequate funding under Sage); and appointment of category or topic editors to spread the editorial workload more efficiently.

Increasing the requisite variety of a journal organization to match a complex and changing environment may be accomplished by creating diversity of representation in the editorial and reviewer roles on a journal. The recently founded journal *Organization Studies,* for example, has its publisher's main office in Berlin, an editor-in-chief located in Britain, a book review editor from the Netherlands, and an editorial board representing several schools of thought and several different nations. The editor-in-chief position is expected to rotate over the years and will include incumbents from different countries and institutions.

THE RATIONAL ACTOR MODEL
OF THE MANUSCRIPT REVIEW PROCESS

The rational actor perspective, one person or many persons acting in consort, depicts governmental decision making in terms of choice among alternatives made by a single, consistently purposeful actor. If an action occurs, it is assumed that there must be a goal or objective that may be expressed in terms of a "payoff" or "preference" function. Understanding decisions made by this unitary actor involves vicariously putting oneself in the decision maker's place in a particular situation so as to understand the actor's goals, objectives, alternatives particular to the situation, and consequences attached to each alternative. Given the constraints of the situation, the actor's choice among alternatives is predicted in terms of optimizing some value of the actor.

The rational actor resembles Merton's (1973) normative scientist who applies objective standards to research. The normative scientist is emotionally detached and consciously disinterested in the outcomes of such research and is objective and detached when assessing research output from any source, including his or her own work. The model can apply to authors preparing manuscripts for submission to journals or to reviewers assessing such submissions because it is assumed they act rationally in making decisions. In terms of the rational actor, the decision to publish or reject a manuscript is primarily a function of the journal editor's preferences, actions, and objectives.

The editor, as a rational actor, decides the fate of a manuscript in terms of one or more purposes, such as to publish manuscripts that contribute significantly to the field or to create or maintain a particular level of prestige or excellence for the journal in the field. The editor's preferences may include emphasis on empirical rather than theoretical work; his or her alternatives may include publication frequency, or the journal size, use of reviewer recommendations, or availability of comparable manuscripts.

Some researchers have studied editors' objectives and preferences in manuscript assessment. Chase (1970) reported "logical rigor" in a research manuscript as the criterion ranked of primary importance to editors in a sample of editors from natural and social science journals. However, she observed differences in criteria rankings between editors of physical (hard) science and those of social (soft) science journals. Natural scientists' high-ranked criteria were "replicability of research techniques," "originality," "mathematical precision," and "coverage of the literature." Social scientists' high-ranked criteria were "logical rigor," "theoretical significance," and "applied significance."

More recently, Lindsey (1978) analyzed responses of 265 editorial board members of psychology, sociology, and social work journals to an inventory of research values comprising 12 items designed to reflect the essential criteria of scientific inquiry. The most important criterion for publication as judged by editors in this study was the "value of an author's findings to the field." Other important criteria included "grasp of design," "sophistication of methodology," "theoretical relevance of material," and "creativity of ideas." These results reflect self-report responses to prespecified sets of publishability criteria and are informative.

Whitley (1970) describes a case study of editorial decision making in two social science journals, one interdisciplinary and one purely disciplinary in focus. He examined the manuscript acceptability decision in terms of reviewer and author characteristics such as professional age and number of publications. Differences were observed between reviewers of the two journals in terms of decision-making characteristics. High-publishing reviewers for the interdisciplinary journal accepted more manuscripts than did low-publishing reviewers. No such distinction was observed among reviewers for the "pure" discipline journal.

Little is known of the ways editors actually choose and order their decision preferences or their purposes or goals. The research cited above only gives an indication of editors' purposes, but this research requires augmentation through modeling what editors actually do in reaching their decisions.

Researching the Review Process. From a rational actor perspective, several existing decision models appear applicable to a study of the editors' decision-making process. In situations where a number of similar decisions are made over time by a decision maker, as is the case with journal editors, it is possible to build a simple model of these behaviors (Slovic & Lichtenstein, 1971). For example, on manuscript review decisions, the accept/reject assignments can be the dependent variable and the characteristics of manuscripts reviewed can be independent variables. A linear regression model can then yield coefficients describing the decision maker's behavior. Using this approach, insights into decision rules can also be obtained for individual reviewers and for editorial boards. Given a sufficient number of manuscript choices over time, shifts in decision rules can be identified or decision rules used by different editors can be compared.

Another approach for aggregating preferences regarding manuscripts is to apply a subjective weighting model. Regression procedures, based on actual choices or ratings of an editor, can be used. Alternatively, decision makers can be asked directly for their preferences and these figures can be used to obtain a coefficient. In such cases, it is usual to separate the scaling of intra-attribute values from the interattribute weighting of importance. This allows for curvilinear relationships reflecting the worth of various attribute values to decision makers (Miller, 1970).

The weighting of importance of attributes can be related to higher order objectives of journals; the instrumentality of attributes in reaching ends higher in some goal hierarchy (such as significant contribution to a field) determines the weighting (Sayeki & Vesper, 1973). Direct assessment models are common to many areas of decision making and have a long history, being represented, for example, in Benjamin Franklin's (1772/1956) "moral algebra."

An alternative rational analytic approach to the study of manuscript review is suggested by research into opinion revision by individuals processing information. Rather than attempting to analyze the processes involved in reviewing manuscripts (attributes of manuscripts, criteria, and so on), one could describe manuscript decisions in terms of the extent to which the opinions of editors (or reviewers) are revised when they consider hypotheses investigated in the manuscript under review with regard to the findings reported. Lykken (1968) develops this approach as a means of determining theory corroboration and conclusiveness of research reports. The value and publishability of manuscripts is assessed, therefore, in terms of the extent of opinion revision, given the nature and outcome of the hypothesis testing process. While authors implicitly or explicitly confirm or revise their opinions on the hypotheses tested, and such considerations no doubt influence decisions on what they will do with the material, it is the nature and extent of opinion revision by editors and reviewers that is most relevant here.

Systematic application of the rational actor perspective to the review process should provide useful insights into how editors (as well as authors and reviewers) make decisions about manuscripts and their publishability. It is unlikely that the perspective will explain all or perhaps even a sizable proportion of variance in the decision process, however. Editors make decisions in the context of organizational constraints. Other variables and processes require consideration if we are to more fully understand the review process. Furthermore, the rational actor perspective as a model of the behavior of scientists has been subject to criticism. For example, Mitroff (1974) observed and described the passionate pursuit of theories by moon scientists and the strong personal bias that scientists displayed in assessing the worth of their own and others' research.

Manuscript review described as an opinion revision process based on overall contribution to knowledge has limitations. Among these are the following: (a) It requires that hypotheses be explicitly stated; (b) relatively large opinion revision is necessary to justify publishing a manuscript; (c) replications, either direct or systematic, are not encouraged; and (d) inputs must be combined if more than one person's opinion (e.g., a panel of reviewers) is involved.

Rational Actor Applications to the Manuscript Review Process

Making explicit to authors the preferences of reviewers and of editors, establishing clearly for authors the ground rules for acceptance or rejection of manuscripts, should aid them in deciding whether and in what way their manuscripts ought to be submitted to any given journal. Moreover, clarification of goals and preferences permits an examination of journal operational policies in the light of objectives of related professions. Clarification of the variables in the rational actor's decision-making process should help make explicit, also, the risk-taking propensity of the decision maker. A particular stance by an editor (conservative or risky) toward publishing manuscripts can be more easily reinforced or altered once it has been clearly articulated. Another way of clarifying the rational actor's decision process would be to publish from time to time shortened versions of "rejected" manuscripts along with comments of reviewers (Nord, 1978). Erickson (1977) describes publication of a manuscript in a criminology journal with accompanying reviewer comments and author responses. Such practices ought to prove valuable to authors and to students of the review process.

THE MANUSCRIPT REVIEW PROCESS RECONSIDERED

In this chapter we have viewed the manuscript review process used by scientific journals from four perspectives and have explored ways to advance understanding and practice of this aspect of journal functioning. The ideological influence, governmental politics, organizational process, and rational actor approaches to decision making offer many concepts and techniques relevant to such an analysis. In addition, our multiple-lens analysis of the manuscript review process suggests a variety of strategies and tactics that might be applied to improve the process. If the accumulated social science knowledge concerning the manuscript review process is to effectively advance journal functioning, it will be necessary for us, as a community of scholars, to examine the quality of our journals, their efficiency, the innovativeness of their content, and the fairness of journal procedures for members of a scientific community. We also need to demonstrate a readiness to implement changes in the manuscript review processes of journals where needed. Before academic journal policies and practices can be modified, individuals in established positions of power in a field must be willing to bear much of the risk inherent in initiating and sustaining changes. Such concerns, issues, and changes appear to us to pose major challenges to scientific fields such as our own in the years ahead. We are hopeful that our professional journals will fulfill their potential for advancing the social sciences.

REFERENCES

Abramowitz, S. I., Gomes, B., & Abramowitz, C. V. (1975). Publish or politic: Referee bias in manuscript review. *Journal of Applied Social Psychology, 5*(3), 187-200.

Allison, G. T. (1971). *The essence of decision.* Boston: Little, Brown.

Bachrach, P., & Baratz, M. S. (1962). The two faces of power. *American Political Science Review, 16*(4), 947-952.

Baldridge, J. F. (1971). *Power and conflict in the university.* New York: John Wiley.

Bavelas, A. (1950). Communication patterns in task oriented groups. *Journal of Accoustical Society of America, 22,* 725-730.

Bedeian, A., Downey, H. K., Price, K. E., & Salancik, G. R. (1980). *Strategies for maximizing acceptance of your research by journals.* Unpublished transcript of symposium presented at the Academy of Management national meetings, Detroit.

Berger, P., & Luckmann, T. (1966). *The social construction of reality.* New York: Doubleday.

Blake, R. R., & Mouton, J. S. (1961). Reactions to intergroup competition under win-lose conditions. *Management Science, 7,* 420-425.

Blau, P. M., & Schoenherr, R. A. (1971). *The structure of organizations.* New York: Basic Books.

Bowen, D. D., Perloff, R., & Jacoby, J. (1972). Improving manuscript evaluation procedures. *American Psychologist, 27,* 221-225.

Buchanan, J. M., & Tullock, C. (1962). *The calculus of consent.* Ann Arbor: University of Michigan Press.

Burke, K. (1966). *Language as symbolic action.* Berkeley: University of California Press.

Burns, T., & Stalker, G. M. (1961). *The management of innovation.* London: Tavistock.

Chambers, J. M., & Herzberg, A. M. (1968). A note on the game of refereeing. *Applied Statistics, 17,* 260-263.

Chase, J. M. (1970). Normative criteria for scientific publication. *American Sociologist, 5,* 262-265.

Child, J. (1972). Organization structure, environment, and performance: The role of strategic choice. *Sociology, 6,* 1-22.

Clark, C. X. (1973). Introduction: Some reflexive comments on the role of editor. *Journal of Social Issues, 29*(1), 1-9.

Clegg, S. (1975). *Power, rule and domination.* London: Routledge & Kegan Paul.

Coleman, J. S. (1966). The possibility of a social welfare function. *The American Economics Review, 56,* 1105-1122.

Coombes, C. H. (1964). *A theory of data.* New York: John Wiley.

Crane, D. (1967). The gatekeepers of science: Some factors affecting the selection of articles for scientific journals. *American Sociologist, 2,* 195-201.

Cyert, R., & March, J. G. (1963). *A behavioral theory of the firm.* Englewood Cliffs, NJ: Prentice Hall.

Dawes, R. M. (1971). A case study of graduate admissions: Applications of three principles of human decision making. *American Psychologist, 26*(2), 180-188.

Deutsch, M. (1949). An experimental study of the effects of cooperation and completion upon group process. *Human Relations, 2,* 199-231.

Deutsch, M. (1962, November). Cooperation and trust: Some theoretical notes. In *Nebraska Symposium on Motivation.* Lincoln: University of Nebraska Press.

Duncan, R. B. (1976). The ambidextrous organization: Designing dual structures for innovation. In R. Kilmann, L. R. Pondy, & D. Slevin (Eds.), *The management of organization design, research, and methodology* (Vol. 1, pp. 167-188). New York: North Holland.

Dunnette, M. D. (1963). Fads, fashions and folderol. *American Psychologist, 21,* 343-352.

Edelman, M. (1971). *Politics as symbolic action.* Chicago: Markham.

Edelman, M. (1977). *Political language: Words that succeed and policies that fail.* New York: Academic Press.

Erickson, R. V. (1977). From social theory to penal practice: The liberal demise of criminological causes. *Canadian Journal of Criminology and Corrections, 19*(2), 170-191.

Filley, A. C. (1975). *Interpersonal conflict resolution.* Glenview, IL: Scott, Foresman.

Franklin, B. (1952). Letter to Joseph Priestley. Reprinted in *The Benjamin Franklin sampler.* New York: Fawcett. (Original work published 1772)

French, J. R. P., & Raven, B. (1960). The bases of social power. In D. Cartwright & A. F. Zander (Eds.), *Group dynamics* (2nd ed., pp. 607-623). Evanston, IL: Row Peterson.

Frost, P. J. (1980). Blindspots in the study of organizations: Implications for teaching and application. *Group and Organizational Studies, 5*(2), 169-177.

Frost, P. J., & Hayes, D. C. (1979). An exploration in two cultures of political behavior in organizations. In A. Negandhi & G. W. England (Eds.), *Cross-cultural studies in organization functions.* Kent, OH: Kent State University Press.

Frost, P. J., Taylor, R. N., & Cummings, L. L. (1981). *Editorial and review processes.* Unpublished paper presented at plenary session, Administrative Sciences Association of Canada, Halifax, Nova Scotia.

Galbraith, J. R. (1973). *Designing complex organizations.* Reading, MA: Addison-Wesley.

Glenn, N. D. (1976). The journal article review process: Some proposals for change. *American Sociologist, 11,* 179-185.

Gouldner, A. W. (1976). *The dialectic of ideology and technology.* New York: Seabury.

Gusfield, J. R. (1976, February). Literary rhetoric of science: Comedy and pathos in drinking driver research. *American Sociological Review, 41,* 16-34.

Habermas, J. (1973). *Theory and practice* (J. Viertel, Trans.). Boston: Beacon.

Habermas, J. (1975). *Legitimation crisis* (T. McCarthy, Trans.). Boston: Beacon.

Hedberg, B. L., Nystrom, P. C., & Starbuck, W. H. (1976). Camping on seesaws: Prescriptions for a self-designing organization. *Administrative Science Quarterly, 21*(1), 41-65.

Heydebrand, W. (1978). Book review of critical issues in organizations. In S. Clegg & D. Dunkerley (Eds.), *Administrative Science Quarterly, 23*(4), 640-645.

Hickson, D. J., Hinings, C. R., Lee, C. A., Schneck, R. C., & Pennings, J. M. (1971). A strategic contingencies theory of intra-organizational power. *Administrative Science Quarterly, 16,* 216-224.

Holden, C. (1980, September). Not what you know but where you're from. *Science, 209,* 1097.

Huff, A. S. (1983). A rhetorical examination of strategic change. In L. R. Pondy, P. J. Frost, G. Morgan, & T. C. Dandridge (Eds.), *Organizational symbolism.* Greenwich, CT: JAI Press.

Israel, J. (1971). *Alienation: From Marx to modern sociology.* Boston: Allyn & Bacon.

Kerr, S., Tolliver, J., & Petree, D. (1977). Manuscript characteristics which influence acceptance for management and social science journals. *Academy of Management Journal, 20,* 132-141.

Kipnis, D. (1972). Does power corrupt? *Journal of Personality and Social Psychology, 24,* 33-41.

Kipnis, D., Castell, P. J., Gergen, M., & Mauch, D. (1976). Metamorphic effects of power. *Journal of Applied Psychology, 61,* 127-135.

Kosinski, J. (1979, February 19). Polish joke: How the publishers got stung. *Time.*
Kuhn, T. S. (1970). *The structure of scientific revolutions* (2nd ed.). Chicago: University of Chicago Press.
Latané, B. (1979a). *Journal of Personality and Social Psychology:* Problem, perspective, prospect. *Personality and Social Psychology Bulletin, 5*(1), 19-31.
Latané, B. (1979b). *Personality and Social Psychology Bulletin:* Five year summary. *Personality and Social Psychology Bulletin, 5*(4), 418-419.
Lawrence, P. R., & Lorsch, J. W. (1967). *Organization and environment.* Cambridge, MA: Harvard Graduate School of Business Administration.
Legge, K. (1978). *Power, innovation and problem-solving in personnel management.* London: McGraw-Hill.
Lewin, A. Y., & Duchan, L. (1971). Women in academia. *Science, 173,* 892-895.
Lindsey, D. (1978). *The scientific publication system in social science.* San Francisco: Jossey-Bass.
Locke, E. A., & Schweiger, D. M. (1979). Participation in decision-making: One more look. In B. M. Staw (Ed.), *Research in Organizational Behavior, 1,* 265-339.
Lykken, D. T. (1968). Statistical significance in psychological research. *Psychological Bulletin, 70,* 151-159.
MacKinnon, W. J., & MacKinnon, M. J. (1969). Computers: The decisional design and cyclic computation of SPAN. *Behavioral Science, 14.*
Mahoney, M. J. (1977). Publication prejudices: An experimental study of confirmatory bias in the peer review system. *Cognitive Therapy and Research, 1,* 161-175.
Mahoney, M. J. (1978). Publish and perish. *Human Behavior, 2,* 38-41.
Mahoney, M. J., Kazdin, A. E., & Kenigsberg, M. (1978). Getting published. *Cognitive Therapy and Research, 2*(1), 69-70.
McNamara, J. R., & Woods, K. M. (1977). Ethical considerations in psychological research: A comparative review. *Behavior Therapy, 8,* 703-708.
McReynolds, P. (1971). Reliability of ratings of research papers. *American Psychologist, 25,* 400-401.
Merton, R. K. (1973). *The sociology of science: Theoretical and empirical investigations.* Chicago: University of Chicago Press.
Meyer, H. H., Kay, E., & French, J. R. P., Jr. (1965). Split roles in performance appraisal. *Harvard Business Review, 43,* 123-129.
Miller, J. R., III. (1970). *Professional decision making.* New York: Praeger.
Mintzberg, H. (1979). *The structuring of organizations.* Englewood Cliffs, NJ: Prentice Hall.
Mitchell, M. B. (1951). Status of women in the American Psychological Association. *American Psychologist, 6,* 193-201.
Mitroff, I. I. (1974). *The subjective side of science.* Amsterdam: Elsevier.
Mulder, M., & Wilke, H. (1970). Participation and power equalization. *Organizational Behavior and Human Performance, 5,* 430-448.
Newman, S. H. (1966). Improving the evaluation of submitted manuscripts. *American Psychologist, 21,* 980-981.
Nord, W. R. (1976). Developments in the study of power. In W. R. Nord (Ed.), *Concepts and controversy in organizational behavior* (pp. 437-450). Pacific Palisades, CA: Goodyear.
Nord, W. R. (1977). Job satisfaction reconsidered. *American Psychologist,* 1026-1035.
Nord, W. R. (1978). Comparison and extensions on Frost's and Weick's analysis of blindspots. *Group and Organizational Studies, 5*(2), 189-197.
Nord, W. R. (1980). Toward an organizational psychology for organizational psychology. *Professional Psychology, 11*(3), 531-542.
Peters, C. B. (1976). Multiple submissions: Why not? *American Sociologist, 11,* 165-179.
Pettigrew, A. M. (1973). *The politics of organizational decision making.* London: Tavistock.
Pfeffer, J. (1981). *Power in organizations.* Marshfield, MA: Pitman.

Pfeffer, J., Leong, A., & Strehl, K. (1977). Paradigm development and particularism: Journal publication in three scientific disciplines. *Social Forces, 55,* 938-951.

Pfeffer, J., & Salancik, G. R. (1978). *The external control of organizations.* New York: Harper & Row.

Rodman, H. (1970). The moral responsibility of journal editors and referees. *American Sociologist, 5,* 351-357.

Rodman, H., & Mancini, J. A. (1977). Editors, manuscripts and equal treatment. *Research in Higher Education, 7,* 369-374.

Sayeki, Y., & Vesper, K. H. (1973). Allocation of importance in a hierarchical goal structure. *Management Science, 19,* 667-675.

Scott, W. A. (1974). Interreferee agreement on some characteristics of manuscripts submitted to the *Journal of Personality and Social Psychology. American Psychologist, 29*(9), 689-702.

Silverman, R. J. (1976). The education editor as futurist. *Teachers College Record, 77,* 473-493.

Slovic, P., & Lichtenstein, S. (1971). Comparison of Bayesian and regression approaches to the study of information processing in judgements. *Organizational Behavior and Human Performance, 6,* 649-744.

Smigel, E., & Ross, H. L. (1970). Factors in editorial decision. *American Sociologist, 5,* 19-21.

Snell, J. C. (1973, May). Editorial standards and authenticity of manuscripts: An earlier generation revisited. *The American Sociologist, 8,* 90-91.

Stinchcombe, A. L., & Ofshe, R. (1969). On journal editing as a probabilistic process. *American Sociologist, 4,* 116-117.

Teghtsoonian, M. (1974). Distribution by sex of authors and editors of psychological journals 1970-1972: Are there enough women editors? *American Psychologist, 29,* 262-269.

Thompson, J. D. (1967). *Organizations in action.* New York: McGraw-Hill.

Tjosvold, D. (1982). Effects of approach to controversy on superior's incorporation of subordinates' information and decision making. *Journal of Applied Psychology, 67*(2), 189-193.

Tjosvold, D., & Deemer, D. K. (1980). Effects of controversy within a cooperative or competitive context on organizational decision making. *Journal of Applied Psychology, 65*(5), 590-595.

Toulmin, S. E. (1958). *The uses of argument.* Cambridge: Cambridge University Press.

Turk, A. T. (1976). Replies to Calvin Peters. *The American Sociologist, 11,* 169-170.

Turner, R. H. (1976). Replies to Calvin Peters. *The American Sociologist, 11,* 168-169.

Wade, N. (1979, May). To accept is to reject: The publishing paradox. *Science, 487.*

Weick, K. E. (1977, Autumn). Organization design: Organizations as self-designing systems. *Organizational Dynamics,* pp. 31-46.

Weick, K. E. (1979). *The social psychology of organizing* (2nd ed.). Reading, MA: Addison-Wesley.

White, M. S. (1970). Psychological and social barriers to women in science. *Science, 170,* 413-416.

Whitley, R. D. (1970). The formal communications system of science: A study of the organization of British social science journals. *Sociological Review, 16,* 163-179.

Wilson, J. (1973). *Introduction to social movements.* New York: Basic Books.

Wolff, W. M. (1973). Publication problems in psychology and an explicit evaluation scheme for manuscripts. *American Psychologist, 28*(3), 257-261.

Wolins, L. (1962). Responsibility for raw data. *American Psychologist, 17,* 657-658.

Yoels, W. C. (1971). Destiny or dynasty: Doctoral origins and appointment patterns of editors of *The American Sociological Review,* 1948-1968. *American Sociologist, 6,* 134-139.

Yoels, W. C. (1974). The structure of scientific fields and the allocation of editorships on scientific journals: Some observations on the politics of knowledge. *Sociological Quarterly, 15,* 264-276.

2

The Social Production of
Knowledge and the Commercial Artifact

STANLEY DEETZ

R esearch in all fields is tempered, if not often forged, by passions beyond the
burning desire to know. Personal, interpersonal, political, and economic
forces (e.g., Lindsey, 1978) as well as cultural trends are widely accepted as
dominant influences on research agendas and data collection and analysis (e.g.,
Wagner & Gooding, 1987). It should come as no surprise that the process of
publishing exemplifies these same forces. Some forces are ad hoc and personal:
A colleague receives a recommendation to save more interesting questions and
field study projects until after tenure. A flurry of publications are more often an
indication that the researcher is coming up for a promotion or wishes to change
jobs than the discovery of a new reality. But other forces are systemic: The "law
of the hammer" is largely evident across research agendas whether thought of in
theoretical or methodological choices. With every trained research capacity
comes trained incapacities. The forces influencing which capacities and incapacities will be developed often have little to do with the social problems we are
called upon to address or the nature of the external world. All research is preju-
diced and all published "knowledge" is artifactual in that it is a result of particu-

lar social factors, historically developed procedures, and a variety of socially derived choice processes.

The intent in raising these claims is not to tear at the already tattered gown of academic research, or to flog the dead horses of objective discovery and intellectual purity, or even to encourage cynicism among the young. And equally important, the intent is not to reclaim a disinterested science freed from its social context on a royal road to Truth. The presence of prejudice gives academic research and publication whatever life and relevance it has. Organizational science should not be disinterested but interesting and interested. But all prejudices and interests are not equal. Some are productive and lead us to better meet a variety of human desires in response to a changing environment. Others are self- or group-serving and play in self-referential systems lacking an openness to an exterior. The cloak of objectivity fostered by privileged methods and procedures and blind review processes has not eliminated prejudices but has made it more difficult to separate productive from unproductive ones. Conceptualizing publication as a communication process motivated by the pursuit of a common understanding rather than the documentation of a fact or a product in a strategic game can help us sort out productive prejudices that contribute to a social dialogue around significant issues from unproductive ones characterized by subjective domination and systematic distortion.

THE CURRENT STATE OF
PROFESSIONAL KNOWLEDGE PRODUCTION

After some 50 years of sociology of knowledge research, no one is surprised by the claim that scientific knowledge is a social product (e.g., Mannheim, 1952; Merton, 1973). Knowledge production is not a result of a neutral, anonymous process but occurs in a politically charged, social/cultural context of real people with real agendas working within important personal relationships and institutional ties. The more that the professional production of knowledge has been studied, the clearer it is that it differs little from the processes by which ordinary everyday people go about making sense of their world with others. This has been most carefully documented in the natural scientific laboratories, where it might be least expected. As Fuchs (1992) summarized the constructionist strain of these studies:

> While scientists in the laboratory are mundane reasoners fabricating knowledge claims in a largely idiosyncratic, indexical, and *ad hoc* fashion, the standard research article

presents objective findings that have erased all traces of social construction, correspond to reality, and were obtained by following rational procedures. . . . facts are constructed by converting the indexical logic of laboratory reasoning into the decontextualized style of the conventional research report . . . facts are first and foremost literary and rhetorical products. (p. 88; see Latour & Woolgar, 1979; Myers, 1985; Woolgar 1980, 1988)

Professionalized knowledge, best exemplified in publication, is connected more to distinguishing its claims by style and pretense from alternative bases of knowledge than to possessing a superior production process (Bazerman, 1988; Simon, 1990). In a society filled with increasingly competitive knowledge claims, professionalized disciplinary practices, training in research methods, and activities of research evaluation often function primarily (even if unintended) as an elite's elaborate attempts to maintain power and dominance rather than engage directly with the larger world (Foucault, 1980). As the speed of change in the society as well as the capacity of other groups to produce and disseminate knowledge increases, the pace of academic research and publication becomes increasingly out of step. More publication outlets and faster, limitless space of electronic journals will only blur the boundaries of professionalized knowledge rather than reduce fundamental tensions. Increasingly, if professionalized knowledge production is to have a place, it will have to be positively judged on its own merits in contrast to other group claims rather than on the status or authority of its maker. But this runs counter to the internal dynamics of professional groups.

The control of knowledge production is central to the maintenance of the profession's social order both internally and in relation to external groups. Increasingly, as Snyder (1973) showed three decades ago, researchers have developed a new elitism "consciously bemoaning the ignorance of the masses while at the same time becoming increasingly abstract and secretive so as to deny the public access to the information and advice so vital for them to make intelligent decisions" (pp. 252-253). Publication has often become more of a credentialing process certifying expertise and assuring stature and appropriate club membership than a pursuit of socially important understanding. Its presence rather than its content allows authors to present prepackaged first-year student-level material to students and managers alike (most often having at best a loose connection to published knowledge). As such, much publication is a terrible waste of time, talent, and trees and leaves competitive professional groups plenty of room for criticism. My complaint is not that these literatures are complex or even difficult to read (problems are often complex and important ideas are difficult) but that their logic more reflects moves in a club's game than addressing issues of significance.

I do not plan here, however, to get into the larger and more radical issues of the relation of power and knowledge (at least in the fundamental sense of a Foucault, 1980, or Lyotard, 1984) or into the legitimacy of claims of expertise or privileged forms of knowledge production. I approach my task here as an insider rather than as an external critic: as a reviewer and editor of the work of others, as a graduate instructor and director, as an active researcher, and as an academic writing an academic essay in an academic publication for an academic audience. For the purposes at hand, I intend to accept the hopes and ideals of professional modernist science. I believe that professional knowledge production can represent long-term social interests that are not well embedded in alternative groups' knowledge production activities. More can be gained by demanding more from it and our own practices of greater responsibility than by dismissal or mere criticism. We must make it more accessible and socially responsive while increasing the conceptual rigor and pursuit of understanding beyond our current language and thought.

In many respects, the postmodern political critiques of professional expertise and the more mundane admission of the political game of doing professional research have allowed many to continue to practice their science cynically as if they believed in its ideal, and reap the benefits thereof but without serious engagement or risks. Research practice is for many a kind of simulation with a simulated knowledge product in a kind of self-referential system with little relation to an outside environment, community, or future. It displays the same type of product/by-product reversal characteristic of the domination of instrumental reasoning in any organization (see Fischer, 1990). It is similar in form to students who pursue grades with learning being an occasional unexpected by-product or companies who pursue profits and sometimes fortuitously fulfill real consumer needs. The cynicism and skepticism of the age have not often encouraged researchers to pursue things they can believe in; rather they often seek advantage in a game in which one cannot believe, a kind of mad rush to book first class on the Titanic even after knowing its fate. One can win in a game that is not worth playing. In such cases, the publication's value is more linked to the personal career of its author/producer than to social needs.

To the extent that the commercial value of having a publication exceeds the social value of its knowledge claim, publication review processes may strive to be fair but the publication process as a whole becomes a strategic game lacking social responsibility, demeaning both its participants and the society that pays for it. I know of no study that demonstrates the successful integration of personal career gains with larger groups' needs for useful knowledge. In an increasingly complex, uncertain, and contested world, the payoff to personal careers appear far more predictable than a significant contribution to any social good. The pressure is not equal even if the logics were in principle compatible, and they may well not be.

I wish to take professional research and publication seriously here not so much because I believe in it or find it defensible in the face of the contemporary critiques but to heighten insight into how it is working, to ask if there is a redeemable project in the current muddle, and to suggest that if we cannot work toward its ideals we ought to start anew rather than compete for the best simulations of the old. I will sketch a conception of privileged knowledge construction based on a model of rational communication, outline the various ways that it has been undermined in current practices, and discuss means of improvement. If this tack seems vaguely reminiscent of the failed attempt to reclaim a conception of the "rational" organization long after its non- and extrarational characteristics were shown, let me suggest that we take seriously the unintended consequences of the alternative. Many of the authors who showed the inevitability of extrarational forces hoped that this would initiate careful consideration and discussion of whose extrarational values were present and who they advantaged—to remove the myth of neutrality so meaningful discussion could be had. The consequences of their work, however, appear more to have provided open license for self-interested politics. The average manager apparently thought, if the organization is inevitably political, I must play the game well. The morality this produced is carefully described by Jackell (1988)—strategic individualism runs wide. Without some concept of reason, power is the name of the game. Perhaps Habermas is right: We might better start with an unjustifiable faith in reason. And if we can broaden the conception of rationality, perhaps we can get a more representative and responsive (adaptive) form of knowledge without a privilege grounded simply in power. It strikes me that at least we might gain some insight by approaching the publication process in this fashion.

KNOWLEDGE PRODUCTION
AS A COMMUNICATION PROCESS

While many think of the production of knowledge as the application of methods and making observations, I think we can get further if we think of knowledge as the outcome of social interactions using claims about people and the world. These claims are supported by observations and methods that become evidence and justifications for the claims in particular social systems. Scientific procedures can be thought of as rhetorical devices in making these claims rather than devices of discovery (Prelli, 1989; Simon, 1990). While removing the certainty of a knowable structure of a real reality as an anchor may create some Cartesian anxiety (Bernstein, 1984), it is not intended to relativize findings. It only suggests that a belief in such procedures is a necessary cultural addition to the scientific action to claim objectivity or certainty in the outcome. By claiming all facts as cultural artifacts (they are produced by following culturally prescribed means and have particular meaning within a cultural discourse) is not to depreciate research findings but to help us attend to the variety of ways that reporting of research is a communicative activity where potentially competitive claims are resolved by many alternative justifications including the rhetorical ploy of objectivity.

Looking at research from a communication perspective allows us to use more general communication theories to examine the process of making a claim to a community, the manners by which resolution of difference happen, and the places of failure or distortions in communication processes. The ideal of science approaches the ideal Habermas suggests for open communication: to pursue a common understanding or unforced agreement as to what is a truth or shared knowledge. Following his development of these concepts, we can ask which parts of the publication process follow or move us toward the ideal communication community and conversely where forces other than the better argument rule.

The focus of communication analysis is on the participatory conditions for the *production* of understanding through social interaction as distinct from the strategic *reproduction* of meaning as expressed by someone toward a target audience (see Deetz, 1992, chaps. 6, 7). Gadamer (1975) and Habermas (1984) have shown how strategic uses of communication are dependent on a more basic communicative attempt to reach mutual understanding. While their conceptions differ regarding the nature of the process, they both emphasize the continual social formation of consensus in interaction beyond the intentions and opinions of the participants. Such a conception is useful in thinking about publications. Mutual understanding focuses attention on reaching openly formed agreement regarding the subject matter under discussion rather than on the agreement of the perspective of the participants (see Deetz, 1990, for development). As Habermas (1984) presented his position:

Processes of reaching understanding aim at an agreement that meets the conditions of rationally motivated assent [*Zustimmung*] to the content of an utterance. A communicatively achieved agreement has a rational basis; it cannot be imposed by either party, whether instrumentally through intervention in the situation directly or strategically. . . . This is not a question of the predicates an observer uses when describing processes of reaching understanding, but of the pretheoretical knowledge of competent speakers, who can themselves distinguish situations in which they are causally exerting an influence *upon* others from those where they are coming to an understanding *with* them. . . . [T]he use of language with an orientation to reaching understanding is the *original mode* of language use, upon which indirect understanding, giving something to understand or letting something be understood, and the instrumental use of language in general, are parasitic. (pp. 286-288)

Figure 2.1 describes the key terms and relations in Habermas's analysis. Such an analysis depends on a careful description of the attempt to reach mutual understanding, a socially based description of morally guided dispute resolution, and a description of communicative difficulties, that is, communicative processes that preclude mutual understanding. From a participation perspective, communication difficulties arise from interaction practices that preclude value debate and conflict, that substitute images and imaginary relations for self-presentation and truth claims, that arbitrarily limit access to communication channels and forums, and that then lead to decisions based on arbitrary authority relations (see Deetz, 1990, 1992, and Forester, 1989, for development). As Habermas's work is well known and summaries readily available (e.g., Thompson, 1984), allow me to be brief with the conceptual development and move fairly quickly to applications to the publication process.

Habermas (1979, 1984) demonstrated that making a knowledge claim implicates a set of relations: (a) a relation of the claim to the author's interior, (b) a relation of the claim to an external world, (c) a relation of the author to others, and (d) a relation of the claim to language. Each of these relations entails responsibilities that while presumptively obligated may or may not actually be fulfilled in a speaking or writing context. The responsibilities following each of these relations are (a) truthfulness, (b) truth, (c) legitimate social relations, and (d) comprehensibility. To the extent that these responsibilities are fulfilled, the communication action is moral and the pursuit of common understanding is enhanced. And to the extent that one or more of the principles are violated, communication becomes distorted (often strategically) and unwarranted advantage exists. These responsibilities serve as a form of normative guidance in social interaction. Investigation of their fulfillment can show places where reason breaks down and knowledge production becomes skewed or disconnected from human needs and human environments. In many different ways, these responsibilities are built into standard journal review processes. Honesty in reporting data is expected, unwarranted biases are to be eliminated, blind reviews reduce power-laden social pressure, and reports are to be clear and understandable. These, to the extent that they are followed, deal with the more obvious cases of irresponsibility, like

These action types can be distinguished by virtue of their relations to the validity basis of speech:

a) *Communicative vs. Strategic Action.* In communicative action a basis of mutually recognized validity claims is presupposed; this is not the case in strategic action. In the communicative attitude it is possible to reach a direct understanding oriented to validity claims; in the strategic attitude, by contrast, only an indirect understanding via determinative indicators is possible.

b) *Action Oriented to Reaching Understanding vs. Consensual Action.* In consensual action agreement about implicitly raised validity claims can be *presupposed* as a background consensus by reason of common definitions of the situations; such agreement is supposed to be *arrived at* in action oriented to reaching understanding.

c) *Action vs. Discourse.* In communicative action it is naively supposed that implicitly raised validity claims can be vindicated (or made immediately plausible by way of question and answer). In discourse, by contrast, the validity claims raised for statements and norms are hypothetically bracketed and thematically examined. As in communicative action, the participants in discourse retain a cooperative attitude.

d) *Manipulative Action vs. Systematically Distorted Communication.* Whereas in systematically distorted communication at least one half of the participants deceives *himself* about the fact that the basis of consensual action is only apparently being maintained, the manipulator deceives at least one of the *other* participants about his own strategic attitude, in which he *deliberately* behaves in a pseudoconsensual manner.

Figure 2.1.

openly strategic action and manipulation in Habermas's scheme, and work fairly well in consensual situations when the grounds for claims are uncontested. They fail to address, however, the more subtle power effects of systematically distorted communication and the weakness of discursive processes in times of more fundamental conflict. This we can show by looking at processes of discourse and systematically distorted communication.

Open Discourse and Discursive Closures

Habermas describes discourse as the process of thematically exploring the grounds for claims in cases of dispute. In these cases, the four presumptive responsibilities are made most explicit. In an idealized case, each of the relations on which these responsibilities are based is explored with an attitude of cooperation and openness. Of interest, published disputes in the management science field rarely operate on such grounds. An adversarial model of discussion/debate with respondent/critics and rejoinders rather than negotiation is nearly always the rule. With such a model, academic discussion often looks more like a divorce court with all the unproductive outcomes than the pursuit of the best position meeting a full variety of community needs.

Further, publications often report the contradictory theories or "findings," support the argument of one or the other, or propose a test to find which one is right but rarely carefully explore the procedures, practices, or assumptions that produce different "true" outcomes. Difference often suggests a complexity that has not been explored and all too often gets left unexplored. As in the media's presentation of national politics, complexity is reduced to contradiction. The system prizes personal expressions of difference but not productive answers that can be mutually supported. (It is small wonder the paying public often feels betrayed, confused, or ripped off.) But it is not just an attitude focused on winning and authority that leads to a constrained interaction rather than shared understanding. Several discursive moves in publication can lead to strategic meaning reproduction rather than open discourse. For illustrative purposes, consider the following for each presumptive responsibility (for development, see Deetz, 1992, pp. 187-198).

Closure of the Inner World. A primary way the inner world relates to knowledge claims is through the presence of values. Because values are most fundamentally present in systems of attention and linguistic distinction, they are often unknown and unexplored. To the extent that they remain hidden, they may be considered ideological. Knowledge claims are frequently ideological, that is, conflicting knowledge claims are based in unexamined value differences. The capacity for each of us to examine our own hidden values and to socially pursue consensus based in openly chosen and shared values arises from the discussion enabled by the difference. *The* world as experienced becomes *a* world to be considered as a possibility among others. In Habermasian discourse, such alternatives are actively pursued as a route to renewed choice over socially determined internalized values and the need to work together in an expanded common world.

Discursive practices in publication can preclude or close off such a discussion. The principal way this happens is through *neutralization*. In neutralization, value-laden research methods, conceptions, and activities are treated as if they were value-free or neutral. Rather than the values being made explicit in the publication or in contestation, objectivity is proclaimed in its place, *a* possible world is treated as *the* world. Rather than objectivity, such a discussion-stopping move only assures subjective domination. In such cases, future publications rarely reveal that conflicts arise out of important value differences that should be explored. In fact, value debate is often treated as nonproductive or extrascientific, private and irresolvable. In most cases, this performs strategic functions by keeping values hidden from critical assessment, by maintaining undefended privilege for one's own group, and by universalization of sectional interests (see Giddens, 1979). In management science literature, this is most clearly seen in continuation of a managerial bias in research and a general inability to address moral questions and issues of social good for the full variety of organizational stakeholders (Carter & Jackson, 1987).

Closure of the Outer World. The outer world is not a simple collection of preexisting, fixed-in-form objects awaiting discovery. Not only is much of the outer world a product of human material and symbolic practices, the "stuff" of nature only becomes "objects" in the presence of human sense equipment and its technological extensions, institutionalized practices, measurement instruments, and linguistic distinctions. Essentialist positions are hard to defend in any careful discussion today whether in physics or the social sciences. Still, our casual professional and everyday talk *naturalizes* the world. The manners by which we produce stable objects are hidden by the implicit claim, preformed by the discursive features of the published report, that objects are by their nature as they appear. Research methods are particular ways of producing objects. The constitutive activity, however, becomes forgotten when they are widely shared in a community. If everyone looks through the same lens, the power of the lens is soon no longer considered.

The active object production by professionally shared constitutive activities soon leads to a false and protected universalization of one's own community's objects. In naturalization, researchers institutionalize a way of expression through "the projection of an 'imaginary community' by means of which 'real' distinctions are portrayed as 'natural,' the particular is disguised in the universal, the historical is effaced in the atemporality of essence" (Thompson, 1984, p. 25). Both the construction and the value-laden nature of construction are forgotten.

Such processes are most obvious when socially produced objects (such as equipment or organizations), social categories (such as labor, management, ethnicity, or gender), research constructs (such as uncertainty, personality, or motivation), and social artifacts (such as productivity or profitability) are treated as natural objects. But they are also present when "problems" that arise in organizations are treated as naturally occurring, requiring researcher solution (as in "institutional research") without critical examination of who is advantaged in this formulation or for whom it is problematic. When research results are contested on the bases of the relations between objects or how many there are, without the possibility of discussing the meaning of producing these objects or relations, discourse over the outer world becomes closed. Theories become evaluated on their ability to mirror this socially-constituted-as-real world, and more basic disputes over preferences for particular theories as ways to practically engage with the world rarely arise (see Deetz, 1992, chap. 3). Feminists have been most active in trying to reopen these disputes (see Harding, 1991; Marshall, 1993), but the basic language of management science report continues to follow a representational language philosophy.

Closure of Relation to Others. Discourse over knowledge claims presumes a freedom from unilateral (including hidden unilateral) social relations based on authority or other conditions of power. Friendship patterns, mentoring relations, funding sources, and other social relations constrain open discourse to the extent that they affect the availability of the expression of positions or the relative weight given to positions. Clearly, social relations do often exert a force. Some of these are interpersonal in form and can be traced in the journals, such as romantic/marital relations, going to the same graduate school, or recommendations by powerful sponsors. Others rest on social concepts of authority. Merton (1973), for example, discovered in his sociology of science studies the presence of what he called the "Matthew" effect: "the social processes through which various kinds of opportunities for scientific inquiry as well as the subsequent symbolic and material rewards for the results of that inquiry tend to accumulate for the individual practitioners of science, as they do also for organizations engaged in scientific work" (p. 606; see also 1988). Not only does perceived authority from past work tend to lead to many more publication opportunities (even in so-called blind review) in one's specialty (which might be warranted on the increased quality of one's claims), it tends to spread to other areas giving privileged access for which it is difficult to find any warrant (e.g., Chomsky's political expressions). Such socially derived advantages are carried in citation patterns that provide little information or guidance to the reader but tend only to buttress the argument by name association.

Closure of the Relation to Language. The point of using language is to relate to an other, but the appeal to comprehensibility does not dictate a particular style. Clarity is a relation to what is to be expressed, not a standard preferred for making different types of claims. Journals frequently implement certain style preferences that preclude research programs resulting in a different kind of report. The long-term prohibition of the use of the word *I* functioned not only to enforce false expressions of neutrality and objectivity but also hampered the direct expression of researcher positionality and self-reflexive consideration of the effects of research procedures. Further, the confusion of difficulty with the lack of clarity can lead to the unwarranted dismissal of new ideas that do not yet fit comfortably within the structure of the natural language or of reports that try to deal with very complex relations.

And, on the other hand, jargon and false linguistic complexity can lend protection and even add weight to positions that otherwise would not stand the test of interrogation. Certainly the development of new terms and precise meanings of old ones are essential to escape value biases and conceptual limitations of everyday language. But the difference between this and jargon that obscures serves as a condition of group membership, and strategically deployed expertise is both significant and ascertainable. All technical terms should answer to the questions of what we can do or think with these terms or definitions that we could not in their absence. Often these questions neither are asked nor can be comfortably asked. As Mehan (1986) showed in his studies, "The authority of the professional report comes from its very incomprehensibility and its obscurity. The psychologist and the nurse [in his study] gain their authority from the mastery and use of a technical language that others do not understand and do not question" (p. 161). "The grounds for negotiation of meaning are removed from under the conversation" (p. 160). The issue of focus should be on whether language usage opens the phenomenon or subject matter to further exploration or functions to stop exploration with implicit claims of authority.

Systematically Distorted Communication

The examination of disputes can show us the normative idea present in communicative action and discursive moves that tend to undermine such ideals, but without a doubt the more significant skewing of the open social formation of

	Random/Ad Hoc	Systematic/Structural
Inevitable	Errors	Standard routines
distortions	Incomplete data or analysis	Trained incapacities
		Blind spots
Strategic	Falsification	Ideologically supported routines and
distortions	Personal relations	criteria
	Individual reviewer bias	Advantages in the production systems

Figure 2.2. Sources of Distortion When Publication Is Viewed as a Communication Activity

knowledge as mediated by publication happens in the more routine situations where no dispute seems necessary. Clearly, some distortion in social knowledge formation happens all the time. A statistical test gives a random false positive, an error is made, data are falsified, a theoretical position is unfairly presented, research routines obscure a significant factor, hidden shared values direct privileged conceptions and avoidance of critical topics, and so forth. One hopes that continued studies will reveal such problems. But this is likely only when two conditions are met: (a) the distortions are ad hoc and random rather than systematic or structural and (b) the distortions are a result of inevitable limitations in the pursuit of common understanding rather than strategically motivated. Figure 2.2 (adapted from Forester, 1989, p. 34) displays examples of different types of distortions categorized by dimensions of these two conditions.

Inevitable distortions arise in human limitations and mistakes. Even the systemic and structural versions of them arise from nonstrategic trained incapacities and the impossibility of studying all things all ways at any given time. Generally these distortions become contested, and because they are unmotivated, contestation is likely to follow a relatively open discourse model. Even strategic moves that are individually motivated, ad hoc, and random do not usually lead to a significant skewing of social knowledge production, although they can cause great embarrassment to the research community (e.g., the David Baltimore case; LaFollette, 1992). *Strategic distortions* embedded in systems and structures, however, are likely to lead to much greater effects and are far more difficult to identify and contest. These qualify as *systematically distorted communication* in Habermas's conception.

In systematically distorted communication, unlike explicit power moves and manipulation, the researcher/report writer deceives him- or herself in some consistent and motivated (advantaging) fashion. Most often these deceptions do not arise from individual pathologies but from community-shared ideologies or ideological practices. These same unexamined (and often protected from examination) values, assumptions, shared routines and instrumentation, and social forces that lead to discursive closures in contestation lead to selectivities in making available research and research reports that go uncontested. The continued presence of ideology not only leads to the censorship of many alternative research programs and their report but more often and significantly to de facto censorship through lack of training, unawareness of options, and perceived effects on personal careers.

Some of these systematic distortions have received considerable attention and need not be developed here. For example, the gatekeeping function of editors and reviewers and generally issues in peer review have been widely studied since Crane (1967; see also Laband, 1990). Differences in criteria for evaluating research programs and their written claims have been summarized well by Morgan (1983) and debated widely in various discussions of paradigms (Burrell & Morgan, 1979). Further, distortions are built into published claims through selective sponsorship of research projects. For example, causal modeling and studies with prediction and control as outcomes are preferred by dominant groups who gain through increased ability to direct the action and thoughts of others. Rarely are these problems solved by the spread of this knowledge to disadvantaged groups or even by disadvantaged groups redefining the content of these studies. What is most lost are studies focusing on invention of that beyond the interests of a group and innovations that foster mutual development.

Importantly, both natural and social sciences have been systematically distorted through the implicit acceptance of dominant cultural values. While claiming neutrality, they are highly politicized in upholding modern conceptions of action, authority, and accountability (see Ezrahi, 1990). Rarely have they demonstrated generative power to *"challenge the guiding assumptions of culture, to raise fundamental questions regarding contemporary social life, to foster reconsideration of that which is 'taken for granted,' and thereby to furnish new alternatives for social action"* [italics in original] (Gergen, 1978, p. 1348).

Additionally, issues of well-intentioned systematic bias arising from privileging certain research methods or theoretical positions are serious and have more often been hidden than corrected by such things as blind reviews. Feminist writers in particular (see Harding, 1991; Marshall, 1993) have revealed many hidden systematic distortions and have suggested alternatives. The gradual acceptance of qualitative research methods in data collection without changing the logic of research activities represents another type of distortion. Continued investigations of these distortions can add an openness and vitality to knowledge production. But here I want to take on briefly a more insidious force of systematic distortion, the commercialization of the knowledge product. Commercialization happens when the expression of knowledge claims becomes economically rewarded apart from its contribution to mutual understanding.

The academic community largely operates from the same faulty assumption held in the larger community that rewarding the individual can be well integrated into contributing to collective goal accomplishment—that is, an individual in pursuing self-interest will contribute to the larger social good. I am not claiming that this cannot be accomplished. With careful relations drawn between group goals and assessment and reward structures, indirect goal accomplishment as an outcome of self-interest pursuit might happen. But these relations are rarely discussed or accomplished. And even where such relations hold, indirect accomplishment often leads to the existence of strategy and game playing rather than the pursuit of common understanding. Often the pursuit of common understanding and career goals conflict, with the result that strategic goal accomplishment across a population can lead to systematic distortions in knowledge production. Most important, we have not investigated well the relation between changing reward structures and systematic effects on knowledge production. Generally self-interest pursuit mediated through a market economy only represents some social interests well (Schmookler, 1993). Here I will only suggest some of the effects we might well investigate.

To the extent that publications are a significant part of reward systems in institutes and universities, we would expect certain consequences. First, internal peer groups give over their decision making to largely anonymous external peer groups. Discussion-based determination of qualities and merits governed by trying to reach mutual agreement is replaced by isolated individual judgments using largely unknown criteria. And to the extent that the locus of the decision is changed, the internal peer group will use more quantitative rather than qualitative judgments in allocating rewards.

Second, the focus on quantity invites a lot of bad publication habits, each of which has distorting consequences for the community's pursuit of more useful knowledge. Among these are the lack of precirculation for comment and revision, one-shot studies and the division of the research project into units of the smallest publishable component, resubmission to other journals without revision based on comments, the selection of methods being based on acceptance and quick turnaround rather than finding good answers, the professionalization of publication strategies in manuals and courses with a focus on getting published rather than doing work that warrants publication, and the development of a rushed lifestyle lacking reflection and broad reading and discussion.

Third, rewarding increased publication activity has consequences for the publication process itself that creates other distortions. Again, a few of these are that largely repetitive literatures are expanded beyond the capacity of individuals to read, journals become back-logged with essays that are losing timeliness and are not being revised, the number of specialty journals expand to the place where little selectivity actually exists and groups centering on particular journals become increasingly isolated without discussion across areas, and inordinate amounts of good researchers' time are spent in review processes that invite judgment but no discussion.

Finally, based on my experience, I believe that greater openness in journals to alternative conceptions and methods has been based more on concepts of fairness in career opportunity than on respect for different truths. This weak form of pluralism more assures that we can all live safely apart than that we grow together. Literatures continue to grow answering only to the internal standards of a relatively homogeneous peer group. A peer group is considered viable whenever it has enough market power to support a journal. The existence of such a journal takes inclusion pressure off mass circulation journals and draws essays away from entering the larger discussion. Fairness is achieved but not contribution and voice.

In this context, professional researchers become like paid performers, seeking audiences, dazzling with the latest twist or trick, being paid for the act rather than the contribution to the art. The problem is not just that this invites strategic shortcuts and cheats (milking the study, like a career-hungry manager does a plant), nor that it puts researchers who choose not to play games at risk; rather produced knowledge itself becomes skewed in ways that make it less valuable in fulfilling human needs. The "variable-analytic" so-called tradition is one natural outcome of this context. Research is done under a logic that if x and y show a statistical relation and y and z show a relation then I can get a publication showing a relation between x and z. Endless studies can be published following likely confirming results with no theoretical meaning or interpretation. Such a logic is good for producing publications but awful for advancing a common understanding. The justification for these studies is often a list of citations showing a gap in a seamless cumulative body but not a reasoning process demonstrating how the study would transform our understanding. The production of "accumulative fragmentalism," as Kelly (1970) called it, is not so much a product of limited philosophies of science as a distortion from a set of practices developed from a reward and motivation scheme.

PURSUING COMMON UNDERSTANDING

Can we create systems and structures that aid the open pursuit of common understanding? I think we can. Fundamental conceptions have to be changed, but changes in publication technologies make the possibilities greater. Problems in profession knowledge production look much like wider social problems arising from the rather strange legacy of enlightenment ideals and liberal democracy. We have emphasized individual expression at the expense of cooperative decision making, we have mistakenly believed that systems that reward individual pursuit of self-interest can lead to collective goods, and we have developed new authority-based forms of tutelage merely replacing older forms of state and church control of knowledge. While I am more interested here in identifying the problems so that they can be more fully explored, I do feel compelled to suggest a couple of directions we might take.

(1) Initially, we should work to disconnect career reward structures from production of knowledge activities. Obviously this is not easy given that universities are big businesses too and a job expectation is to publish. But there are ways to at least better align the needs of social knowledge production with university reward processes. For example, promotion, merit, and/or tenure packets might be limited to the inclusion of only one publication from each year. Attention could then be better directed at quality and importance. In addition, reviews of essays might be published with the essays. This would aid quality discussions and assessments that have been made virtually impossible in number games and citation indexes. These changes are still limited even if they are accomplishable. Significant changes can happen in the publication process, but ultimately I agree with Maddox (1989) in his review of the current state of journals: "Some means must be sought for abating the pressure to publish quickly, or to publish in the leading journals, or even to publish at all. In the long run, there will have to be better means by which the academic community can make judgements of the quality of its members" (p. 11).

(2) Traditional refereeing processes should be ended. There are many reasons for this. Refereed publications have acquired a status that is not clearly warranted. There is little evidence that refereed publications are of higher quality or better represent the full variety of significant positions on issues than those published in invited special issues, or as book chapters for that matter. Many of the most important theoretical advances would never pass through a traditional referee process (Maddox, 1989). Repeated questions have been raised regarding

selection of reviewers, interreviewer reliability, and bias protected by the cloak of anonymity. Cicchetti (see Bower, 1991), in a study of 20 years of publishing in a variety of physical and social sciences, showed consistently low agreement among referees and, in the social sciences, few or no changes in rejected essays before resubmission. Clearly, some evidence does support some value added in the review process (e.g., Laband, 1990), but this results from the proper matching of paper and referee rather than from blind reviewing.

The availability of electronic journals means we no longer have limited space needing allocation. Electronic publications truly can be marketplaces of ideas guaranteeing freedom of expression, assuring more timely availability, and allowing continuous critique and discussion. Remaining paper journals should focus on making sure that all important positions are available for a public to decide on important issues. They should provide a type of expression suggested by the model of open discourse. Clearly, such journals could become biased and controlled by inside groups, but such problems are both more visible and more easily solved than the systematic distortions already present. The privilege of the refereed publication has not provided a higher quality product nor generated timely discussions of important ideas; rather it has used up endless hours of good researchers' time in editing and evaluation that could be used in formative and interactive discussions. The refereed journal form embodied the philosophy of the possibility of a board certified truth rather than emphasizing truth as an important social product.

(3) Journal space should be used to focus on problems and provide answers rather than provide isolated expressions of claims. A solution orientation to problems has had important payoffs in applied contexts. Such an orientation makes the differences among possible participants a value through clarifying the need for alternative positions and facilitates explicit value discussions. Similar gains could be made in professional knowledge production. Further, it allows for the adjudication of conflicting claims by referencing the problems that drive research rather than the incommensurate language systems of specific scientific communities. Editorial boards, especially those representing professional associations, could spend their time in determining significant problems that need to be addressed and the variety of stakeholders needing representation in problem definition, thus helping direct research agendas to significant concerns and increasing the relevancy of professional knowledge. I see this as considerably different than special issues on contemporary topics. These often still invite the parallel expression of positions rather than focus on what we can say together. As the hope for a truth grounded in a universal and atemporal order fades, situ-

ated and temporal studies grounded in social needs provide a reason to pursue a common understanding. The focus on problems invites genuine struggles with others rather than abstract posturings or largely disconnected topical literatures. It also can give life to our theories as a way to engage in the world rather than being simple abstractions of it. This does not mean that our journals should become more "applied." There are major, long-term social problems that we should be addressing that are not well addressed by other knowledge claimants.

If we approach major problems with consensual procedures, we can change our claims from isolated findings put in the hands of adversarial groups to constructive decision aids (see Ozawa, 1990). We should be able to have important innovative discussions that reveal genuine value differences and advance the role of professional knowledge in a more ideal democracy. At least we might better warrant the use of our time, energies, talents, and what remains of a public trust.

REFERENCES

Bazerman, C. (1988). *Shaping written knowledge: The genre and activity of the experimental article in science.* Madison: University of Wisconsin Press.

Bernstein, R. (1984). *Beyond objectivism and relativism.* Philadelphia: University of Pennsylvania Press.

Bower, B. (1991). Peer review under fire. *Science News, 139,* 394-395.

Burrell, G., & Morgan, G. (1979). *Sociological paradigms and organizational analysis.* London: Heinemann.

Carter, P., & Jackson, N. (1987). Management, myth, and metatheory: From scarcity to post scarcity. *International Studies of Management and Organizations, 17,* 64-89.

Crane, D. (1967). The gatekeepers of science: Some factors affecting the selection of articles for scientific journals. *The American Sociologist, 2,* 195-201.

Deetz, S. (1990). Reclaiming the subject matter as a guide to mutual understanding: Effectiveness and ethics in interpersonal interaction. *Communication Quarterly, 38,* 226-243.

Deetz, S. (1992). *Democracy in an age of corporate colonization: Developments in communication and the politics of everyday life.* Albany: State University of New York Press.

Ezrahi, Y. (1990). *The descent of Icarus: Science and the transformation of contemporary democracy.* Cambridge, MA: Harvard University Press.

Fischer, F. (1990). *Technocracy and the politics of expertise.* Newbury Park, CA: Sage.

Forester, J. (1989). *Planning in the face of power.* Berkeley: University of California Press.

Foucault, M. (1980). *Power/knowledge: Selected interviews and other writings, 1972-77* (C. Gordon, Ed.). New York: Pantheon.

Fuchs, S. (1992). *The professional quest for truth: A social theory of science and knowledge.* Albany: State University of New York Press.

Gadamer, H. (1975). *Truth and method* (G. Barden & J. Cumming, Eds. and Trans.). New York: Seabury.

Gergen, K. (1978). Towards generative theory. *Journal of Personality and Social Psychology, 36,* 1344-1360.

Giddens, A. (1979). *Central problems in social theory.* Berkeley: University of California Press.

Habermas, J. (1979). *Communication and the evolution of society* (T. McCarthy, Trans.). Boston: Beacon.

Habermas, J. (1984). *The theory of communicative action: Vol. 1. Reason and the rationalization of society* (T. McCarthy, Trans.). Boston: Beacon.

Harding, S. (1991). *Whose science? Whose knowledge? Thinking from women's lives.* Ithaca, NY: Cornell University Press.

Jackell, R. (1988). *Moral mazes: The world of corporate managers.* Oxford: Oxford University Press.

Kelly, G. (1970). An introduction to personal construct theory. In D. Bannister (Ed.), *Perspectives on personal construct theory* (pp. 1-6). London: Academic Press.

Laband, D. (1990). Is there value-added from the review process in economics? *Quarterly Journal of Economics, 105,* 341-352.

LaFollette, M. (1992). *Stealing into print.* Berkeley: University of California Press.

Latour, B., & Woolgar, S. (1979). *Laboratory life: The social construction of scientific facts.* Beverly Hills, CA: Sage.

Lindsey, D. (1978). *The scientific publication system in social science.* San Francisco: Jossey-Bass.

Lyotard, J. (1984). *The postmodern condition.* Minneapolis: University of Minnesota Press.

Maddox, J. (1989). Where next with peer-review? *Nature, 339,* 11.

Mannheim, K. (1952). *Essays on the sociology of knowledge.* London: Routledge & Kegan Paul.

Marshall, J. (1993). Viewing organizational communication from a feminist perspective. In S. Deetz (Ed.), *Communication yearbook* (Vol. 16, pp. 122-143). Newbury Park, CA: Sage.

Mehan, H. (1986). The role of language and the language of role in institutional decision making. In S. Fisher & A. D. Todd (Eds.), *Discourse and institutional authority.* Norwood, NJ: Ablex.

Merton, R. (1973). The Matthew effect in science. In R. Merton, *The sociology of science* (pp. 439-459). Chicago: University of Chicago Press.

Merton, R. (1988). The Matthew effect in science, II: Cumulative advantage and the symbolism of intellectual property. *ISIS, 79,* 606-615.

Morgan, G. (Ed.). (1983). *Beyond method: Strategies for social research.* Beverly Hills, CA: Sage.

Myers, G. (1985). Texts as knowledge claims. *Social Studies of Science, 15,* 593-630.

Ozawa, C. (1990). *Recasting science.* Boulder, CO: Westview.

Prelli, L. (1989). *A rhetoric of science: Inventing scientific discourse.* Columbia: University of South Carolina Press.

Schmookler, A. (1993). *The illusion of choice: How the market economy shapes our destiny.* Albany: State University of New York Press.

Simon, H. (1990). *The rhetorical turn: Invention and persuasion in the conduct of inquiry.* Chicago: University of Chicago Press.

Snyder, R. (1973). Knowledge, power, and the university. In G. Remmling (Ed.), *Towards the sociology of knowledge.* London: Routledge & Kegan Paul.

Thompson, J. (1984). *Studies in a theory of ideology.* Berkeley: University of California Press.

Wagner, J., III, & Gooding, R. (1987). Effects of societal trends on participation research. *Administrative Science Quarterly, 32,* 241-262.

Woolgar, S. (1980). Discovery: Logic and sequence in a scientific text. In K. Knorr-Cetina & M. Mulkay (Eds.), *The social process of scientific investigation* (pp. 239-268). Dordrecht, the Netherlands: Reidel.

Woolgar, S. (Ed.). (1988). *Knowledge and reflexivity: New frontiers in the sociology of knowledge.* London: Sage.

3

Looking at
Ourselves as We Look at Others
An Exploration of the
Publication System for Organization Research

WALTER R. NORD

In the poem "To a Louse," Robert Burns wrote of how wonderful it would be if we had the gift to see ourselves as others see us. I believe a second gift is equally important to those of us who make our living by observing other people and organizations—the ability to see ourselves as we see others.

This chapter applies this second perspective to the publication system in our own field of organization behavior. It asks: What might we discover about our publication process if we examined it in the same way we analyze core elements of other organizations? More specifically, if we examine problems many of us see in our publication system as outcomes of the way we are organized in the same way we might treat complaints that other people voice about their systems, what might we discover? What policy implications and action steps might we suggest?

AUTHOR'S NOTE: Portions of this chapter were presented at Academy of Management meetings in Dallas, Texas, August 1983.

For this exploration, I ask you to imagine a case discussion in a second-level MBA course in organization design. Today's case treats an organization whose product is published research on organizations and organization behavior. In other words, the organization referred to in the case is the set of people, processes, and structures that together (a) mine and/or produce information about formal organizations and (b) transform this information into documents that are either published or disseminated in some other form to relevant academic professional audiences. In short, the organization analyzed was our own publication system.

In preparation for this specific session, the students have read a Harvard-type case that described the salient issues about the publication system in organization behavior. The instructor, Dr. Black, had put the case near the end of the course so that the students would have completed most of the required reading, which included Mintzberg's (1979) *The Structuring of Organizations,* Pfeffer's (1978) *Organizational Design* and (1981) *Power,* and Weick's (1979) *Social Psychology of Organizing.* There are a few doctoral students in the seminar who are familiar with a broader spectrum of literature.

The case contained a number of key points about the organization. For one thing, it described the turmoil within the field about the dysfunctional consequences of current control methods in the organization's major communication system—its journals. Also, it reported that some members of the organization—sometimes called rabble-rousers or radicals by ranking members of the field—have been most vocal in their complaints. The case write-up also emphasized that the journals play a major role in the allocation of rewards and tenure in the field. In fact, publication of at least several articles in the leading journals was described as a "rite of passage" to permanent membership.

The organization itself was portrayed as not being very effective; in fact, in important respects it was failing. For example, in comparison with members of similar organizations within its immediate environment such as finance, accounting, and even marketing, participants in this system had relatively low status. Moreover, in comparison with similar but more remote organizations such as those in the hard sciences, the output of the organization had not been particularly useful in building theory, attracting support from external constituents, or even producing data that people within the field (much less outside it) viewed as high quality. In fact, both members and outsiders had charged that the organization has contributed little beyond what is common sense (Gordon, Kleiman, & Hanie, 1978; Lundberg, 1976; Thomas & Tymon, 1982). On the other hand, the case also noted that there is a strong potential market for the types of products this organization seeks to produce. In fact, several products based on information from this field have recently been long-term best-sellers on the *New*

York Times book list. (This fact led one of the accounting majors in the class to ask another student before class, "Did the case say whether these books appeared on the fiction or nonfiction list?")

Most of the 28 students in the class were in the second year of the MBA program. However, a few doctoral students from psychology and sociology were enrolled; their general familiarity with a broad spectrum of the literature had given the class a more academic flavor than often is found in an MBA class.

The cold morning rain had induced more people than usual to drive to the university. The inevitable minor traffic problems had increased the difficulty of finding an acceptable parking place. As a result, it was a few minutes after 8:00 a.m. before most of the students had managed to purchase a cup of coffee and slide into their chairs. Before the last two had settled, Dr. Black had begun to introduce the case and start discussion with his typical question: "How do you diagnose the situation?"

The first student Dr. Black called on attempted to hide his lack of preparation by attacking the case itself. He argued: "The case does not refer to an organization. I don't understand why this case was assigned in a course on organizations."

Some lively discussion followed, but most people agreed that the publication system could be described as the outcome of organizing in the Weickian (1979) sense. In this view, organizing is like a grammar; it is a systematic account of rules and conventions by which sets of interlocked behaviors are assembled to form social processes that are intelligible to the actors. They also agreed that the case treated rules for forming variables and causal linkages into meaningful structures (cause maps) that summarize the recent experiences of the people who are organized.

Impatient to get to the meat of the issue, Dr. Black said: "Let's assume that we are talking about an organization. Mr. Johnson, how did you diagnose the situation?"

Mr. Johnson reported that he began with an analysis of the task that the publication system was attempting to accomplish and then examined the current structure to see if it fit the task. He argued that the manifest or stated goal of the system was to disseminate valid, important information to researchers in the field. Citing Perrow (1970), he argued that the current technical system appeared to be particularly well adapted to handling relatively routine materials where stimulus variability was low and problems were analyzable. Citing guidelines for authors from leading journals from an appendix to the case, he concluded that indeed the criteria were well specified, operational, and extremely consistent with doing thoroughly routine tasks. Moreover, because the scientific method was well-known and science required replicable, detailed oriented activity, Mr. Johnson concluded that the current rather centralized control structure was highly appropriate. In fact, he said, "If there is a serious problem it is not the lack of innovation but the lack of replication that the current system fosters."

Ms. Jones agreed with Mr. Johnson, at least in part. She asserted that many of the tasks were routine and that the current structure fit them quite well. However, she maintained that these routine tasks are only part of the process by which knowledge is uncovered. Building her case around Mintzberg's (1979) hypotheses about the importance of fashion at the time of an organization's founding and the tendency of organizations to be guided by fashions that may not be appropriate for them, she argued that the current structures were too mechanistic. She speculated that many of the requirements for advancements in knowledge are much more consistent with structures like those of adhocracies than they are with professional bureaucracies or machine bureaucracies, which seemed to be the types of organizations Mr. Johnson had described. Dr. Black noted that, while there was much in what Ms. Jones said, there was also a need to consider the need for even greater routinization. He reported how frequently several of his colleagues who were doing meta-analysis complained that the journals did not require authors to include information needed to interpret their results fully.

Mr. Robinson supported Ms. Jones and added that the real problem was one of creating balance between bureaucratic and more amorphous, unstable patterns. Drawing on Hedberg, Nystrom, and Starbuck (1976), he argued that objectivity should be fostered, responsibilities delegated, and conflicts resolved impersonally on substantive criteria; however, simultaneously, expertise should be diluted, authority ambiguous, statuses inconsistent, responsibilities overlapping, activities mutually competitive, rules volatile, decision criteria varying, communication networks amorphous, behavior patterns unstable, analytic methods unsophisticated, subunits conflicting, and efficiency a subordinate goal. He continued, "These latter features increase the likelihood that the organization will remain open and avoid gravitating into stagnant waters." Citing Hedberg et al. again, he noted that structures supporting such flexible activities are analogous to tents rather than palaces but that, based on the description of the structure of the publication system provided in the case, most journals have become palaces. He concluded, "Clearly new structures are needed, not necessarily to replace the current ones but to balance them."

Another student noted that, while those who had spoken so far had analyzed the publication process correctly, they had limited their analysis to journals. She concluded by saying, "Much communication in the field of organization research is informal. There are numerous meetings, conventions, colloquia, and an 'invisible college' through which working papers are circulated. These less formal networks supplement the journal system so effectively and the production cycle that transforms manuscripts into published papers is so long that, at least for people doing cutting edge work, the journals are not an effective communication medium. They are more like archives than communication systems." She concluded, "Any idea that is worthy of consideration has ample opportunity to be communicated to scholars in the area. The journal system is best at dealing with fairly routine tasks; however, the total communication system is adequate for handling the nonroutine tasks." Other students tended to agree. For example, Ms. Larson, based on analysis of a so-called typical Academy of Management Convention program printed in the appendix, argued that at least 30% of the program was devoted to highly speculative topics of all sorts. Another student added that several people in the case had even complained that the leading journal in the field had even gone too far in publishing speculative work. Overall, these students concluded that, collectively, the publication system, defined a bit more broadly than journals, was balanced and served the task requirements quite well.

Sensing the consensus on the analysis of the formal structure and task requirements of the publication system, Dr. Black asked, "If what you seem to be saying is true, why then is there so much conflict, debate, and discontent among the members of the organization—particularly some of the lower level participants—about the publication system?" Having recently completed Pfeffer's (1981) book on power, the students were really ready for this one. In rapid succession, a number of ideas emerged. First, journal space is a scarce resource and conflict develops around scarce resources. Individuals who control the resources, having won past contests for control, will seek to institutionalize their control. They will set rules and procedures that favor the type of work they do. They will build and solidify coalitions with others who share some of their interests. They will attempt to routinize the control system by making it appear impersonal and objective. In response to these control tactics, those who currently lack control over the resources will seek either to develop an alternative basis of power by establishing their own journals and/or to challenge the legitimacy of criteria embodied in the rules and procedures institutionalized by the more powerful.

Some students saw this as a wasteful process, but others followed Salancik and Pfeffer (1977) closely and concluded that, while the debate will be heated, and there will be name calling, labels assigned, and so forth, it is through this type of contest system that needed readjustments can be made in systems where the criteria are not unambiguous, authority is not centralized, resources are scarce, and decisions are important. The existence of such conflict is inevitable and is functional in the sense that the results of the struggle are useful in helping the organization to allocate power internally in a manner that leads to mapping the organization's external environment in ways that will help the organization to survive. A consensus appeared to be emerging that struggles were normal and—particularly in an adhocracy—would quite probably lead to realignments of power for effective functioning.

However, Mr. Rodgers was not happy with this conclusion. He pointed out that Pfeffer (1978) had also suggested that organizations get trapped by their own histories and that Mintzberg (1979) had argued that for long periods of time institutionalized patterns of relationships emerge that keep the organization from being in touch with its environment. Consequently, major reorientations are required periodically. Because current leaders are too slow to change, such major reorientations may require removal of the existing elites. After all, he concluded, "What is the 'iron law of oligarchy' all about anyway?"

At this point, a light seemed to go on for Ms. Cohen. She blurted out, "It seems to me we may have missed the point. We have been treating the publication system as a communication system when in fact its real function is a control system. While there are a variety of mechanisms through which ideas can be communicated, not all channels are equally powerful ones to use. Those who control the most important channels exercise disproportionally more power than the others. In fact, one might argue that the less potent channels are useful co-optation devices. Give the critics a place in the formal scheme of things—but a relatively weak position—and this is the best way to protect existing routines."

Pleased that the issue of control had come out so clearly, Dr. Black said, "Let's look at the control aspects." Several points were brought out. Some students focused on the manifest consequences of the system. They argued that, like all control systems, the publication system ensures quality. It protects consumers from fraud, forces high standards among the producers, and protects the status of the profession. Evidence that the system was working included the high number of rejections that the leading and even somewhat secondary journals in the field boast. Clearly, such severe controls, some students argued, screen out a great deal of low-quality work.

A student with a physics background pointed out that, in the highest prestige journal in physics, only 50% of the articles are rejected. This point led to a discussion of what the high rejection rate in the social science journals might indicate. Reasoning from Pfeffer (1981), one student observed that the low paradigm nature of the field results in a lack of explicitly agreed upon criteria. In such contexts, individuals and groups can exercise considerable power. If nothing else, the high rejection rates mean that powerful actors in the social sciences are exercising power.

Several students took a different position. They argued that, while the control system had many functional consequences, it had a number of direct and indirect costs. They pointed to publication lags, the screening out of novel material, and reviewer bias. (On this latter point, a doctoral student from the psychology department noted the low referee agreement on papers reviewed in consumer psychology and the low reliability—.26—reported by Scott, 1974, on articles submitted to the *Journal of Personality and Social Psychology*.) Dr. Black indicated that the low reliability by itself did not indicate bias. He said that low reliability could in fact indicate that editorial boards were heterogeneous. Heterogeneity would lead to diverse evaluations. Thus low reliability could indicate a very open process. Alternatively, high reliability could indicate that people with narrow homogeneous points of view were doing the reviewing. He said that data from Mahoney's (1977) study were probably more indicative of possible bias. Mahoney sent pseudomanuscripts to reviewers who were known to have certain positions on the issues treated in the manuscript. The papers were identical except for the results. The results were manipulated in such a way that it was possible to send "self-confirmatory" or "self-disconfirmatory" outcomes to referees—*self-confirmatory* meaning that the direction of the results would agree with the assumed position of the referee. Mahoney found that there was a strong tendency for reviewers to accept confirmatory results and reject disconfirmatory results. Thus some case for bias seems possible.

At this point, Ms. Cohen reentered the conversation by returning to the control theme she had developed earlier. She maintained that the most vital consequences of this control system were its institutionalizing effects rather than its direct outcomes and that the journal system exerts major and perhaps functionally autonomous pressures on the socialization and selection processes; these processes determine who enters and who continues in the field. She indicated that the case said that individuals who, after the first five or six years, had not published several articles in important journals were often forced out of the organization. She concluded, "The real influence of the journal system is that it determines who will teach in the field and who will not."

At this point, Mr. Cains entered the fray. Mr. Cains was a finance/economics major who the instructor suspected was taking the course for an easy grade. He typically appeared bored, so his vehemence on this issue got everyone's attention. He began, "Let's assume that what Ms. Cohen said is true—journals are the most important channel of communication—not so much because of their manifest consequences but because of their latent consequences—that is, evidence of publishing in them is the most heavily weighted selection criterion in the field. Moreover, let's assume, as we have discussed, that the journal technology is more attuned to routine than nonroutine inputs. Under these conditions, the incentive structure seems rather clear cut. People just entering the field would be well advised to follow a risk-averse strategy. Their entire careers hinge on the small number of manuscripts they produce shortly after entering the field. They are faced with low probabilities of acceptance, a short time period, considerable error, and quite probably a conservative bias in the process. Under such conditions, the risk-averse strategy would be the rational one—any rational maximizing decision maker would direct their resources toward traditional topics and methods. Thus not only are risky papers not published, but there is little incentive to even attempt such projects."

Another student interrupted, "That is just nonsense. There are three statements on page 16 of the case from journal editors who assert vehemently that they have for years sought innovative contributions and in fact have published several clearly nonmainstream articles."

Mr. Cains countered that all the rhetoric and those few examples really changed the expected values little, and then continued on another subject: "What bothers me most about this whole discussion is that no one has compared the present allocation of resources with the optimal pattern. You haven't dealt with the fundamental issues that are, in essence, economic ones.

"First, what are the real costs of the current process? From what I can tell, there are substantial direct costs for printing, mailing, editorial staff, and so on. Moreover, the indirect costs are even more significant. Some of the best scientists become editors and spend huge amounts of their time in quasi-administrative tasks. Similarly, reviewers no doubt are some of the top people in the field. While, of course, they benefit from reading new work and perhaps from their power, they devote a great deal of their time to reviewing. Moreover, since rejected manuscripts are usually submitted elsewhere, several teams of reviewers are involved before a final resting place is determined; these multiple submissions mean the total costs of evaluation can be very great. In short, large direct expenses and significant indirect resource commitments that are not recognized in the financial statements of journals are expended by the current system. Suppose we were to start the system *de novo*—how would we allocate these resources to achieve the communication goals?

"Second, there is a 'bundling problem.' Many of the specific issues of journals contain a great deal of information that is irrelevant to a particular scholar. In short, if I wanted to buy a journal that meets my needs, I'd have to buy a lot of articles that I do not want.

"Third, who are the actual consumers of journals? Most journals seem to be founded by people who are looking for publication outlets, not in response to readers demanding such a journal. The real consumers are the people who compete for the scarce journal space to enhance their own prestige, legitimacy, and career chances. Charging submission fees would shift some of the burden to these consumers who are now getting a free good and might help reduce the multiple submission process. Other major consumers are third parties such as university administrators and faculty from other fields attempting to make personnel decisions within their organizations. They use the journals—not for their content but as tools for evaluation.

"However, I think the most important thing that you have left out has to do with property rights. People in my field, such as Douglas North (1981) and Harold Demsetz (1967), have shown that progress requires ways for individuals to get personal benefits from their contributions. The organizational research community as a whole has few mechanisms whereby an individual can capture economic returns from his or her research. The financial resources the field attracts accrue primarily to third parties—book publishers, management associations, consultants, and trainers—who pirate the material with at most minor payments for reproduction fees back to the research community. The individuals in the profession who capture financial resources are typically the consultants and textbook writers who benefit as individuals by summarizing and translating the materials that are published in the journals. It would seem that the leaders of the organization in the case need to find some mechanisms to turn public interest in their field into resources that can be used to develop the profession—to increase journal space if nothing else."

A bit defensively, Dr. Black acknowledged that Mr. Cains had made some very interesting and novel points. He suggested that perhaps the recent purchase of the popular magazine *Psychology Today* by the American Psychological Association might be a model to consider for capturing economic returns by the profession. Through such publications, proceeds from subscriptions and from advertising revenue would accrue to the profession rather than to other publishers.

At this point, the class was almost over and Dr. Black made a few observations. First, he amplified some of the earlier discussion about the history of the publication process and Mintzberg's (1979) notion that organizations tend to be heavily influenced by their age, the period of their founding, and their initial purposes. He suggested the importance of exploring the history of the journal process in more depth. Drawing heavily on Bernal (1939), he indicated that academic journals arose several centuries ago when the mode of science was basically a pastime of the rich who, to get the most from their hobbies, established ways to communicate with each other about their activities. As things developed, an important function of these journals was to control the charlatans and quacks as science became a profession rather than a hobby. Thus a basic historical function of the journals has been control as well as communication. These two functions are partially incompatible and have been wedded together in ways that may be dysfunctional for the development of science. He suggested the need to make conscious choices about the trade-offs between the benefits of control versus the costs of more free flows of information. Second, he indicated that the current process might be even more dysfunctional for scientific progress than the students had imagined. He noted that prospective authors (rightly or wrongly) perceive journals as wanting to shorten manuscripts severely. Moreover, university administrators are often victims of number magic. These two facts seem to induce people to try to cut their research reports into as many pieces as possible rather than to pursue a coherent, systematic development of their product. Moreover, he reported on hearing colleagues talk in ways that indicated that publication possibilities were being given considerable weight in their choices of both problems to be studied and methods to be used. In short, the means, in important ways, had become ends. The medium influences not only what can be sent but what is available for sending.

Dr. Black also indicated that the class had overlooked some important considerations. In particular, the incentive structures for journal editors may also cause them to be risk averse. One type of error they might make is to publish articles their peers view as deficient; these errors are visible and consequently a stimulus for sanction. On the other hand, not publishing a manuscript, however insightful it may be, is an error that is less likely to cause problems for the editor. Thus Kerr's (1975) notion of rewarding A while hoping for B applies to editors as well as authors, inducing members of both groups to be less innovative.

On the other hand, Dr. Black also questioned how important a particular "missed case"—that is, screening out of an important innovative piece—really is. If science is a cumulative process, there are often several people working and thinking the same way at the same time. Consequently, any individual missed case is apt to be relatively unimportant in the development of science—it will be corrected by another paper in the near future. The real costs of such a system are to the individual scientists rather than to scientific progress itself. He used the development of the periodic table in chemistry as an illustration. Several years prior to Mendelev's "discovery" of the ordering of the elements, an English scientist, John A. R. Newlands, had his manuscript postulating the periodic table rejected by leading journals; Mendelev, several years later, published very similar information. While there was some time lag, and we can pity Newlands whose creativity, for some period of time, led him to be ridiculed rather than praised (see Dickerson, Gray, & Haight, 1979), historically, the important idea won out. However, Dr. Black added, if the research system is undermanned, as Staw (1982) suggested, then such missed cases could become more important.

Dr. Black, eager to move things to a conclusion, asked, "Suppose you were a participant—a leader or a member of this organization. What would you do?" A number of ideas were offered.

One student suggested that an obvious problem was that there was too little publication space—particularly in the highly esteemed journals.

"What would you do?" Dr. Black repeated. The student suggested that finding ways to raise resources to provide more outlets would be required, and returned to the property rights theme suggesting that professional organizations ought to design ways to benefit from those who use the knowledge. He indicated that films, journals such as *Psychology Today,* and other forms of communication that generate revenue might be used to provide additional resources not only for journal space but also for research support. Another student proposed vertical integration into the textbook business; certainly books sanctioned by leading professional groups would have a comparative advantage in the marketplace. Another student suggested that, while such vertical integration is worth considering, it involves a curious mixture of possibilities and pitfalls. On the one hand, it would give the academic community more influence in presenting its findings appropriately to users and other publishers. On the other hand, the new activities might be so far outside the normal expertise and roles of the research community as to be very risky.

Another student, who could always be counted on to present the Weickian view, suggested the following. First, recognizing that organizations create their own environments, she suggested that efforts must be made in the field to stimulate the organization to be concerned with discovering ways to partial out the effects of its own interventions from what would have happened had the organization not intervened—asking such questions as the following: "What didn't we do?" "What next step best preserves our options and does least damage to our repertoire?" "What do these bruises mean?" "How did we ruin that equipment?" (see Weick, 1979, p. 169). Moreover, ways to complicate the controller must be found. Mechanisms she proposed are appointment of editorial boards of quite different persuasions, publication of articles that maybe only one reviewer sees as being significant, perhaps even forcing a distribution of provocative, speculative, controversial articles. She then stressed the importance of discrediting—

doubting what is believed and treating as certain that which is doubted (see Weick, 1979, p. 221).

Picking up on her lead, another student proposed the value of stretching metaphors. He asked, "If the function of journals is, or at least ought to be, an efficient communication system, what type of communication system should it be? Should it be a formalized bureaucratic one where messages are edited and monitored by central groups and then sent to everyone, or should it be more like a post office where people desiring to send messages and those desiring to receive messages about a particular topic are provided with a means to expedite that process? Sometimes a paragraph could convey an important idea; other ideas require a monograph." Stretching the post office metaphor, he suggested the need for the medium to be rich enough to handle one short idea that could be sent on a postcard, detailed case studies that require large packages, and all things in between. The instructor noted that, almost a half century ago, Bernal (1939) had proposed the post office model for scientific communication. Drawing on this discussion, several students observed that developments in data processing have provided computer users with access to sophisticated data banks. Developments in information technology may make journals obsolete. One proposed task force should be set up by professional organizations to investigate these possibilities. Specifically, he observed that journals will be replaced by floppy discs that can be updated periodically and that perhaps central data banks indexed appropriately and accessible by personal computers would virtually eliminate the need for journals and eliminate the bundling problem Mr. Cains had described. Staying closer to the existing system, another student pointed out that there must be greater rewards for negative results. Citing material from *In Search of Excellence* and from cases the class had considered on the management of the R&D in industry, she indicated how managers of these enterprises recognized that a major element in their success stemmed from rewarding the competently done, creative failure.

Mr. Markley indicated that, in view of the foregoing discussion, which had indicated the great need for replication but absence of reward for it, some specific mechanisms to reward replications ought to be devised. He proposed that each journal devote 10% of its space to the publication of manuscripts that were replications of studies the journal had published. Such an allocation of scarce journal space might encourage investigators to attempt to replicate previous research. He noted that such manuscripts could be very brief because the literature reviews and descriptions of method would need only refer back to the original piece. Moreover, he argued this proposal required very little change in basic routines; in fact, it was a simple procedure for institutionalizing a widely held scientific principle.

Another student suggested that, if journal editors are sincerely interested in having the opportunity to publish truly innovative work, ways to effectively communicate this to scholars in the field must be developed. He suggested that fuller statements of this intent and efforts to define criteria in the editorial policies might be a start.

Yet another student suggested that, in view of the data that exist on the faultiness of the review process, mechanisms to revise it might be considered. Obviously, procedures for appointment of review boards, assignment of manuscripts, and so on need description and evaluation. Perhaps greater accountability of reviewers might be considered so as to equalize the power relationships. As one student pointed out, "If, in fact, an adhocracy-type structure is needed, the literature suggests the importance of more equalized power among the participants."

The final comment was from one of the more erratic students—he was nearly always provocative but sometimes seemed to be responding to a different case than the rest of the class. He argued that really very little could be done, because the current organization had enacted an environment in which the current journal procedure was perceived as indispensable. Paraphrasing Pfeffer (1978), he said, "The organization is trapped by its own history. Universities have created routines to evaluate people that are based on the present system of refereed journals and unless a large number of more powerful fields (e.g., finance, accounting, marketing) changed simultaneously, any significant changes in the journal system for organization research would be suicidal. Members of the organization could not let it happen. It's a prime example of alienation—people being controlled by their own creations."

POSTMORTEM

At the end of class, Dr. Black complimented the students on their insights. As he was returning to his office, he began to think about what had been said. Which solutions were feasible? Which were far too revolutionary for the field to possibly implement?

As one of the critics of the current process, he was even more pessimistic than before. Had journals become palaces? Could they possibly be made tents? Who would publish in a tent? Weren't the palaces in fact necessary for members of the field to gain legitimacy in their own individual universities? On the one hand, he was convinced of the need to provide richer media and agreed with many of the criticisms that the students had made of the current process. Yet, he realized how often he and his colleagues told students and clients that it is only possible for systems to change through a disjointed incremental process—especially systems as loosely structured as a scientific publication system. Why should his organization be different than others? Perhaps he was expecting far too much of this particular human system. He recalled the feelings of powerlessness a retiring journal editor (Campbell, 1982) had expressed. Still, many of the proposals such as Mr. Markley's idea of devoting a specific amount of space to replication studies seemed clearly incremental. Perhaps the major problem was simply the prevailing tendency to view the publication system as a self-correcting scientific routine rather than as a human organization that to be effective needed to be redesigned in a conscious and deliberate manner. This prevailing view kept those who could change it from engaging in the required diagnosis. In any case, he was convinced of the merits of examining the research process as an organizational problem—that is, trying to see ourselves as we see others—and decided to write down what he could remember of the class discussion. He believed the students had some valuable insights. Maybe they were publishable somewhere— although probably not in a refereed journal.

REFERENCES

Bernal, J. D. (1939). *The social function of science.* London: Routledge & Kegan Paul.

Campbell, J. R. (1982). Editorial: Some remarks from the outgoing editor. *Journal of Applied Psychology, 67,* 691-700.

Demsetz, H. (1967). Toward a theory of property rights. *American Economic Review, 57,* 347-359.

Dickerson, R. E., Gray, H. B., & Haight, G. P., Jr. (1979). *Chemical principles* (3rd ed., pp. 276-277). Menlo Park, CA: Benjamin/Cummings.

Gordon, M. E., Kleiman, L. S., & Hanie, C. A. (1978). Industrial-organizational psychology: Open thy ears O House of Israel. *American Psychologist, 33,* 893-905.

Hedberg, B. L. T., Nystrom, P. C., & Starbuck, W. H. (1976). Camping on seesaws: Prescriptions for a self-designing organization. *Administrative Science Quarterly, 21,* 41-65.

Kerr, S. (1975). On the folly of rewarding A, while hoping for B. *Academy of Management Journal, 16,* 769-783.

Lindsey, D. (1978). *The scientific publication system in social science.* San Francisco: Jossey-Bass.

Lundberg, G. C. (1976). Hypothesis creation in organizational behavior research. *Academy of Management Review, 1*(2), 5-12.

Mahoney, M. J. (1977). Publication prejudices: An experimental study of confirmatory bias in the peer review system. *Cognitive Therapy and Research, 1,* 161-175.

Mintzberg, H. (1979). *The structuring of organizations.* Englewood Cliffs, NJ: Prentice Hall.

North, D. C. (1981). *Structure and change in economic history.* New York: Norton.

Perrow, C. (1970). *Organizational analysis: A sociological view.* Belmont, CA: Wadsworth.

Pfeffer, J. (1978). *Organizational design.* Arlington Heights, IL: AHM.

Pfeffer, J. (1981). *Power in organizations*. Marshfield, MA: Pitman.
Salancik, G. R., & Pfeffer, J. (1977). Who gets power—and how they hold on to it: A strategic-contingency model of power. *Organizational Dynamics, 5,* 3-21.
Scott, W. A. (1974). Interreferee agreement on some characteristics of articles submitted to the *Journal of Personality and Social Psychology. American Psychologist, 29,* 698-702.
Staw, B. M. (1982). Some judgements on the judgement calls approach. In J. E. McGrath, J. Martin, & R. A. Kulka (Eds.), *Judgment calls in research* (pp. 119-127). Beverly Hills, CA: Sage.
Thomas, K. W., & Tymon, W. G., Jr. (1982). Necessary properties of relevant research: Lessons from recent criticisms of the organizational sciences. *Academy of Management Review, 7,* 345-352.
Weick, K. E. (1979). *Social psychology of organizing* (2nd ed.). Reading, MA: Addison-Wesley.

Relevance and Rigor in Publishing
Introduction

L. L. CUMMINGS

PETER J. FROST

I t is not possible to talk for very long about publishing in the organizational sciences without addressing issues of the relevance and rigor of what we publish in our field. We asked two colleagues to speak to these issues. Each has graduate training in the organizational sciences. Each has specialized to some degree in a different arena—Professor Staw in research and Dr. Price in management. Each has received recognition from his peers as having achieved excellence in his respective area of expertise. Collectively, they span three arenas to which we believe publishing in the organizational sciences ought to speak: creating knowledge, teaching/communicating/translating knowledge, and applying it in the field. Their reflections on relevance and on rigor are instructive.

As Staw points out in his chapter ("Repairs on the Road to Relevance and Rigor: Some Unexplored Issues in Publishing Organizational Research"), two aspects of the relevance and rigor issue seem fairly clear cut. First, where one comes down on the question of the relative importance of relevance versus rigor in the work of our fields depends in large measure on what we think a field is about and where we believe it ought to be headed. Second, it is not easy to

maximize both relevance and rigor at the same time. There are other aspects of
relevance and rigor in the context of publishing, however, that do emerge from
the discussions and speculations of the authors of these two chapters. Some of
these are discussed here.

ON RELEVANCE

Both authors see relevance of ideas and findings in terms of the contributions
these make to new knowledge. Knowledge, for each writer, refers to that which
helps us better understand what goes on in organizational settings and what organizations are about. They each talk about the importance of research that helps
us see organizational phenomena differently, which in Price's words, "challenge[s] causal assumptions," as well as research that meaningfully extends existing theory. It is knowledge if we find it interesting, knowledge if it clarifies
and illuminates our thinking.

Professor Staw differs from Price on the issue of research application. He
does not focus on application, while it is a crucial dimension for Price. Relevance does not include, for Staw, the use of research to manage or change organizations or organizational events.

Dr. Price in his chapter ("A Customer's View of Organizational Literature")
is unequivocal about the importance of the applied dimension of relevant published research. Not only should research give the practitioner a way to look at
problems differently, but it should be of assistance to him or her in trying to
resolve these problems *now.* He sees relevant research as that which tries to answer the "So what?" question, is informative on issues of organizational effectiveness, and is prescriptive in tone.

Expanding Our Thinking on Relevance

Both authors are innovative in their efforts to go beyond the conventional
definitions and treatments of relevance. Professor Staw distinguishes contributions to knowledge from those to the literature, the latter serving an archival
rather than a generative function. He examines the way we conceptualize relationships between variables as a means to creating knowledge that advances the
field and suggests that our research might become more relevant if we are prepared to take risks, to be more adventurous in our studies.

Dr. Price provides us with an interesting operationalization of relevance from
the professional-in-the-field's perspective. It is a perspective that we feel is a

reasonable approximation to that of the practicing line manager who seeks information and knowledge from published sources. Relevance of a published article hinges, for Price, on whether it is interesting, attempts to relate findings to organizational dilemmas; helps him see/think about problems and issues differently; extends existing theories meaningfully; summarizes/integrates important, topical, or interesting ideas in the field; helps him see trends among the current mix of organizational and societal affairs; or builds bridges from behavioral to other organizational functions (such as marketing, finance). His final criterion for relevance—"Can I recommend this to a manager?"—is novel and intriguing. In some senses, it is a useful quick test of whether we judge a publication to be relevant, whether our reference point be research, teaching, or practice. If we believe a publication might inform others' ideas or work, might increase their understanding of an organizational issue, *and* we recommend it, we have signaled quite clearly, through our action, how we assess its relevance.

While not all of his criteria apply to all published research, and it is not clear whether some are more important than others, Price's application of the scheme to several highly regarded journals in the organizational sciences is illuminating. Perhaps we should not be surprised that he found little of relevance to him in the research journals. Does it matter? Their intended customers are not practitioners. But the journal editors should perhaps be more alert to his message. The question: "For whom are our research publications relevant?" will be addressed briefly, later in this commentary.

ON RIGOR

Looking across these chapters, we find less emphasis given to the issue of rigor in relation to the publication process. Not surprisingly, Staw, as the researcher, is more explicit than Price in examining the question of rigor. His discussion of rigor and of the interaction of rigor and relevance adds to our knowledge on the subject. For Professor Staw, the rigor of a research report lies in the strength of the inferences that can be made from the study findings. He discusses the implications of this perspective for our traditional treatment of rigor as bound up in considerations of quantitative analysis and statistical significance. He discusses the trade-off we typically make between rigor and relevance when the subject matter of the research is novel and the cost of error is high. In his view, we ought to take risks, be more lenient in our demands for rigor than we presently are, when assessing such studies. He draws from his own experience as a reviewer in arguing this point.

Price focuses little attention on rigor. In a sense, his treatment of rigor of published research is implicit. He takes for granted that what he reads in journals has been screened in terms of rigor. The quality control is built into the system.

In another way, Price does deal with the rigor question. Price implies a willingness to make the judgment on the rigor of a research paper himself. His need for research information that is useful to his current organizational preoccupations (resolving an organizational problem) drives him to sources other than traditional journals for that information, such as conferences, workshops, and informal connections from which such information is more readily available. Such sources and networks are less accessible to someone in Price's situation, because he is located away from where much of the organizational science research takes place. Nevertheless, he too is likely to have his networking accesses to current research results. The point is, the consumer of unpublished ideas (in the traditional sense of the term) must take more responsibility for determining the rigor of the product. The customer has to make the judgment him- or herself. There is no "seal of approval" label on the package.

There is nothing inherently wrong with this approach. In fact, both authors want the evaluation of manuscripts and responsibility for reputation to be pushed down further into the communities in which they have their primary interests. The problem, which is not necessarily unsolvable, lies in ensuring that, as customers, we have the expertise within ourselves, or in our community, to help us decide on the quality of the product. Knowing whether a publication is relevant or not may be more idiosyncratic to the customer than deciding on whether one can place confidence in its findings and conclusions.

OTHER OBSERVATIONS

Both authors are dissatisfied with the way journals in our field function. Each represents different customer segments in the market. Professor Staw sees creativity being stifled by the publication process. Dr. Price sees our prestigious mainstream research publications as unhelpful to him. They are not producing interesting knowledge and they in turn seem insensitive to his needs as a translator of basic organizational research issues for those who are grappling with such issues in the field. He asks with concern: For whom do the journals produce? Who is the customer? It is our belief that we ought not ignore these customers' complaints. We ourselves are customers. What do we want and need and how do we get what we wish for?

The authors do attempt to answer the "How do we change the status quo?" question. Many of their suggestions have links with earlier chapters in the book by Frost and Taylor, Deetz, and Nord. Staw's distinction between contributions to knowledge and to the literature, and Price's discussion of the reader-as-customer, augment those earlier discussions.

Taking Professor Staw's argument that much of what appears in journals is archival and combining it with Dr. Price's reader-as-customer image, one can argue that our journals serve well a particular segment of the market, those in the field who need archives. Much of the material in our journals serves normal scientists. It is bleached white and it is "dated," it is "made safe," and it is sterilized so that it can be used with confidence by those who go into the archives for their information. Such information, for those who want to use it is, at the best of times, both relevant and rigorous.

We are left with two problems, however. One difficulty is that journals, as primarily archives, cannot meet the needs of customers who need other products. This dilemma might be manageable, given that the condition was recognized as a problem, if the issue were made explicit in these terms. However, even with the founding of journals to meet consumer needs, the press, as Professor Staw points out, is still toward the archival model. Journals, unless reconceptualized and managed differently, serve as screening devices, as deviance-removing mechanisms that narrow the range of possibilities and products and make the product unsatisfactory for many customers. To prevent this outcome, it takes a clear perception of the issues involved in delivering the desired product and an awareness of the traps and biases that can cause subversion of the goal of a journal to meet its customers' needs. Otherwise, the outcome, over time, will be to produce the conventional archival publication. Ensuring that a journal such as *The Organizational Behavior Teaching Review,* for example, stays sensitive to its readers' needs requires energetic, thoughtful, and constant attention to the objectives of the journal, to the nature and meaning of the reviewing and decision processes in that journal. We are sure that the editors and review board of that journal will attest to this point.

The other problem, which Staw identifies so eloquently in his chapter, has to do with the way we, as researchers, define and evaluate relevance and rigor. His suggestions for change in this regard are provocative and important. Unless we are vigilant and attend to issues such as those he raises, the publications that are in the archives will be such that they are useless even to those who draw on them most. We will be storing useless information.

Both authors wrestle with the time frame within which publications typically reach their audiences. Researchers need knowledge they can use in their current research projects. Typically the researcher time frame is measured in terms of projects that operate over a period of months and years. Teachers look for knowledge that will update their next teaching assignment. Sometimes this is for the next class meeting. More frequently, it is for the course next semester. Practitioners want the knowledge today. Their problems need attention in a very short time span. Dr. Price's message is that if it is old knowledge it is of no use to him or his manager. Archives do not appear to assist him at all.

Finally, it is interesting to note the emotional stances that the authors believe should accompany our research so that it may become more relevant and so that we may assess rigor intelligently. Professor Staw urges us to be adventurous, to take risks. Dr. Price encourages us as researchers to be courageous, to study organizational phenomena in the field rather than to stand back and treat only the abstractions, to reach out to practitioners and help them with their problems, to confront our research with the "So what?" question and to share the answer with those in the field. Both authors express or imply that we should be unafraid to make our own judgments about the rigor of what we read. Each of the authors communicates his own commitment to the emotions he expresses. They write boldly, with passion, courage, and a zest for their topic.

4

Repairs on the
Road to Relevance and Rigor
Some Unexplored Issues in
Publishing Organizational Research

BARRY M. STAW

S ome obvious thoughts crossed my mind when I was asked to write on relevance and rigor in publishing organizational research. Should publication
standards encourage more rigorous research, should journal articles be more
relevant, or is there an inevitable trade-off between rigor and relevance? Certainly what is relevant may not be rigorous, what is rigorous may not be relevant,
and it is extraordinarily difficult for research to be high on both of these dimensions. Although I considered these issues for some time, none of these thoughts
made it into the present form of the chapter.

In writing this chapter, I realized that we are rather fully informed on relevance versus rigor, at least as these concepts are usually juxtaposed. Depending
on one's definition of these research dimensions, prescriptions for more or less
relevance and rigor come down to either a statement of values about where the
field should go or an obvious pronouncement that it is hard to be high on both
of these dimensions. Therefore, rather than try to prescribe any particular level

of relevance or rigor, I will make some observations on the concepts themselves and how we use them in research publications. I will attempt to point out some aspects of relevance and rigor that are often omitted when evaluating research manuscripts. I will also struggle with the issue of what makes an article a significant contribution, and offer some thoughts on the constant tug between normal science and more creative advances. Although my remarks will, I am sure, read more like a set of work notes than a coherent and consistent argument, my hope is to provide material for more meaningful discussions in the future.

SOME NOTES ON RELEVANCE

Relevance is often used as a term that means practical implications or meaning to outside publics. However, from a research perspective, relevance comes closer to depicting the importance of a finding or idea for the advancement of knowledge. A relevant article in organizational behavior would therefore be something that helps one understand behavior in organizational settings or the behavior of organizations themselves. Such knowledge might certainly have practical implications for those who manage, but, in my usage, relevance will pertain more to our understanding of how organizations function than to change efforts to improve their functioning.

By defining relevance as knowledge rather than implementation, I have delimited the term but not necessarily resolved its ambiguity. One problem that constantly plagues our discussions of relevance, for example, is the confusion between a contribution to the literature and an advancement in knowledge. Although we like to think of our literature as the repository of knowledge on organizations, this is not always the case. Too often, topics in the literature take on a life of their own because of the availability of theory or the ease of data collection, regardless of their importance in organizational life. In fact, we routinely judge the significance of a research paper by its contribution to the pile of studies already conducted and archived in the journals rather than by its contribution to our understanding of organizations.

When research is literature- rather than theory-driven, contributions to knowledge are more conservative and incremental than they need to be. Because authors focus more on how their research fits with the previous literature than on the organizational problem itself, their research inevitably becomes directed toward controversies and gaps in the literature rather than toward a fresh look at the issues being studied. The review process also contributes to this conservatism. Because deviant methods and ideas are screened out in the review process, authors are usually hesitant to break open new topics or to drop established procedures in dealing with organizational problems. The only thing that seems to break this stagnation is the occasional paper that somehow "slips into the literature," perhaps by error or oversight in the review process. The deviant paper may create a storm of controversy and interest, but once such a deviation is published, it is frequently followed by a rush of new papers attempting to address the freshly legitimated topic. Researchers assume, I suppose, that a dominant coalition or set of wise individuals (e.g., the journal editor and the editorial board) have carefully decided to turn research to this new and fruitful area.

What Makes a Significant Contribution? If making a contribution to the literature is not synonymous with contributing to knowledge, how can we judge the significance of an article? We might ask whether it provides new understanding, or whether it extends, clarifies, and provides verification of old knowledge. Some might argue that the most important contributions are those that refute common sense or provide answers where common sense can go either way (e.g., Aronson, 1976). Others might argue that the role of research is to validate our common sense rather than to defy it (e.g., Homans, 1961). A more radical view might be for social science to provide new forms of organization or social interaction where common sense and everyday knowledge are not now applicable (Argyris, 1976; Gergen, 1978). Certainly, there is not now an easy resolution of these alternatives and probably should never be. If knowledge building is our goal, then the only contributions that are clearly insignificant are those in which we have little interest in the major predictions of the study, regardless of how the data turn out. Unfortunately, into this small category one might place a large proportion of the current literature.

Proximal Versus Distal Predictions. The most flashy and controversial studies are often those with a great distance between independent and dependent variables. Some examples are McClelland's (1961) prediction of societal achievement by themes in children's literature from an earlier time period, Brenner's (1979) finding that mental hospital admissions can be explained by unemployment data, and Phillips's (1982) prediction that single-vehicle car accidents are influenced by suicide stories in television soap operas. These are all bold and brazen attempts to link variables that are very distant empirically, coming from totally independent data sources. They are also studies that link variables that, on the surface at least, would seem to be very distinct conceptually (e.g., unemployment as a variable has little to do with mental health). Yet, they are the jackpots of social science. They generate interest, controversy, and sometimes even findings that hold up under substantial scrutiny.

Toward the opposite end of the research spectrum are studies that capitalize on a narrow separation between independent and dependent variables. Some examples would be predictions of turnover from the individual's desire to remain in an organization (Mobley, 1977), the hypothesis that job satisfaction should be associated with perceptions of task characteristics (Hackman & Oldham, 1976), and the prediction of job performance from assessments of work motivation (Nadler & Lawler, 1977). I have not singled out these studies as especially bad but, instead, as being rather typical. They are typical in the sense that they rely on independent and dependent variables that are very close conceptually and empirically. In some cases, the independent and dependent variables are both attitudinal variables measured by a single questionnaire. In other cases, the relationship between attitude and behavior is rather narrow and obvious. Few of us would argue that this organizational research is completely tautological given that there is some distance between the independent and dependent variables. Yet, the overlap between outcomes and predictors does make us suspicious about whether a real contribution is involved.

Where One Variable Ends and Another Begins. Central to the issue of conceptual distance is the problem of separating a strong relationship *between* variables from coherence *within* a single larger construct. The use of a multitrait/multimethod matrix to separate variables is a valuable empirical exercise, but it is often not much help theoretically. Where one variable ends and another begins is a judgment call that must be defended conceptually rather than simply assessed, post hoc, with the empirical association of indicators. The line between a tautology and a valuable contribution is very thin; it may vary between variables and the stage of research on particular theoretical constructs.

Pfeffer and Salancik's (1974) work on power in organizations helps illustrate the tenuous division between variables. They operationalized power, in part, by representation on committees that control resources in the organization, using the organization's actual allocation of resources as their dependent variable. A conceptual problem with the study is that we are not sure whether resource allocation should be included as an outcome variable or a measure of departmental power itself. However, the field tended to excuse Pfeffer and Salancik on this score because of the early stage of empirical research on power and our inherent interest in resource allocation as an outcome. In contrast, a study that correlated job involvement with job satisfaction would have been likely to suffer stiffer criticism in the review process. We would have asked for clearer separation, both conceptually and empirically, between these two variables before examining any findings that could have related the two constructs.

Where does this discussion of conceptual distance leave us? It should, I would hope, sensitize us to the rather vague boundaries between tautology and valuable prediction, making us less likely to rule out arbitrarily any contribution that uses independent and dependent variables that are close and making us hesitant to blithely grant research status to anything that relates two distinct variables. My own prejudice is that we need, in general, to stretch the distance between variables, becoming more risk-taking in our empirical investigations. As research matures on any given topic, there should be a willingness to make more rash predictions, ones that push our predictive powers to the limit. Too often, research proceeds from the brash to the boring, moving from some initially interesting findings to the conclusion that we really cannot say anything with confidence on new as well as older research topics.

SOME NOTES ON RIGOR

Rigor is sometimes conceived as having numbers to represent variables and statistical analyses to demonstrate causal relationships. Qualitative and descriptive work are often considered nonrigorous, because it is difficult to identify separable pieces of data and nearly impossible to conduct standard statistical analyses on these sources of information. Rigor is more than quantification, however, and these additional dimensions of rigorous research tend to blur the distinctions between quantitative and qualitative work.

I would define rigor in terms of the strength of inference made possible by a given research study. By this definition, many quantitative investigations are nonrigorous because a preponderance of alternative explanations can make their conclusions empirically vacuous. Likewise, some qualitative data are so compelling as to make their conclusions much stronger than any other available hypothesis. Rigor therefore is more than either the quantitativeness of a study or the level of statistical significance shown by the data. It is also somewhat more than the level of internal validity contained in traditional hypothesis testing (e.g., Cook & Campbell, 1979). Controls against threats to internal validity will no doubt strengthen the inferences made in a given research study, but so will other more qualitative features of a quantitative study.

The Qualitative Side of Quantitative Research. McGrath, Martin, and Kulka (1982) have elaborated many of the qualitative aspects of quantitative research. These include the many dilemmas that one must address, if not solve, in designing an empirical study. For example, there is an inevitable trade-off between standardized procedures and the ability to generalize to a world of varying properties. And, there is the dilemma between studying a larger sample of individuals on a small number of variables versus a smaller sample on a larger number of variables. As McGrath (1982) notes, these issues are not solvable in a traditional sense, nor are they reducible to textbook instructions. They are dilemmas with which we grapple qualitatively, using informal knowledge or "street smarts" rather than textbook solutions (Martin, 1982).

In addition to the qualitative aspects of *conducting* quantitative research, there are a number of qualitative issues in judging the rigor of a contribution. Most of the threats to internal validity mentioned by Campbell and Stanley (1966) and Cook and Campbell (1979) are questions of logical rather than statistical inference. But there are other logical issues in judging the rigor of a study not considered by these authors. One is the strength of the argument presented in the research write-up—that is, the logical consistency of the theoretical hypotheses and the conceptual overlap of the empirical tests. A strong argument results from carefully articulated theory and a set of analyses that fit the theory in a construct validity sense. A strong argument also results from multiple operationalizations and several logically, if not statistically, independent tests of a given hypothesis. A third component of a strong argument is the demonstration of when, theoretically, effects should be intensified or weakened. If a predicted effect can be made stronger by heightening a logically consistent set of antecedents, then much greater confidence can be placed in the theoretical hypothesis. Too often, moderating variables are isolated in an atheoretical manner, providing empirical limits to a finding rather than offering any insight on the theoretical mechanism itself.

As an example of using moderating variables for strengthening rather than weakening an argument, I would like to consider a recent study by Pfeffer (1977). He argued that the social class of business school graduates would, controlling for other demographic variables, predict career success. The theory underlying Pfeffer's prediction was that individuals use social similarity and consensus to resolve ambiguity in decision making. Thus, when making personnel decisions on hiring and promotion (which are inherently ambiguous), executives would be predicted to reduce uncertainty by replicating themselves, choosing those individuals who display similar social characteristics and mannerisms. Pfeffer indeed found a significant relationship between indicators of social class and achievement in business, but did not stop there. He also predicted that this relationship would be moderated by line/staff distinctions. Because the monitoring and appraisal of performance is more ambiguous in staff than in line jobs, it was predicted that achievement in staff positions would be more closely associated with social class. The line/staff distinction did in fact moderate the effects of social status on the success of business graduates (as indexed by their level of earnings). The important point is not the result, but the fact that Pfeffer used a moderating variable to strengthen rather than weaken his theoretical argument. Usually, moderators are considered simply as limiting conditions (e.g., social characteristics don't have much of an effect in line positions), serving to trivialize results after several such conditions are accumulated in the literature.

The Quantitative Side of Qualitative Research. Qualitative research can also differ in terms of rigor. Although data may be in the form of verbal descriptions rather than numbers, there may be multiple observations of a phenomenon across several case studies. And, more important, within a single ethnographic study there may be multiple observations of a theoretical mechanism, process, or product. Campbell (1975) has described this notion as the "degrees of freedom in a case study," meaning that multiple predictions are available even when investigating a single culture, group, or organization.

Weick (1974) has offered several examples of making multiple predictions from a single case. In studying a single university, one might, for example, look for several independent outcroppings of an authoritarian culture, ranging from library checkout privileges, to dormitory rules, to certain symbols or artifacts on campus. A strong or rigorous argument about the nature of an organization's culture would therefore involve multiple checks on one's hypothesis from relatively independent (or at least nonoverlapping) data sources. Thus, while statistical tests are unavailable for verbal presentations of case studies, the rigor of the argument can depend on logical replication and conceptual degrees of freedom.

A Glitch in the Trade-Off Between Relevance and Rigor

The relevance or importance of a paper is often viewed as a compensatory factor to rigor in decisions to publish. A study in a new area with few precedents would therefore be allowed more methodological flaws or ambiguities than manuscripts within well-worked territories. An exception may be studies whose significance is achieved largely from the contradiction of existing literature or prevailing theoretical assumptions. With contradicting or nonobvious results, a greater level of rigor is often demanded than with commonsense or more mundane findings. This built-in conservatism can be very frustrating when it appears that lower standards are being used for less significant research or when inordinately high standards are being used to preserve ideas that deserve to fail.

I have often felt victimized by the conservatism effect, which fails to substitute strengths in relevance for weaknesses in rigor. However, perhaps as often I have been a purveyor of conservatism through the review process. Probably the best example of the dilemma of rigor and/or relevance was a paper I once reviewed on extrasensory perception. The idea of the manuscript was that successful managers possessed a special gift for forecasting change and anticipating reality. To test this idea, a sample of highly successful and less successful entrepreneurs were given a table of random numbers and asked to guess the next number in the sequence. Results showed that successful entrepreneurs were the best guessers, and the difference between the two groups reached standard levels of statistical significance. As a reviewer, I faced a classic dilemma. Here was a study that was certainly important, and with data that would pass normal levels of methodological scrutiny. I took the easy way out. I praised the author for courage and ingenuity but asked for a replication of his data before publication.

The way I reviewed the ESP study is very threatening to our notions of scientific progress. Is there a trade-off between rigor and relevance only when the stakes are relatively unimportant or the cost of error very minimal? On important or costly issues, are relevance and rigor interactive, such that high levels of relevance require even higher levels of rigor? In answering such questions, one can imagine two equations, one in which scientific contribution equals rigor plus relevance, and another equation in which a study's contribution equals rigor minus relevance:

1. Contribution = Rigor + Relevance
2. Contribution = Rigor − Relevance

When relevance or the cost of error is low, our intuitive judgment seems to rely on the first model in which rigor and relevance are additive factors. When relevance and cost of error are high, we appear to use the second judgment model in which rigor and relevance are subtractive factors.

SOME NOTES ON NORMAL
SCIENCE VERSUS CREATIVITY IN PUBLISHING

An inevitable issue in journal publication is the trade-off between normal science and creativity. Normal science strives to achieve a set of replicated findings and clarified theoretical relationships, usually through the standardization of conceptual terms and methodological procedures. More creative advances move in alternative directions, both theoretically and methodologically. They may venture into theoretically uncharted ground, reorganize existing knowledge, or deny accepted facts in a given research territory. Often these creative leaps will need to be taken without standardized procedures, because the new ideas may themselves have been blocked by the accepted methodology or have at least not been accessible by its usage.

I believe that journals rarely make conscious decisions to follow a creative versus normal science route. Sometimes the issue comes up at editorial board meetings, but most of the decision making is diffused among the submission and review processes over time. Gradually journals take on a reputation for publishing certain types of articles, and this reputation determines the type of material people send. At present, for example, the *Journal of Applied Psychology* has a distinct reputation for normal science—so much so that the editor must occasionally make pleas for more interesting work. *Administrative Science Quarterly,* on the other hand, has the reputation of *not* publishing articles that replicate or extend rather than attempting to open new areas or upend existing views. To counter this reputation, *ASQ* has now specifically invited normal science submissions in its notice to contributors. Thus, while journals can attempt to tinker with their mixture of creative versus normal science, the overall direction of a journal seems to be set by the researchers and readers it serves over longer periods of time.

Toward More Creativity in Publishing. From my point of view, it almost always appears that publications are biased toward normal science. Our own creative ideas are criticized as shallow, ungrounded, inconsistent with existing theory, or just plain wrong. Our methods are often viewed by reviewers as deficient, flawed, and inappropriate, when they are of course cleverly adapted to the new theory or type of data. As authors, we try to innovate but are soundly rebuffed. We get angry and go off and review someone else's paper in the same way for the same journal.

Is there a solution to this dilemma? Can we have journals and a review process that are more amenable to creative advances, yet retain some selectivity in terms of quality? I think not, at least as we currently conceptualize the problem. Most procedural solutions suffer from the fact that any selection process will inevitably discard ideas and methods that are deviant. One could, for example, create separate journal sections for major versus minor advancements, hoping to stimulate more interesting and substantial contributions. This would of course have the disadvantage of possibly creating greater competition for space within the "major contribution section," prompting even more restrictive standards than for space in the "minor" category. One could also imagine the creation of a separate journal section for tentative and even "premature" ideas, yet I am not sure how journals would actually decide on what to print in these pages. Would there be a place for "findings that deserve to be true" even though they are contradicted by current empirical evidence, or would this simply be yet another section for theoretical notes and logically defensible propositions? As these examples may show, any procedural solution seems to trade off creative versus normal science, often in ways we are not currently prepared to accept.

JOURNALS AS A SOURCE OF VARIATION
OR AS A SELECTION-RETENTION MECHANISM

Many of the debates about whether journals should be more flexible in their publication standards revolve around differences in views about where the field is and where it should be going. Is the field suffering from a limited set of theoretical models and a surfeit of empirical studies testing these few models? Or is the field suffering from a lack of verifiable facts—findings that can be replicated easily without too many qualifications and limiting conditions? Depending on their answers to these questions, researchers will prefer journals to be stimulators or suppressors of theory, trying to remove excess models from the literature or attempting to move theory in alternative directions.

Although there is no agreement about whether we suffer from normal science or no science at all, some light can be shed on the role of journals by drawing analogies to evolutionary processes. The study of creativity, like any other knowledge process, can be viewed from a social-evolutionary point of view. As noted by Campbell (1960), creative thought can be described as a product of blind variation and selective retention. Creative individuals, for example, can be understood as ones who can generate a large number of alternatives and who at the same time can sort the good ideas from the nonsense. Creative groups, likewise, are able to generate wide-ranging information and viewpoints, and then make quality decisions on these data. Thus an important aspect of stimulating both individual and group creativity is making sure a wide range of alternatives or variation is encouraged before any editing or selective retention mechanism is activated.

In understanding creative advances within the field of organizational behavior, one could view the array of individual researchers as the source of variation and the publication process as the selective retention mechanism. This formulation of the publishing process is, in fact, probably very close to the current view of how journals should optimally function. Unfortunately, this way of viewing the publication process may not be helpful to research creativity. Because creativity usually necessitates the open and free elicitation of alternatives before divergent ideas are discarded, journal publishing, as it is now structured, may be contradictory to creative advances. Under current practices, when a paper is disliked by two of three referees, it is likely to be rejected outright. When a paper is disliked by one referee, it is likely to go through substantial revision, usually softening its impact (and influence) on other imagined readers who might share the objector's viewpoint. Thus the most divergent papers (and ideas) may never make it out to the field or may not survive in a forceful enough tone to be truly provocative. They have been prematurely selected out before they could be either praised and widely adopted or thoroughly scorned and rejected by the field.

From the social-evolutionary perspective, the chief dilemma for journal publishing appears to center on where the selection-retention mechanism should properly be placed. Should journals function as the primary screening mechanism, picking those studies that should be retained in the library of ideas, or should journals work as communication devices devoted to spreading the word and facilitating the variety proffered by individual researchers? The first model is what we have now. Under the second model, ideas would be selected and retained *by the research community rather than the journals.* Under the second model, knowledge in organizational behavior would be built by the research community and not by the published literature.

Using journals as communication rather than selection devices creates some difficult but surmountable problems. First, although there may be a communication overload, one can argue that we have one already. In fact, some researchers now say that they only read articles first screened by graduate students, because they do not have time to read all the papers in their own subfields. Second, one might argue that false information will be distributed by journals that are primarily communicators rather than selectors. However, some researchers already say that "everyone knows a certain finding is garbage," even though the literature is still highly supportive. Finally, some of our colleagues are praised for their contributions to the field *in spite* of their published writing, being highly influential through conversations and personal influence rather than the quantity and quality of their articles. These are all signs that the research community can and already does make knowledge judgments without the journal selection process.

By taking a social-evolutionary view of journal publishing, we can see that small procedural changes may not be enough to make a real difference in the way the field functions. If we really want to increase the creative potential of the field, we may therefore need to rethink the basic function of journals, moving them from a selective retention mechanism to a generator of variety. Shifting journals from a screening to a communicating role will of course open a number of potential futures for journals not now seriously considered. These possibilities could range from sending on-line news items in the form of computer mail, to periodic compendiums of bright ideas, to live debates on controversial issues. Somewhat akin to presentations at annual meetings of professional societies, journals of the future would become dispensers of live information (with perhaps even a social science research channel or wire service). Annual meetings, by this reasoning, would have to be reserved for what many already believe is their only real function—socializing, job searching, and the exchange of gossip.

CONCLUSION

This chapter has moved rather eclectically across the territory of relevance and rigor. It was first noted that relevance involves some difficult distinctions between tautology and relationships between variables. It was then noted that the differences between qualitative and quantitative research are often more subtle than we realize, and that strength in argumentation is central to rigorous work in both qualitative and quantitative realms. Some exceptions to the assumed trade-off between rigor and relevance were then noted, and, finally, social evolutionary concepts were used to examine the screening process practiced by journals.

These are but a few of the issues that might be raised in examining relevance and rigor in journal publishing. My discussion has provided few answers for the perfect publishing process. Yet, if successful, this chapter may stimulate some new content issues in the debate over journal publication—issues that go beyond simple preferences for more or less relevance and rigor.

REFERENCES

Argyris, C. (1976). Problems and new directions for industrial psychology. In M. Dunnette (Ed.), *Handbook of industrial and organizational psychology.* Chicago: Rand McNally.

Aronson, E. (1976). *The social animal* (2nd ed.). San Francisco: Freeman.

Brenner, M. H. (1979). Health and national economy: Comments and general principles. In L. S. Ferman & L. Gordis (Eds.), *Mental health and the economy.* Kalamazoo, MI: Upjohn Institute for Employment Research.

Campbell, D. T. (1960). Blind variation and selection retention in creative thought as in other knowledge processes. *Psychological Review, 67,* 380-400.

Campbell, D. T. (1975). Degrees of freedom and the case study. *Comparative Political Studies, 8,* 178-193.

Campbell, D. T., & Stanley, J. L. (1966). *Experimental and quasi-experimental design for research.* Chicago: Rand McNally.

Cook, T. D., & Campbell, D. T. (1979). *Quasi-experimental design: Design and analysis issues for field settings.* Chicago: Rand McNally.

Gergen, K. J. (1978). Toward generative theory. *Journal of Personality and Social Psychology, 36,* 1344-1360.

Hackman, J. R., & Oldham, G. R. (1976). Motivation through the design of work: Test of a theory. *Organizational Behavior and Human Performance, 16,* 250-279.

Homans, G. C. (1961). *Social behavior: Its elementary forms.* New York: Harcourt, Brace & World.

Martin, J. (1982). A garbage can model of the research process. In J. E. McGrath, J. Martin, & R. A. Kulka (Eds.), *Judgment calls in research.* Beverly Hills, CA: Sage.

McClelland, D. (1961). *The achieving society.* New York: Free Press.

McGrath, J. E. (1982). Dilemmatics: The study of research choices and dilemmas. In J. E. McGrath, J. Martin, & R. A. Kulka (Eds.), *Judgement calls in research* (pp. 69-102). Beverly Hills, CA: Sage.

McGrath, J. E., Martin, J., & Kulka, R. A. (Eds.). (1982). *Judgement calls in research.* Beverly Hills, CA: Sage.

Mobley, W. H. (1977). Intermediate linkages in the relationship between job satisfaction and employee turnover. *Journal of Applied Psychology, 62,* 237-240.

Nadler, D. A., & Lawler, E. E. (1977). Motivating individuals in organizational settings. In J. R. Hackman, E. E. Lawler, & L. W. Porter (Eds.), *Perspectives on behavior in organizations.* New York: McGraw-Hill.

Pfeffer, J. (1977). Toward an examination of stratification in organizations. *Administrative Science Quarterly, 22,* 553-567.

Pfeffer, J., & Salancik, G. R. (1974). Organizational decision making as a political process: The case of a university budget. *Administrative Science Quarterly, 19,* 135-151.

Phillips, D. P. (1982). The impact of fictional television stories on U.S. adult fatalities: New evidence on the effect of the mass media on violence. *American Journal of Sociology, 87,* 1340-1359.

Weick, K. E. (1974). Amendments to organizational theorizing. *Academy of Management Journal, 17,* 487-502.

5

A Customer's View
of Organizational Literature

RAYMOND L. PRICE

M ost organizations exist to meet the needs of some customer. While there may be several other organizations that transform the original product, ultimately there is an end customer who will use the products or services provided by the organization. In the businesses with which I am most familiar, we have "original equipment manufacturers" (OEMs), who take basic electronic equipment, add other hardware or software to it, and make a final product that will meet the needs of customers. Essentially, they take a basic product and make it easily usable by an end customer.

Applying this analogy to the organizational literature, we would try to identify both the end customers and the OEMs. If the purpose of the literature (as stated in *Administrative Science Quarterly*) is "to advance the understanding of administration," a plausible end customer of this information could be the managers and employees in organizations. If we are advancing the understanding of organizations and the behavior within them, then people faced with working in these organizations should be interested in that understanding.

Using the interest in the popularized renditions of organizational behavior themes as an indicator, the sales of books like *In Search of Excellence, The One Minute Manager, Theory Z,* and *High Output Management* clearly demonstrate that people are interested in organizational behavior. Managers, professionals in organizations, and the public in general are currently more interested in organizations, management, and effectiveness than they have been in the past 20 years. Is the current academic literature influencing this interest and capturing the imagination of these potential customers?

Many academics could persuasively argue that the books mentioned above should not have a major impact on the public at large due to oversimplification of the complex relationships in organizations, poor data, or prescriptions that are not based on solid evidence. Academics could also argue that the academic literature cannot further the understanding of organizations if it also tries to be popular. In their view, rigor and popularity are frequently mutually exclusive.

Given that many academics would argue that academic literature should not reach the end customers directly, who are the OEMs for the literature? Who are the people or the organizations who take academic literature and transform it into something that people in organizations can use? Many academics perform this function through their consulting and writing for more popular journals. Additionally, consulting and training organizations help make this translation for their clients. Finally, there are groups of people inside organizations in management and employee development functions who are capable of linking the academic literature to use in organizations.

The following observations and comments come from the perspective of both a final customer and a potential OEM of academic literature. As a customer I will describe some of the things I would like to see in academic literature that would help me with the problems I face. While these observations are neither very original nor very profound, they are worth stating and I think worth considering seriously.

CRITERIA FOR CUSTOMER SATISFACTION

Most of the people I work with on a daily basis are trying to make their organizations or the people in them more effective. They are asked to constantly improve or at least to maintain their personal effectiveness and the effectiveness of their organizations. For either a manager or another employee to do this, they have to (a) recognize the important issues facing them, (b) understand the issues more completely, and (c) act with respect to that understanding. Every day, managers and employees have to act on the information and understanding available to them. If they are to use any new understanding about organizations, they have to be able to integrate it almost immediately into their view of the organization. As one of our more astute managers said when examining some research being done inside the company, "If I can't use it tomorrow, it won't do me any good." If an article is not sufficiently powerful to affect the way you look at situations or your reactions to them within a day or two, there is little chance of the article making any difference to the manager or employee.

Given this action-oriented environment, there are two major factors I consider when personally determining the value of an article. First, does it provide some new insight that will incrementally broaden my ability to understand what is happening to me or to the organization in which I work? Second, does it provide me with a tool for influencing someone else in the organization? That is, would I recommend the article to someone else? Within these two broad factors there are several specific criteria I look for in articles.

Relevance

The first criterion I use when looking at an article is the relevance of the topic to the issues I am trying to understand. This is the most subjective of my criteria because it depends totally on my biases and interests. Yet it is probably the most important, because if an article does not pass the first screen it will not be read. Although I am clearly biased, I propose that my biases are congruent with those of most managers and employees in my organization and the managers of other, similar organizations.

My concern with strategies, organization structures, management development, and employee development provides an opportunity to link most studies to current organization problems and challenges. While many links between theoretical concepts and organizational problems are easy to make, it certainly helps if the author makes an attempt to relate the findings to problems or dilemmas in organizations.

Challenge Causal Assumptions

Some of the most memorable articles I have read have been those that caused me to think about problems differently. The arguments in these articles may be counterintuitive or at least counter to the most common current perspectives. March's garbage can theory of organizational decision making, Ferris's analysis of productivity leading to job satisfaction, and Pfeiffer's situational analysis of leadership are a few memorable articles that have argued convincingly against the norm.

Significant Extensions of Current Theories

Because one person's significant extension is another person's trivia, this criterion is also hard to objectively assess. However, there clearly are some studies that do tell us significantly more than other studies. Does the extension tell us something we did not know before, or does it only confirm what the basic theory already told us? It is much safer to do small variations of an accepted theory than to discover major new perspectives. Providing some new understanding and not just demonstrating the obvious or rehashing old ideas is more likely to produce a useful article.

Categorize

Summary and review articles that classify and categorize previous research can be very useful in understanding trends and putting different findings in perspective. Series of articles, like those on cultures in the September issue of *ASQ*, are effective in pulling together different views in one place where they can then be more easily compared and contrasted.

Future Orientation

In analyzing a body of research, there are usually trends that continue for some time before there is a structural shift that causes a major revolution. Articles that attempt to identify or propose major structural changes or new paradigms can have a major impact on readers and on the field. I would like to be able to understand current trends, why the trends are occurring, where they might lead, and what the likely time frame is. Is there something happening in the environment that could have a major impact on the organization? The book *Megatrends* is a classic example of what an article could do on a smaller scale.

Current Business Topic

Some articles are interesting just because they address issues currently important to me or others in my organization. These topics are often related to each of the major functions and are currently the focus of significant improvements.

These types of articles could be classified under extensions of current theories but that would not give a totally accurate picture of their use.

Recommend It?

Because most managers are very action oriented, or I could say less tolerant of academic literature, an article has to meet the other criteria exceptionally well to pass this final test. The article could be shared with a few people interested in a particular topic or it could be included in our training programs and reach a much broader audience. A potential question for self-analysis is this: "Would you give this article to a potential consulting client to demonstrate how you could help him or her on a particular issue?"

Although it is probably not appropriate to write academic articles totally in lay terms, there has to be some attempt to place the findings in a context useful to astute managers. If this cannot be done, I would not recommend the article and would question the overall worth of the research.

I HAVE NOT BEEN A SATISFIED CUSTOMER

Under the mundane pressure of organization life, I have turned to reading the *Harvard Business Review, Organizational Dynamics, Business Week,* and *Fortune* instead of *Administrative Science Quarterly, Academy of Management Journal,* and *Academy of Management Review.* In the past I had not been a satisfied customer and now I could hardly be considered a customer. Not having perused the academic journals in some time, I had to check to determine if I had been missing something. Although there were a few exceptions, my previous experiences were reinforced.

For example, examining the three key articles in the March 1983 edition of *Administrative Science Quarterly* was not one of my more enlightening experiences. I learned in the first article that both managers and nonmanagers use talk to try to control the other party particularly in staff meetings and informal hallway meetings. Second, I learned that the laws passed by state governments can influence the laws passed by cities within those states. I am not sure what I learned from the third article. The abstract said, "This study examines the connective and directional continuity of all ties disrupted accidentally among 1,131 large U.S. corporations between 1962 and 1964 to determine the relative likelihood that different types of interlock ties facilitate relationships of formal coordination." I immediately grasped the essence of the argument and moved on.

Overall, the relevance of these articles to me personally was much less than I desired. This lack of relevance may be attributed to my personal biases and my being unrepresentative of the broader population. Or it may be attributed to the topics, how they are examined, and for what purpose they are examined. For example, telling anyone who has tried to influence someone else that talking to them is a common, maybe even useful, method is neither very surprising nor very useful. However, an examination of the effectiveness of different patterns or methods of talking to someone would be much more interesting and potentially useful. The authors of this study seemed more enamored with the methods used than with the end results. My values are quite different. If the final results are not interesting, I do not care much about how they were achieved. But, if the results are interesting, then I will examine the methods to see if they can reasonably lead to the conclusions.

"A Study"

To determine if I had unfairly judged the academic literature on the basis of one issue of *ASQ*, I did a brief analysis applying my criteria to the main articles of the 1983 editions of *ASQ, Harvard Business Review,* and *Organizational Dynamics* and the 1982 editions of *AMJ* and *AMR*. After reading the abstracts and the conclusions of these articles, I judged how many passed the "relevance" test and how many passed the "recommend it?" test. If an article passed the relevance test, I then placed it in one of the following categories: Challenges Causal Assumptions, Extends Theory, Classifies Previous Research, Future Oriented, or Current Business Topic. Table 5.1 shows the results of this "study." To be represented in Table 5.1, an article had to pass the "relevance" test; that is, it had to be interesting to me.

Although there were some interesting articles in all the journals, the percentage that passed the "relevance" test were lower than one might hope, particularly for the academic journals. It could be argued that given my orientation these results would be expected, and indeed they would be. But why don't more of the articles pass my "relevance" test? What would the results be if the reader did his or her own "relevance" test?

Perhaps more interesting than the results of the "relevance" test is the result that none of the academic articles (at least the ones that passed my "relevance" test) challenged causal assumptions and only one was future oriented. Most of the articles extended the current most popular theories or classified previous research. As stated before, the reader may do a similar classification of articles of interest to him or her.

TABLE 5.1 Classification of the Articles From Specific Journals That Meet the
"Relevance" Criteria

Criteria	Journal				
	ASQ	AMJ	AMR	HBR	OD
Challenge causal assumptions	0	0	0	2	0
Extend current theories	3	2	3	2	5
Classify previous research	2	0	2	0	1
Future oriented	0	0	1	1	1
Current business topics	0	0	0	11	1
Recommend it?	0	0	0	5	2
Total relevant	5	2	6	16	21
Total articles	24	49	63	62	21
Percent relevant	21%	4%	10%	26%	38%

The other result, and one that was somewhat unexpected, was the number of *Harvard Business Review* articles that were of interest to me but fell in another discipline like quality, manufacturing, R&D, and marketing. There is much talk about the interdisciplinary nature of organizational behavior, but we have done very little to integrate the other disciplines into our view of management. Maybe the integration of these subjects is more within the boundaries of business policy but I would like to think that organizational behavior could make a significant contribution here.

If the results of the "study" and my own preferences for reading are any indication, I am not a major customer of the academic literature. However, the question of whether I should be a major customer still remains. For the research done in business schools and schools of administration, I think I should be a major customer or at least a major OEM. If not me or people like me, are there any customers outside the confines of academia? As a potential customer, I have some suggestions for what I would like to see in the academic literature.

SUGGESTIONS

Understanding Organizational Behavior

As I read many of the articles, I kept getting the impression that the research was done without a sincere interest and desire to understand behavior in organizations. Too frequently, the research was very far removed from organizations or the people in them and there was no effort to tie the results back to the organizations. Even though the theories and concepts are extremely important in research, they are abstractions from the behavior and phenomena originally of interest. Many of the studies were only building on the abstractions of previous researchers without the understanding and the experience to make those abstractions meaningful. As a result, they lost the richness of the situations by being faithful to the abstractions rather than the behavior.

Case studies, stories, anecdotes, and field studies are appealing because they have the richness of the situation and have not been filtered through so many abstractions. A reader is able to see much more vividly the richness, ambiguities, and incongruencies that are part of organizational life.

I would not suggest using only field studies, anecdotes, and stories. But I would suggest the necessity for truly understanding organizations and the behavior in them rather than relying solely or even primarily on previous abstractions.

Although it is important to reach a level of detail that is controllable and understandable, it is also important to fit the research into a larger context. If we have this additional knowledge, what problems will it help us solve? What phenomenon will we understand more completely?

One of the first lessons I learned as a graduate student was to ask the questions, "How do you know?" and "So what?" While the need to answer the "How do you know?" question is pervasive in academic literature, we must not lose sight of the "So what?" question. Does the research make a difference? Does it tell us something we did not know before? Does the research really help us gain a better understanding of organizations and behavior in them?

Effectiveness

The concepts of individual performance and organizational effectiveness immediately raise red flags to many academics; assessing effectiveness is often quite subjective and always difficult. But effectiveness is a major concern for many people in organizations. With almost any topic, the implicit or explicit concern of organization members is effectiveness.

As managers, if we attempt to change our culture, will we be more effective? As an employee, will I be more effective in this culture than that culture? While few people would expect direct answers for specific unique circumstances, few people would expect the question to be avoided.

One of the appealing factors about books like *In Search of Excellence* and *The One Minute Manager* is that they clearly suggest what is effective and what is not effective. They may not be accurate or complete but they do not avoid the topic.

Prescriptive

If effectiveness is a major variable in the research, the step to being prescriptive is quite small. Although it is difficult to understand many situations in organizations, it is much harder determining what to do. Understanding a situation and knowing the most important variables certainly do not guarantee knowing how to respond to the situation. Managers and other people in organizations desire to understand situations but they desire even more to know how to behave in the different situations they face.

Prescriptions force the author to think through the implications of the study, to ask the "So what?" question, and to relate the study to the behavior of people in organizations. Prescriptions are much easier to intuitively validate than analysis; the analysis may sound reasonable but may not be sufficiently reasonable to warrant action based on the conclusions.

Academics frequently support their bias toward theory by quoting Kurt Lewin, "There is nothing as useful as a good theory." We do need good theories—theories that are useful and can help guide our actions. We currently focus on theories of analysis; we desperately need better theories of action.

A Perspective on Customer Suggestions

In our company, we try to understand our customers' problems and what they are trying to do so as to help them accomplish their tasks more effectively. We are not always able to provide the best solution; we sometimes completely miss the market; but we are always willing to listen. When we don't listen, we rarely invent an appropriate solution.

Even if we listen very well, we usually will not try to address the immediate problem as the customers describe it, because by the time we could create a solution they will have solved the problem and moved on to other problems. Neither do we always accept their definition of the problem; nor do we give them exactly what they think they want. Instead, we combine our understanding of their problems with our technical research and development knowledge and create better processes to solve their problems. Our customers will realize we have a better solution to their problems if we are to be successful.

As a potential customer of academic research, I realize that I may have very specific short-term needs that will not be met in the near future. While people like me and others in organizations may not be the primary customers of academic literature, we should be seen as potential customers. Having customers in organizations, listening to them, and letting their inputs influence the type of research and how it is reported may have a significant positive impact on the academic literature in organizational behavior.

Positional Perspectives
Introduction

L. L. CUMMINGS

PETER J. FROST

This section of the book positions various contributions according to our model of the transitions and states that scholars take as they enter and progress through the maturational and developmental processes of the publishing enterprise. We go beyond the perspective of the positions "inside" the enterprise to offer reflections on our products and our experiences as seen through the eyes of commentators from outside our field.

We view these transitions and states as composed of three perspectives: those entering the field (the "newcomers"); the insiders, who take on varying roles as "in place" within our disciplines; and those who have had little or no direct intellectual experience in our disciplines ("outsiders") but who, in our opinion, would have valuable and unusual insights to offer about what we do, how we do it, and our cognitive and emotional reactions to both.

When one speaks of an implied continuum from outside, through entering, to inside, one raises the question of the dimensions along which such transitions might be expected to occur. Our framework for the next 11 chapters centers on the elaboration of four such dimensions:

Temporal Positioning. How long has one been performing a role or roles within our disciplines? Is our contributor speaking from a perspective of before, during, or after a transition between multiple roles? Is the temporal vantage point one of the past, present, or future?

Proximity or Distance. Is the contributor speaking from a position at the core or center of the web of intellectual and political forces operating in a discipline (as a respected, long-term editor of a major journal might be expected to be doing)? Alternatively, is the writer expressing warranted uncertainty and ambiguity as he or she is entering the scholarly role? Is the writer "in process" across the typical progression of roles between occasional ad hoc reviewer, *to* regular ad hoc reviewer, *to* member of an editorial board, *to* associate editor, and, possibly, *to* editor of a significant scholarly journal? Of course these transitions of proximity toward the core of a discipline via the reviewing and editing routes are very likely to be paralleled by increasing visibility along other routes such as having one's own scholarship recognized and respected, changes in institutional affiliations, promotions through the academic ranks, and increasingly accountable positions of responsibility within the relevant professional associations. The transitions toward centrality (some would add toward conservatism as well) are interdependent and feed upon one another. In the chapters to follow, we will hear several senior scholars articulate the linkages, the boundaries, and the systematic nature of these transitions from beginner to midcareer challenges to senior status. There are surprises, both pleasant and unpleasant, along the way at each stage.

Emotionality. That is, the stages of feelings experienced as one anticipates, experiences, and reacts to the happenings of the transitions. The fears, uncertainties, challenges, pleasure, and pains, in their aggregates, do not necessarily increase or lessen as one matures within the publishing enterprise. On the other hand, from the contributions that follow, it is clear that they change in their focus and context. Issues, problems, and opportunities seem to shift, and in rather systematic ways. Newcomers experience many similar emotions, as do intermediate stage colleagues, as do the more established. Fortunately, our collaborators offer both a cross-sectional view (i.e., comparing subsections "Entering the Field" and "From Inside the Field") and retrospective longitudinal self-analyses (e.g., chapters by Pondy, Perrow, and Schneider).

Of course, Chapters 15 and 16 present perspectives by two psychiatrists, which should both reflect and stimulate our thoughts about the centrality of emotionality to scholars who are pursuing the advancement and dissemination of knowledge by publication. These two commentaries should make us feel less alone when we confront the emotional side of our enterprise. The psychiatric message seems to be twofold: (a) Emotionality is a valuable part of the human experience when that experience centers on issues central to one's definition of self and efficacy, and (b) the human is immensely adaptable given the emotionality of his or her work. At least to us, this perspective is particularly encouraging given the public nature of much of our publishing enterprise; that is, our successes and failures are frequently exposed to our friends and colleagues. Our adaptability to keep our victories and our defeats in perspective is heartening.

Conceptuality and Linguistics. To what extent are the constructs and language used in our publications (which are, in turn, presumably reflective of our disciplines' underlying structure) subject to meaningful interpretation by professional linguists? What do our products appear to mean and imply about our thinking, our customs for expression, and the deeper structure of our disciplines? We offer one chapter (Chapter 14) that analyzes the syntax, semantics, and synesis of our expressive modes. These contributions are intended as supplements to the standard issues surrounding constructs, design, measurement, and presentation. In no sense do we argue that they are more important. It is our conviction, however, that our expressive modes are fruitful bases for learning about ourselves and our disciplines. Beyond that, they are relatively unstudied as a basis for such learning.

Entering the Field

Commentary

L. L. CUMMINGS
PETER J. FROST

Entering any new world frequently brings forth anxieties. Anxieties focus not only on the uncertainties about expectations of others but also on issues of value compatibilities, assessment and testing of competencies, and the challenges of leading a balanced life in the face of the unending opportunities available in our disciplines.

Becoming consciously aware of these anxieties, subsequently using the resulting energies in constructive manners, and coping with occasional unexpected consequences of such coping each require courage, tenacity, and creativity.

Our contributors to this subsection accepted our challenge to speak openly, vividly, and even provocatively about these uncertainties, dilemmas, and anxieties. Neither they nor we can claim that their testimonies are shared by all new entrants to the mainstream of the discipline.

Postdoctorisms take many forms: Some transitions are smooth, others are rough; some anticipated, others surprising; some are guided by available models and mentors, others are sketched on untraced ice. Graham and Stablein, and Schoorman, vividly portray the entire spectrum.

But their commentaries and revelations are significant not only in the light of the crossing of boundaries into new territory. They also can be viewed as ground against which the generally greater certainty and lessened anxiety, even wisdom, of the established and the establishment should be viewed (see subsection, "From Inside the Field"). What are the processes and rites of passage that surround these changes? Are the anxieties and dilemmas resolved as each of us moves toward a comfortable positioning within our field? Alternatively, do the more experienced dodge, ignore, or bury the centrality of the issues raised by the newcomers? Do the processes through which people self-select to stay or leave our field, coupled with the progressive reinforcement of those who stay, eventually produce an unquestioning conservatism toward the issues? Is it now more difficult to get published as a new scholar in the field? Are we in our fields making it so difficult and time consuming for new scholars to get their work published that we are destroying motivation? Are we "eating our young"? We should ask ourselves to reflect upon these questions not only as we read from "the entering" perspective but also as we reflect upon what "the insiders" have to say. They are, respectively, the figure and the ground of this subsection.

6

A Funny Thing Happened
on the Way to Publication
Newcomers' Perspectives on
Publishing in the Organizational Sciences

JILL W. GRAHAM

RALPH E. STABLEIN

PROLOGUE

We originally envisioned this chapter as a conceptual article but, to our amaze-
ment, it has become an empirical study instead. Our methodology is participant
observation, and the sample size is small ($n = 2$); actually this is a case study
written by the human subjects. What they/we discovered is that the rate of attitude change about publishing in the organizational sciences can be extremely
high as one moves from being an outsider to an insider in the discipline. That
discovery is how we make sense of the widening gap in our opinions over the
course of writing this article.

As fourth-year graduate students, we were asked to write this chapter in June
1983. After meeting with one of the editors, who told us the background and
scope of the proposed book, we tentatively agreed to the assignment. Neither of
us had finished our dissertations at that point, and both had new jobs to start in
the fall, so we didn't begin work on the article right away. At the 1983 annual
meeting of the Academy of Management in Dallas, however, one of us attended
a very provocative symposium on the topic of publishing in the organizational

sciences. That stimulus led us, right there in Dallas, to have our first long talk about what we might say. Several more talks followed during the fall, and by November we had worked up a fairly detailed outline of the several sections we envisioned in the article. Our talks were very stimulating, we agreed on virtually everything, and each of our contributions complemented the other's in a way that had us concluding: "Now we understand why people do joint research—the ideas flow so much better!"

Meanwhile, both of us had assumed full-time teaching responsibilities at a new school, and one of us had finished her dissertation. Finding time to write a first draft of the paper was difficult, but more so for the one still working on his dissertation. As a result, one author's parts of the chapter were composed at a more leisurely pace than the other's. When the parts were finally combined, they didn't fit very well together. Stylistic differences were apparent, but we thought those could be worked out. The more difficult discrepancy was one of tone: One of the authors (the one with the completed dissertation) no longer felt quite so strongly about some of the criticisms contained in the chapter.

Whether it was a self-fulfilling prophecy or just coincidence, the author's changing perspective had been predicted in an early draft of the chapter. She had written, "The socialization process of newcomers contains within it factors which shift priorities, loyalties, and self-interests." As the two authors worked to put the pieces of their chapter together, academia didn't seem to one of us nearly as brutal an environment as it had only a few months before. Nice things were happening; doors were opening; she was beginning to feel legitimate.

But perhaps all this is but a temporary honeymoon, with a reality trip scheduled next; or maybe it is all a form of devious co-optation. How would one study the matter?

INTRODUCTION

The overall theme of this chapter is an answer to the question the authors posed to us: "What does publishing in the organizational sciences look like to an outsider, more particularly to a would-be insider, that is, a newcomer to the field?" In one word, the answer is—fearful. We fear uncertainty, we fear failure, and we fear pain. We also fear being changed into people we don't like. The perils of the publishing process we see include threats to idealistic values and humane instincts, rejection and/or ridicule of one's creative labor, thwarted career goals, and perpetuation of a system that batters egos in the name of bettering human understanding.

Not wanting to sit still for all that (and having been offered a forum), we felt that we had things to say to four different groups involved (to various degrees) in publishing in the organizational sciences. Ordered roughly in terms of social distance, those constituencies include other newcomers, advisers/mentors, reviewers, and gatekeepers. This chapter includes a section directed to each of those four groups. Our overall purpose is to offer support and comfort to other newcomers, to (re)sensitize mentors and reviewers to the newcomer experience, and to challenge those who find current publishing practices to be both defensible and satisfactory.

We have tried to write this chapter in a style that is consistent with its substance, that is, advocacy of human communication that is honest, humane, thoughtful, and fun; we hope you find the same qualities in this chapter. As mentioned in the Prologue, the last few months of our lives have been both busy and bizarre in several ways. In the final section of the chapter, we share some critical self-reflections about what we have learned in the process of working together on this project.

MESSAGES TO OTHER NEWCOMERS

What do we have to share with other fledgling academics in the organizational sciences? We do not pretend to have much in the way of wisdom to offer, but we can share our current perspective on the publish-or-perish world we have all chosen to inhabit. In this section of the chapter, we describe our perspective on the world of publishing in three parts: (a) our values or preferences for that world, (b) our feelings or emotional reactions to the status quo, and (c) our options or ways of living in the world of publish-or-perish.

Value Preferences

The values that shape our preferences for living in the publishing world include idealistic applications of scholarly activity, humanism in the scholarly process, and balance in the personal lives of academics. Each of those value preferences is discussed in this section.

Why try to publish? Because publishing is essential to one's career success? While that answer may appear sufficient to explain (soon to be) observed behavior, we believe there is more to it than self-interest. We are avowed idealists; we want to try to make a contribution to knowledge that can help people's lives. And we think it is valuable to retain our idealism while involved in the important, but

116 PERSPECTIVES ON PUBLISHING

not all-important, business of "making it." We want to get tenure. We want to be promoted. We want to have our work cited. We want to be recognized as stars. But we also want to increase understanding of organizations and even to affect organizational behavior. We want the world, and organizational life in particular, to be a better place as a result of our work.

We know that sounds both preposterous and presumptuous. But we suspect that many in our field are idealistic. On occasion we have heard both newcomers and old hands express a sense of idealistic purpose about their work, but we hear cynicism more often. Perhaps with time and experience as practicing scholars we will become disillusioned. Idealism may yield to pragmatism. Pretensions of scholarly contribution may fade as we humbly settle for the satisfactions of the lifestyle allowed by an academic career. But for now we affirm the definition of publishing as communication to a community of scholars for the purpose of human progress. We hope to help one another sustain our idealism against the threat of worldly cynicism.

A second value position that we wish to communicate is process oriented rather than goal oriented. We prefer to live in a work world where humanistic values prevail. One of us entered the field through organizational development. The other worked in both human service and human rights organizations. Both of us go to church regularly. Our value stance derives from those sources, though other routes lead to humanism as well. Where we come from is not as important as how we would like to get where we are going. We would like to travel a path marked by signs of compassion, friendship, fun, and community. We have seen those signs among our peers, but we would like to see them in the publishing world as well.

The publishing process absorbs an incredible amount of time. It is a very important part of our lives as junior members of the faculty. Yet we do not care to limit such a central activity to our intellect; we would like the rest of our humanity to be involved as well. A paper represents an investment of considerable emotional and spiritual energy as well as creative intellectual effort. It is not just an objective research report independent of the personal energy that went into it. Such an understanding of publishing leads us to advocate greater acceptance of the fullness of humanity in all phases of the publishing process: in graduate training, in interactions with coauthors, in the review process, and in critiques of published work. The product (i.e., published work) could also benefit from that prescription. For example, published material could include an explanation of the author's *non*intellectual motivation for pursuing a research question.

Feelings

We argued in the previous section that emotional energy was an integral part of the publishing process. In this section, we discuss particular feelings that we associate with publishing: uncertainty, frustration, fear, and anger. We do so because, in the spirit of the previous section, we wish to make a small contribution toward humanizing reflection and discussion in the organizational sciences. We also hope that our words will strike a responsive chord in other newcomers. Somehow it is easier for us to keep on and enjoy our work when we know we are not alone.

Our overriding emotional response as we take our first steps in this new world is a profound sense of uncertainty. There are so many things we don't know. We have grown comfortable with ambiguity when it concerns the *content* of the field; furthermore, our training has provided us with the means for attempting to do something about those unknowns. But the uncertainties surrounding publishing are legion, and we lack any tools for their reduction. We just don't know the operative rules, although the espoused rules are generally accessible.

A list of some of our questions follows:

- How do you envision the publishable outcomes of a research effort in advance?
- How do you carve up your dissertation or other large project into separate pieces? How much is enough for a given article?
- How do you choose what *not* to include in your write-up? How detailed should a procedure section be? How speculative should a discussion section get? How much ex post facto logic is ethical?
- What is the appropriate journal for a given article?
- Do you have to "go along" to get published? Are there barriers to publishing on topics not already in the literature? Is there a bias against radical perspectives and topics? Can you publish nonquantifiable empirical work?
- How important to getting published is networking, going to conventions, becoming known by the "right" people?
- Do publishable articles have to be written in a boring style, or does it just happen that way?
- Just how original and new must an idea be to be publishable?
- Is coauthorship a liability?
- How blind is blind review?
- Which journals "count"? Do book chapters "count"?

Perhaps we will find answers to some of those questions elsewhere in this book. We hope we don't have to learn all the answers by trial and error.

Uncertainty is our constant companion. Often our sense of uncertainty is generalized, so that it is difficult to identify a specific cause of the feeling. In contrast, our frustrations are more focused. There are two types: frustration with ourselves and frustration with others.

We are our own greatest source of frustration. We don't seem to be creative enough to meet our standards. We can't maintain our concentration and we keep getting distracted by outside pursuits. Everything takes us longer to read, to write, and to understand than we think it should. In sum, we are frustrated that we are not brighter, quicker, more creative, and more diligent than we are. We feel that we should be able to do better.

Other people can frustrate us as well. Often this frustration arises when others don't understand the importance of what we are doing. We can't figure out why some people think goal-setting research is boring or that principled organizational dissent is of marginal interest to the study of organizations. Thus we are frustrated by the difficulty we experience in securing research sites or quick turnaround time for comments on drafts we have written. We certainly recognize the potential benefits of our studies and the hazards of continued ignorance. Others' obtuseness makes us frustrated!

Another way others frustrate us is by missing deadlines. Joint authorship or other forms of collaborative effort create a situation that is ripe for mutual disillusionment. Especially in the case where one has almost missed a deadline him- or herself, the fact that a coauthor did not stay up all night to get his or her part done *too* is extremely vexing. Our experience with this chapter—a coauthored piece in a book with two authors—has helped us to understand that frustration. Punctuality is discouraged by a series of solid deadlines from book authors that melt into insignificance. We find ourselves playing the game of psyching out the "real" deadline and meeting *it,* ignoring the "official" due dates.

We have chosen a career in academia. Publishing is the measure by which we demonstrate our worth to ourselves and others. For academics, frequent publishing in the better journals is the critical criterion defining "the right stuff," just as flying experimental aircraft was for pilots in Tom Wolfe's book of the same name. Our achievement needs can no longer be satisfied by classroom grades, grades nearly guaranteed to be high due to grade inflation and curving. But we are not sure how our outlier position on the bell-shaped grading curve will transform onto the Poisson publishing curve. The resulting feeling is fear.

Some of the fear is straightforward and conscious, such as the fear that a manuscript that represents a good deal of work and heartache will be rejected. But some of our fear is deeper seated and less conscious. At some level we suspect that all those grade reports and test scores were matched to our names in error. Now, in this new evaluation arena, we will be found out. We are about to be unmasked, revealed to the world as the intellectual weaklings, the pretenders to competence we've long suspected ourselves to be. Perhaps even more than conflicting obligations and time constraints, that fear explains our slowness to convert our research into submitted articles.

The most unsavory feeling stirred up by the publishing process is anger. We experience it when a friend (or we ourselves) has (have) a manuscript rejected. The anger is focused on the reviewers who have proven their poor judgment by the very act of the rejection (and also on the editor who sent the piece to such a lousy reviewer). Although we can always produce a legitimate, plausible rationale for our anger, on reflection we realize that we are angry primarily because a friend (or oneself) has been hurt. It matters not that the hurt may be "good for him or her" in the long run. For the moment, someone we care about is hurting, and we are mad at the immediate cause of that suffering.

Options

Fragile though they may be, our egos are not underdeveloped. Thus we cannot resist the opportunity to give advice. In recognition of its dubious value, we offer the following as "options" rather than as "recommendations." These options are strategies we have found useful in our attempt to build competency as academic, publishing-oriented professionals. The three strategies are not mutually exclusive, but neither are they completely complementary. Individually, each author has followed a different mix of the various strategies. We both agree, however, that it is important to minimize "convenience publishing," that is, peripatetically joining in on others' projects instead of pursuing one's own coherent research program. Sustaining individual initiative and purposefulness is a common theme through all three options.

The basic strategy of one of the authors for surviving and actually enjoying the prepublishing initiation rite called graduate school was to act "as if" his preferred world were the "real world." That meant treating fellow graduate students and faculty members as colleagues from the first day on campus. Explicit or implicit recognition of status differentiation and submissive behavior was avoided. No one can completely control the definition of the world, but the author was pleasantly surprised to discover the extent to which people were willing to go along.

Such a strategy has its risks. The world you create and your role in it can constrain your freedom to behave. For example, the role described above might increase the difficulty of asking elementary questions (such as those posed as areas of uncertainty earlier in this chapter). Furthermore, others may challenge your world and role definitions or misinterpret them (e.g., "What an arrogant student!"). When the "others" are powerful, the consequences can be significant and harmful. Thus it is important to determine the limits of your willingness and ability to bend to others' world definitions in advance of any potential contests. Be prepared to be flexible and play another's game if you can, but know when you can't. For the author pursuing this strategy, the limit was a goal of holistic personal development and self-control over his life as a graduate student. He was able to complete the program without violating that limit, but it has taken longer than anticipated and has had some negative impact on his career progress.

The second strategy for successful entry into a publishing-oriented profession is vertical networking. It involves establishing relationships with recognized contributors to the literature. The mentor relationship is the most common form of that strategy. Mentors have presumably acquired wisdom through experience, and their advice and opinions can be helpful. They can, for instance, help resolve the uncertainties we listed above. Mentors can guide a protégé through the research and publishing process as the protégé works on the mentor's research and/or the mentor supervises the protégé's research. Association with a prestigious mentor can also lend legitimacy to a protégé's unconventional research topic. Finally, mentors can provide personal support in times of fear and frustration.

Being a mentor's protégé, however, is not without its costs and risks. At the extreme, one's work may be expropriated. The protégé may be required to assume a submissive role. His or her research interests and opportunities may be constrained by the interests of the mentor. The mentor may move to another school or lose interest in the protégé or his or her work. Having a mentor may also involve protégés in destructive academic politics. Mentors sometimes exacerbate rather than heal the emotional traumas of their protégés.

Many of those risks can be limited by broadening the base of vertical networking. One of the authors survived graduate school by pursuing what could be termed a "multiple mentors" approach. She sought out opportunities to study with or work for *several* scholars (from several disciplines) whose work and thinking she particularly admired. That approach provided high-calibre personalized learning experiences from different sources, thereby allowing her to compare and contrast diverse perspectives. It also provided entrée into several different information and influence networks, so that leads on "who would be a good person to talk to about . . ." were readily available on many subjects. The multiple mentors approach also allows a student to play a role in the continuing education of mentors themselves, either by being the communication link among mentors who do not normally communicate directly or by challenging the mentors with the student's own new ideas. It's lots of fun, a heady experience, and has been extremely helpful in getting a good start in academic life. The dangers of the multiple mentors strategy are dilettantism (from learning only superficially from one's various mentors) and mismanagement of multiple mentor-student relationships (by letting any one mentor get his or her nose out of joint because of time spent with another).

A general concern we have about all forms of the vertical networking strategy stems from its inherent conservatism. It assumes that what worked well in the past will also be relevant for the future. The validity of that assumption is debatable. The danger is that protégés will fail to break with the past and move into the future. There may be tempting short-term rewards for reproducing the accomplishments of the past rather than building on them or even rejecting them in favor of a wholly new approach. In implementing the vertical networking strategy, therefore, it is important to assess both the gains and the chains of linking up closely with the past.

The third strategy for getting started in academic publishing is horizontal networking. Here the emphasis is on building links to graduate student and junior faculty peers both at one's own and other institutions. Today those peers may not have much knowledge about the publishing process, but most of the new ideas and empirical research to appear in the next few years will originate in this group. It is their working papers we should be reading and to which we should be responding, both for their benefit and our own. Over time we and our peers will gain knowledge about the publishing process. Previously established networks will facilitate sharing that information. An important benefit of networking is the opportunity to build the friendships that humanize our work world. We are already grateful for the intellectual stimulation, practical advice, support, and love we have received from our colleagues. Thanks go to those who are responsible for our ability to write the previous sentence.

MESSAGES TO ADVISERS AND MENTORS

To those of us from the pre-sex education generation, publishing is a lot like sex. It's a central but taboo topic of conversation in formal settings, and it is difficult to initiate a discussion of it with one's elders. Instead, we learn about it from our equally ignorant peers. The result is an abundance of shared ignorance, superstitious learning, misinformation, and uncertainty.

As the curriculum is not likely to include "Publishing 101" at most institutions, mentors can play an important role in filling this gap in graduate student or junior faculty education. The content of that education should include answers to questions such as those we listed above as the uncertainties we experience as newcomers.

Mentors should take note of our sex analogy. Despite the importance to newcomers of knowledge about publishing, we often do not ask for help. As with sex, we don't want to admit our ignorance. We'd like to pretend we are more knowledgeable and experienced than is actually the case. With respect to publishing, the situation is aggravated by the evaluative aspect of the mentoring relationship. We know mentors have both developmental and gatekeeping roles to play. We don't know whether our questions will be interpreted as commendable curiosity, regrettable but correctable ignorance, or evidence of unsuitability for the profession. (As a mental exercise, ask yourself how many of the questions we asked earlier made you wonder about the authors' competence.)

We have seen many honest queries lead to negative attributions about the questioner's intelligence; thus we tend to avoid appearing "stupid" by limiting our requests for assistance. Generally, we stick to immediately necessary areas such as help with administrative hassles, substantive questions about course material, and guidance on the dissertation. We forgo the opportunity to learn the publishing skills that will be so important to us in the following years. As junior faculty members, the perceived need to avoid signs of weakness in front of senior colleagues may continue, due to promotion and tenure worries. It would be useful if mentors would take the initiative and offer information even though their graduate students or junior colleagues have not asked for it.

It is interesting that one of the authors finds asking questions more difficult than the other. This difference may be gender related. Where the male author fears the appearance of weakness, the female author is comfortable acknowledging differences in experience. It may be more culturally acceptable for women than men to ask "dumb" questions. It can also be argued that the appearance of ignorance is most forgivable at the very beginning of one's career, making that the time when it is least costly (in terms of negative attribution) to ask a lot of questions.

MESSAGES TO REVIEWERS

What does a reviewer review? Is a paper full of words and ideas nothing more than an inanimate object? Isn't it also a human product, that is, evidence of the expenditure of intellectual, emotional, and spiritual energy? Taking the latter perspective raises issues concerning two very human, very animate phenomena: feelings and interests. We mean to include in "feelings" the full range of human emotions, especially those that affect motivation. We mean to include in "interests" the core values and essential premises that provide the assumption base on which intellectual (as well as other) effort is built. This section of the chapter deals with the implications of recognizing that neither authors nor reviewers are devoid of human feelings and interests.

Recognizing Human Feelings

First-time critical reviews are a shock to newcomers in the field. Some may never try to submit a paper again. Is ability to withstand criticism the optimal selection criterion for admission to the field? Others become fearful and skittish, more risk-averse than they used to be in choosing topics and conducting research. In a field where progress depends on the development of new knowledge, aren't pressures to be conformist dysfunctional? It is hard to believe that anyone is unaffected. It is painful to learn that your work is unimpressive, flawed, uninformed, ill-conceived, and so on. Perhaps one develops callouses with experience, so it doesn't hurt as much—or at least it doesn't shock as much. Perhaps one's batting average improves too, thus effecting a change in the reinforcement schedule. But that is all in the future. The reality of the here and now for the newcomer, critical review in hand, is that it is very painful.

The question we want to address is this: Is there anything reviewers can do to be more sensitive to the pain at the receiving end of negative feedback? We suspect there is. And we do not think that the only possible way of showing sensitivity is to withhold negative feedback, thereby violating a major purpose of the reviewing process. Nor do we ask for special treatment for newcomers. There are two reasons to reject that course: First, because such treatment compromises, at least to some extent, the goal of concealing the identity of the author; and, second, because we suspect that receiving negative feedback will *always* hurt, and so the problem is not one suffered only by newcomers.

So what can reviewers do? The keystone is respect rather than ridicule. One device is to imagine that the unknown author is a close friend. That does not mean ignoring the negative and touching only on the positive (we have higher standards for friendship than that) but delivering the message in such a way that the dignity of the other person is respected. Clarity in identifying shortcomings, suggestions of ways in which they might be overcome, all stated in a constructive, supportive tone, would be helpful. The newcomer whose work is flawed but not without redeeming merit would especially like to read that "several of the concepts developed here show real promise, and this reviewer looks forward to additional work from the writer." Our insecurities are truly legion, and past accomplishments pale in comparison with our uncertain futures.

We have given some thought to the humanity of the reviewers too. The act of writing a *hostile* review (a special form of negative appraisal) is dehumanizing to its writer, in addition to the adverse impact such a review has on its ultimate recipient, that is, the author whose work is under review. Hostile reviews serve no useful academic purpose, so we wonder why they occur at all. One possible explanation is that reviewers are venting the hurt that they (as authors) have suffered at the hands of other reviewers, that is, that they are engaging in a form of displaced aggression. A system that creates such a self-perpetuating pattern of destruction and harm-doing is diabolical. We need to help one another establish a more humane approach.

Another possible explanation for the perceived hostility of some reviews results from an insensitivity to the effects of status differences. Some would like to imagine that "colleagues are colleagues," and that a senior professor's appraisal of a junior colleague is received no differently than an appraisal by someone of equal rank. While the question could be researched empirically, we suspect that criticism from above is perceived very differently than peer review or criticism from below. Ilgen and Feldman's (1983) comments on separating the coaching and controlling components of supervisory feedback support such a speculation. Especially for newcomers, journal reviewers are assumed to be superiors. While criticism should not be condescending, reviewers might imagine that each paper they are reading (and of which they are inclined to be critical) is some junior person's first submission. We feel the resulting humaneness in reviews would be a benefit to us all.

Some might argue that we are being overly sensitive to negative feedback, that it is time to "grow up." They might advocate hardening our hearts, toughening our skin, and so on, rehearsing the virtues of macho toughness. We believe, however, that the capacity to feel pain is linked to the ability to empathize with others. We would retain our sensitivity, therefore, in the hope that we might be deterred from replicating any harm-doing we experience.

Where a paper is an empirical one, the human element can be seen not only from the perspective of the author and reviewer but also from that of the subjects or the respondents/interviewees. Treatment of human subjects should be used as a criterion in reviewing empirical research papers. Deception of subjects as an intentional part of the research design requires a compelling argument in its defense (e.g., that the research question was an important one *and* that no alternative designs would have been appropriate). Reviewers should require evidence that the study received "human subjects review" at the author's university or went through a comparable procedure elsewhere. In sum, an ethical criterion concerning the manner in which the research was conducted should become a more important part of the review process.

Recognizing Values and Interests

Knowledge seeking can be evaluated in terms of both ends and means. While methods (another term for *means*) sections are standard fare in research articles (at least those with an empirical base), comparable attention is rarely given to ends. A study may be positioned relative to previous empirical findings and conceptual material, the rationale behind specific hypotheses may be outlined, but the overall purpose of the research is rarely made explicit or its importance defended. That neglect can be faulted on at least two grounds. The first is that the skills involved in discerning the motive force behind one's search for knowledge will atrophy with disuse. Such a capacity for critical self-reflection is crucial in the perpetual struggle to be free of the constraints imposed by traditional ways of seeing and thinking. The second reason to require an explicit treatment of ends concerns public disclosure of the interests and assumptions of the author. Reviewers should ask: "What function is served by this research?" "Whose interests are furthered?" "Why has the author *not* chosen to include an analysis of his or her data from labor's perspective rather than only from management's (or vice versa)?" Partiality ought to be accounted for, not merely acknowledged. Failure to ask such questions reinforces a disinclination (and, ultimately, an incapacity) to engage in critical analysis.

The values and ideological component of reviewers' ends or goals also have important effects on the publishing process. The fear that articles on radical, nontraditional research topics and methods will be disproportionately rejected by reviewers discourages risk taking. Such a fear may not be justified objectively (arguments are heard on both sides), but it persists nonetheless. To a newcomer, the resulting situation has a catch-22 quality: While editorial statements in journals typically call for fresh new ideas, and mentors warn that to succeed one must not only work hard but be bold and original, there is something else deep in the soul that tells us to play it safe. First tenure, then temerity.

Where does the voice in the soul come from? Is it merely a handy excuse to stay on well-trodden paths, never venturing far from the mainstream? Does one newcomer spread false rumors about reviewer conservatism to frighten off other contenders for recognition as "radical newcomer of the year"? Is this but another illustration of a chronic "young turk" phenomenon? Or is the screening process for nontraditional material actually more stringent than it is for conventional topics and approaches? Most important, is it reasonable to expect that newcomers to the field will risk their fledgling careers to find out? Do we have any choice?

Even if it is objectively false that reviewers are more severe with radical material, is there anything to be done to overcome the contrary belief? In the annual report of submissions and rejections, perhaps journal editors might summarize the *reasons* for rejections. Would "author's perspective is too far out in left field" be a category any reviewers would admit to?

Concluding Messages to Reviewers

The review process has both short-term and long-term goals. In the short term, it serves as a screening mechanism for publication in journals of certain types and reputations. In the longer term, it has a lasting effect on authors and their research and on the progress of the field. The reviewing process can inflict pain, toughen the skin, and instill a yearning for vengeance. It also has the potential to stimulate greater sensitivity to human subjects and scholarly colleagues, develop scholarly research skills, and encourage the practice of critical self-reflection. Because reviewers play a legitimized control function in the publishing process, they can be held accountable for the exercise of their authority. We ask that human factors—both emotional and ideological—be part of that accountability process.

MESSAGES TO GATEKEEPERS

Critics of prevailing publishing practices in the organizational sciences are themselves subject to criticism. The argument defending the status quo typically has three components: (a) Journals rightfully play a gatekeeping function so as to maintain and/or increase the stature of the field and the quality of the work done in it; (b) convincing empirical evidence proving that nontraditional topics, methods, or ideologies are disproportionately rejected by editors and reviewers has not been presented; and (c) those who complain that their work does not get the hearing it deserves in refereed journals are expressing sour grapes—the truth is that their work is not very good and/or that they are envious of those who occupy important gatekeeping positions.

This section of the chapter is a response to the gatekeepers' argument. The shortcomings of that argument are discussed in three parts: academic parochialism, inconsistently applied motivational analysis, and (of special note here) relegation of newcomers to impotent quiescence until they are so much a part of the establishment that criticism might be self-destructive.

Academic Parochialism

As is noted elsewhere in this book, there are many ways of knowing, each of which is acquired differently, is assessable by its own criteria of adequacy, and serves a particular interest (Morgan, 1985). The kinds of knowledge are not ordered in any hierarchical manner, so no one kind is better than another in any absolute sense; each serves a different interest. To assess knowledge of one kind by the adequacy criterion of another kind is therefore inappropriate; each needs to be "framed" (Culbert & McDonough, 1980) in its own terms.

The dominant knowledge type in the organizational sciences has been in the functionalist paradigm (Burrell & Morgan, 1979). That is the type of knowledge that the gatekeepers require to be convinced that nontraditional research does not receive a fair hearing in the journals. Evidence from a different paradigm is unacceptable to them. That situation is analogous to an English-speaking government official insisting that Spanish-speaking citizens who feel themselves to be discriminated against on account of their language file their complaint in English. The critic is placed in a catch-22 situation.

By refusing to consider as knowledge anything demonstrated outside of the functionalist tradition, critiques that are by their very nature outside of that paradigm (e.g., the radical structuralist view that those in power will inevitably abuse their positions of trust to further their class interests) are automatically relegated to the area of nonknowledge. The parochialism of the gatekeepers' argument defending the status quo thus limits its falsifiability. But a nonfalsifiable defense of things as they are does more than put radical critics in an awkward position. Such a defense also robs the prevailing system of self-corrective mechanisms. Even if the system is "right" today, how will it ever find out if its performance begins to decline? That, in the long run, is a major threat to standards of excellence in the field.

Inconsistent Motivational Analysis

Defenders of current publishing practices are quick to assume that the motives of critics cover up their own shortcomings, that is, that the critics are expressing sour grapes. Certainly mixed-motive behavior is a common occurrence, and interpreting criticism is complicated by the need to distinguish that which is legitimate from that which is purposely obfuscatory. But if motives are relevant to criticism, aren't they also relevant to countercriticism, that is, to defense of the status quo? The temptation to allow self-interest to affect opinion is omnipresent, whether that opinion favors or opposes the prevailing system. While a moralist might bewail that fact, a realist would try to build in safeguards to cope with it, noting that the greater the stakes the greater the need for safeguards. Those who are currently in positions of power have more to lose from successful criticism than do the powerless from successful countercriticism. Thus the temptation to skew opinion in the direction of self-interest is greater for those already entrenched. If a greater threat is posed by the biases of the powerful than by those of the powerless, there is a greater need for self-reflective critical analysis from the haves than the have-nots. The question to be answered is this: How can those in power be sure that the criteria they use to assess criticism are legitimate, and not simply devices to deflect criticism?

Impotence of Newcomers

Newcomers, using the gatekeepers' logic, can't be credible critics of the status quo. Such a role is denied them because of the suspicion that their criticism is but anticipatory defensiveness stemming from a fear of trying and failing to meet current standards. To assume the role of critic, a newcomer must establish credibility by playing and winning under the current rules. Having proven his or her worth, the ex-newcomer may then criticize. But, having succeeded in the system, the "critic" has to challenge the value of her or his own achievement in gaining acceptance.

The socialization process of newcomers contains within it factors that shift priorities, loyalties, and self-interests. So if newcomers must be socialized into the system to become credible critics, the system (intentionally or not) defends itself from "outsider" attacks. The operational definition of being credible is having nothing left to say that is critical.

Concluding Messages to Gatekeepers

A system that is well protected from criticism, that is, that has effective mechanisms for deterring criticism by labeling critics as malcontents, or deferring criticism until it is outdated or forgotten, is unlikely to change in response to constructive internal debate. Such tightness of control may be efficient in the short run but is not effective over the long haul because it reduces the system's capacity to adjust to a changing environment. The challenge is in creating mechanisms to sustain both the capacity for self-reflective critical analysis *and* the motivation to engage in it. What would such a system look like? Does publishing in the organizational sciences look like that now? From a newcomer's perspective, we have serious reservations about giving an unqualified "yes" to the question.

SELF-REFLECTIONS

In this section, we reflect upon the chapter we have written and the thoughts and feelings that went into its making. We do so in the hope of discovering what we have learned about publishing and about ourselves. Because of that personal component, we have written individual self-reflections.

From Ralph

In our messages to peers, we had hoped to provide courage and support for our junior colleagues through sharing our values and feelings. It appears we have done so only insofar as "misery loves company." We are disturbed by our generally negative tone concerning the central activity of our professional lives. We must conclude that there is something wrong either with the system or with us. But we know we are not alone in many of those negative feelings. Much of what we have described seems to be a classic negative reinforcement system where the desired behavior removes a lot of aversive stimuli. We have also described the classic problem with such a reward system: insufficient direction regarding the paths leading to the desired outcome. In addition, we suspect that many of the "rats" refuse to play in this maze. How high is the opportunity cost to the field of lost contributions from Ph.D.s who publish little beyond their dissertation or tenure requirements? Are we really giving out all those Ph.D.s to people who don't have anything to add to our collective scholarship?

There must be ways to change the rewards, climate, structure, culture, and so on of a system that generates bad feelings regarding its central activity. There would seem to be little that we, as newcomers, can do about it on our own. But we need not accept our social world as fixed. We can move toward a more positive world in many modest ways. We can actively support each other in our work.

We can celebrate the completion of a manuscript. We can provide considered and considerate feedback on our peers' ideas and papers. We can commiserate with our rejected colleague. We can refuse to accept the cynical definitions of the field. We can strive to live a career that contributes to the growth, application, and dissemination of knowledge about organizational life, a career of intellectual challenge, personal growth, social responsibility, and developing friendships.

From Jill

Writing from a position of avowed ignorance, as we are in this chapter, is at once a liberating, frustrating, and challenging experience. It is liberating because, as newcomers neatly labeled as "outsiders," we are free to say absolutely anything we like. We needn't do an extensive literature review or worry ourselves about issues of accuracy or representativeness; we have been asked to "tell it like it is" as we see it right now. Our arguments are unassailable because they only purport to reflect our personal perspectives. Who could prove we are wrong?

Who would bother to try? That is the frustrating part. We are encouraged to put on public display all of our prejudices, insecurities, and stereotypical views about a subject on which our only claim to fame is near-total ignorance. It's embarrassing. Those are not our prettiest parts. And it can certainly be argued that nothing we have written should be taken seriously (if read at all) because we are totally lacking in credibility. The frustrating thing is that, if there is even one helpful insight in what we have written, it is likely to go undetected amidst the less redeeming material.

At this point, we could fairly be asked why we agreed to participate in this project. After all, getting into print because of incompetence is unlikely to impress those who will review us for promotion and tenure. (Maybe, a little voice whispers, they won't actually read the chapter, so they won't find out what it's really about. Or maybe it will do our careers good to be seen in the company of so many fine characters as our coauthors.) Or maybe—we hope this is part of it—putting on display not only our ignorance but our willingness to be honest, and our attempt in this last section to be unpretentious, will be a useful demonstration to others that a humble yearning for learning is OK. We want to try hard to keep to our personal values of honesty, humanity, and humility. We don't know if we will ever "make it" in academic publishing. But if anyone knows where to find us 10 years from now,[1] please ask us how well we've kept to our chosen path.

EPILOGUE

The concluding section of a research article usually includes a discussion of the limitations of the data. We close with observations of a similar sort.

This chapter was described in the Prologue as a case study written by the human subjects. In addition to the problem of bias inherent in such a research design, we also had to face the reality that our subjects, while not uncooperative, refused to sit still while we studied them. Our first reaction to that fact was one of annoyance. We had collected and analyzed the data, and formed it into a neat package; then it fell apart. It soon occurred to us, however, that we had come upon *new* data, information that was interesting on a different dimension. Exploring that dimension led us to several important insights:

It is challenging (if humbling) to contemplate the apparent power of situational variables (e.g., the removal of aversive stimuli in a negative reinforcement system) on individuals who always believed they would have been among the nonconformists in the Asch and Milgram experiments.

It is an exhilarating (if exhausting) experience to be forced to shift gears and come up with a radically new perspective on material we thought we had already figured out.

It is possible to disagree with one another, to experience the world differently, and still be patient and understanding and supportive friends.

NOTE

1. Professor Graham is now tenured at Loyola University–Chicago and Professor Stablein is now tenured at Otago University–New Zealand.

REFERENCES

Burrell, G., & Morgan, G. (1979). *Sociological paradigms and organisational analysis.* London: Heinemann.

Culbert, S. A., & McDonough, J. J. (1980). *The invisible war: Pursuing self-interest at work.* New York: Wiley.

Ilgen, D. R., & Feldman, J. M. (1983). Performance appraisal: A process focus. In L. L. Cummings & B. M. Staw (Eds.), *Research in organizational behavior* (Vol. 5, pp. 141-197). Greenwich, CT: JAI Press.

Morgan, G. (1985). Journals and the control of knowledge: A critical perspective. In L. L. Cummings & P. J. Frost (Eds.), *Publishing in the organizational sciences* (chap. 3). Homewood, IL: Irwin.

7

Publishing in the Organizational Sciences
The Dilemma of Values

F. DAVID SCHOORMAN

For a newcomer to the field of organizational science, the issues involved in the publishing process are much broader than the mechanics of seeing a finished product through the review and editorial process of a professional journal. The more fundamental issues that need to be resolved concern the nature of the product, the values inherent in this product, and the process of creating the product. Only when these issues are resolved can the strategies associated with the dissemination of the product be dealt with, and these strategies are inextricably tied to the choice of values. This chapter is an attempt to explore this diversity of values and the dilemmas associated with the choice among values related to the creation of knowledge in organizational science. The implications of these choices for the dissemination of this knowledge are also discussed.

ENTRY INTO THE FIELD

There are many doors that allow entry into the general field of organizational science. The truly interdisciplinary nature of the field allows entry through training in psychology, sociology, business and management, education, journalism, and less frequently through other disciplines. The newcomer to the field would do well to take this as the first clue that this is not a field where there is "one best way" or where consensus is likely to be the rule. The early socialization that occurred during graduate training will have exposed the newcomer to a particular set of values and will have set the stage for the newcomer's struggle to find a niche that is comfortable and compatible in this vast domain of values. The compatibility of values must first relate to the creation or production process that is to be undertaken and the specification of the outcome of this process. Once this is accomplished, compatibility of values concerning dissemination or marketing of the product will be sought.

THE CHOICE OF PRODUCT

As an earlier section of this book suggests, there are choices that the organizational scientist is faced with regarding the product that is to be created. These choices include the production of (a) new knowledge, (b) educated students, and (c) organizational change. The roles associated with these products—researcher, teacher, and practitioner/consultant—are more familiar. However, many of us work in universities, conduct research, and apply it to organizations, thereby accomplishing the tricky balancing act among roles that is all too familiar while effectively avoiding a definitive choice.

The choice among the three products is actually very important with respect to the publishing process. Publications are most critical in the researcher role because the product of this role is the most intangible, and the evaluation of the researcher is based primarily on publications. For the teacher role, publications are much less critical. Published material is used in the teaching process and therefore is important, but the quality of the product of this role can be evaluated independently of the publications. The practitioner/consultant role relies least on publication, the outcomes of an organizational intervention being the measure of role success. Publications do, however, play a role in the visibility of the practitioner. While each of these roles contains its own unique dilemmas of values, for the purposes of this chapter, we will focus on the researcher role because this is where the values associated with publishing are most clearly defined. We will further assume that this researcher role is being carried out in the context of a university department complete with all the complexities involved in managing the conflict with the teacher and practitioner roles.

THE PRODUCTION OF KNOWLEDGE

In an effort to adequately represent opposing views, the discussion that follows will depart from the traditional style (norm) of writing in our field and take the form of a conversation that might occur between a newcomer to the field and one or more members of the field. The question asker in the following discussion is the newcomer to the field. The responses of the "field" to the questions of the newcomer may be interpreted as representing either different individuals' values or the response of a single individual with multiple personalities with many of the personalities responding. The visual image of the latter seems to capture for this author an excellent caricature of the experience of a newcomer. (In either case, the use of the personal pronoun *I* does not imply that the view expressed is that of the author.)

> "I am really excited about my first job. There is so much more to this field than I realized. This job could be an excellent opportunity to learn new things about this field. However, I am a little unsure as to whether I should approach the job this way. Should I take the time to learn more about aspects of the field that I am less familiar with?"

Yes, by all means take advantage of the opportunity for learning that your new job presents. Learning is the most exciting aspect of this profession and when you stop expanding your horizons you will stop enjoying your work. Through learning you will accrue the added benefit of being able to have intellectual exchanges with your colleagues and perhaps even collaborate with them in a newly mutual interest.

No, you have already spent many years in intensive study in your field of interest. The field is too large for you to reasonably expect to become an expert on all topics, and if you attempted to achieve this you would have little time to do anything else. You are an expert in your areas of interest and have been well trained. Concentrate your efforts in these areas and you will be respected by your colleagues for your special expertise.

> "This sounds similar to the arguments I've heard in favor of eclecticism of research interests on the one hand and programmatic research on the other. Could you help me decide which approach is more appropriate?"

You should definitely pursue an eclectic research program. Remember that you are a faculty member in a university community. You will need to have a broad range of interests so as to educate the students in your program and to guide them in developing new ideas of their own. You will be called upon to represent the broader interests of the field and you should be able to fulfill this responsibility adequately and confidently. If you take an eclectic perspective, your day-to-day work will have greater variety and therefore be more interesting and stimulating. You will be less likely to experience professional burnout.

As a newcomer to the field, the only sensible course is that of programmatic research. Pick a single area that is of interest to you and direct all your efforts toward this area. This will allow you to establish a name for yourself in a particular area, which is much harder to do if your research is scattered across different topics. You will be much more productive if you follow a program of research because you will not have to spend time keeping up with new developments in multiple areas. You are much more likely to receive tenure early if you establish a single program of research.

"What are the issues that I should consider in the selection of a topic?"

You should pick a topic that is in the mainstream of current interest in the field. Your own contribution to the knowledge on the topic should be the development of one particular aspect of the topic. This will help to identify you as an "in-group" member of the field rather than one who is on the fringes of the field.

Pick an area of research that is relatively unexplored. Develop a way of making this research an accepted topic in the field. This will make you the "leading authority" on your particular topic. You should not settle for being one of the masses studying, for example, the relationship between satisfaction and performance.

"If there are more and less acceptable topics, are there also more and less acceptable research strategies?"

Yes, there are some critical choices among research strategies, the most important of which is the need to do field research and collect real data. Too many researchers in organizational science forget that this is an applied field concerned with real problems. Research conducted in the laboratory with college students or other convenient samples may be acceptable in social or cognitive psychology, but it just does not contribute much to industrial psychology or organizational behavior. I cannot imagine that this department would ever hire an organizational scientist who did his or her research in the laboratory.

Yes, the most important of which is the difference between laboratory and field research. Many researchers are so anxious to rush out in the field and solve the problems of the world that they forget that they are supposed to be in the business of doing science, not miracles. They have little sense about experimental design and even less sense about adequate control and end up with "real world" data that can be explained in at least a dozen ways. Learn to do research in the laboratory and it will make you a better scientist. When you have learned as much as you can in the laboratory (and not until then), you should consider exploring the complexities of field research.

"Is this related to the philosophies of inductive versus deductive reasoning?"

Yes it is. Field research is often based on an inductive philosophy because much of this research is not theory driven. The designing of laboratory research on the other hand requires the a priori development of a conceptual framework and research hypotheses.

No, the philosophy of research one adopts is independent of whether research is conducted in the field or the laboratory. It is just as important to conduct research based on deductively reasoned theory in the field as it is in the laboratory. While inductive research plays an important role in suggesting possible relationships among variables, it is the deductive research that sets up a critical test of a network of relationships that advances science.

"Most of the research that I have read in the organizational sciences used a survey method to collect data. Is this the most accepted method of research in our field?"

Yes, it certainly is the method of the organizational sciences. The survey, when carefully designed with good psychometric properties, can be the most versatile tool of the organizational scientist. Using surveys we can gather data about attitudes, or behaviors, about individuals, groups, and even about relationships. We can determine if the data are reliable, and valid, and we can even build in mechanisms to detect if the respondent is taking the survey seriously. As a young researcher you would do well to master this procedure and use it often.

The survey method is indeed overused in this field. While surveys do have many advantages, they are not the best method by which to study many of the issues of interest to organizational science. Surveys are best suited to the measurement of individual attitudes. Measurement of behaviors with surveys is open to questions about the accuracy of self-reported data, and measurement of group- or organization-level concepts is fraught with problems of aggregated data. In addition, because surveys yield cross-sectional data, it is difficult to answer questions about process and causal relationships.

"Should I try to use other methods in my research? How do I make a decision about what method I use?"

You should let the problem you are investigating suggest the appropriate method to be used. When the study requires strict controls and the question is not specific to a particular organizational context, an experimental method, simulation, or role-playing study might be appropriate. If you are interested in behavior over time or in questions about process, you might consider an observational method. Interviews are very useful for gathering data when you are not certain about what you are likely to discover. An important aspect of the latter two methods is that they generally yield qualitative data, which require very different analytic techniques than quantitative data. You should also consider the possibility of using multiple methods in the same study, which will yield a much richer perspective of the problem you are studying.

The problems associated with other research methods such as observation, simulations, and unstructured interviews far outweigh their benefits. Do not underestimate the versatility of surveys. We now have psychometric techniques that overcome many of the problems attributed to survey data. We can examine causal relationships and test hypotheses about processes with survey data. With surveys, one is able to reach a larger, more broadly based population, at a minimal cost, thereby increasing the power of the statistical techniques used in analyses. While you might use other methods under special circumstances, surveys seem to be the most pragmatic method of research.

"If I were to conduct a field study and would like to use a survey, are there standard surveys available? And if I put one together, should I be writing my own items or using previously developed scales?"

There are several fairly well-known complete surveys that you can use for your research. You should take advantage of them whenever possible because they have been used in previous research and extensive norms are available for interpreting your data. You can also use the reliability and validity data that previous research has provided. If you create your own survey, you should use established measurement scales for as many of your variables as possible for all of the reasons cited above. A related strategy that you may consider is to obtain a data set that has been collected by an independent research organization using a standard survey and spend your time and efforts on analysis and interpretation. I know of one researcher in our field who is well known as an expert on the organizational characteristics of a particular type of company. This researcher has not had to be (and has never been) in an organization of this type.

I cannot imagine any reason that you would want to reuse a complete survey unless you are doing a replication of a study. There are some advantages to using established measurement scales that have good psychometric properties. However, you should use these scales only if the concept being measured by the scale is exactly what you intend to measure, and if the scale was developed for a population and a context similar to those you wish to study. If not, or if you are in doubt, write your own items. This will make sure that the scale will measure exactly what you intend, and it will be tailored to the context. Write multiple items to measure concepts that have a complex or multifaceted conceptual space, and sometimes a simple straightforward issue may be captured by a single item. Remember that, although there are many good arguments for being able to demonstrate through internal consistency statistics that you have a reliable measure, it is a very fine line between reliability and redundancy in measurement. One final note, do not ever be tempted to build a research program on a data set that you did not participate in collecting. You may discover many interesting statistical relationships but you will be no closer to understanding what actually happens in those organizations. Remember that the data you collect are only as good as the care and diligence that go into the process of collecting the data. If you relinquish control of the data collection process, you can never be sure of the quality of your data.

"If I am engaged in an ongoing program of research, how often do I need to publish? How much new information needs to be generated before I have the content for a publishable paper?"

I am glad you raised this question. Think of your research program as the process of solving a jigsaw puzzle. You should wait until you collect enough adjacent pieces to the puzzle to have a meaningful pattern of information to report. Writing an article about every single piece to the puzzle does not enlighten anybody and only serves to clutter the literature with unverified trivia. Be careful not to attract a reputation as an author of such "quick and dirties." Most of the prominent scholars in any field tend to be associated with a single piece of research, often a key article that advances the field. Give yourself the opportunity to have the same success; make your contributions count.

There is one clear answer to this question to any scholar in our field and this answer is only more emphatic to a young scholar. Publishing is the name of the game. Publish as often as you can. Do not worry about how good or how important it is (that is what editors are for), just get it out there. Remember that you are working against a clock and no matter how much people tell you that the quality of your work will be evaluated at promotion and tenure time, five articles always look like higher quality than one article.

"Throughout this discussion, we have talked about research and data collection as though they were the same. Is all research in this field empirical? Is empirical research more acceptable? What are the alternatives to empirical research?"

As a young scholar in this field, you should be concerned with doing empirical research. While there are other ways in which researchers can contribute in our field (for example, through review articles and theory development), this role is reserved for more senior, well-established organizational scientists. As a young researcher, you will be judged on your ability to conduct empirical research and nonempirical work may even be detrimental to the development of your career.

Research in any field should include integration, theory development, and empirical testing. The success of the field depends on how well all three of these functions are performed and on how well they are coordinated. This field does have a bias toward empirical research to the exclusion of theory development and integration. In addition to this, the coordination among the three functions is poor. It is relatively easy to learn how to do empirical research and much harder to build good theories. As a young scholar, you should try to be good at all aspects of research and concentrate in particular on the most difficult skill of theory development. The norm of leaving the tasks of integration and theory building to senior scholars has not worked well. We must try to change this pattern. An important way to change is to recognize that integration, theory development, and empirical research are interdependent functions. We should write articles that incorporate all three components rather than segregating them to different articles for submission to specialized journals.

BALANCING THE ROLES

"As a faculty member at a university, I will be required to teach. What is the relationship between research and teaching? How should I approach my teaching responsibilities?"

You already know that as a young scholar you are faced with serious time constraints in terms of establishing yourself as a researcher before your tenure review. No matter how you look at it, teaching takes up time—time that could otherwise be spent doing research. There are those who would argue that teaching graduate students is not as detrimental to research as teaching undergraduates, but this is based on the premise that you would spend less time on teaching activities at the graduate level, which is not necessarily true. You should make every effort to reduce the time you spend in teaching-related activities and I have outlined some strategies for doing this: (a) Compare schools on the basis of teaching load and use this in your job choice. There are significant differences. (b) When you negotiate the terms of your job, there is always room for negotiating a reduced teaching load, particularly in the first year. (c) Negotiate for summer support for which you do not have to teach. (d) Try to get as many teaching assistants as possible and delegate as much of your teaching responsibilities as possible. For example, you should do the highly visible, short-duration activities such as a 45-minute lecture to the entire class but not the low visibility, long duration activities such as grading examinations and projects or conducting preexamination reviews for smaller sections of the class. (e) Try to get research grants that will allow you to buy time off from teaching. This has the double benefit of improving your research credentials at the same time. (If you are especially good at the art of persuasion, you may be able to get time off to write the research proposal that, when funded, will get you more time off.) (f) Take on any administrative or service responsibilities that will relieve you of some teaching responsibilities if the total time commitment is reduced by the trade. (g) If you cannot reduce the number of courses you teach, try to reduce the number of preparations. Get your teaching "act" down to a routine that requires minimal preparation time. (h) Consider the utility curve associated with the quality of your teaching. Frequently, teaching at a level that is anything above adequate has a negative marginal utility.

The view that teaching inhibits the research process is highly exaggerated. This view is, however, reinforced by the field, which tends to define each of the roles such that it excludes the other. A very important aspect of the research process is the dissemination of the products of research. Dissemination can occur in a variety of ways. The research findings can be communicated in writing in the form of journal articles or books as well as through oral presentations. Oral presentations of research findings can occur at professional meetings and at invited addresses but most frequently occur in the classroom. The audience in the classroom (particularly at the graduate level) is, arguably, the most important audience to which one can disseminate research findings because they are the future professionals of the field, the ones who are likely to add to our current base of knowledge. The context of the classroom also increases the probability that the information is adequately assimilated. Unfortunately, the field of organizational science rules this out as an acceptable form of dissemination of knowledge. It is particularly unfortunate because more scholars will find out about your research in the classroom than read about it in a journal. Do not rule out your classroom as a vehicle for dissemination. A second reason that teaching is compatible with research is that teaching students about new knowledge is often best accomplished through the research process itself. Collaborations with students on research projects can successfully combine the research and teaching processes and prove to be very rewarding.

"Should I consider consulting opportunities with organizations? What are the advantages and disadvantages of doing this? Will consulting facilitate or inhibit my research?"

Consulting is a very important aspect of being a researcher in the organizational sciences. You must remember that this is an applied field and, to have any credibility in your views, you must have experience as a practitioner in ongoing "real world" organizations. In addition to this experience, consulting also establishes contacts in the business community that make it easier to find a research sample when you need one. You can actually make your consulting work count as research if you contract with the organization to allow you to publish the results of any interventions you conduct. In situations such as this, the consultation is your research and makes for a very efficient use of time, because you will also get paid for your consultation. Other advantages are that your department and colleagues may value your reputation as a consultant and see you as a potential facilitator of entry into organizations for research purposes, while the university may view your consultations as a valued community service.

The most obvious advantage of consulting is that you can increase your income. However, like teaching, it is a role that consumes time, which reduces the time available for research. Many scholars in our field believe that consulting can be treated as research and they actually try to publish reports of their consulting. These reports neither add to their credibility as researchers nor advance the knowledge of the field. Because consulting represents interventions that are problem oriented, and frequently diagnosed and requested by the organization, a series of consultations has very little in common with a research program. In addition, the department you work for and the colleagues you work with may resent the fact that you spend as much time as you do away from the university and therefore do not contribute as much as you should to the department. Be careful to not get a reputation as a "consultant type" because many academic departments would be very reluctant to hire you if you decided to move.

PUBLISHING THE FINISHED PRODUCT

The dilemmas discussed in the preceding sections have serious and predictable implications for publishing in the organizational sciences. The same conversation mode is used in this section to explore some of these implications. However, the response to the newcomer's questions represents a more integrated, universal perspective.

> "We have talked at length about the process of doing research, but we have not talked about publishing. How do the issues we discussed relate to publishing in the organizational sciences?"

The choices you make with respect to the issues we have discussed concerning the process of doing research have a significant impact on your ability to publish. The following are a series of observations and experiences by scholars in our field as to how these issues affect publishing.

I once submitted an article that included a deductively reasoned theory that was followed by an empirical test of *a part* of it. The editor remarked that much of the paper was irrelevant to the study and that I should delete it in a revision of the paper if I hoped to publish the study.

I have been amazed at how many reviewers and editors have a consistent bias against laboratory research. The arguments are always the same; laboratory research is not generalizable to "real" organizations and is therefore not worthy of publication.

I had a similar experience with an editor who insisted that the title of my article should be changed to begin with the phrase, "A laboratory study of . . . ." I presume he felt that unsuspecting readers deserved an early warning system.

That is not any worse than the trouble I have had with "laboratory types" as editors. I don't need a control group in my research and laboratory data cannot tell me any more about causal relationships than I already know.

I had an article rejected because a key variable was measured with a single item and I could not report an internal consistency statistic. How many ways can you ask a person whether he or she has made a particular decision previously?

The rest of you have nothing to complain about. You should try publishing a study that used an observational method and qualitative data. There are no publishing outlets for my work.

> "If this is what the review process is like, how does one ever get anything published in this field?"

It is not as complicated as it seems. Given that there are a wide range of values regarding the process of conducting research, and that editors and editorial boards (gatekeepers) have particular biases, it follows that each publication outlet will have a unique configuration of values about what gets published. If you have any doubt about this conclusion, share some of your work with some of your senior colleagues and ask them for advice about where to submit it. To a newcomer, this may seem to be a peculiar question because it does not inquire about the quality or readability or logic of the paper. However, the senior faculty will treat the question as a perfectly reasonable one, and when they have read the articles they may well make statements such as the following: "This is a good *ASQ* piece," or "You should shorten this to a *JAP* article," or "I think *OBHP* would go for this." What they are telling you is which journal has a configuration of values that are compatible with your article. (If you know your colleague well, and know his or her own values about research, the statement about where you should publish the article may be a thinly disguised comment about how "good" he or she thinks it is!) Pay close attention to these values and you will soon learn the configuration of values represented by each journal. It will not be long before you fall into the trap of conforming your writing with a particular journal in mind. (Whether you do this or not is also a decision about values that you will make. The consequences of this decision are quite serious.)

"Given the variety of perspectives we have discussed, how do editors get agreement among multiple reviewers on a particular article?"

This is an excellent question to which there are probably many answers. First, let me make two points about this issue of multiple reviewers. On the positive side, it is a credit to our field that most of the journals use two or three reviewers for each article. On the negative side, editorial boards tend to reflect compatible value perspectives and outside reviewers tend to be colleagues or associates of the editors, hence the potential range of values is not represented. However, in response to your question, very few scholars in this field have not had the experience of receiving multiple reviews on the same article that made contradictory recommendations. The fate of such an article is generally decided by the editor. Ultimately, the responsibility for accepting or rejecting an article is the editor's. A colleague recently showed me a review of an article that said it was an outstanding piece of research and should be published with no changes. It was unquestionably the most positive review that either of us had seen. The article was rejected by the editor without even a request for a revision.

"Do certain prominent scholars get special treatment when they submit articles to journals?"

This is a difficult question to answer for two reasons. (a) It is hard to discover clear evidence that special treatment does occur, and (b) the implications of such a charge are very serious, both for the field and for the individual making the allegations. The research of prominent scholars may represent more acceptable values in the field and therefore be more easily published. On the other hand, the current research of a prominent scholar may be published on the strength of the scholar's reputation rather than the merit of the research. In this matter we have little choice but to trust the integrity of the editors of our journals. There are some differences in policy across journals that may make the process more objective. Some journals conduct the review process such that the reviewers are blind to the author of the article. This goes a long way toward eliminating questions about favorable treatment. Perhaps we can start exploring strategies by which the entire gatekeeping function is blind to the authors of the articles. As a reviewer, I have seen correspondence between editors and authors that has reflected at least a poor choice of situations in which to discuss personal friendships.

"How should I decide where to publish?"

Ideally, you should produce the kind of research that reflects your own values about the process and then disseminate it where there is a market for it. This means that if there is no journal where your work is "valued," you may be faced with the choice of publishing your work as a book or disseminating your ideas through your interactions with others in the field. However, there are other more pragmatic considerations that you should think about. (a) Certain journals will be more acceptable to the senior faculty in your department. Remember that these faculty will have a major impact on your acceptance in the department and on your prospects for promotion and tenure. (b) Different journals are more valued in various professional networks and organizations. (c) You might consider the audience you wish to reach. Journals are very different in terms of their cost, circulation, and diversity of readership.

"What are the advantages of publishing books, or chapters in books, rather than writing journal articles?"

One of the major advantages of writing a book chapter is that it presents one of the rare opportunities in our field to publish theory development. You can also use the opportunity to integrate literature, develop theory, and provide empirical evidence to your readers in one paper. Book chapters often tend to be longer than typical journal articles, which facilitates this type of integration. Unfortunately, to write a chapter for a book, one has to be invited to do so by the editor of the book. The editors of such books generally invite only prominent scholars in the field to contribute chapters because their names help to sell the book. In fact, the choice of the particular scholars is frequently less a function of their expertise in the issues to be addressed in the book than it is a function of their national visibility. As a result, one can expect to find a remarkably similar group of contributors to books on topics as diverse as leadership, organizational effectiveness, motivation, performance appraisal, organizational change, careers, and higher education. A careful examination will even reveal that many of our prominent scholars have the same thing to say about each of these topics. In several areas within our field, there are regular volumes that publish reviews of developments in particular topics. These reviews are an excellent source of integrated knowledge and an "almost real time" indicator of how the field is progressing. These reviews are also written by invitation, and these invitations are also extended exclusively to senior scholars. There is a curious notion in this field that seniority makes for better integrators and theory developers.

"Aren't you being too cynical about this issue? Isn't the simpler explanation that editors are more aware of the prominent scholars, and therefore invite them, a reasonable alternate explanation?"

Perhaps I am being too cynical. However, I do not believe that the alternate explanation you suggest accounts for the choice of contributors. Let me tell of an incident that supports my view. A senior scholar in our field was invited to contribute a chapter to a book. He did not feel he had the time or the interest to devote to this chapter and was about to decline when a former student, a relative newcomer to the field, convinced him that they should collaborate in writing the chapter. The senior scholar was reluctant at first but, when assured that the younger colleague would do much of the work and would be the first author on the paper, the senior scholar agreed. The arrangement was discussed with the editor, who also agreed. As the process continued, the young scholar completed initial drafts of the paper, which were reviewed very positively by the editor. When the final draft was completed, the senior scholar realized that he had not participated or contributed to the final product and suggested to the young scholar that he should be the sole author of the paper. The editor reacted angrily to the suggestion and after several discussions indicated that unless the senior scholar's name was on the paper it would not be published. The authors discussed the implications of this ultimatum and decided that the paper should be a single-authored paper. It was not published.

"How 'perfect' should a paper be before I send it to a journal for review?"

Most young scholars worry about this question of whether their work is perfect enough to be submitted to public scrutiny. While I do not want to suggest that striving for a perfect product is inappropriate, the issues we have discussed with respect to research suggest that the goal of perfection is very elusive in this field. There are as many definitions of perfection as there are unique configurations of values in our field. Frequently, revisions suggested by reviewers are attempts to make an article more consistent with an alternate set of values, thereby making the revised version of the paper less perfect by the author's standards. For example, I have almost always felt less positive about the published version of my own papers than I have about an earlier draft. The difference between drafts generally represents the compromises of values that have occurred. This process of revising the manuscript is much easier to cope with if you frame the conflict as that which occurs among multiple value configurations, all of which are acceptable to the field. The less energy you spend in the "perfecting" process, the easier it is to deal with the eventual compromises.

"What do you do if your paper is rejected and you feel that the rejection was on the basis of incompatible values?"

This is very likely to happen to you, and perhaps happen often, during your career. It is very important that you learn to recognize when a rejection is on the basis of a difference in values. It is usually unwise to send a revised manuscript back to the same journal because the policy of most journals requires that the same reviewers be consulted on the revisions. Their values about research are not likely to have changed in the interim. It is useful to realize that, if fate had dictated that a different group of reviewers be chosen when you first submitted the article, it is entirely possible that the outcome would have been different. Following this argument, if you can be assured by the editor of an independent review, you will have a much better chance of success. *Chance* is indeed a key word that describes the likelihood that the values of the reviewer are compatible with your own. As with events based on chance, the more independent opportunities for such a match to occur the higher the probability of a fair review.

An argument that a young colleague has about this process (which, although representing an extreme version of this view, is quite compelling) is that you should assemble a list of all the acceptable journals in the field in ascending order of the average turnaround time for reviews and submit your paper to each journal sequentially, with the rule of never making revisions (that relate to values) until the article is accepted. This will maximize the probability that you will find a group of reviewers who agree with your values while minimizing the time to publication. You will understand the motivation for this form of pragmatism when you have waited six months for a review that encourages you to revise and resubmit (on the basis of value differences), you have resubmited the revision a month later, and then have waited another six months to hear that it was rejected.

CONCLUDING REMARKS

The premise of this chapter has been that there are multiple configurations of values about research in the organizational sciences that lead to conflicts that surface in the publishing process. This chapter has not been concerned with the issue of competency. There are, of course, varying degrees of competency among researchers in the execution of research regardless of the values they hold. Incompetently conducted research should not be published, and often the rejection of articles is on the basis of a question of competence and not of values. There also are occasions when reviewers of articles are incompetent and the errors they make may be of the false-positive or false-negative variety. Questions of incompetency among reviewers arise most frequently with respect to their familiarity with the literature and their knowledge of analytic procedures. While having an article rejected because a reviewer misunderstood a statistical analysis is no less frustrating than having one rejected on the basis of values, this chapter has focused exclusively on issues regarding values.

Finally, this chapter is not intended to be a pessimistic report on the field, nor is it intended to discourage newcomers to the field. On the contrary, it reflects a measure of optimism about the field. One of the most positive aspects of this field is that it encompasses many disciplines, many traditions, and many values about how science should proceed. This is a sign of a healthy, vibrant field. This optimism is, unfortunately, dampened (as noted in the chapter) by the fact that the field has not always recognized this diversity as a strength. If the field could learn to acknowledge, nurture, and encourage this diversity of values, a great deal of frustration experienced by researchers in the publishing process could be avoided. (On the other hand, this may just be a value held by the author!) To the extent that a discussion of the values involved can help newcomers to the field understand and anticipate some of the dilemmas that they will encounter, it will make their socialization into the field much easier and more enjoyable.

From Inside the Field

Commentary

L. L. CUMMINGS
PETER J. FROST

This subsection presents three perspectives from within the field: those of reviewers, of established authors, and an empirical study of publishing from both reviewers' and authors' viewpoints.

The four reviewers we invited as contributors are Professors Denise Rousseau, Richard Daft, Louis Pondy, and Elaine Romanelli. We intentionally invited these five as representing differences in reviewing perspectives across at least four dimensions. We believe that our anticipation of these differences has been fulfilled in the chapters that are presented.

We wished to capture the effects of

1. differences in tenure as a reviewer, with Romanelli, Rousseau, and Daft (the latter two in 1985) being less experienced than Pondy;
2. differences in formal responsibility in not only a reviewing capacity but an editorial capacity as well, with Pondy and Daft having experience in the editorial saddle with *Administrative Science Quarterly;*
3. differences in conceptual and disciplinary perspective, with Rousseau having been trained as an industrial/organizational psychologist at Berkeley and now teaching in a graduate business school, Daft trained at the University of Chicago in sociology

and organizational theory and now teaching in a business school, and Pondy trained at Carnegie Mellon University in decision theory and administrative sciences and now a department head in a business school (at the time of the first edition); and

4. differences in philosophy and reputed practices of reviewing.

Of course, categorizing one's colleagues along lines of orientation toward reviewing is a risky endeavor. Both Professors Rousseau's and Daft's orientations were expected to be a combination of the evaluative and developmental perspectives on their roles. Professor Pondy was explicitly invited to articulate his posture as a highly developmentally oriented (not without critical capacities and expression, of course) reviewer. In fact, the title of his chapter portrays the reviewer as defense attorney within the nexus of orientations involved in scholarly reviewing. Thus we feel that our four contributors on the reviewing process have indeed fulfilled our hope of presenting multiple perspectives, which, when viewed in the aggregate, provide a rather full, balanced insight into the essence of the reviewing enterprise.

Elaine Romanelli's chapter journals the "passages" that she has experienced over the time frame since she began reviewing. She was invited to enter the review process at a very early stage of her career and she provides an insightful account of the changes occurring within her perspectives on reviewing. One of the most insightful is her transition from a reviewer focused on writing reviews for "the" editor to writing for the author. She also provides useful commentary on the roles of efficiency, thoroughness, and development in reviewing—particularly from the point of view of the competitive tugs and pulls among these three outcomes.

Likewise, we aimed to provide a broad perspective on publishing as seen through the eyes of two established, highly regarded, well-published authors. Again, orientations from sociology and organization theory (Perrow) and from industrial and organizational psychology (Schneider) were invited. The resulting range of contributions not only reflects these aspirations but our three established authors go well beyond. Perrow offers us a revealing, challenging, longitudinal self-analysis of his career as an author. He draws vivid prescriptions and lessons for others from his reflections. Professor Schneider's analysis is directly prescriptive. He never claims that his "how-tos" are based on broad empirical evidence beyond his own active experience as an author. He offers us a glimpse not only of his successes but of his failures and summarizes the lessons to be drawn in propositional form. We interpret his propositions as useful schemata within which to interpret many of the experiential accounts and cases of editorial decision making presented elsewhere within this book.

8

Publishing From a Reviewer's Perspective

DENISE M. ROUSSEAU

For a researcher and reviewer, the review process is a difficult subject to write about. In writing on the reviewer's perspective, it is necessary to distinguish between the reviewer role as it *should be* and as it *is,* though these need not be far apart. The *shoulds* derive from personal training, beliefs, and what the philosophy of science says about scientific critics. It is tough to write about what is because it's difficult to isolate the experiences of a reviewer from the other ways a researcher encounters the review process. The experience of a review board member is distinct from that of an occasional reviewer reviewing for various journals on selected topics. These are distinct from the experiences of a review recipient. All of these roles differ from the part we all occasionally play as source of consolation, social support, and rationalization for students and colleagues who have received reviews that have produced varying degrees of confusion and trauma. None of these is a disinterested role, all involve internalized professional standards, personal beliefs, and individual judgments. In this chapter, I will present my perspective on the review process in journal publication by first describing my perception of the reviewer's role and then what I have personally experienced through this role. Finally, I offer some recommendations to authors to enhance the contribution and publishability of their work and to reviewers and editors to reconcile some differences between what I think should be and what seems to be.

THE REVIEWER'S ROLE

The journal reviewer is generally the first formal critic to which any research or piece of scholarship is subjected (excluding for the moment the review panel overseeing grant proposals). The responsibilities of this role are to comment upon, critique, and direct a written description of research toward an end state consistent with the objectives of a particular discipline. The ultimate objective of a science is to add to the knowledge base. But what knowledge is remains an unanswerable question. It's easier to ask what is the information and to generate some criteria by which to make judgments about it. In my opinion, the reviewer is responsible to the field for (a) identifying what is information (and for advising the journal editor as such), (b) providing the author with direction for enhancing the information value of the present work (where possible), and (c) informing the researcher of shortcomings in his or her current work to enhance the information value of future research (when the present effort does not provide sufficient information for publication). He or she is also responsible for treating the author as a fellow professional entitled to both courtesy and constructive criticism.

Criteria for evaluating what is information are innumerable but could include the logical presentation of new ideas, better specification of existing constructs, articulation of preexisting constructs into new theory, and also the identification of the boundaries (limits) of existing theory. Scholarship meeting any one of these criteria adds information to the discipline. A reviewer's job is in part to identify what is information in a piece of scholarship and to make recommendations regarding how this information might best be presented to the field. A second responsibility of the reviewer is to promote the generation of information by directing authors to better conceptual or methodological approaches to dealing with the issues they address.

This role is obviously subject to all the sociological forces to which any science responds. Of necessity, the review process has a gatekeeping function. This function is mostly beneficial to the science and the fulfillment of its objectives. But in a few cases, it is not. Reviewers are probably far better able to cope with the evaluation of scholarship based on refined scientific theory than on works addressing emergent models—where personal orientations, training, and values are more likely to promote bias. But it is also true that the passage of time leads to better articulation of theories. Thus the hesitation and reluctance that often characterize the reception of new ideas and models stem in part not from the reviewer's lack of understanding but from the true state of the art. For the reviewer's part, he or she must know how to *value* (or, even better, *appreciate*) something new. Part of that appreciation is the ability to read something different and ill-specified and to see in it possible implications and insights the authors might not have developed. Here it is important for the reviewer to act as a commentator and mentor in addition to acting as a critic. To quote Lakatos (1978):

> One must treat budding programs leniently: programs may take decades before they get off the ground and become empirically progressive. Criticism is not a Popperian quick kill, by refutation. Important criticism is always constructive: there is not refutation without a better theory. (p. 6)

The same applies in the case of researchers working on established models. The reviewer should play the role of mentor in addition to critic: to do otherwise risks creation of an advisory relation between researcher and reviewer—a bad mindset for either party. How constructively the reviewer presents his or her feedback is critical to how the researcher receives and responds to it. From the reviewer's perspective, writing a review to the umpteenth study of _____ (fill in the blank for yourself) might be justifiable grounds for a tart reply. But it could well be demoralizing to an author who has not yet written umpteen articles.

One essential problem reviewers face, I think, is dealing with the doctrine of falsification that Popper and other philosophers of science have addressed. Popper (1959) argues that every genuine test of a theory is an attempt to falsify it. Science advances by disconfirming hypotheses when rival hypotheses exist. From this concept of falsification come criteria for evaluating a "good" theory. It should contain prohibitions, that is, the specifications of contradictions to it that cannot exist if the theory be true. The more the theory prohibits the better. Thus falsifiability, refutability, and testability are qualities reviewers look for, though a bias to confirm tends to characterize researchers (Twenty, Doherty, & Mynatt, 1981). Even a correct hypothesis is subject to disconfirmation when data quality are low, specification of the relations of hypotheses to data are poor, or incorrect or incomplete specifications are made of one or more details of the hypothesis. All these conditions can evoke reviewer criticism and possibly recommendations for rejection. But in a new area where hypotheses cannot be well specified, such conditions of falsification may be too harsh.

For example, case study data, limited as they are from a causal inference perspective, can have value when developing and assessing emergent models. A reviewer with an appreciation for new ideas will see the distinction between an emergent concept and existing ones, will recognize the perspective brought to a problem, a case, or other phenomenon by the concept or by a new combination of concepts (new theory). Here a case study exemplifying a new concept or a new relation between old ones can be informative. But to evaluate such a study, the traditional criteria of falsification must be replaced by concern for concept specification and development.

So far this discussion of the journal reviewer's role has focused largely upon responsibilities to the field in dealing with novel ideas or approaches. Responses to innovative research are telling regarding the function of reviewers as gate-keepers. But this is not to overestimate the amount of time reviewers spend dealing with conceptual or paradigmatic breakthroughs. In the vast majority of cases, manuscripts deal with incremental additions to an established area.[1] The body of research on expectancy theories of motivation exemplifies the incremental nature of most research. Studies of innovation suggest that there are two major classes of innovation: *alpha* change, where breakthroughs occur introducing qualitatively different approaches to technical or scientific problems, and *beta* change that adds incremental improvement to existing models and methods. Far more innovations are incremental, in continuity with previous approaches, than are those that are disjunctive. The reasons for this are many. Obviously, beta innovations are more easily conceived. Moreover, approaches to research emphasizing falsification lead to increasing refinement of data gathering, precision in linking data to hypotheses, and specification of constructs. As Kuhn (1962) argues, a scientific community will seldom embrace a new theory until researchers solve all or almost all of the quantitative puzzles that have been treated by its predecessor. Beta-type manuscripts can reflect a disciplinewide need for closure.

In addition, the predominance of beta-type manuscripts lends support for those who argue as does Mitroff (1974) that *scientists* seek confirmation, even if *science* itself advances through disconfirmation. Advocates for a point of view generally identify with it, pursue its elaborate specification, and seek to place it in the public view. Aside from intrapsychic reasons for this being the case, the tenure system rewards people for pursuing a consistent, continuous line of research with which the individual is strongly identified. The reviewer therefore spends most of the time he or she serves the field in this capacity in the review of incremental research. The ultimate criterion for such scholarship is technical perfection (as Szent-Gyorgyi, 1976, has argued in his discussion of the Apollonian and Dionysian approaches to science[2]). Perfection is sought through, ironically perhaps, the pursuit and yet avoidance of falsification. Incremental lines of research search for limiting conditions to the generalizability of a theory. They do so by the identification of moderator variables, specification of relevant populations for generalization, and refinement of method. In the micro areas of organizational study, the prevalence of moderator variable articles in leadership research and methodological discussions in job design research exemplify the incremental approach, as does the frequent publication of macro-level research specifying theoretically consistent operationalizations of structure.

Given these forces operating within a scientific discipline, the reviewer's role is to view the research in the context of past studies and to ask the following questions:

1. Does this research make more precise the concepts past work has detailed?
2. Does its design specify more limits to the generalizability of the theory than did past research?
3. Was the theory put to a test where disconfirmation was really possible? Or, in other words, if the study supports the theory, were there events that might have occurred within it that could have refuted the theory?

These questions could be asked of any incrementally oriented manuscript where original data have been presented or when past research has been reviewed and synthesized. In addition to these three questions that are derived from a falsification approach, I would add two others; I always ask myself:

1. What do I know now about the theory I did not know before? How does the design of the research tell me this? (This is to pinpoint whether it is the study itself that provides the insight as opposed to personal introspection [!], and to identify the study's critical design features.)
2. How does the presentation of the research interfere with the reader's grasp of its points? How could it be said better?

Whether one reviews alpha- or beta-type manuscripts affects the kinds of criteria used to evaluate them. This differential evaluation process is endemic to the reviewer's formal role. Other formal conditions that affect the criteria a reviewer uses include the status of the reviewer—board member or occasional reviewer. A board member is more likely to have received at some time or another direction from the journal editor regarding plans for the journal, types of topics to be emphasized or pursued in future issues, and possibly problems with previously published works that should be avoided in the future. As such, the board member has a relationship to the editor and to the journal that might give rise to the use of additional evaluation criteria, including appropriateness for the journal and consistency of manuscripts with the journal's overall strategy. An occasional reviewer has a much looser relationship to the journal and its editor. That individual is not necessarily aware of such editorial concerns. In addition, there is an interaction between reviewer status and the subject matter of manuscripts assigned to reviewers. Occasional reviewers generally are chosen because of some special knowledge or expertise regarding the topic of the manuscript. The topic may, in fact, be an extension of the reviewer's own previous work. Closeness to the area brings special knowledge and insight as well as the reviewer's own special perspectives and biases into the process. Board members review many manuscripts quite unrelated to their own research and might therefore find it easier to play a dispassionate role.

Personal Experiences

From my experience as a board member and occasional reviewer for a variety of journals in organizational science and related areas, I have constructed a set of beliefs about what a reviewer does, should do, and actually accomplishes. I say "constructed" because my perspectives on reviewers come from experience and not from professional training. In graduate school, I do not think it is very common for students to critically review the work of others, and my training was no exception. By the time we finish the dissertation and other requirements for the degree, we may be reasonably knowledgeable and able to make helpful suggestions to others, but there is often little time or opportunity to do so. Though some instructors incorporate critical reviews as exercises in graduate seminars on such topics as research methods, the critical review is not typically a part of our training.

Nonetheless, as a graduate student, I saw reviewing as a very professional, prestigious, and important thing to do. To make comments on someone else's work prior to publication meant a chance to shape what gets published. After reviewing for several years, averaging 25 or so journal reviews a year, I still believe reviewers do significant and scientifically crucial work. But they have an impact quite different than what I once thought. Rather than as a source of constructive help on manuscripts, I see much of the task of reviewing as a rough cut, a veto process separating wheat from chaff. The reason for this shift in view is the low base rate of manuscript acceptance. Because few of the manuscripts read and commented upon actually are accepted, the reviewer is primarily a screening device rather than a molder of ideas and presentations. Personally, this is frustrating because there is often little help one can offer to the author but to tell him or her what to do next time. I believe that I approach each manuscript to some extent as the author's advocate, trying to identify what is informative about the piece and how its value can best be highlighted. But lots of times I have not felt I was given much to work with (I used to think it was the editor's doing—sending all the publishable papers to someone else to review). Inadequate method, unreliable measures, restrictive sampling (e.g., on the dependent variable) cannot be corrected after the fact. But conceptual difficulties, especially fuzzy concepts, can be equally difficult to correct once operationalizations have been made. Reviewers can really have a constructive impact only upon a handful of manuscripts. However, this might be as it needs to be. Only a portion of submitted manuscripts have the potential for fruitful revision. These provide some real satisfaction—particularly when on the second or third go-around the manuscript looks "tight." It does, however, leave unanswered the question: What impact has the reviewer had on those authors whose works were rejected and who cannot make sufficient changes to meet reviewer objections and concerns? Reinforcement theory would predict that future work would tend to conform to the reviewer's recommendations or that the authors would become less likely to submit to that journal. The impact of reviewer feedback on the future work of those authors whose manuscripts are rejected is a significant issue about which little is known.

Personally, as a professional researcher, reviewing has provided me with three significant experiences. First, it's made me articulate my professional standards. (Often enough so that I have become aware of changes in my thinking about what constitutes "good" research.) It's made me take a stand and state a position (to myself as well as the author) about the methods that advance organizational study, the criteria pertinent to evaluating these methods, the role of theoretically driven versus wholly empirical (dust bowl) research. All of this is particularly true for research that has neither conceptual nor methodological overlap with my own work. As a case in point, qualitative studies of women's roles I might do in my head at home, but they are not my professional forte. Nonetheless, I seem to have reviewed a lot of these (What can that mean?) and they have helped me develop personal criteria for evaluating qualitative methodologies, for gauging the value and publication merit of exploratory studies, and for assessing the logic underlying a study coming out of a literature with which I am not too familiar. This experience has been invaluable to me as a teacher of graduate students who often are interested both in areas far afield of my own and in using methods that are new or not well specified. In my case the recent increase in qualitative or ethnographic studies has meant reviewing works that in no way conform to the research traditions and practices of my industrial/ organizational psychology training.

Second, it's brought me a feeling of integration into the field. When I was given the opportunity to do a journal review as a graduate student, it was the first time that I really felt part of the field. In my case, it followed acceptance of my first publication; but being asked to review for a journal made me feel more of a scholar than getting my own manuscript accepted. The fact that most opportunities to do a "first" review come from some personal contact with an editor or board member implies that one has a place in the "network." Some professional integration is a prerequisite for the opportunity.

Finally, it has been instructive in overcoming the Nobel syndrome. It is hard for a young researcher to know when a manuscript is ready to submit to a journal. The question always remains: Is it good enough? Seeing the state of papers that come in for review makes it a little easier to submit one's own work to the test— it may also compound the already high rejection rate. In all these ways, reviewing has been a professionally developing experience for me. And having participated in this process, it has been instructive regarding how to get research published.

RECOMMENDATIONS TO AUTHORS

What to Avoid

Entanglements. Reviewers might be positive about many aspects of the manuscript but the editor only picks up the negative in the feedback letter to the author. To me this means lack of editor support and interest in the paper. When the editor arrives at such an opinion, this could mean the editor did not like the paper and is using selected reviewer comments to justify the opinion or that, while the reviewers mixed positives and negatives in their feedback to the authors, their comments to the editor were more negative. This situation leaves the author in no way the wiser about what to do regarding the paper vis-à-vis that particular journal. It might be best to seek publication elsewhere. (The problem of what to do with those unreconciled reviews remains, however, and is addressed in my recommendations to editors.)

One's Own Myopic Tendencies. Check the reference section of the manuscript. Is it heavily laced with the citations of publications of one theoretical perspective, of scholars from one institution or type of background? These may be endemic to the topic under study. But they might also indicate an overly narrow view of the problem. As a reviewer I am sensitive to a too narrowly focused view. I also think that representativeness is valuable. Papers with a too limited view are often inbred—based on the research and theory of scholars from one institution (and their students who might now be members of other faculties).

Work That Dots the "I's." Marginally incremental research may be of little value (depending on the significance of the issue) and often appears to be piecemeal. Incremental research is necessary for refinement of theory. But the potential for providing information to the field of course corresponds to the size of the increment!

Piecemeal Publication. If the reviewer labels it piecemeal in the feedback, that probably means that not only was the work shaving off a large block of data but also that it was relatively meaningless, out of relation to the other data gathered. It is hard to make a contribution or publish a paper that will be remembered with this strategy. (The belief persists that piecemeal publication makes careers— which is an issue that is addressed somewhere in this book, I am sure.) A variation on piecemeal publication as a chip off a block of data is *piecemeal (or selective) reporting* of data. The use of computers in data analysis allows computation of more statistics than was ever attempted by a research assistant equipped with a 20-pound Monroe calculator. When the analysis strategy is a hunt for statistically significant results, rather than hypothesis testing, the selected analyses reported can seem contrived. As a reviewer the significant question here is this: Would someone have gone to all the trouble of collecting the data to find *that* out? The ultimate sin here is misrepresenting the decision-making process in hypothesis testing (Was the hypothesis generated before or after the analysis?). The penultimate sin is triviality. It can happen that, in the course of testing one hypothesis, analyses reveal an unexpected finding in a related statistical test. Though the representativeness of that finding is an issue, it could have meaning. The problem lies in the case where the hypothesized relation does not materialize but a tangential post hoc one does. Despite the inclination against publishing negative results, I recommend presenting both the a priori and post hoc analyses. If the data are good enough to make the failed hypothesis test meaningful (good theory, good sample, good measurement), it will add meaning to unexpected findings.

A classic example of such a situation is moderator variable research. Few studies testing moderator effects are primarily interested in the moderator variable (e.g., need growth strength in job design research, task characteristics in leadership studies). I am enormously skeptical of manuscripts purporting to test for a moderator effect where there was no theoretical basis for such effect a priori. Unless the study presents a replication in another sample, the generalizability of such a finding is questionable. In this situation, I feel it is most appropriate to address the reasons for the failure of the a priori hypothesis and to pose the moderator relation as one of many possible explanations or limitations on the predicted relation. Another instance of selective reporting occurs where a good deal of data have been gathered and a small slice are reported for which a strong theoretical rationale is lacking (e.g., when a few variables based on self-reports in a large sample are the purported topic of the research project). Here the reported significance levels might well be meaningless. I believe this type of reporting is a departure from established scientific procedures and, unless the complete database is acknowledged, highly unethical.

Faith in Small Numbers. Some manuscripts seem to "rush into print" novel or atypical findings based on a single study without replication. When the last 10 studies in an area produce one pattern of results and a study comes along that contradicts it, one question that must be asked is this: How representative is this new finding? Is it a case of sampling bias? If the sample is small or unsystematic, I am skeptical. Research capitalizing on chance occurs not only by asking a lot of questions and reporting those yielding significant results but also by asking them in nonrepresentative ways.

Bending Over Backward. How far should an author go to accommodate a reviewer's comments? As far as these are helpful in improving the manuscript. But a manuscript has its integrity and the reviewer represents only one opinion. If accommodating means saying what the author really does not believe, say so. As a reviewer once wrote in a review of one of my own manuscripts, "It's not our purpose to beat you into submission." I greatly appreciate and share this view. Therefore respect your paper's integrity. I suspect most reviewers are concerned more with helping the author say what he or she has to say well than with gatekeeping *what* is said.

The Approach

Develop Research That Tests Competing Hypotheses. This is better science than the traditional null versus alternative hypothesis approach, provides richer information that can be productively integrated into theory, and is more interesting to write about and to review. Twenty et al. (1981) describe the natural inclination of human beings to pursue one hypothesis at a time. However, there are two advantages to testing competing hypotheses: It avoids the narrowness that plagues much research (see "One's Own Myopic Tendencies," above) and, given the predilection for confirmation, increases the odds of finding some interpretable effects.

In choosing a journal, check your reference section to see which journals are represented. This gives an approximate though not completely accurate indicator of where the manuscript would fit into the professional literature. It also indicates where reviewers are likely to have been supportive of similar research.

Choose Research Topics You Care About. Although there is debate about the appropriateness of an advocacy approach to hypothesis testing, I would like to make a pitch here for sincerity in research! The research process is a long and complicated one. It is often necessary to be at once meticulous and anal retentive as well as open, flexible, and creative. Successful scholarship might, in fact, require the Apollonian and Dionysian approaches in the same research program. To pay attention to detail when that is what is needed (i.e., to keep reading relevant literature, to pursue precise operationalization) and to be open to new ideas (to drive to and from work thinking of the problem in different perspectives) is easier when the issue is important to us personally. I wonder if a researcher who is truly interested in the answer to the questions his or her scholarship asks ever could burn out—or write a paper that had no insight. Research shows that scientists who strongly identify with a pet theory or view also are the most influential (Twenty et al., 1981). This might demonstrate the institutional value of bias. On the other hand, it might suggest that, in the long term, we do best what we care most about.

Be Thick-Skinned. Even the most inflammatory reviews can be written by reviewers who appreciate what one's research is about. You may be responding more to style than substance. If not, apparently negative reviewers might eventually give in, come around, or be overridden by the editor.

Don't be discouraged.

RECOMMENDATIONS TO EDITORS

Resolve Reviewer Disagreements. It is frustrating to review a manuscript and have disagreements between reviewers go unreconciled to the author (even more so, of course, for the author). Obviously, it is more desirable to give the author as clear a direction as possible for improving the contribution of the manuscript. Some editors are consistently careful about this; others are not. If the editor does not feel able to give clear direction about what to change, what to elaborate upon, and so on, I feel that additional reviews should be sought before sending comments back to the author. To throw a manuscript back to the author without consistent direction (do this/do that/forget it) is not fair to the author or to the reviewers who tried to be constructive.

Screen Caustic Reviews or Comments. There is no reason I can think of to allow the way feedback is given to interfere with its information value or to sour the relationship between journals and researchers. When feedback is couched in flip or even caustic terms, I feel that editors should white-out that part of the reviewer feedback to the author and let the reviewer know what was done and why.

Openly Address Editor/Reviewer Disagreements in Author Feedback. The feedback most journals send to authors consists of a letter from the editor informing the author of the decision on whether or not to publish, request a revision, and so on as well as copies of the reviewers' feedback to the author. Both as a reviewer and as an author, I have known situations where the reviewers seem very positive and the editor gives a negative decision. Two conditions can account for this: (a) The reviewers really were positive in the feedback to the editor (seen only by the editor) but the editor disagrees with it or (b) the reviewers gave supportive comments to the author but were more negative in the evaluation they reported to the editor. I think it is important to the author's ability to form a reasonable judgment about the value of the manuscript and its problems that the editor make it clear if the decision is a consensus or a judgment call on the editor's part. Of course, the reasons for the *editor's* decision should be presented.

CONCLUSION

In writing this chapter, I note that three roles seem to characterize my personal orientation and attitudes toward reviewing: the mentor, the advocate, and the critic. These roles are three styles a reviewer might adopt sometimes in succession (from mentor to critic) and sometimes simultaneously (advocate and critic). What to an author (or perhaps even the editor) might seem conflicting comments might in fact be the demonstration of two styles at once. To be an effective critic, I think it is necessary to play either the mentor or the advocate as well.

NOTES

1. Note that the Organizational Behavior Division of the Academy of Management does not give its New Concept Award annually as was once intended.

2. Szent-Gyorgyi in a letter to the editor of *Science* magazine argued that there are two primary types of researchers: Apollonians, who follow an established road toward perfection, and Dionysians, who pursue their intuitions and insights in nonlinear, emergent, and generally ill-specified directions.

REFERENCES

Kuhn, T. S. (1962). *The structure of scientific revolutions.* Chicago: University of Chicago Press.
Lakatos, I. (1978). *The methodology of scientific research programmes.* Cambridge: Cambridge University Press.
Mitroff, I. (1974). *The subjective side of science.* Amsterdam: Elsevier.
Popper, K. R. (1959). *The logic of scientific discovery.* London: Hutchison.
Szent-Gyorgyi, A. (1976). Dionysians and Apollonians. *Science, 176,* 966.
Twenty, R. D., Doherty, M. E., & Mynatt, C. R. (1981). *On scientific thinking.* New York: Columbia University Press.

9

Why I Recommended
That Your Manuscript Be Rejected
and What You Can Do About It

RICHARD L. DAFT

No one can learn to write an excellent paper based on examples of failure. No one can expect to have a paper accepted at a major journal by hearing about papers that have been rejected. Research and publication are learned through trial and error. Scholars learn by doing. Yet this chapter is about failure, the reasons for failure, in the journal submission process. Why concentrate on the shortcomings of papers previously submitted to journals in the organization sciences? There are several reasons.

For one thing, we are a community of scholars. In a community, people learn from one another. By sharing previous errors, the number of trials required for new scholars to publish their work may be reduced. Moreover, examples of excellent papers are already in the journals. The good papers are out there for everyone to see, but many colleagues do not have insight into the problems, mistakes, revisions, and previous rejections asscciated with excellent publications.

Another reason is that the journal review process is central to each scholar's growth and development. Thinking back over my own publication experiences, the high and low points were associated with journal reviews. A number of reviews were absolutely devastating. The reviewers seemed determined to be destructive, hurtful, and narrow minded. But I have also been buoyed, supported, cheered, helped, and encouraged by reviewers, and constructive criticism has improved my work dramatically. The review process can have enormous impact, either positive or negative, so it seems important to share views about it.

A final reason for analyzing the review process is that there are several points that need to be made, some tricks of the trade that should be passed on to authors. I find that reviewing is more subjective than objective. Manuscripts give off many cues, and these cues form a gestalt. Factors that influence this gestalt include such things as writing style, tone, and method of theory building. Subtle, intangible cues often cause me to like or dislike the paper, and hence to support or not support the paper for revision or publication. These intangibles are hard to put a finger on, and they are crucial to the paper's acceptance, yet are hard to explain in the written review given back to the author. The intangible side of the review process needs to be analyzed as one way to help authors get their work published.

The purpose of this chapter is to present my perspective on the review process. Because this is my personal perspective, I will put my biases on the table. My training was at the University of Chicago, where I was imprinted with the belief that the goal of research is theory development. Data collection and analyses are important, but data are intended to illuminate a path of insight into organizational behavior and processes. Theory gives meaning to data. I can also say that I am challenged and excited by the review process. I enjoy sharing my views and suggesting ways authors can improve their papers. I have been reviewing papers for journals for about six years, and I am not tired of it. Each paper is a new challenge. I enjoy the review process.

In this chapter, I will present an analysis of my reviews for journal manuscripts, and I will propose seven guides for overcoming common manuscript problems. My analysis and suggestions are written with the desire to shorten the publication cycle for colleagues, to crystallize some of the intangible elements that annoy and turn off reviewers, and to facilitate those high points of science—those successful researcher-reviewer transactions—that are exciting and constructive and lead to the publication of new ideas and important discoveries in the organization sciences.

ANALYSIS OF REVIEWS

The approach used to bring order to my observations was to analyze the content of my own reviews of journal submissions. The reviews were limited to manuscripts submitted to *Administrative Science Quarterly* and *Academy of Management Journal* because these journals are in the mainstream of the organizational sciences. Most papers were on organization theory topics, although a few were in closely related areas such as business policy. Most papers were empirical and reflected traditional fieldwork methods, although several used what would be called qualitative methodology.

The sample for my analysis included 111 reviews over the last four years. Some overlap existed among these reviews because several papers were reviewed a second or even a third time. The revised manuscripts were included as separate entities in my analysis because a paper's gestalt can change substantially with a major revision. Solving one problem often calls attention to other problems.

My procedure was to read each review and note up to three reasons the paper was weak and needed a major revision or was rejected. The reasons listed were then consolidated into categories. The categories grossly oversimplified the unique characteristics of each paper, but the categories do identify common problems that existed in the papers sent to me by *AMJ* and *ASQ*.

Why I Recommended That Your Manuscript Be Rejected

The results from the analysis of 111 manuscript reviews are in Table 9.1. Table 9.1 lists 11 problems and the frequency of each problem. The content of these problems is described here.

No Theory. Theory means explaining what the variables mean and why they are related to one another in organizations. Fully one half of the papers I reviewed had little or no theory to explain relationships among variables. Theory need not be formal or complex—theory should simply explain why. Theory provides the story that gives data meaning. The measurement of variables, procedures for data collection, and techniques for data analysis are important parts of the research process, but they are not sufficient for publication. The essential point of research is to provide an understanding about human behavior and processes within or between organizations. The purpose of theory is to interpret data to provide insight into real behavior.

TABLE 9.1   Problems Found in 111 Manuscripts Reviewed for *AMJ* and *ASQ*

Problem	N*	Percent of Problems	Percent of Manuscripts
1. No theory	56	(21.7)	(50.5)
2. Concepts and operationalization not in alignment	35	(13.6)	(31.5)
3. Insufficient definition—theory	27	(10.5)	(24.3)
4. Insufficient rationale—design	27	(10.5)	(24.3)
5. Macrostructure—organization and flow	26	(10.1)	(23.4)
6. Amateur style and tone	23	(8.9)	(20.7)
7. Inadequate research design	22	(8.5)	(19.8)
8. Not relevant to the field	20	(7.7)	(18.0)
9. Overengineering	11	(4.3)	(9.9)
10. Conclusions not in alignment	6	(2.3)	(5.4)
11. Cutting up the data	5	(1.9)	(4.5)
	258	(100)	(100)

*N = 258 major problems identified in the 111 manuscripts.

Consider, for example, a hypothetical study of resources, environmental contacts, centralization, and the introduction of new products. The investigator may hypothesize that fewer slack resources will be related to greater centralization and fewer environmental contacts, and environmental contact in turn will be positively related to new product introductions. The role of theory is to explain why these relationships exist. Perhaps resource scarcity leads to conflict among departments so that managers are forced to centralize decision making. Centralized decision making might mean that employees feel less responsibility for contact with customers. Customer contacts may be an important source of ideas for new products, so fewer contacts would mean fewer ideas and fewer new products.

This story could be developed in more detail, but some type of story must explain the relationships among variables. So many manuscripts miss the essential point of research, which is theory construction. Without a theory, there is nothing to pull the study together, nothing to justify why the variables should be studied. Simply reviewing the literature and showing that each variable appeared previously is not enough. The theory organizes the variables into a set and is the basis for new insight into organizations.

Concepts and Operationalization Not in Alignment. The frequency (35) of this problem surprised me because it seems so obvious, but often the operational base of the research did not reflect the variables or model under study. Sometimes level of analysis was the problem. The investigator might propose to study organization technology and structure. Then the investigator surveyed individuals in a single organization and analyzed the responses for individuals rather than for departments or the organization as a whole. The sample thus precludes any opportunity to learn about the relationship between organization-level technology and structure.

Other examples of poor alignment included the use of number of hospital beds as a measure of organizational complexity, and percentage of university graduates as a measure of organizational control. Number of beds is an indicator of size, and size may be associated with complexity, but using beds as a measure of complexity requires a thoughtful and convincing rationale. To some extent, educational level may be associated with the extent of clan control, but educational level means a number of other things as well. Simply calling a variable "complexity" or "control" does not make it so, especially when the operationalization measures another concept.

No operationalization is perfect, and perfection is not expected. But authors often did not select measures or a sample to fit their concepts. Manuscripts sometimes read as if new labels were created for old data in the hope of getting published. But to attain publication, investigators have to maintain congruence between concepts and operationalization, between theory and research design.

Insufficient Definition—Theory. Insufficient definition is similar to the notion of no theory but is even more basic. This problem occurred when authors did not explain what the concepts meant. Authors did not provide definition, explanation, or reasoning for some of their variables. Instead, authors simply proposed variables because of appearance in previous studies or because the variables seemed like a good idea. If administrative ratio had been reported in previous publications, that was offered as sufficient rationale for studying it again, and the reader was expected to know what it meant and why it was important.

Concepts in the social sciences are fuzzy, and an explicit definition is usually required to let the reader know exactly what is meant. In a study of information processing, it helps to define information and to say how it differs from data. If the study pertains to information load, information density, or information form, each of these concepts must be made explicit. Frequently a "correct" definition is not available in the literature. The author should enact a definition. Otherwise the reviewer is in the dark about what the author is thinking and studying. Defining exactly what each variable means is an important part of the theory construction process.

Insufficient Rationale—Design. Again, insufficient rationale was a problem, but in this case the manuscripts lacked explanation of study procedures. The author should introduce the reader to the true operational base of the research. Simple things, like describing the sample, saying who completed the questionnaires, providing example questions from the questionnaire, and reporting means and standard deviations, all bring the reader close to the basic data. If, for example, the author elected to sample one firm in each of three industries and to survey 20 managers in each firm, the reasons for those selection decisions should be explained. Nothing is obvious to me as a reviewer. The author has to explain why the sample and procedure are appropriate to test the proposed research question.

The absence of rationale about design issues was frequently a cause of my conclusion of poor alignment between theory and method. Without full disclosure and openness about method, I could not understand whether the method was appropriate. For example, in a study of ideology, routine versus nonroutine technology was used as the measure of ideology without careful explanation, and in a study of business strategy the presence of a large computer in the organization was used as a measure of strategy. These design decisions must be explained. Without adequate rationale, the author's logic is suspect, and the reviewer is likely to reject the paper because the research procedures are unclear.

Macrostructure—Organization and Flow. Macrostructure means whether the various parts of the paper fit together into a coherent whole. *Microstructure* pertains to individual sentences and paragraphs, which are satisfactory in most papers. But the macrostructure is a harder problem to solve. The theory portion of the paper may make sense by itself but be out of alignment with the conclusion section. The results section may be well written but not test each hypothesis proposed in the theory section. Scholars must make a special effort to visualize the entire paper—especially the interconnections among the parts—and be confident they are effectively constructed before submitting the paper for publication.

A number of clues indicated macrostructure problems in manuscripts I reviewed. The author might introduce measures in the method section for variables that were not identified in the theory section. Occasionally an author introduced new tables and analyses into the conclusion section, almost as an afterthought. Frequently the results section did not explicitly test each hypothesis raised in the theory section. Or the conclusion section might draw conclusions about theories and variables (e.g., organizational effectiveness) that were unrelated to the paper's explicit research question (e.g., information processing). In most cases the author saw an implicit connection, but the reasoning was not made explicit to the reader.

Other indicators of macrostructure problems were an insufficient number of subheadings to provide an obvious road map for the trip through the research, frequent parenthetical statements or footnotes to explain things (frequent parenthetical statements are distracting), asking the reader to see other papers in order to understand what something meant (see Campbell, Daft, & Hulin, 1982, for details), referring ahead to future parts of the paper for explanations (I will explain this point in the conclusion section), or simply submitting a paper that was far too long for the research at hand.

Any of these elements gives the paper a disorganized, poorly conceived look. A good paper is extremely disciplined. A good paper does not jump around, is internally congruent, and doesn't open up new areas late in the paper. Author self-discipline is needed because the study itself may have been conducted in a disorganized way, as is most research. But that disorganization must be removed for the reader to understand what happened. The paper should take the reader from A to Z in a logical sequence without deviations. Then the paper can tie back to A in the final section by summarizing what new has been learned about the research question.

Amateur Style and Tone. Style and tone are intangibles, but they have enough impact on me as a reader to sometimes cause rejection. Style and tone can signal that the authors do not know what they are doing, that they are amateurs. One indication of amateurism was contrived emphasis—the frequent use of underlining or exclamation marks. If the point is made properly, contrived emphasis seems *very* silly and inappropriate, and actually *takes away* from the point. Another problem was the use of "straw men." The importance of the research topic was grossly exaggerated to make the case for publication. One example was the argument that bureaucracy should be studied because bureaucratic processes are oppressing individuals in all organizations. The paper was written in direct response to Weber and ignored all the literature in between (loosely coupled systems, informal organization, garbage can model) that indicates bureaucracies are not as tight as Weber proposed. The avoidance of exaggeration is so critical that authors must understand it or they will never be published again!

Yet another indicator of amateurism was an overly negative approach to the previous literature. Authors often tore down previous work to justify their study rather than show how their paper built on previous findings. (That is, the reason this chapter is so good is that the other chapters left out many ideas, are poorly developed, and their databases are smaller and less accurate than mine.) Previous work is always vulnerable. Criticizing is easy, and of little value; it is more important to explain how research builds upon previous findings than to claim previous research is inadequate and incompetent. A related problem was when amateur authors wrote as if their research project were going to correct all previous findings on the topic. They believed their study was going to prove once and for all that organization size was related to formalization and administrative ratio, or some such thing. The authors did not acknowledge the realistic limitations of their own research. Yet their findings were a function of their specific sample and measurement techniques and were not any more valuable than the previous research that was supposed to be corrected.

Inadequate Research Design. When this problem appeared, it was typically fatal. Design cannot be corrected because the research has already been executed in an invalid manner. Graduate schools must be doing something right, because this problem appeared in only about one fifth of the manuscripts I reviewed. Sometimes the true problem was lack of explanation. On the other hand, additional explanation often revealed the paucity of the design. But only about one fifth of the papers were rejected due to unsolvable design problems.

An inadequate design revealed itself in various ways. A closed-ended questionnaire survey was mailed out to a random sample of managers to study subtle and intangible political or decision-making processes. Survey questions cannot capture these equivocal processes, and the whole procedure lacked face validity. An investigator surveyed top managers and asked questions pertaining to details of departmental activities and technology about which the respondents would have little information or insight. Another example was to use an undergraduate student sample to analyze the selection of business strategies by corporate executives. Undergraduates have virtually no experience at upper levels of organizations, and they often have a hard time even understanding strategy concepts. To use undergraduate students as representative of senior managers is grossly inappropriate. In each of these examples, the design error was basic and major, the study lacked validity, and the problem could not be corrected after the fact.

Not Relevant to the Field. Sometimes papers simply were inappropriate or irrelevant to the organization sciences. Sometimes papers were written from a finance or economic orientation, almost as if the papers were rejected from journals in those disciplines and were retooled toward organization theory as a way to get published. These papers typically lacked depth and insight for organization theory questions. Sometimes papers had a strong mathematical base and attempted to understand organizational processes through mathematical proofs. This approach was valid enough but was of no value if the author did not discuss organizations or organizational relationships. Some papers simply came across as a rehash of old issues. No single flaw killed the paper, but the parts did not add up to sufficient new knowledge to warrant publication.

One hidden factor that influences a paper's contribution is the maturity of the topic matter. Research topics behave like the product life cycle described in marketing. When the topic is new, a lot of research activity is generated, and most projects contribute new knowledge. But as the product matures, and a large number of studies have been published, it becomes more difficult to conduct a study that produces genuinely new insights. In organization theory, size and administrative ratio is a mature topic that has been overstudied. In organizational behavior, the topics of motivation and job satisfaction have matured. A new study on a mature topic may use a novel sample or organizations, or include a new variable or two, but the insight into organizational processes is typically small. The case for publication is easier if the topic is new, fresh, and poorly understood rather than mature and overstudied.

Overengineering. Sometimes authors overdid methodology so that it became an end in itself. The strength of the study was the operationalization of perhaps 50 or 100 variables. Or perhaps the authors used exotic and sophisticated statistical techniques to analyze data. In this type of manuscript, the engineering mechanics were emphasized to the exclusion of what the data meant. Sometimes the case for publication could be made for a well-engineered study, but typically the emphasis on engineering took away from the underlying theoretical contribution. As data were combined through factor analytical techniques and were run through interactive data analyses, their meaning was further and further abstracted from the operational base of the organization sample. Sophisticated techniques are fine, but when the concepts become far removed from organizations, new insight into organizational processes is impossible. The ultimate justification for a study is to learn about organizations. Simply measuring and manipulating variables, no matter how sophisticated the techniques, does not provide new understanding sufficient for publication.

Conclusion Not in Alignment. This problem occurs just often enough to be worth mentioning. A publishable paper should have a strong concluding section that tells the reader what the findings mean. This section should interpret the findings, show how the data add to or modify the original theory, and state explicitly how the study adds to the developing knowledge base within the field. Sometimes the conclusion section was limited to a paragraph of the papers I reviewed. The authors wrapped up as if they were in a hurry to get away from the research. They left it up to me to figure out what the findings meant. Other times the conclusion section generalized far beyond the data. Some generalization is important, because authors need freedom to think beyond the data. But jumping into unrelated topic areas, or using findings from a single study to reorganize the field, typically struck me as unrealistic. The discussion should not become too far removed from the operational base of the research. Some statement about research limitations is also worthwhile, but the concluding section should not dwell on methodological issues. The important thing is to use the conclusion section to fully develop the theoretical contribution and to point out the new understanding from the study. The conclusion section should build on and be congruent with previous parts of the manuscript. The conclusion section deserves as much attention as the theory, method, and results sections, because the conclusion section explains what it all means.

Cutting up the Data. This problem occurred when the paper under review for one journal overlapped by 80% a paper under review for another journal. Sometimes the paper contained the same data as previously published papers but under somewhat different names or with slight modifications. This did not happen often, but when it did the impression on me was terrible. Other reviewers and I called it to the attention of the editor, who immediately went back to the author. Attempting to multiply publications from a single database wastes everyone's time and is a breach of professional ethics.

There are well-established precedents for publishing multiple articles from a single database. The Aston group studies of organization structure during the late 1960s and the early 1970s are an example. Each article was a complete meaning unit that contained a significant portion of the overall study and was directed toward a specific theoretical topic. Follow-up papers made explicit reference to previous publications and stated exactly how the new research added to the previous paper in a building block manner. When this procedure is followed, reviewers have no problem with multiple publications from the same database, and indeed will admire the author for undertaking a large study. But when a small study is analyzed to death to get multiple publications, everyone involved is left with a bad taste.

THE QUALITATIVE COUNTERPOINT

The above discussion assumed a traditional, theory-based, hypothesis-testing approach to empirical research. But an increasing number of qualitative studies are being submitted to such journals as *Administrative Science Quarterly* and the *Academy of Management Journal.* I reviewed several manuscripts that used qualitative procedures. The major shortcomings in qualitative manuscripts were the same as for traditional research, but the problems were revealed in a different way. The two biggest problems, lack of theory and incongruence between theory and method, can be understood by comparison with traditional methods.

No Theory. The single biggest problem I found with qualitative research was lack of theory, which surprised me because the purpose of qualitative research is to build theory. The problem was that the researchers did not define new concepts or create new theory. In qualitative research, concepts and models should be defined at the end of the manuscript. The point of going out to observe organizations is to construct theory based upon the investigator's observations and interviews. The research goal is to end up with a well-defined set of constructs and a model that can be used to guide future research.

The same rule applies to both qualitative and quantitative research—theory is more important than data. Theory is the contribution to knowledge. Researchers should use the paper to crystallize a model that explains their observations. Many authors seemed too timid to stick their necks out, to go beyond the data, to enact a model from the myriad details they observed. Without the final model, the paper came across as long and meandering without a point, without a conclusion. The paper was rejected not because referees did not like qualitative research but because the investigators had not used the manuscript to build theory, which was the purpose of the research in the first place.

Concepts and Operationalization Not in Alignment. Practically every reviewer will agree that qualitative procedures are as valid as quantitative procedures. But qualitative procedures have to be tailored to the right research problem.

Most research projects can be placed on an imaginary continuum that reflects the extent of previous theory development. On one end of the continuum are research topics for which a great deal of previous research and understanding exist. Theory is well developed, so the goal of new research is hypothesis testing. To test explicit hypotheses, data have to be gathered in a sufficiently quantitative way to permit systematic comparisons and hypothesis rejection.

The other end of the imaginary continuum reflects research topics that have little previous theory development or systematic knowledge. The goal of research on these topics is to develop a theory or model for future tests. A successful research outcome is a tentative model based on observation and conjecture that can facilitate new research on this topic.

Quantitative procedures work well for topics on the hypothesis-testing end of the continuum. When frameworks are explicit and hypotheses can be tested, it makes sense to gather data in a quantitative way so the hypotheses can be accepted or rejected based on statistical tests. Qualitative studies, on the other hand, fit on the exploratory, theory-building end of the continuum. Qualitative procedures provide the freedom to ransack one or more organizations for new ideas and to consolidate these ideas into a plausible model.

The design problem occurs when the wrong procedure is used. When there is an extensive research literature so the author can formulate explicit hypotheses, then a loose, open-ended, qualitative procedure is not adequate to accept or reject the hypotheses. The procedure seems impressionistic; qualitative findings are too vague to contribute new knowledge to a well-defined topic. At the other extreme, when quantitative studies are used to study topics that are poorly developed, the result is premature rationalization and oversimplification. The quantitative procedure lacks the richness to build new theory. Thus, when qualitative procedures are used to test explicit hypotheses or when quantitative procedures are used to explore new topics, the research design came across to me as inadequate for the research problem.

Learning to Play Golf

The 11 items in Table 9.1 capture the bulk of the serious problems discovered in the 111 manuscripts I reviewed for *ASQ* and *AMJ*. There are also two overall patterns in the data that should be noted.

Theory Versus Design. The first pattern is the disparity between theory development and research design as the cause of failure, as indicated in Table 9.2. A problem with theory was five times more prevalent than a problem with design. One reason theory was a frequent problem is that theory building is hard to learn. Textbooks tell us how to design studies, but theory is learned through experience with both organizational research and real organizations. Theory requires both creativity and practical insight. One reason many authors had trouble explaining what the data meant or writing a story about the relationship among variables was that they had never seen the phenomenon about which they wrote. The

TABLE 9.2 Theory Versus Design Problems as the Cause of Manuscript Failure

Theory development problems	114
Research design problems	_22_
Total	136

authors learned to do research from behind university walls and had no face-to-face experience with the organizational subject matter. Theory building is more difficult to learn than research design because it does not come from textbooks or classrooms. But theory building can be mastered through experience and effort once researchers see that their contribution to knowledge comes from explanation, interpretation, and theory construction.

Three Skills. The second pattern pertains to the skills needed to produce winning research. I have read that an excellent golf game requires the mastery of three separate games—the woods, the irons, and putting. Each part of the overall game requires a different skill, and all three skills must be mastered to be a top pro. Weekend golfers may do well on one or two parts of the game, but they do not excel at all three.

The golf analogy fits the research game. Three skills are needed to be a top pro in the organizational sciences—theory skills, writing skills, and design skills. Manuscripts are rejected because of insufficient skill at one or more parts of the research game. Table 9.3 organizes the data according to the skills needed to correct the deficiencies I found in the manuscripts.

For 149 of the criticisms, the publication solution was through additional theory building skills in the authors. Greater skill with theory would enable the authors to go beyond their current manuscript with respect to definition of concepts, telling the story that connects the concepts to one another, clarifying how concepts relate to the operationalization, and showing why the study contributes to the field of organization sciences. An important point is that many of the 149 problems could have been prevented before journal submission if the researcher had worked at theory building and acquired the skill. Learning to build theory takes time and requires several revisions and feedback from colleagues, but theory building skills can be learned.

Writing skill was the reason for 82 criticisms. Writing pertains to how things were expressed. The act of putting words into sentences or forming sentences

TABLE 9.3 Skills Needed to Overcome Manuscript Problems for Publication

	N*	*Percent*
Theory Skills (define concepts, enact models, write stories, develop theory, integrate variables)	149	59
Writing Skills (flow, style, tone, integration of parts, rationale, openness, A to Z then back to A)	82	32
Design Skills (inadequate method, wrong method, no validity)	22	9
	253[a]	100

*N = 258 major problems identified in 111 manuscripts.
a. The five cases of cutting up the data are not included in the table.

into paragraphs was generally OK. The problem occurred when the paragraphs and sections did not convey specific insights to me and other readers, or when the sections did not complement one another. Writing skill means that concepts and issues are conveyed to the reader with precision and clarity. Writing skills are used to convey the rationale for design choices. Writing skills provide a consistent organization and flow, a professional tone, and a tight integration of theory, method, findings, and conclusions.

Finally, only 22 criticisms reflected poor research design skills. Research design skills were better developed than theory or writing skills for the manuscripts I reviewed. When poor research design occurred, however, the paper could not be improved through additional revisions or skill acquisition by the authors.

A paradox in Table 9.3 is that most problems were preventable. Theory and writing represent 90% of the problems, and they could be overcome through practice and revision. Yet only 10%-15% of manuscripts are accepted for publication. The explanation seems to be that researchers cannot learn theory building and writing skills easily. These skills take time, commitment, hard work, and an extension of self beyond the techniques learned in graduate school. These skills are not analyzable and teachable, as experience and practice are crucial, just as golfers must play every day to learn driving, approach, and putting skills.

AND WHAT YOU CAN DO ABOUT IT

Authors can do a number of specific things to increase their skill level and the probability of satisfying reviewers. The guidelines below can help authors overcome most of the problems identified above. Some of these guidelines are quite easy to follow; others are more difficult. But each guideline is an explicit point against which a manuscript can be compared before it is submitted to a journal. Authors can check whether they have gone as far as possible toward accomplishing theory and writing skills.

Tell a Story

One technique I have found to overcome the lack of theory in a manuscript is for authors to think of each variable in the study as a character in a story. The author's responsibility is to fully describe each character, and then to explain how and why characters interact with one another. Storytelling explains the "why" of the data and gives meaning to observed relationships. Storytelling is difficult because we are trained to be rigorous and precise and to stick to the data in literal fashion. Storytelling requires conjecture and going beyond the data; it is the opportunity to fill in the blanks between variables. The story provides a larger framework within which each variable has a logical place. The explanation gives us insight into organizational processes. The story explains the why of relationships in organizational terms. The why is important, and researchers should be creative and ruthless in pursuit of it to solve the theory problem (Weick, 1974). The why, not the data, is the contribution to knowledge.

Another aid to storytelling is a visual figure or model. If the investigator creates a contingency table or series of boxes and arrows to summarize the theory, then storytelling is easier. The story explains the reasons behind each box and arrow. For traditional hypothesis-testing studies, a visual representation strengthens the early part of the manuscript and can be revised in the conclusion section. For qualitative studies, a visual representation at the end of the manuscript is an ideal way to crystallize the theory developed from personal observations.

Discuss Fully Your Procedures and Thought Processes

Openness is a refreshing and positive characteristic in a manuscript. Many authors seem to hide the details of their research procedures, as if they fear that reviewers will criticize and reject the paper for those weaknesses. There is no better way to defuse criticism than to admit the weaknesses and point out the problems. Describing thought processes and rationale may be difficult when decisions were made intuitively. But the rationale for the selection of variables, design decisions, and analysis procedures needs to be explained. Reviewers gain a more positive impression from full disclosure, including weaknesses and problems, than from partial disclosure that appears to hide something.

Concentrate on Macrostructure

Many problems in a manuscript are caused by poor coordination among sections of the manuscript. The theory has to be congruent with the method, the method with the results, the results with the discussion section, and all sections with each other. The paper should flow logically in a straight line of thought, without digression. Each section should come across as a self-contained unit, and the sections must add up so the entire paper is a coherent meaning unit. Most writers find the macrostructure hard to manage, and several revisions may be required. If the macrostructure is clear, the microstructure will normally take care of itself. Make sure the overall logic and flow are in order before sending the manuscript to a journal.

Find the Operational Base of Your Research and Stick to It

The core of an empirical research paper is the operational base of the research methodology. The theory, results, and discussion must all correspond to the operational base. Authors who think in terms of the operational base make a clearer presentation than authors who think in terms of abstract concepts. Descriptive information on the organizations in the sample, questionnaire items, means, standard deviations, procedures, and all relevant details about the operational base should be included in the manuscript. Other parts of the paper should correspond to this operational base. If the study measures organizational size in the method section, there is no reason to propose a hypothesis about organizational complexity in the theory section. If the operational base measures technology, there is no reason to write a concluding section about organizational ideology. The operational base is the focal point for the research, and the other parts of the paper must be coordinated with it.

The operational base should also be reflected in writing style and interpretation. For a questionnaire survey that reports a positive correlation between elements of structure, the finding can be accurately reported as follows: "Perceived formalization was associated with perceived decentralization." The operational base does not measure actual constructs when we rely on the perceptions of others. Correct operational interpretations and appropriate phrasing suggest that researchers are in touch with the true operational base of the study.

Listen to Your Reviewers

Authors become supremely involved in the internal logic of their manuscripts. They are often dismayed when reviewers do not receive the message that was sent. Reviewers provide important feedback because they do not know the background of the study; they see only the written manuscript. Reviewers evaluate it with the cold eye of objectivity. If the author's message does not get through, then the message should be changed. Do not blame the reviewer. Reviewer feedback can help you revise the manuscript toward the right message and content. Remember, reviewers are on your side. Reviewers are practically out searching for good material; they enjoy helping transform a good paper into an excellent one. Also keep in mind that sometimes a paper simply is not very good. Sometimes a design has flaws that cannot be corrected. Research is trial and error, and some trials don't work. When the study is flawed, reviewers will be quick to point it out, but the flaw is not their fault. Incorporate their suggestions as best you can. If the paper is unpublishable, use it as a learning experience and move on to the next research project.

Allow the Manuscript to Ripen Naturally

The analysis of manuscript problems in Table 9.3 indicated that most papers have difficulty with theory development and writing. These skills require thought and practice rather than mechanical technique. Theory development takes time; good theory follows a maturation process. The same is true for good writing. It takes time to draw out the implicit reasoning underlying research decisions, to see all the insights, to discover all of the important factors within the research. With each revision, the paper ripens. Expose your paper to the fresh air and sunshine of collegial feedback. With each discussion, new ideas emerge. The ripening process is facilitated with hard work and frequent revisions. When a paper fares badly with reviewers, the paper was still green—it probably was submitted prematurely. Allow the paper to ripen naturally with the passage of time, lots of sunshine, and many revisions as a way to develop theory and writing skills.

Don't Exaggerate

An underlying law of reviewer reaction is that understatement is more persuasive than overstatement. Nothing kills an argument so quickly as exaggeration. Nothing will motivate a reviewer to find flaws like overstatements and contrived emphasis about research results and importance. Exaggeration tells the reviewer that the author is not in touch with the true base of the study. Understatement, by contrast, can engage the reviewer on your side. The reviewer can see that the results are even stronger than you suggest and can agree with and support your interpretation.

To implement this guideline, avoid statements like "the findings prove," "certainly," "obviously," and "very strong relationships." No matter how strong the correlations, it is better to substitute phrasing like "the findings suggest," "tentatively," and to talk about "moderate relationships." This phrasing is more accurate and defendable for social science research. Everything we find is tentative. I think overstatement often is inadvertent rather than intentional. But exaggeration inserts a tone of amateurism to the paper and says that authors are not aware of what they are doing. Exaggerations can be excised from the paper and replaced with tentative understatements, which are more accurate and persuasive and will increase opportunity for publication.

CONCLUSIONS:
THE RESEARCH DUALITY

No one can write an excellent paper by hearing about failures. No one can be certain of having a paper accepted at a major journal by reading about papers that were rejected. Yet this chapter was about reasons for failure and rejection. My purpose in this chapter was to illuminate reasons for manuscript rejection. I analyzed the problems defined in my reviews of 111 manuscripts submitted to *AMJ* and *ASQ*, which revealed 11 major reasons for failure. My analysis suggested that most failures were due to theory rather than to method, and that three distinct skills—theory, writing, design—are needed to produce an excellent manuscript. Seven guidelines were proposed for developing manuscripts that can be published in major journals.

The findings from this analysis parallel two other projects of mine that examined the research process. The projects involved interviews with prominent scholars about significant and not-so-significant organizational research (Campbell et al., 1982) and a proposed model of research as craftmanship (Daft, 1983). The outcome of the interviews with prominent scholars suggested that research is significant when it embraces a special kind of duality. Significant research excelled at both method and theory and was characterized by both objective and subjective elements, by both organic and mechanistic processes. The description of research as a craft implied something similar—that the soft, theoretical side of research had to be integrated with the hard, methodological side to achieve significant outcomes.

The duality also appears in the analysis in this chapter. The findings suggest that good research requires both a theoretical base and a solid methodology. An excellent manuscript masters the intangible factors, including tone, style, and integration, along with the tangible factors of research description and solid research design. A well-written paper sticks to the operational base of the research, yet tells a story that goes beyond the data.

The research duality creates a tension for scholars. The dual elements may seem mutually exclusive. How can an author stick to the operational base and go beyond the data at the same time? This is the challenge facing authors. The finding from my analysis is that most manuscripts did not meet the challenge. They fell short on the subjective, theoretical side of the duality. Most of my criticisms pertained to theory rather than to method, to tone and style rather than to design. This suggests to me that the softer, theoretical side of the research duality is more difficult to learn. To master our craft, we must master theory and writing skills in addition to research design skills. The skills on the intangible side of the duality take more time, more work, and cannot be taught through formalized course work in graduate school. Yet mastery of this side of the duality is what distinguishes the truly excellent papers and allows them to be published in the leading journals.

The emphasis within the duality required for publication probably depends upon respective disciplines and journals. A journal such as *Administrative Science Quarterly* emphasizes the theoretical end of the duality. Without strong theoretical development, a paper is less likely to be published in *ASQ*. The *Journal of Applied Psychology* or *Management Science* emphasize the end of the duality where method and design procedures are important. But excellent papers typically capture both aspects of the duality to some extent when they are successful and have impact.

Most papers I reviewed handled the design and method portion of the duality satisfactorily, which is important. But they fell down on storytelling, the coordination of one part of the paper with other parts, tone, rationale, or letting the paper ripen naturally. Most authors need to work hard at these elements before submitting their papers for publication. Improving the theory and writing will please and delight the reviewers and increase the chances for publication.

REFERENCES

Campbell, J. P., Daft, R. L., & Hulin, C. L. (1982). *What to study: Generating and developing research questions.* Beverly Hills, CA: Sage.

Daft, R. L. (1983). Learning the craft of organizational research. *Academy of Management Review, 8,* 539-546.

Weick, K. E. (1974). Amendments to organizational theorizing. *Academy of Management Journal, 17,* 487-502.

10

The Reviewer as Defense Attorney

LOUIS R. PONDY

E valuating and publishing a scientific manuscript is in some ways like conducting a criminal trial. The author plays the role of defendant, who, although technically innocent until proven guilty, potentially stands accused of many crimes: failing to cite the relevant literature, stating hypotheses in nontestable form, using improper methods of data collection and analysis, interpreting results incorrectly, going beyond the data to state speculative conclusions, and so forth. All authors cringe at the expected litany of sins that will surely flow from the courtroom proceedings.

There are other actors in the drama as well. The editor plays the role of trial judge, charged with the responsibility of controlling the flow of facts and arguments into evidential status, and finally of pronouncing the sentence—accept, reject, or revise and resubmit. Copy editors, especially at some journals, are like wardens, parole officers, or rehabilitation specialists who shape up a manuscript and civilize it for public presentation. The role of final jury is played by the readers of the journal, who pass judgment on the ultimate merit of the published manuscript.

What role do the reviewers of the submitted manuscript play in this legal metaphor? To be mere witnesses for and against the defendant is too passive;

reviewers do more than respond to questions put by the trial judge, the editor. They themselves frame accusations against the defendant and demand responses. It seems clear that the reviewer plays the role of prosecuting attorney. His or her task in the trial is to marshall the evidence against the defendant, to build the strongest possible case against publication of the manuscript, to discover errors of method, to assert the triviality of findings and conclusions, to protect the public against the criminal act of faulty research.

And yet, we are troubled by the incompleteness of the metaphor. Is there not a crucial role that is missing from the courtroom drama? Must the defendant remain defenseless against the imposing array of trial judge, warden, jury, and prosecuting attorney? Must the author, like the client who has a fool for a lawyer, provide his or her own defense? Who, indeed, plays the role of defense attorney for the author? Who helps the author to shape his or her argument, to marshal his or her evidence, to give him or her confidence that his or her case is stronger than it appears, to call witnesses on his or her behalf, and to counter accusations from the prosecution? One might argue that the author's own colleagues should play this role; but they have no formal standing, no credentials, no license to practice in the court of manuscript evaluation. Does it not make eminently good sense that one of the reviewers or referees should be assigned the role of the author's defense attorney, his or her advocate and friend in court? Surely it does.

But where shall we find such defense attorneys? Our present corps of reviewers have been trained and conditioned in a prosecution mentality, in large part through observing how their own manuscripts have been treated by an earlier generation of reviewers. The norms of reviewing are passed down from generation to generation in a subterranean exchange between author and reviewers, an exchange that is almost entirely hidden from public view. Because the reviewing process is not publicly visible, we have only limited means to change it. What little information surfaces publicly includes selective complaints from authors about the toughness of their review or selective boasts from reviewers about their high standards. (I know of one person in the field who claims *never* to have recommended a manuscript for publication.) Thus reviewers who define themselves as defense attorneys for the author are not likely to emerge naturally from the existing process. Most reviewers do, of course, have positive things to say about some papers amidst the criticisms, but there is no guarantee that this will happen.

One proposal is to have the editor specifically assign to one of the reviewers the role of author's advocate. The reviewer/advocate would be responsible for making the strongest possible case for publication of the paper. The strength of this advocacy review would be balanced off against a more critical review from the other referee in the editor's decision to accept or reject the paper.

NEED FOR A ROLE MODEL

Even with this structural solution to the problem, there is little guidance on how a referee should review a paper when acting as defense attorney. As we have said, the exchanges between authors and reviewers are almost entirely hidden from public view, so social learning cannot take place in the profession. We have no publicly available role model for conducting an advocacy review, a role model in which the reviewer strongly supports the author's manuscript and encourages him or her to move beyond the correction of technical errors to discover and articulate the best possible paper that is contained in the submitted manuscript. We need a role model that shows how to give an author hope and courage to do more than satisfy editorial criticisms to gain publication. To fill this void, I would like to enter into the public domain for public discussion and debate one such role model, an actual exchange between an author and a reviewer that illustrates how the defense attorney model of reviewing might work in practice.

In the June 1978 issue of the *Academy of Management Journal,* Dick Daft published a paper titled "A Dual Core Model of Organizational Innovation" (Daft, 1978). I had the good fortune to be selected as one of the reviewers of Daft's manuscript by Larry Cummings, then editor-in-chief. Both Daft and Cummings have given me their kind permission to publish our exchange.

Daft originally submitted the manuscript in October 1976 under the title "The Innovation Process: Administrator Initiative, Employee Professionalism and Collaborative Strategies for Success."

My comments on Daft's original manuscript were as follows:

This is a lovely, exciting paper. It's lovely because its intelligible prose is a welcome change from the turgid jargon that I suffer through with most manuscripts. It is exciting because it suggests a fundamental restructuring of our ideas about organization. Let me be very specific. Thompson's model of organization contains only a single core—the *technical* core. But your data support an alternative conceptualization of organization that contains *two* cores—a technical core *and an administrative core!* Essentially what you are saying is that innovations can take place in either core, and the two cores may be only loosely coupled. That is, most of the time a core will propose and implement its own innovations. But under certain conditions, e.g., low professionalism in the "host" core and high professionalism in the "other" core, innovation will be initiated in the "other" core. This is a slight extension and generalization of your basic argument, but I think it simplifies your explanation (in a revolutionary way!) and is still consistent with your data. In fact, I would like to suggest an alternative title for your paper that captures this notion: "The Dual Core Model of Innovation."

I would like to suggest that you send a copy of your paper to John Meyer in the Education School at Stanford. He has some ideas (and a loose form of data) that suggests that the administrative core (my term, his idea) needs to be buffered from *its* environment. Ask for the paper that he and Bryan Rowen presented recently at the conference on loosely coupled systems. There are several other people who would be interested in the paper and I encourage you to send it to them, if you have not already: Ian Mitroff at Pitt, John Kimberly at Yale, Dick Scott at Stanford, Ed Morse at Tulane, Gerry Gordon at Boston University, to name a few.

As good as the paper is, it could be strengthened even more by tying it into the implementation literature. See especially the classic paper by Churchman and Scheinblatt (*Management Science,* about 1965). Their concept of "mutual understanding" (between scientist and manager) is parallel to your concept of "collaboration."

On page 8, your reference to "pool of new ideas" suggests the notion of a "gene pool," which in turn suggests that you might build on Weick's idea of evolutionary processes in organization. Specifically, Weick suggests that an organization should have both crediting and discrediting elements in the variation and selection processes. This in turn suggests that the two cores are isomorphic to those crediting and discrediting processes.

Take a look at Edwin Mansfield's books on technological innovation for both a nice methodology and some substantive results that parallel some of your own.

On page 13: One of the reasons that administrators sometimes initiate technical innovations, but teachers seldom initiate administrative innovations, is that most administrators were once teachers, but not vice versa.

On page 15, you say that administrators initiate a larger percentage of innovations. But is it possible that the number of administrator-initiated innovations is roughly constant, and what varies with professionalism is the number of teacher-initiated innovations?

My guess is that collaboration is most likely when teacher and administrator professionalism are roughly equal—sort of a power-balance model.

The "dual-core" notion suggests that you need a Table 7 headed "Summary of Teacher Strategies for Innovation."

Could you develop a more systematic and exhaustive analysis of when collaboration is likely to take place?

Take a look at Chapter 7 of March and Simon for what they have to say about the occasions of innovation.

Top of page 19: Perhaps that's because the administrative component of educational systems tends to be tightly coupled (i.e., efficiency-oriented and highly programmed) whereas the technical part of educational systems tends to be loosely coupled. I wonder if you couldn't work in Bob Duncan's notion of the "ambidextrous organization" and "switching rules" here, too. Tightly coupled systems are good at implementation, but loosely coupled systems are better at idea creation. So you would expect a higher percentage of proposals for administrative innovation to be adopted, but a higher *rate of proposals* for technical innovations (but fewer adopted).

I have made a few comments in the margins of the paper itself.

In that review I attempted to do several things:

1. refocus the main theoretical contribution of the paper
2. put the author in touch with others working on related problems
3. tie the analysis into other related literatures
4. make specific comments that would strengthen the argument
5. encourage the author that he was working on an important idea
6. persuade the editor that this was an important paper

In January 1977 Daft submitted a revised manuscript. The other reviewer was less enthusiastic and raised questions about the rigor of Daft's methods. Caught between contradictory reviews, he tried to steer a narrow course between them. He expressed this in his cover letter to Cummings:

Dear Larry:

I am surprised by the divergent opinions expressed by the two reviewers. To accommodate one reviewer may aggravate the other. I have incorporated all the suggested revisions that I could, and want to make a couple of comments for you to use in your decision.

Reviewer number 1 caught the spirit of the paper, which was to dig out data on internal organization processes to learn what is really going on when organizations innovate. This approach offers a rich opportunity for new insights that correlation-type studies miss. Reviewer number 2, however, was concerned with theoretical and operational rigor. His/her comments are valuable and I've included several in the revision. But, Larry, this is not a hypothesis testing study with a rigorously specified theory followed by statistical testing. The theory is a research guideline, and the data analysis is fairly unsophisticated.

But the methods fit the research problem. And, oh, the new insights. As reviewer number 1 said, the paper "suggests a fundamental restructuring of our ideas about organizations." This statement goes a bit far, but the findings give us substantial new insight for rethinking our ideas about innovation.

If reviewer number 2 won't accept the paper, would you ask a third reviewer to read it—preferably someone who cares about innovation knowledge rather than method.

Note how Daft used my review to frame his intent in the paper. One hypothesis is that an advocacy review can give the author some leverage in his negotiations with the editor on the acceptance decision and on revision of the manuscript.

In his specific response to my review, Daft rejected my suggestion to use the dual core idea, largely because the other reviewer had already criticized him for going "beyond the data," and he suggested that someone else should develop the idea instead. He did, however, pick up on several other suggestions. His response was as follows:

The responses to specific reviewer comments are listed below. Paragraph numbers refer to the number of the reviewer's paragraph. A copy of the original reviewer's comments is also attached.

#1. Thank you for the comment on readability.

The dual core is a marvelous idea (the title too) but I don't think I should use it. One reason is that while I can see that a dual core exists in most organizations, I don't demonstrate that administration is truly a core. Innovation activity is not good evidence for a core because innovation can occur in multiple cores or territories around the organization, depending upon the division of labour. These data point toward a dual core simply because there are two major centres in school districts. Other aspects of cores, such as having buffers, are not touched upon at all in this paper.

Another reason for not including the dual core idea is that the other reviewer feels the conclusions already go far beyond the data, and is inclined to reject the paper. A further generalization, even one as nice as this one, will reduce the chance for publication.

#2. I've sent papers to a couple of these people. After revision I will send to others. Perhaps ideas of dual core can be developed in a paper by Meyer and Rowen, or by you, or by me. Incidentally, I have data on university innovation that supports the same dual process of innovation.

#3. I see your point. But this paper is really not a study of implementation, which I make clear in the revision. This study is examining the source of proposals and the reasons for proposal and adoption. But as you point out, collaboration is really an implementation strategy, and I acknowledge this in the revision as well as the Churchman and Scheinblatt ideas.

#4. Hummmm, I like this idea too, but it would only fit a theoretical framework that goes beyond the data. I am reluctant to go further beyond what I already have in this paper.

#5. I am familiar with Mansfield's work on innovation adoption. His analysis and conclusions are sufficiently different from mine that I don't think they apply here. For example, he observed the first adoption only and correlated this adoption with other organizational characteristics. That is quite a different approach than my examination of internal processes.

Or do you mean his later work on research and development, where coupling with the rest of organization is associated with higher success rates for new products. That doesn't quite apply here either.

#6. Good point. I have included that explanation in the revision.

#7. The Table 3 data indicate that administrators initiate both a larger percentage and a larger absolute number of innovations in the low professional districts. Teacher

professionalism also explains some differences in percentage of proposals, but I don't think that constant administrative activity explains the Table 3 data.

#8. I never thought of that explanation. In Table 3, collaborations are highest for medium professional districts, which is modest support for your explanation. I've included this point as a possible explanation in the revision. Thanks.

#9. I would like to stay with the leader perspective. The study was designed to take a macro perspective, which is most applicable to top administrators. "Teacher Strategy" implies a strategy individuals can take to secure adoption of a single innovation. I am studying individual innovation behaviour separately, and prefer to report the findings separately. (We found that idea champions advocate ideas and obtain support for them through a variety of means.)

#10. Yes. I have elaborated a bit in this discussion section, but much of it is speculation because data on collaborations are not detailed. I stumbled onto collaborations when collecting data and got what data I could, which wasn't much.

#11. O.K.

#12. This interpretation forces me to make a distinction between proposals and adoptions. I do not have data on whether educational versus administrative components are loosely or tightly coupled. But I do have data to test Duncan's notion of "switching rules." I don't have his latest paper, but I think the ideas are similar to the ones expressed in the Zaltman et al. book. I have added the finding that nearly all proposals are adopted. Proposals and adoptions are synonymous in these districts. This does not support Duncan's theory, and I discuss why in the revision (p. 22). This is an important finding which I was going to use in another paper, but I think it fits in here very nicely.

#13. I received them and revised the text in a couple of places.

What is most interesting about this response is that it reveals a good deal of the negotiation and bargaining that frequently goes on between author and reviewer. The author not only submitted a revision but attempted to justify which changes he did and didn't make.

My reaction to Daft's revision and to his responses to my original comments were quite strong, almost bullying as I look back at them now. I had become more an advocate of the dual core idea than of the author, and indirectly I was arguing with the other reviewer, not just Daft. What was centrally at issue was the legitimacy of "going beyond the data" in scientific theorizing, and the other reviewer and I had clearly taken opposing sides of the issue. My comments were as follows:

I was mildly disappointed that you chose not to use the idea of a dual core model, but I was profoundly depressed by your reason—that you were afraid to go beyond your data. If Einstein had been afraid to go beyond the available data, he would never have come up with the theory of relativity; if Darwin had been afraid to make the intuitive leap beyond his data, he would never have invented the idea of natural selection; if Newton had been afraid to go beyond his data, he could never have invented the concept of gravitation that integrated swinging pendula, falling bodies, and planetary motion; if Freud had been afraid to go beyond his data, he would not have created the idea of a subconscious; in fact, if Jim Thompson had been afraid to go beyond his data, he would not have invented the concept of a technical core. I agree that you should not claim *conclusions* that you have no data to support, but we're not talking about conclusions. We're talking about root metaphors or organization within which empirical research and explanations take place. But one never "proves" a root metaphor. The best one can say is that the metaphor is or is not useful for making deeper sense of things than some other metaphor. And in this case, the metaphor of a dual core is a very powerful device for liberating a new insight into one specific organizational process. I think you're turning your back on an opportunity to make a major contribution to our thinking about organizations. But that's your business. As it stands, the paper will make a pleasant, ordinary contribution, but it could have been a classic. It should be published, but there's no rush. Sigh. I guess I'll look around for a field where the good young people aren't afraid to go beyond their data.

You said you took a look at March and Simon, but you don't reference them. Let me suggest, as they do, that innovation is stimulated by failure. But it's important that failure be defined properly as the shortfall of actuality from expectations or aspirations. I would argue that professionals have higher or more elaborate aspirations than non-professionals, so they will perceive more "failures" and will be more motivated to innovate. Your explanation suggests that professionals innovate more because they are more competent. Can you rule out my explanation? If not, you are obligated to report both explanations as possible conclusions.

I like your highlighting your unexpected findings. Please take a look at a paper by Murray Davis called "That's Interesting" in the 1971 *Philosophy of Social Science.* You're using one of his devices for making your paper more interesting by focusing on deviations from expectations. The same goes for the finding related to the Zaltman-Duncan theory. Can you give that finding a bit more prominence in the write-up?

Given the other reviewer's viewpoint, I had no idea how the author (still unknown to me) would respond to my urgings. Of course, the other key actor in the debate was Larry Cummings, the editor. I tried forcefully to influence his opinion in a cover note to him in hopes that he might persuade Daft to incorporate the dual core idea. But I was prepared to recommend acceptance of the paper in its present form:

Larry—

The paper is publishable in its present form, although there are a few minor things he might do to improve it a bit. But what I'd really like to see you do is to try and persuade him that he ought to use the dual core idea. I'll even give up my footnoting rights. Just seeing the idea exposed to the light of day would be satisfaction enough for me. I hope my comments to him aren't too grandiose. I really do think that the paper could become a classic if he used the dual core metaphor, and that of course would redound to AMJ's reputation as well as the author's. I'm really bugged by his reluctance to "go beyond his data" in giving us a new model to work with. I guess I'll just have to publish a paper called "The Dual Core Model of Organization," myself.

I do not know the details of what Cummings subsequently told Daft, but Daft did ultimately incorporate the dual core idea and change the title of the paper, using the more modest "A Dual Core Model . . ." rather than "The Dual Core Model . . ." His final response to my suggestions was as follows:

> Yes, you are right, of course. It is interpretation, insight, extensions and revisions of extant theories that count, not the mere facts of the data. If everyone was afraid to venture beyond their data, we'd still be in the middle ages.
>
> I found it awkward to set up the paper as a test of the dual-core model, so I have introduced the dual-core notion at the end of the paper as an explanation for the findings. It is an extension of Evan's trickle-up, trickle-down innovation theory and Thompson's technical core. I have also drawn the Zaltman-Duncan finding into the dual core discussion (paragraph 4 of your comments) because the dual core seems to explain why their theory was not supported. Organizations don't need different structures of "switching rules" for handling innovation proposals versus innovation adoptions. They need a structure to reflect the innovation activity required in the technical versus administrative core. When the technical core requirements dominate, then the structure should be decentralized, low formalized and loosely coupled to complement the bottom-up innovation process. When the administrative core dominates, the structure should be centralized, low on complexity, high formalized and tightly coupled to fit top down innovation needs.
>
> *Re:* your comment on March and Simon. I think you are absolutely right. Professional employees are activated by high aspirations and the resulting performance gap. They are also exposed to new ideas which may make current procedures look inadequate. I didn't mean to imply that professionals innovate simply because they are competent (and non-professionals incompetent). I trust this comes through more clearly in the revision. I have probed this matter more deeply elsewhere. The apparent disagreement with March and Simon (also Cyert and March) is that successful organizations— no failing ones—report more problems and are more likely to try new ideas, all because of aspirations.
>
> Other changes in this revision: The introductory theory based upon Evan's ideas has been shortened. Table 2 (summary of Table 1) has been dropped. So has Table 6 (Administrator strategies for innovation).

What can we learn from this case study of a reviewer acting as defense attorney for the author?

(1) A published manuscript is sometimes (perhaps frequently) the cumulative result of a complicated interchange and negotiation among author, editor, and reviewers. Too often in my three year stint as associate editor of *ASQ,* I saw

authors willing to make *any* changes demanded by reviewers just to have their papers accepted for publication. Daft was willing to argue and debate the points to preserve the integrity of his manuscript. But the bottom line is that publishing research is an intensely *social* activity involving several key actors.

(2) The reviewer acting as author's advocate can provide the author with moral support to withstand the methodological and other criticisms of another reviewer. The editor, too, plays an important role not only in selecting reviewers and making the final decision but also in providing guidance to the author in how he or she should weigh the suggestions of competing reviewers.

(3) Perhaps most important, the simple act of making such a series of exchanges public for the first time permits us to examine how an advocacy review might take place. It provides one possible role model for the reviewer to follow as author's defense attorney before the editor/trial judge.

CONCLUSION

Suppose we take seriously my proposal that journal editors assign the role of defense attorney to one of the reviewers of each submitted manuscript, and that the refereeing process be set up as a dialectic between competing reviewers. What are the possible consequences for both the amount and the quality of published research? Can we say anything about the optimal balance between the prosecuting attorney and defense attorney models of the reviewing process?

Use of the prosecuting attorney model of reviewing is likely to minimize the chance of incorrectly publishing a faulty piece of research. But it maximizes the probability of failing to publish research that may have merit.

Defining the role of reviewer as that of prosecuting attorney makes most sense when the amount of journal space is limited relative to the number of manuscripts being produced, and when the average quality of manuscripts is low relative to the research standards of the field. The prosecuting attorney model also makes sense when the field wishes to tip the balance away from novel definitions and approaches to research problems and toward reinforcement and elaboration of the reigning research paradigm.

In contrast, the reviewer as defense attorney takes the position of developing a rationale to support publication of the manuscript. More important, the defense attorney model places the reviewer in the position of helping the author to shape his or her arguments, of defending his methods of data collection and analysis, of drawing significant interpretations from the data, and of placing the study in a literature context that maximizes its scientific impact.

The defense attorney model reduces the chance of failing to publish a piece that may have scholarly merit and value. But it increases the risk of the opposite type of error—of overloading the journals with papers of questionable significance based on faulty methods. This latter risk is, however, moderated by the part that the reviewer qua defender plays in shaping and improving the manuscript. Heavier use by a scientific community of the defense attorney model is likely to undercut the conservative nature of the field's research paradigm, and to tilt the balance, for better or worse, in the direction of more novelty in both method and content.

Organizational behavior, like all fields of scholarly research, faces the basic policy decision of striking the right balance between the prosecuting and defense attorney models. Operationally, the balance is controlled by journal editors who select manuscript reviewers. Editors, through experience with individual reviewers, know with some confidence who is likely to take a hard line, and who not, on any particular paper. They can tilt the balance toward either a conservative or a liberal judgment of the manuscript through the selection of reviewers. The balance is also controlled by the reviewing norms of the field, as we have said. Organizational behavior as a field has within its power, through its editors and through the reviewing norms, the discretion to alter the balance between prosecuting and defense attorney models of the reviewing process.

Acceptance rates at leading OB journals such as *Administrative Science Quarterly* and the *Academy of Management Journal* approximate 10% to 15% of the manuscripts submitted. (In leading physical science journals, the acceptance rates run much higher, as much as 80% to 90%.) To say it another way, seven to ten times as many manuscripts of a given length are submitted as can be published, given available journal pages. If we want a greater percentage of submitted manuscripts published, we must expand available journal space, shorten average manuscript length, or reduce the number of manuscripts submitted. If none of these alternatives is viable in the short run, then we will have to continue to live with a 90% rejection rate. If the rejection rate continues at the 90% level, then the pressures and incentives on editors and reviewers will be heavily tilted, as I think they are, in the direction of favoring the prosecuting attorney model of reviewing to justify negative decisions.

Even though high rejection rates create pressures for a prosecution mentality, use of the defense attorney model of reviewing is not necessarily inconsistent with low acceptance rates; it is just more difficult to support and rationalize. One of my purposes in this chapter has been to develop an independent rationale for the defense attorney model that can withstand the natural pressures of high rejection rates that are pushing us as a field in the direction of the prosecution model. Furthermore, I have argued that a persuasive rationale for the defense orientation cannot be supported without a clear exemplar of how the defense attorney model might function in actual practice. By providing such an exemplar, I hope that I have made it somewhat more possible for authors with novel ideas to secure a fair hearing in court. And perhaps I have also provided a model for reviewers who wish, or are assigned by the editor, to act as defense attorneys for the author.

REFERENCE

Daft, R. (1978). A dual core model of organizational innovation. *Academy of Management Journal, 21*(2), 193-210.

11

Becoming a Reviewer
Lessons Somewhat Painfully Learned

ELAINE ROMANELLI

A s I begin this chapter, there are three manuscripts sitting on my desk awaiting review. One is already late, and I am feeling guilty. Two are due within the next week, and I am feeling pressured. Editors' protestations notwithstanding, I know that new manuscripts will arrive within a week or two of my returning these. I am also dimly aware of several manuscripts under revision that will probably return to my desk for second review sometime in the near future. In more than 10 years of reviewing now, it seems that there have been only a few short time periods when I have not had at least one manuscript to review. It strikes me, then, that one of the most basic challenges of reviewing is handling the ubiquitous deadline. The question I have struggled with during all that time is how to write a good review efficiently.

What does *efficiency* mean? It means that the review is begun and ended in a relatively short time period. There are lots of ways to do this. One way that I have heard espoused by many colleagues is just to start writing comments, section by section, paragraph by paragraph, as many as are needed, until the entire manuscript has been addressed. Only one thorough reading is required. Another way, also frequently espoused, is to skim the manuscript quickly, making notes about important problems or questions until two or three, or some number deemed sufficient by the reviewer, have been found. The reviewer can then simply write up these few central problems and recommend revision or rejection depending on the severity of the problems. In rare cases, when few or no major problems are found, the reviewer can note this fact, point out a few major contributions, and recommend acceptance.

I believe there are positive aspects to both approaches. The first is certainly thorough. The author will be treated to a detailed exposition of virtually every question and issue that occurred to the reviewer. The second is probably very effective at gatekeeping for the journal. Manuscripts that exhibit a few basic problems need a revision. Manuscripts that exhibit more than a few probably merit rejection because the likelihood of successful revision tends to be low. I don't believe, however, that either approach satisfies an objective of writing a *good* review efficiently. In my experience (and I have tried all the ways), the first is comprehensive but fails to clarify key problems that the author should address. The second approach is satisfactory for evaluation and probably points out some of the central difficulties but fails to provide constructive help.

So what is a good review? Today I think there are some rather straightforward answers to this question, all of which, I must acknowledge, are well presented in the major journals' "instructions to reviewers." A good review clearly identifies key contributions and problems in the manuscript. A good review provides constructive suggestions to the author for improving the manuscript. A good review provides consistent support for a recommendation to the editor about the disposition of the manuscript and does so without necessarily revealing the recommendation. Unfortunately, while these objectives are straightforward, and I have always understood them in my mind, they have not been easy to achieve in a practical sense. Nobody taught me how to spot key contributions quickly. Nobody taught me the difference between constructive criticism—although it seems like I remember something from fifth grade on this—and just an elaborated list of a paper's deficiencies. Like too many aspects of an academic's job, the good review can be described, but the lessons for writing one are left to individual experimentation, self-doubt, and random conclusions.

It has been an interesting task, in contemplating this chapter, to consider what I have learned about reviewing, and when I have learned it. In keeping with the motivations for this book, I think the best way I can tell the story of my learning is through the personal "passages" that I have experienced. As I look back at literally hundreds of reviews, what is most clear is that the audience for the reviews—the audience in my mind, of course—has changed quite substantially. I once wrote for editors; now I write for authors (more on that below). In part, the audience has changed because I have grown more secure and more confident in my abilities to write a good review. In part also, though, the audience has changed because I have grown more caring about the objectives of my reviews. The following sections identify changes in audiences and describe the lessons that have promoted the changes.

FIRST REVIEWS:
WRITING FOR EDITORS

I received my first manuscript to review when I was still a doctoral student. I felt both honored and challenged by the assignment. I had no published papers, only one book chapter accepted, and just a few conference presentations. Like most academics in the early stages of their careers, I had dreams of becoming a well-known and well-respected member of my profession. As I observed my mentors, I saw that they spent a rather large amount of time reviewing manuscripts. They were proud of being invited to serve as members of editorial boards of top-tier journals. As I scanned the lists of names on editorial boards, I saw that they comprised a lot of famous people whose names I also saw as authors of articles in the journals. Reviewing, apparently, was a route to status. I wanted to become a reviewer.

Thus, when I got that first manuscript—and I am a little embarrassed to say this—before ever reading a word, I had only one objective: to get a second manuscript. Getting manuscripts, of course, is controlled by editors. I had to figure out how to write a review that would impress the editor.

In truth, I hadn't a clue. I thought I had to show that I was "up" on my literature, and that I knew the relevant research questions. I thought I should demonstrate competence at research methods. No fatal flaw should get by me. In keeping with the "instructions to reviewers to take into account clarity of writing," I supposed I should also help the authors to write more clearly. Thus I set out to comment, having now read the paper maybe once, on virtually every aspect of the manuscript.

Needless to say, efficiency was nowhere on my mind. (I didn't know then that it would be a problem to worry about.) I spent at least a week worrying about the review and writing it, all the while ignoring the dissertation proposal I was supposed to be writing. I looked up and read many of the paper's important references. That first review was more than eight single-spaced pages long, organized according to subheadings used by the author. I patiently explained problems in each of the sections and, with some pedantry, described how the author could do better. I didn't know then, and I don't know now, who that author was, but I hereby offer an apology.

As I look back at the review (and, yes, I still have it), I think maybe the only objective it met was thoroughness. At least the editor got plenty of fuel for the rejection that the paper received. The review was highly evaluative. While I offered many suggestions for improvement, I don't believe the author got much constructive help for a revision. Mainly, I criticized.

A few months later, I received that second manuscript to review. And then I got a third, and a fourth. Apparently, I was now a reviewer. I followed much the same procedures for reviewing the new manuscripts, but two things seemed wrong. First, I was beginning to notice, and feel frustrated, that reviewing took an awful lot of time. I was reading lots of articles—authors' references—that had little to do with my own research. The reading didn't seem to be helping much with the reviewing anyway. I was also beginning to notice that editors were only once in a while mentioning my reviews in their letters to the authors. It is a strange fact of reviewing that the only feedback we ever get directly on individual reviews is the editor's letter to the author. How come my comments weren't guiding the editor's decisions and instructions?

I thought that maybe my reviews weren't sufficiently to the point. Almost certainly, this was true. Perhaps my review should focus more directly on the major problems in the manuscript. Maybe I should just concentrate on the central problems of the manuscript so that the editor would have clear issues (that I had identified) to point to in the decision letter.

My reviews got shorter. I adopted the approach of identifying and discussing a few key problems. My reviews got quicker. I didn't have to read the paper in detail, and I didn't have to write a comment on every issue that the paper addressed. I guess the real truth is that I didn't have to bother helping the author to write a better paper. As we all know from grading students' papers, evaluating is easier than explaining. For a while, it seemed that I had learned how to review efficiently. Simple gatekeeping was the ticket.

LATER REVIEWS: WRITING FOR MYSELF
(OR, THE PAPER I WOULD HAVE WRITTEN)

But not so fast: I learned some hard new lessons on reviewing when, during my first year as a junior faculty member, I got some reviews on a paper of my own. I will never forget Reviewer 2, who called my hypotheses "vapid and inane." Those words set the tone for virtually every comment in the review. The review was evaluative in the extreme, and constructive not at all. Once I was done cursing the reviewer for meanness, cowardice, and stupidity, not necessarily in that order, I was left to revise the paper so as to convince a reviewer who was on record for plain hostility toward my work. I was angry that I would have to respond to this reviewer in a tone that was "appreciative" for help that had not been given. I didn't know how to begin.

The other reviewers were more helpful. Reviewer 1 praised the study's basic research question. This was a very useful focusing device. Through that reviewer's restatement of my objectives, I could see what main line of argument my paper should follow. The revision was easily initiated just by jettisoning all the extraneous discussion and fascinating nuances that were intelligible, in retrospect, only to me. Reviewer 3 liked the data but pointed out ways in which they might be better analyzed. This reviewer, too, worked hard at linking the analyses to the questions of principal interest. These reviewers showed me how to revise the paper.

Somewhere about this time, I had a conversation with a senior colleague who was then an associate editor for a top-tier journal. He talked about writing, and reviewing, and editing. He suggested that the best papers—that is, those that advanced understanding of organizations and got cited a lot—were those that had mainly only one good idea to present and clarify. I thought this was useful advice for me as a writer; maybe it wasn't such a good idea to integrate *all* the literature and solve quite all the empirical problems every time I wrote a paper. I also decided that it was a good guideline for me as a reviewer. Other reviewers had helped me to see what was interesting and important in my own work. Here was a positive contribution that I too could make. From that point forward, and to this day, my reviews always begin with a short statement of what the useful contribution of the paper might be.

I also vowed never to be callous in my comments to authors. I had learned too well how debilitating it was to contend with a hostile reviewer. It takes a lot of time to be angry and hurt. If I was not so "vapid and inane"—yes, it still rankles—as Reviewer 2 thought, then maybe I owed a commensurate credit to the authors that I was reviewing. I was pleased to see recently, in the "instructions to reviewers" of one top journal, *Administrative Science Quarterly,* some specific admonishments against scornful or dismissive remarks. The editors pointed out that the damage of a rude review extends well beyond just the author's hurt feelings. Authors who are too cavalierly dismissed or insulted may be reluctant to submit to the journal again. Some of the authors may someday write very good papers.

So, I set out to be positive in my tone and helpful in my suggestions for improvement. One important thing I discovered quickly was that I changed my mind more often about a manuscript. Sometimes, especially for papers that seemed poor on first reading, when I tried to state their central contributions I discovered new value. Sometimes a rejection became a revision. Maybe this is only a halo effect from my efforts to write the contribution. Nevertheless, it seems good to err on the side of supposing that the author has something to say.

Of course, this positive reviewing also opened up three new traps for me to fall into. First, there was growing disparity between the positive tone I was taking with the authors and the often negative evaluations I was presenting to the editors. I found myself writing long letters to editors trying to bridge the gaps. Second, increasingly it seemed that I was spending vast amounts of time (and paper) explaining to authors just exactly how I thought they should revise their papers. Finally, none of this was very efficient. The reviews were getting very long again, and I was expending rather a lot of creative energy on somebody else's paper.

I don't know that I've ever solved the first problem satisfactorily. I still write letters to the editors, though they are shorter. I still worry, especially when I get a revision to review, that authors haven't fully "heard" my requests for major revision. Perhaps it is true that the tension between evaluation and constructive help cannot be completely resolved. One small solution I have hit upon is to close the review with a restatement of what I like about the paper, but also a summary of the revision I think will be required. Mainly, though, I think I still leave it as the editor's job to communicate the likelihood of successful revision, assuming that revision is the decision.

For the second problem, another senior colleague provided much useful help. A few years ago, at an editorial board meeting, this colleague called into question what he considered the pervasive practice of asking an author to write the paper that the reviewer would have written. "Guilty," I thought. It is not the reviewer's job to describe the perfect paper that the author might write. It is arrogant to believe that a reviewer could know enough, or even read enough, to do competently all the research that their authors have tackled. It is really only the job of the reviewer to show how the author might better have done his or her identified research.

My reviews got shorter again. They also got quicker.

CURRENT REVIEWS: WRITING FOR AUTHORS

I began this chapter by talking about efficiency and the career concerns that dominated my early reviews. While it seems obvious that neither efficiency nor career should drive the reviewing process, I believe that both, in subtle but powerful ways, do direct the objectives of reviewers. At least this has been true for me. I would like to close this chapter by talking about what efficiency means to me today, and also about how some career changes have affected my reviewing processes.

Efficiency seems a mundane and possibly even a dangerous place to begin an essay on reviewing. On the mundane side, I do not suppose that what I have written is particularly new or insightful for any experienced reviewer. Certainly there are reviewers who have learned these lessons faster and better than I have. On the dangerous side, it would be wrong to convey that efficiency alone is an appropriate objective for reviewing. Efficiency is only a plain flat need for those of us who review frequently.

Efficiency became a silent objective in my reviewing because I seemed always to be struggling to meet the deadlines. As you can see, from the opening paragraph of this chapter, I still struggle with deadlines, but in a different sort of way. Ten years ago, the deadlines were tough because when I began a review I never knew how long it would take to complete. The process was wholly unstructured. Today, when I approach a review, I know that it will be done in just a few hours' time. Deadlines are a problem only because I tend to procrastinate.

I hope it is clear that the keys to this hard-won efficiency are focus and collegiality. Focus saves time by directing comments toward fundamental problems that need to be fixed and away from extraneous issues. For example, if the data overall are inappropriate for the research question, additional amounts of effort don't need to be spent explaining problems with measurement. If the author has made major errors in describing the arguments of other theorists, then the hypotheses that are premised on the errors don't have to be explicitly criticized. The reviewer may wish to offer a brief comment or two about improvements in measures, or describe how hypotheses might change if theories were properly presented, but great detail is unnecessary. The rule of thumb that I use goes as follows: If revisions to improve the fundamental problems in the paper would clearly eliminate associated problems, I spend little time on the associated problems.

Note: I think this is also fair to the author. Nothing annoys me more, as a writer, than a reviewer who nitpicks his or her way through every detail of a manuscript after already calling for "a complete overhaul." Not only may I have to respond to all those comments, even though they may no longer be relevant, I feel somewhat humiliated. I would like a reviewer to give me a little credit, and a little room, to revise my paper myself.

Which brings me to collegiality; collegiality saves time because it assumes that the author is a competent professional who can probably revise a paper given some good, general guidelines. Less detail about minor problems can mean more focus on the broad strokes that most revisions require. If the author can successfully address the large problems, the details can be handled in the second review. Given that the details will always change in a revision, why spend time in the first round identifying them all? It is not efficient and, in the end, it is not helpful.

Career changes also have led me to greater focus and collegiality in my reviews. Today, I think it is a little funny how concerned I was, 10 years ago, about getting that second manuscript to review. Little did I know that demand for reviewers is so great that reasonable intelligence and general familiarity with the basic questions and methods of our field are about all that is required. But perhaps my ignorance was a good thing. My desire to impress an editor, first to get a second manuscript and later to be the reviewer who gets cited in the editor's letter, led me to care a great deal about the quality of my review. I am uncomfortable, though, that impressing the editor may not be the best objective for producing a helpful review for the author.

Eventually I was invited to serve on an editorial board. This was a very nice reward for what had been, by then, several years of hard reviewing work. Of course, it also increased the workload. Efficiency became even more important. Changes in my attitudes also began to evolve. For a while, I was concerned with justifying the confidence that had been placed in me by the board membership. I wanted the editors to know that they'd made a good decision. Over time, however, as I got more and more secure about my abilities and my credentials as a reviewer, slowly, slowly, I stopped worrying about impressing the editor.

Today, I am a member of three editorial boards, and I have been a member of two more. While I still feel honored to be invited, the achievement has lost just a bit of its excitement. In some funny way, I don't really care anymore whether I get papers to review. It goes without saying, but I'll say anyway that reviewing is a service that we provide to our profession and to our colleagues: a service—not a rung on a career ladder.

Maybe learning this deep down is the final stage of becoming a reviewer.

12

Journaling Careers

CHARLES PERROW

This is a chapter proposing ways to use journals to advance one's career, with illustrations of successes and failures from my own history. (*Journaling* is a stockbroker's term for moving assets from one of the client's accounts to another.) But I must start with an apology. Pontification is inevitable in a piece like this. The authors requested a chapter from the perspective of the "established author," which is an invitation to self-serving tale telling, illustrating large generalities. More important, any such account is largely retrospective judgment and, as such, may have little to do with the actual names, dates, and dynamics that one dwells upon in the tales. Rejoinders from all of the named and unnamed persona in my own Canterbury Tale would be appropriate.

I have a series of propositions, all rather shakily supported by personal experience:

AUTHOR'S NOTE: A graduate student, Lee Clarke, and several young faculty members (Neil Bennett, Paul DiMaggio, Matt Hamabatta, Phil Leaf, and Walter Powell) gave me good comments on the first draft of this chapter.

(1) Mainline journal publication is a must for those starting their careers, as destructive and difficult as it might be at the time.

(2) The setting (generally the department) that one works in probably explains about 35% of the success rate in careers. Success is favored by a setting that emphasizes high standards, provides tough critics, and has good graduate students. (I argue below that 40% is luck and 25% talent.) If you find the setting does not produce rigorous critiques of your work, use the mail to compensate and listen especially hard to the referees of articles and research proposals and hope they are tough. Develop the existing graduate students as best you can: Their value is that they bring the views of other faculty members to you and read more of the literature than you can read.

(3) After you have gained a bit of a reputation from journals (or, better yet, a published dissertation), and while one should return to the journals from time to time, the best work is that produced for unrefereed outlets (so is the worst, unfortunately). Refereed journals are a good place to summarize your ideas but are inhospitable to the process of working them out. (Thus combining 1, the need to publish in major journals, and 3, the inhospitality of major journals to exploration and development, the young are instantly at a disadvantage; but, because they are brighter than the old, there is some justice here.)

(4) Extraordinary talent will out; Professor Maurice Zeitlin will get his radical critique published in the *American Journal of Sociology* in spite of an initial rejection by the editor. A few others with extraordinary talent, such as Charles Tilly, will publish their way out of infertile settings. They will push aside the established authors—but . . .

(5) Luck is even more important than setting. The journeyperson sociologist may prosper if he or she has the luck (a) to be in a prestigious university that spreads its halo over its members, provides conference invitations, easy access to research sites and data resources, easy access to ideas and other disciplines; (b) to have the fortuitous configuration of faculty interests in a department that generates some synergy independent of the department's overall quality; (c) to pick an area that the federal government then becomes interested in and supports with grants; (d) to find he or she is riding a popular wave; or (e) to be sponsored by a prestigious member of the profession. While talent and setting may play a role in the above, I would argue that they are much more a matter of luck. It is notoriously difficult to judge the talent of new Ph.D.s, so, of two equally talented people, one may end up at Weed State University and the other at an Ivy League university. The latter gets all the breaks and the candidate selection prophecy is

self-fulfilled. (Extreme hard work and sacrificing such things as family life, I take for granted.)

First, the following is evidence for proposition 5, luck. My luck was extraordinary. How many people do you know who were born and reared in Tacoma, Washington (Bing Crosby, Janis Page)? After a journey around the Pacific Rim and the country, I decided to be a novelist. By the time I had spent a quarter at the University of Washington, two years at Black Mountain College in North Carolina, a year in what would later be called the counterculture of the Lower East Side, six weeks at Reed College in Portland, and another year in the rooming house section of Oakland, California, I entered yet another school, Berkeley. No novels had materialized and even my short stories were whimpering and self-indulgent. As an undergraduate at Berkeley, I took an extraordinary year-long course on the Idea of Progress given by Kenneth Bock (it was a bad idea, he concluded) and found that sociology was my calling. Reinhard Bendix and Robert Nisbet were also in the department, but one could hardly say as yet that I was lucky to be there. The department was so bereft of civility and stature that a distinguished member of the philosophy department had to be persuaded to step in and chair it. But my luck turned. Herbert Blumer was recruited as chair and, over my undergraduate and graduate years in the department, he added Philip Selznick, Kingsley Davis, William Kornhauser, Tamatso Shibutani, William Peterson, Seymour M. Lipset, and Erving Goffman. I became a graduate student in 1953 and shared that status over the next five years with Bennett Berger, Arlene Daniels, Fred Goldner, Tom Scheff, Art Stinchcombe, and Gunther Roth. Amitai Etzioni and Juan Linz were also there. I can only call this extraordinary mix of faculty and students a stroke of luck for me.

The wisdom and difficulty of proposition 1, to write for the mainline journals at the beginning of one's career, was illustrated in my first job at the University of Michigan. One of my early publications was not refereed and was in a non-mainline journal, *Social Research* (Perrow, 1964-1965). The piece was an attack, still rather uncommon in the early 1960s, on pluralist theory and the excessive emphasis upon norms and values at the expense of political power and economic realities in the work of such functionalists as Parsons, Smelser, and Kornhauser. The chair and some other wise people suggested that I should give up that line of inquiry and publishing outlet. They pointed out that it was the *American Sociological Review (ASR)*, the *American Journal of Sociology (AJS)*, and perhaps *Social Problems* and *Social Forces* that counted. They were right in both respects; one's credentials needed to be established before ideological criticism of major figures in sociology will be accepted, and the mainline journals did the credentialing. I gave up criticism and concentrated on mainlining.

(I hope I may be forgiven an irrelevant anecdote. The paper in question was to be presented at the Montreal ASA annual meeting in a great hall with a great crowd and Canadian television coverage. It was never read. I was the last speaker on the program and the other speakers had run on so long that the one preceding me had to be interrupted in flight by Peter Blau, who stormed into the hall shouting: "This meeting is already 10 minutes overtime and the business meeting must start." The chair, Dennis Wrong, finally got the speaker off and graciously said that all was not lost; Perrow had written a very good abstract of his paper and the audience could read it in the published proceedings. It was my first ASA convention appearance. Another undelivered paper was for a section of the Michigan Sociological Society annual meeting when only two people showed up. We went for coffee. It had to get better.)

Meanwhile, I had expanded parts of my dissertation and published a bit in *AJS* (it was initially rejected by *ASR*) and another bit in *ASR* (one keeps trying) (Perrow, 1961). It was a lot of work; colleagues at Michigan were relentless and the drafts were numerous and even then the journal referees and editors insisted on improvements. But what a bounty from those two mainline, refereed pieces! Mainstreaming your work when you are unknown brings invitations to write chapters for edited volumes and attend conferences and symposiums where your presentation may also find published outlets. (Being at prestigious Michigan also helped, of course.) Now we come to proposition 3: In papers for conferences, symposiums, and edited collections, which are not refereed, you can expand, develop, experiment, and take risks. If we were only allowed to work on first-rate articles and books in our early career, there would be insufficient motivation, because of the risks and difficulties, for most of us to try to leap those high hurdles. Lower hurdles provide practice and respite, along with the less expensive rewards.

I had seen a remarkable paper in a political science journal outlining a political theory of organizations by James March (1962). I did not know him, but I sent him my two mainline pieces on prestige and on goals in hospitals. I felt they were consistent with his views and did not think he would ordinarily come across them. It just so happened (good fortune again) that March needed a piece on hospitals for the *Handbook of Organizations* he was preparing, and asked me to review the hospital literature for the *Handbook* (Perrow, 1965). I reviewed the literature in passing but took the occasion to try out and develop an idea about technology and social structure. I knew I had the freedom to do so in an edited volume. I knew because the volume editor is not likely to reject a commissioned manuscript just because it does not quite fit. The editor of a journal can be more demanding, however.

This invitation to review the work on hospitals was the first chance I had to work out my ideas about technology. Though the ideas had come from what was then a very large-scale comparative study of organizations—reform schools—in which I was the study director, the two principal investigators of the project favored a leadership interpretation over my task and structure interpretation. As a result, the notion that staff practices and organizational structure depended heavily upon the techniques adopted by the organizations, regardless of leadership, barely surfaced in the published volume (Street, Vinter, & Perrow, 1966). Both the Michigan department and the project I was on did not lend generous support to critical papers or new ideas about organizations. But Michigan provided something much more valuable in the long run, although I was not aware of it for some years. They demonstrated that the setting in which one does one's work is vital. This is proposition 2, and my evidence follows.

There was much that I did not like about the University of Michigan in the early 1960s. The chair required me to shave off a summer beard before teaching; he kept the courses in organizations for himself or his favorite graduate students; the junior faculty taught introductory sociology and we were expected to use a dreadful text written by the senior members of the department; my salary, when I left in 1963, was about $7,200 for the academic year; and I was told, when I got an offer from the University of Pittsburgh in 1963 and inquired about my tenure prospects at Michigan, that to get tenure I had best go over to the University of Michigan Survey Research Center and collaborate with someone there to produce a hard cover book with "hard" (questionnaire) data. But as unpleasant as all this was, I now see that it was irrelevant. The collegial resources, graduate students, and quality demands were extraordinary. On the project I had directed, I was nominally in charge of such research assistants as Rosemary Sarri, David Street, and Mayer Zald. The tenured staff was full of luminaries such as Harold Wilensky, Morris Janowitz, Amos Hawley, Guy E. Swanson, and Albert Reiss; and Herbert Blalock, David Bordua, and William Gamson were among the juniors.

Let me indicate what happened when I violated my rule about the importance of setting by moving to Pittsburgh. I will give you a concrete example of what it meant to do work in a place like Michigan, as compared with my next post, the University of Pittsburgh, where the faculty were more concerned with theory than research.

Among the many expected advantages of Pittsburgh was the time and research support to explore my ideas about task and social structure among organizations where the test would be more stringent than it had been in reform schools and hospitals. I could focus upon a variety of industrial organizations with technologies ranging from routine to nonroutine. At that time we were just learning of structural differences between custodial and treatment-oriented hospitals and assumed the structure of firms was much more unvarying. Pittsburgh allowed me to spend a trimester doing exploratory work in the field—just getting to know two moderate-sized firms. Then I was ready to write a big grant proposal. I felt I knew all about proposals for big studies from my Michigan experience. After I had submitted it to the National Science Foundation, I was stunned to get a call from the sociology director of NSF, Carl Bachman, who said the idea was quite interesting but the proposal was lousy. Very little literature was referenced; no sample interview or questionnaire items were included; the proposal did not make clear how the firms would be selected; there were no propositions that would be tested by the survey that were clear enough to be tested; and the *theory* was too vague to be dignified by that term. But, if I wanted to completely redo it, the deadline was in three weeks.

I cursed Carl Bachman for two and a half weeks and then realized in the third that I should have blessed him. My idea became a full-blown theory because I was forced to be rigorous to meet his criticisms. It is not something one does naturally or even very willingly; thinking through one's ideas in a rigorous way is very hard work. At Michigan, because one sees several others doing this, one is encouraged to undertake the effort. This did not seem to be the case at Pittsburgh, where the working style was far more leisurely. I suspect that a lot of good ideas are not flushed out of the thicket of casual papers and casual conversation in such settings. But program directors at foundations, journal referees, and tough colleagues at other institutions can help overcome the deficits of the setting.

But, even so, the Pittsburgh setting continued to defeat me. I received the NSF grant and started work with confidence in my experience. At Michigan I had directed a large survey of hundreds of inmates and staff, and the questionnaire we created was, I still believe, excellent. The research climate at Michigan was such that I insisted that every question proposed for the survey by the staff and the principal investigators had to be justified with a table showing the expected distribution and the contribution to the theory that would be made. Much blood was even spilled over whether to have five or seven responses for each question. Thus I felt I was well prepared to conduct another large study, this time of several industrial firms in the Pittsburgh area. But there was no Mayer Zald on the project to argue with and no Morris Janowitz or Robert Vinter on the faculty to run it by. I did such things as leave out standard items for comparison with other surveys and had key questions with only three possible choices and as a result much serious skewing of the responses. I redid and expanded the survey when I later went to Wisconsin and made no such mistakes; just as at Michigan, it would have been unthinkable at Wisconsin. At both places (and at my next berth, Stony Brook), such technical aspects of the craft were palpable forces.

Proposition 3 asserts that the best developmental work is done for nonrefereed journals, but it is also true that the results of that work belong in the major journals, not just for career purposes but for the good of the discipline. I have a much cited and reprinted theoretical article in *ASR* that grew out of the NSF grant proposal and the Pittsburgh part of the industrial study (Perrow, 1967). The ideas were worked out in the *Handbook* chapter mentioned earlier, some fugitive conference papers, the grant proposal, and papers at meetings. When it was ready, I worked it over and over for a mainline journal.

There are two important exceptions to proposition 3. First, there are a few people who appear to burst into their career with a stunning work, with, as far as I know (but I could be wrong), few prior nonrefereed developmental pieces. Most of us cannot expect to launch ourselves with something like Peter Blau's *Dynamics of Bureaucracy*, Philip Selznick's "Foundations" article in the 1948 *ASR*, Kai Erickson's *Wayward Puritans*, or, for more contemporary examples, the books and articles of Eric Wright or Theda Skocpol. Luminaries such as these do not need the advice given in this chapter.

Proposition 3 also does not apply with equal force to those who work in well-established paradigms. In sociology these include demography, the status attainment literature in stratification, perhaps criminology, and certainly the reinterpretations of Durkheim and other masters. This work will fit with and be welcomed in the mainline journals. The format is established, the references extensive, the empty spaces of the paradigm clearly revealed, and the referees chosen by the journal editors will share the perspectives. (I am not as clear about paradigms in the "organization sciences," but the main brands of leadership theory, small group theory, research and development management, and contingency theory strike me as having formats, rules, and consensus.) If one is fortunate enough to work in such mainstreams, the major journals will accommodate you. In fact, despite routine disclaimers by each new editor that they will encourage more diversity, the momentum of the field controls editors' choices. The most well-crafted articles are likely to be in the mainstream, which is where most of the people work, including those at the most rigorous settings; the field has grown, producing an abundance of mainstream research; and there has been little expansion of prestigious journals. The consequence, I shall shortly argue, is that the mainstream journals increasingly publish the work of younger people, and the older scholars have established a variety of nonrefereed outlets. But, first, an illustration of proposition 4—that talent will out.

The *American Journal of Sociology* has the reputation of being less conservative than *ASR* and occasionally publishes long, unusual articles. One of the best of the great late 1960s and early 1970s pieces was Maurice Zeitlin's (1974) long essay attacking the article of faith that control of the modern corporation had shifted from owners to managers. As I recall, Zeitlin sent *AJS* a short piece summarizing some recent work that suggested that the Berle and Means hypothesis, now accepted as unquestioned fact, was not true. Instead of being controlled by managers, perhaps a third of the largest corporations were family owned and another large group were closely held by investors. Social class was more important than technocracy. More important, even in firms with management domination, the behavior of managers is not any different than that of owners: They are forced to maximize profits.

In some journals, such as *AJS*, when an article comes in it is first screened by a hired professional, called the managing editor, who works full time at editorial tasks. Then it is passed on to the editor, who is a faculty member doing this work as a professional service (the university generally gives them one or more courses off). The editor picks the referees to receive the submitted article. The managing editor of *AJS* did the first screening. (Managing editors can wield much power, incidentally.) She did not, as I recall, send it to the editor but instead called Zeitlin and said that on such an important topic much more evidence and discussion was required. "Would you allow me 50 to 60 pages in the journal?" Zeitlin asked. "Well, that would be unusual, but it is possible." Zeitlin then spent about six months thoroughly researching the matter and sent in a long manuscript. The editor now came into the picture, sending out the article for reviews. Judging from the response of two of these, they were quite possibly people whom Zeitlin had vigorously attacked. (It is a good idea to send such a piece to at least one of those attacked; but that is a targeted review. Two others more neutral should also review it.) The manuscript was rejected.

Zeitlin called the managing editor, who confessed annoyance about the outcome but counseled patience. The editor's term of office would soon be up, she said, and Zeitlin should submit it again. He did and the new editor thought it was brilliant; for all one knows, the new editor may have sent it out only to people who would be sympathetic to it, and the rest is history. It wrapped up one era in the topic of corporate control and power, and commenced a new one. I think that, even if it had been rejected the second time, it still would have appeared someplace, but probably in a book of essays or an annual edited by a friend of Zeitlin, where it would have had a readership of perhaps 300 to 400 people for the first year or two. Eventually it would have been more widely recognized. An imaginative, controversial work will generally find its audience in overdue time, but one hopes for a speedy hearing though the mainline journals. Recall that proposition 4—virtue is rewarded—is weaker than 5—luck counts for more.

I have not made a study of the matter, but I suspect that many agree with proposition 3, that creative work is more likely to appear outside of the mainline journals. This is a recent development; until perhaps the 1960s the mainline journals were more open to innovative and controversial work. Since then there has been more controversial work, but there has also been more "normal science" that develops established paradigms or reinterprets the classics in minor ways. The number of prestigious journals expanded very little, so they found less room for controversial articles, except in the occasional "special issue." The evidence for this view is that the mainstream journals are filling up with the work of graduate students and new Ph.D.s, mostly working in established paradigms, as perhaps they should, while those interested in more exploratory, unconventional, and reflective work have created new outlets. (Walter Powell tells me that the new outlets are largely a result of the expansion and profitability of commercial monograph publishing houses. See his 1985/1988 *Getting Into Print* for a complete discussion, and implicitly, much valuable advice.) For example, more and more of the people that I think are imaginative are publishing in edited series. One of these, edited by Barry Staw and Larry Cummings, had two articles that won awards and two more have just been nominated. There are at least three such series in organizational theory alone, one of which is published in England. The English one enabled me to place a long essay (Perrow, 1982), with tentative and preliminary ideas about "normal accidents," and get some feedback, and I knew that I was not bound by those formulations in a subsequent book (Perrow, 1984). But I know that unrefereed outlets, or those with only modest refereeing, are bound to publish some low-quality material, and even material of moderate utility will be read by a very small group. The "proceedings of a conference" volume is likely to have the lowest quality and the most restricted readership. But it may be the best way to seriously explore a novel subject. Let me illustrate.

A conference on organizational paradigms gave me the opportunity to explore the work of one of the participants, the economist Oliver Williamson. His 1975 book, *Markets and Hierarchies*, received much attention because it argued that the costs of conducting transactions (contracts, price setting, surveillance, and so on) in the market were greatly reduced if the purchasing firm simply integrated, forward or backward, by absorbing suppliers and distributors or setting up their own facilities. Giant firms were the result of efficiency. The motive, I thought, was not reduced transactions costs but market control and labor control. As the historian Alfred Chandler, in his 1977 classic *The Visible Hand,* also argued for the increased efficiency of large, multidivisional firms over market transactions among small specialized firms, and ignored labor and market control, I included his work in my criticism. While I welcomed the all too rare attention of both an economist and a historian to organizational analysis and the history of organizations, I was worried that the role of class and power was being neglected.

The conference allowed me to explore this work in an essay that I think would never have been printed in a conventional journal (Perrow, 1981). In addition, Williamson would have the opportunity to rebut my critique in print, and one of the conference organizers, Andrew Van de Ven, even asked Chandler to respond, although he was not a part of the conference. Chandler not only produced an important response, but I was able to respond to Chandler in print. (He came back with the last, though certainly not the correct, word.) The result was an extended debate over an issue that is rarely raised, and my critique of both scholars was, to my knowledge, the first extended one ever to appear in the four or so years since the publication of their very important works. (Subsequently, Richard DuBoff, historian, and Edward Herman, economist, published a better critique of Chandler in *Politics and Society,* 1980.)

Two further anomalies that only such unrefereed conference volumes can produce: James March showed up without a paper and told a few stories, but then wrote an important paper on theories of choice for the volume, and William Starbuck gave one of the most thorough and devastating critiques of a paradigm that I have ever seen, that of the Aston researches. It is a critique that would be unlikely to appear in any of the conventional outlets, whether journals or edited volumes (March, 1981; Starbuck, 1981).

One last personal story—it illustrates the flexibility and inflexibility of the mainline journals and suggests one more reason that we "established authors" find it a lot easier to go the unrefereed route (unless we have a paradigmatic formula that the journal embraces). I inadvertently had an article published in the mainline journal *Administrative Science Quarterly* (Perrow, 1983). It was neither submitted nor refereed, something one might consider the best of all possible worlds. This is what happened.

I was talking with Karl Weick, the innovative editor of *ASQ,* and asked him if he knew where I might publish a technical report I had done for an agency on the subject of human factors engineering. (Human factors engineers try to ensure that equipment is designed with the operators and maintenance personnel in mind.) The report, I thought, was far too specialized for *ASQ* and too elementary in its human relations approach to organizations, and I wanted to get it into a journal that had an engineering and policy-oriented audience. I knew that several prestigious leaders of the human factors community disliked the piece, so it was unlikely to be accepted in their mainstream journals. (Mainstream journals are much the same in all disciplines.) Weick said he knew of some journals that might publish my report, that I should send it to him and that he would check it out. He read it and passed it on to the managing editor, who liked it. She, in turn, passed it on to the two associate editors, and, to my surprise, she said *ASQ* decided to publish it, though I should make unspecified changes to make it more appropriate for the journal.

I deleted some elementary organizational theory and gave it a more academic flavor and returned it. Now it went to the manuscript editor, who rolled the paper flat and covered it with what I call *ASQ Asphalt*. No amount of gentle irony, humor, evocative phrasing, even active verb construction, let alone any unscientific hesitancy, was allowed. Even those of you who have had your own journal articles returned, covered by those hen's feet and chicken droppings that pass for editing, would be surprised by the attack upon my piece. Virtually every line was changed. In addition, several sheets accompanied the manuscript listing over 100 comments and queries.

Now some of the editing was very good indeed; the manuscript editor was a demon for logic, clear construction, and would have caught any non sequitur in the Ithaca Metropolitan Area (if there is one). I had to painfully rethink and rewrite some messy passages and simply dropped, in desperation, one of my key points because, although I believed in it, it would not wash after all those chicken droppings. But that you expect and hope you get. The asphalt, however, was too much. I got on the phone with Linda Pike, the excellent managing editor, who apparently shared my dismay, and we spent three hours together putting back a part of the hills, valleys, and green grass that had been there. I then recalled a stimulating piece by Howard Aldrich and a colleague that I had read in manuscript form. To my surprise, when I looked at the *ASQ* published version, very little of the reflective, suggestive, and exploratory virtues of the piece remained. I think the highway department got to it, and even Howard Aldrich, one of two associate editors, succumbed.

The moral? Journals will occasionally take an out-of-the-way piece, but even then the familiar organizational processes of standardization, formalization, and specialization take over. It is a formidable institution, the mainline journal, even with innovative editors, and you are not alone if you find it dehumanizing. But let me repeat: Go to the mainline journal first; the dissertation or early work is most likely to be well thought through and close to established paradigms. The mainline journals may provide devastating critiques, but after revisions (sometimes two or three), publication there may give you the opportunities elsewhere for exploration and for unremarked failures. When one is once again at that stage where something important has been worked out, go back to them. The discipline needs to have that kind of work in visible places, not in obscure yearbooks, conference volumes, or volumes such as this. (Author's note: Of course, Cummings and Frost are taking exception. That is, Perrow's contribution here, as well as those of others in this volume, are likely to receive enhanced visibility because [a] they probably would not have been written without invitation and [b] appearing together in a focused book increases impact.) Even a measure of standardization, formalization, and specialization in format and subject matter is vital for the mainstream of a discipline, and without the mainstream, there can be no tributaries.

Think of two or three years of mainlining it, followed by two or three in unrefereed places, then go back to the mainline journals. If, after that, you want to move about intellectually, as I do, I hope you will be in the setting where you can and will return to the mainstream every few years to tell colleagues what you have been up to. The first six or so years of your career is not a long apprenticeship, and the freedom of the craftsperson that comes after it is extraordinary. Luck is something I cannot help you with, but the growth of the organizational sciences and their interdisciplinary character suggest that you are already blessed with some luck—to be in a field that is not only exciting but expanding at a time when much else in the social sciences is withering under the chilling effect of political orthodoxy.

REFERENCES

Chandler, A. (1977). *The visible hand.* Cambridge, MA: Harvard University Press.

DuBoff, R., & Herman, E. (1980). Alfred Chandler's new business history: A review. *Politics and Society, 10*(1), 87-110.

March, J. (1962). The business firm as a political coalition. *Journal of Politics, 24,* 662-678.

March, J. G. (1981). Decisions in organizations and theories of choice. In A. Van de Ven & W. Joyce (Eds.), *Perspectives on organization design and behavior* (pp. 204-244). New York: Wiley Interscience.

Perrow, C. (1961, January). Organizational prestige: Some functions and dysfunctions. *American Journal of Sociology, 66*(4), 335-341.

Perrow, C. (1964-1965, Winter). Sociological perspective and political pluralism. *Social Research, 31*(4), 411-422.

Perrow, C. (1965). Hospitals: Technology, goals and structure. In J. March (Ed.), *Handbook of organizations* (chap. 22, pp. 910-971). Skokie, IL: Rand McNally.

Perrow, C. (1967, April). A framework for the comparative analysis of organizations. *American Sociological Review,* pp. 194-208.

Perrow, C. (1981). Markets, hierarchies and hegemony: A critique of Chandler and Williamson. In A. Van de Ven & W. Joyce (Eds.), *Perspectives on organization design and behavior* (pp. 371-386, 403-404). New York: Wiley Interscience.

Perrow, C. (1982). Three Mile Island: A normal accident. In D. Dunkerley & G. Salaman (Eds.), *The international yearbook of organization studies* (pp. 1-25). London: Routledge & Kegan Paul.

Perrow, C. (1983). The organizational context of human factors engineering. *Administrative Science Quarterly, 28,* 521-541.

Perrow, C. (1984). *Normal accidents: Living with high risk technologies.* New York: Basic Books.

Powell, W. (1985). *Getting into print.* Chicago: University of Chicago Press. (Paperback edition published 1988)

Starbuck, W. (1981). A trip to the elephants and rattlesnakes in the Garden of Aston. In A. Van de Ven & W. Joyce (Eds.), *Perspectives on organization design and behavior* (pp. 167-198). New York: Wiley Interscience.

Street, D., Vinter, R. D., & Perrow, C. (1966). *Organization for treatment: A comparative study of juvenile correctional institutions.* New York: Free Press.

Zeitlin, M. (1974). Corporate ownership and control: The large corporation and the capitalist class. *American Journal of Sociology, 79*(5), 1073-1117.

13

Some Propositions About
Getting Research Published

BENJAMIN SCHNEIDER

A series of 10 propositions is offered about getting research published in scholarly journals. In brief, the propositions recommend persistence, writing to get read, avoiding data glut, avoiding journalism, publishing in scholarly outlets, planning on delayed gratification, *not* castigating others, worrying about problems but not statistical significance, collecting data prior to writing theory, and writing.

I n this brief chapter, I offer a series of propositions that summarize my experience in trying, with occasional success, to have my research published in refereed scholarly journals. The phrase *occasional success* is true, especially recently. I have about 12-15 papers that I have yet to publish, try as I might; I have never had a paper accepted without relatively extensive revisions; the most laudatory review a paper of mine ever received yielded an outright reject by the editor of the journal (without a third reviewer); and at least five papers I have published were initially rejected by the journal in which the paper eventually appeared. Given this background, let me offer my propositions with commentary.

Proposition 1: Getting published requires persistence.

In addition to good ideas, appropriately accomplished research, and good writing skills (the latter two can be learned), it takes persistence to get published. First, it takes persistence to turn ideas and/or data into a potentially publishable manuscript. A publishable manuscript is one that is straightforward, clear, follows the rules of the game in terms of format, and, in general, answers reviewers' questions before being sent out for review. Can this be accomplished? Yes, if you use your diverse colleagues and friends as critics, have people with perspectives different than your own review successive versions of your efforts, and persist in creating a publishable manuscript by obtaining feedback and by constant rewriting.

The second kind of persistence required is the kind stimulated by a review process that focuses on negative feedback. Negative feedback must be desired and accepted and used as a stimulus to produce a better and more publishable paper. We all claim to want feedback but we mean *positive* feedback. Trying to publish in refereed journals is not a path to positive feedback.

The third kind of persistence required concerns the rejected manuscript. Authors must be committed to publishing a paper prior to sending it out for review, but the commitment has to be to the data and ideas in the paper, not to "getting a pub." When the commitment is to the ideas in the paper, then the paper can be defended where it was rejected and/or, in the light of feedback, it can be changed to be made acceptable. Low commitment to the ideas in a paper will yield low persistence in pursuit of publication.

Proposition 2: Try to get read, not just published.

A career as a scientist is not established by getting published, it is established by getting read. A series of propositions could be written about this one proposition alone, and I will offer a few below, but the important point here is that a long-term career as a researcher/scholar depends upon a certain amount of notoriety ("reputation") and the only way that happens is for others to read your work and cite it. One of the best things that can happen to a career is for a researcher to publish something new and different, controversial, counterintuitive, or, in Davis's (1971) terms, "interesting." Others *read* interesting papers because they tend to be infrequently occurring events.

It is important to note that it is hard to learn to do interesting work but it is relatively easy to avoid uninteresting ideas—just content-analyze the last two years of the articles appearing in the journals that constitute your reference and membership groups. Whatever most people are doing will generally be uninteresting.

The second major strategy for getting read is to do *integrative* work. Integrative papers usually are reviews of literature; at best they are reviews plus theory. Scientists love to read reviews for three reasons. First, reviews cut down on them spending their own time to learn a topic. Second, reviews save them time when looking for references, and, third, reviews facilitate teaching. All of these time-savers allow more time for research and writing, which, of course, are the bases for publishing. A paper that can save another person time will be read. Perhaps more important, graduate students read integrative reviews in preparing for their comprehensive exams, and they *really* remember articles that are helpful.

Proposition 3: Avoid data glut.

Data glut exists when a researcher has collected too much data. Too much data means having more data than can be integrated into a coherent theme in one paper. Data glut is a result of two problems. The first problem is the absence of a conceptual framework or specific question to guide data collection. The second problem exists because researchers never fail to pass up an opportunity to collect as much data as possible; this compulsiveness is due to the fear that no data collection opportunities will ever be available again.

The first issue, failure to articulate a conceptual framework or a specific question, is the major shortcoming of the contemporary journal literature in OB. OB seems to be going through an atheoretical phase in which the theoretical frameworks of the 1960s and 1970s (expectancy theory, contingency theory, job characteristics theory) have yet to be replaced by theories of the 1980s and 1990s as coherent frameworks for research.

The absence of coherent models requiring elaboration and testing makes it difficult to know precisely what to study, so the tendency is to try and study many (all?) potentially interesting issues. Because the presence of mark-sense answer sheets and computers facilitates the collection and analysis of too much data, data glut is certainly a product of technology. But technology alone cannot explain the phenomenon; poor conceptual work and fear of not having data are the best explanations.

Fear is, of course, a great motivator. Here *fear* is being used synonymously with *anxiety*. The fear is that a present data collection opportunity will be the last one. This particular fear can lead to disastrous glut even when a conceptual framework has been developed. Thus data are collected to test a framework/model/hypothesis *and* data are collected because they might be "interesting."

However it happens, data glut impedes publication in two ways. First, once data are collected, the compulsive researcher (Are there any other kinds of researchers?) proceeds to analyze them. This, of course, takes time, especially when the analyses turn up "interesting" findings and an attempt is made to integrate them into a coherent theme. The second inhibition comes from the production of a lengthy, convoluted manuscript. Usually a manuscript over 25 pages total length including tables, figures, and references will have difficulty getting published. Data glut produces tables without end, which, in turn, leads to confusion on the part of reviewers. The confusion arises because all tables need to be explained and reviewers are unable to keep more than a few relevant themes in their heads at any one time; they will think that your paper "lacks coherence," "fails to be thematic," "lacks thrust," "confounds the reader," and so on simply because the paper tries to do too much. An article should inform readers by doing the hard work *for* the reader; the writer's responsibility is to be parsimonious, to simplify complexity. (*Parsimonious* means cheap, but scientists use it to mean straightforward, i.e., without extraneous adornment.)

Proposition 4: Scholarly journals publish research and theory, not journalism.

If one desires a career as a researcher/scholar, one publishes in journals that are acknowledged outlets for research and theory. Journalism fails to meet standards of reproducibility, public verifiability, reliability, and so on—the current standards for research in our positivist tradition. Research that deviates from the positivist tradition will have to defend itself or it will be considered journalism.

A number of strategies exist for the publication of case studies and/or nonquantitative research efforts that will keep them from being rejected as journalism. First, the paper needs to acknowledge relevant conceptual models that already exist—the paper needs to show how the new framework *contributes* to or *enhances* the understanding of, rather than is *clearly superior* to, older models. A paper need not *alienate* a reviewer for it to be interesting; a paper can *educate* a reviewer by framing issues in ways that are understandable to him or her and that illuminate previously hidden or unexplored phenomena. Needless to say, the new framework needs to indicate how it responds to potential critiques and it must be logically tight.

The second technique for avoiding the "journalism" critique is to conduct the research in a systematic fashion, using multiple sources and kinds of data to test an idea or to make a particular point. A good example of this technique can be found in Levine's (1980) analysis of Bernstein and Woodward's research/

journalism for *All the President's Men*. Levine makes clear the journalism-science continuum and shows, dramatically, how the standards/guidelines of the two can contribute to superior work in both domains.

My perception is that high-quality nonquantitative research will be relatively easy to publish in the future, with the emphasis on high quality. Here, *high quality* means conceptually tight writing, on a topic that is shown to be important, with data collected in systematic ways using multiple data sources (see Morgan, 1983, for useful extended discussions of these issues).

Proposition 5: Publications in scholarly journals count more.

In addition to the journalism-research continuum regarding kinds of research, there is another important continuum, research-practice. People in OB who want to be known as researchers/scholars need to publish in scholarly outlets. They can publish in practitioner journals also, but their work needs to pass through the scholarly gatekeepers (reviewers) before the researcher will be taken seriously in the field. This comment also applies, incidentally, to publication in edited volumes; they count most *after* one establishes a reputation as a scholar.

Because organizational researchers see themselves as conducting relevant research, the urge to publish in practitioner outlets is understandable but, early in a career, it is best suppressed. First, early in a career, the journal style of writing needs to be learned and anything that detracts from learning this skill is detrimental. Writing for practitioners not only takes time away from learning how to write in journal style but it can lead to negative transfer, making it even *more* difficult to develop a style acceptable to scholarly outlets.

Especially in business schools, where a combination of consulting opportunities and teaching MBAs exists, the urge to publish for the practitioner must be very great indeed. However, long term, the research career will be grounded in scholarly publication, not "knocking out" pablum for the practitioner audience. Perhaps the recent popularity of respectable outlets for schizophrenic articles (articles having both some scholarly and some practitioner merit) makes this proposition less relevant today, but it still merits consideration for the person interested in a career as a scholar.

Proposition 6: Plan to delay gratification, but plan to get it.

A very difficult aspect of the publishing game is the delay of gratification. The typical length of time for a research project, from idea to actual publication, is probably a minimum of three years with five years being the norm. With rejection rates in the more prestigious journals at 80% or more, this means that many projects may never yield gratification. There are three rules for eventually attaining gratification. First, always be working on more than one interesting project. Second, always have different interesting projects in different stages of completion. Third, do your projects with interesting methods and in logical stages.

Working on more than one project makes life interesting and also operationalizes the idea that gratification of the desire to publish requires something to publish! What this means is that if one project is a disaster there are other projects that can take its place. Disasters, unfortunately, come in many forms, most of which are not recorded in any books or articles. In fact, the first thing a researcher learns is that research is not actually accomplished in the way the journal articles imply: neat, straightforward, easy, and no sweat.

I tried to publish a paper once in which I described losing over 800 completed questionnaires on a bus from New York to Maryland; I had to argue for retaining this fact in the paper (Schneider, Parkington, & Buxton, 1980). In 1966 I began the data collection for my dissertation and finished that project in 1974. A set of criterion data that I was promised for use in a project never arrived so all I had was the predictor data! A CEO who was my sponsor in a company was fired just before I turned in my report; his successor would have nothing to do with anything my sponsor had touched so a year's diagnosis to be used as background to a major project resulted in nothing to publish.

The second rule—have projects in different stages of development—is particularly important for field researchers; one must capitalize on good opportunities when they appear (but remember data glut). I have found that it takes a minimum of about two years to collect and prepare a good set of data regardless of whether it is a survey, an interview, or an observational project. Given this time problem, if you are not working on periodically starting projects, then you run out of good data quickly.

It can be argued, of course, that it is silly to start a new project until you have answers to the questions you asked in the prior project. This is true, however, only if in the prior project all of the interesting questions were asked. My experience has been that simply getting a project started raises interesting questions; the *only* alternative is to find another site to pursue the answers. What constitutes programmatic research is the pursuit of asking and answering interesting questions through a series of integrated and overlapping research efforts. Programmatic research is accomplished relatively quickly by field researchers only if their research program is active in starting (and, of course, finishing) new projects.

A third rule to follow to enhance the probability of gratification is to design research so that it can be accomplished in stages. Because field research projects take so long to complete, it could be years before anything publishable is accomplished unless projects early in the career are designed to yield interesting findings/insights along the way. In other words, while each research project should have a coherent major goal, intermediate stages in, for example, a longitudinal effort may constitute meaningful contributions to the literature. In addition, the methods developed to achieve the goal may be novel—and publishable. Each project, then, offers numerous opportunities for creativity on the way to an "ultimate" research goal, and those creative methods or intermediate stages can be prepared for publication.

I have found this not only to be a pragmatic process but, much more important, the insights gained from pushing myself to develop and use new techniques and methods have yielded findings that were far more important to my way of thinking than the presumed "ultimate" goal of the project. Of course, frequently the "ultimate" goal turns out to be one of those disasters referred to earlier. In that case, a great deal of gratification can be obtained from having pushed to try a new method and/or to design a project in various stages to answer some other meaningful questions.

> *Proposition 7: Write what you think and what you did,*
> *not what someone else failed to do.*

Most researchers set out to prove how right they are, and that is bad enough. However, in addition to trying to prove they are correct, they set up a "straw person" they can knock down. Articles that begin by speaking about previous failures of theory, method, or interpretation in the literature turn readers and reviewers off. Conversely, papers that propose interesting ways to answer interesting questions by building on prior literature, and papers that show how they will help resolve previously divergent or competing hypotheses, will find a receptive audience.

It is very clear that the easiest task for a researcher is to critique other research. In fact, one of my favorite hates is the thought that the reviewer of a research paper of mine is someone who has not tried to publish data-based papers. Until a person has tried to do data-based research, he or she really has no appreciation of the issues. My worst nightmare is to submit a paper where $N = 23$ organizations, and the reviewer's critique of the paper emphasizes the small sample size! The point is that research is very easy to criticize and authors of papers submitted for publication are appropriately upset at rejections based on "picky" issues.

Those same aspiring authors, however, can write the pickiest critiques of already published research to substantiate their own theory and/or project. But this reversal of positions does not make criticism more appropriate, especially when the best research is forward looking. In short, then, this proposition urges the writer to allow the reader to draw conclusions about how wonderful the paper is.

Proposition 8: Nonsignificant results are publishable if the research is significant.

Research carried out carefully that fails to yield expected findings is publishable. The secret here is in the word *carefully*. Careful research has a sound theoretical and/or logical rationale, hypotheses that conform to the theory and are logically deduced, or an approach that *generates* sound theory that is logically deduced, and appropriate methodology and data analysis. Failure to support hypotheses when these standards are met is publishable.

What is not typically publishable is research that is nonsignificant in many ways: It attempts to answer minor questions about theoretically or practically unimportant issues, it uses questionable methodology (methods not appropriate for the question), and/or the data analyses are weak. In other words, *statistical* nonsignificance is only significant when the research effort itself is insignificant.

Examples of this kind of research are numerous and, unfortunately, they do get published (others say the same things about my research). Generally, research of the response-response sort (method bias) that fails to test *competing* hypotheses (i.e., the correlation between X and Y under condition A will be significantly greater than under condition B) is not worth publishing even *if* some kind of statistical significance is achieved.

Carefully accomplished research that fails to support commonly held assumptions about significant issues is publishable. Do significant research and do not worry about statistical significance.

Proposition 9: Write theory to become famous; collect data first.

The most prominent people in the field are known for theory; data collectors are not so prominent. Theory captivates and promotes research activity but that activity is rarely if ever as noteworthy as the original theory. Even if shown to be incorrect, theory prevails over data in terms of impact because it is usually parsimonious and it promotes research activity.

Probably the clearest example of this phenomenon in OB is Herzberg and his colleagues' (Herzberg, Mausner, & Snyderman, 1959) proposals regarding satisfiers and dissatisfiers—the infamous two-factor theory. Essentially every study of the two-factor formulation showed it to be in error (Locke, 1976). However, practices and principles following from the theory, especially those connected with job enrichment, have yielded both practical (Ford, 1973) and theoretical (Hackman & Oldham, 1976) benefits.

I have been curious about the centrality of theories to the field especially because it is not only academicians who react favorably to them. People in business and industry, especially executives at the top of organizations, frequently seem to "buy in" to behavioral science based on an idea, a philosophy, or a theory. Certainly the popularity of Peters and Waterman's (1982) journalistic accounts of some apparently successful companies suggests that the adoption (and creation) of behavioral science approaches to corporate excellence is based more on philosophy/values and less on data.

Theories are useful because they help to simplify the world around us. In contrast, most data are messy, nonprecise, and, in short, complex. The nuances of mean differences or differential predictability, on the one hand, or the calculation of "passion ratios" (Pettigrew, 1973), on the other hand, are lost in the grand sweep of theory.

Then why collect data? For two reasons: First, the discipline requires perspective and the testing of competing ideas; research data provide these. Second, and perhaps more important, most theoreticians go through a data collection phase and that phase sharpens their thinking. My impression is, then, that the operationalization of ideas—the conversion of ideas into procedures for testing them—is one of the most important steps in the development of any scholar. Simply trying to design ways of answering questions has the impact of clarifying the questions being asked.

For example, McGregor (1960) operationalized his constructs as a practicing manager; Katz and Kahn (1978) conducted numerous research efforts long before (e.g., Katz & Kahn, 1952) even their first book (Katz & Kahn, 1966); Likert (1932) developed the most frequently used attitude scale almost 30 years prior to his major theoretical works (Likert, 1961); and so on. It appears to be true that, while theoreticians become famous, a step along the way is data collection and analysis.

Proposition 10: Write up what you've been doing and thinking.

The previous propositions have some overlapping themes. The most persistent one is to keep working at *doing* research; now I add to keep working at *writing* it. The most fundamental proposition, then, is that, in the absence of articles being submitted for publication, no one will get published. If researchers fail to share their ideas and findings with a wide audience, they cheat that audience of those ideas and findings.

Clearly it is difficult to write, and for two reasons. First, there is the skill issue. Writing journalese takes a certain skill. Second is the issue of rejection. The chances are that what gets written will be rejected and, because what you write is *you*, you, and not the paper, are rejected. But you must persist. And to get published, you must write.

Many authors find that they are most productive in their writing first thing in the morning. They claim they are "fresh," "full of ideas," and so on, only in the morning. A few writers deviate from this norm and I am one of them. I find that I am *too* fresh, *too* full of ideas in the morning to concentrate on writing; I am able to focus, to concentrate, only later in the afternoon or early evening when I am somewhat less energetic and can sit for extended periods.

I also find that the best stimulus for getting a paper written is to publicly set a goal. Sometimes I fail to make the precise goal (as Cummings and Frost will attest!) but, without it, too many other "emergencies" arise. Each emergency prevents the establishment of blocks of time for writing, and I can usually only write in a minimum block of two hours. My point here is that writing takes time and making the time requires commitment to *making the time.* Writing only happens by doing it and it is the necessary (although not sufficient) condition for getting published.

The most basic sufficient condition for getting published is to submit what is written. My impression is that numerous writers fail to submit papers they have written or tried to write. They do this because the paper fails to meet their own very high standards for what a publication should be. Generally speaking, there are two kinds of activities authors should not be trusted to do: criticize their own work and proofread their own work.

It is absolutely essential for writers to have colleagues/friends/spouses they can trust to provide them with feedback/suggestions. Colleagues are better than friends and spouses because they are in the same boat (although some colleagues are, of course, also friends and/or spouses). In any case, the rule here is not only to write but to seek feedback, and then to rewrite—and eventually to submit what is written.

CONCLUSION

Getting published is a very personal endeavor and a unique challenge. Delay of gratification is very long, you lay yourself open before your peers, you "fail" as often as you succeed, you have to play at least somewhat by other people's rules, and the payback is nebulous. Most people never publish because of these horrors and uncertainties.

What I have tried to share with the reader are some personal learnings and observations. Surely there are other processes that have yielded some success but these capture the ones with which I am familiar. They were not conscious strategies, although they certainly read as if they were; I wish I were that clever! Like a written report of research, however, I've tried to share what *has* been learned, not everything I had to do to learn it.

REFERENCES

Davis, M. S. (1971). That's interesting: Towards a phenomenology of sociology and a sociology of phenomenology. *Philosophy of Social Science, 1,* 309-344.

Ford, R. N. (1973, January-February). Job enrichment lessons from AT&T. *Harvard Business Review,* pp. 96-106.

Hackman, J. R., & Oldham, G. R. (1976). Motivation through the design of work: Test of a theory. *Organizational Behavior and Human Performance, 16,* 250-279.

Herzberg, F., Mausner, B., & Snyderman, B. (1959). *The motivation to work* (2nd ed.). New York: Wiley.

Katz, D., & Kahn, R. L. (1952). Some recent findings in human relations research in industry. In G. W. Swanson, T. M. Newcomb, & E. L. Hanley (Eds.), *Readings in social psychology* (2nd ed.). New York: Holt, Rinehart & Winston.

Katz, D., & Kahn, R. L. (1966). *The social psychology of organizations.* New York: Wiley.

Katz, D., & Kahn, R. L. (1978). *The social psychology of organizations* (2nd ed.). New York: Wiley.

Levine, M. (1980). Investigative reporting as a research method: An analysis of Bernstein and Woodward's *All the President's Men. American Psychologist, 35,* 626-638.

Likert, R. (1932). A technique for the measurement of attitudes. *Archives of Psychology,* 140.

Likert, R. (1961). *New patterns in management.* New York: McGraw-Hill.

Locke, E. A. (1976). The nature and consequences of job satisfaction. In M. D. Dunnette (Ed.), *Handbook of industrial and organizational psychology.* Chicago: Rand McNally.

McGregor, D. M. (1960). *The human side of enterprise.* New York: McGraw-Hill.

Morgan, G. (Ed.). (1983). *Beyond method: Strategies for social research.* Beverly Hills, CA: Sage.

Peters, T. J., & Waterman, R. H. (1982). *In search of excellence.* New York: Harper & Row.

Pettigrew, A. M. (1973). *The politics of organizational decision-making.* London: Tavistock.

Schneider, B., Parkington, J. J., & Buxton, V. M. (1980). Employee and customer perceptions of service in banks. *Administrative Science Quarterly, 25,* 252-267.

14

The Grand Scrivener
Text and Commentary

MICHAEL PACANOWSKY

MARY S. STRINE

Dear Reader, I am growing tired. You probably wouldn't know it to look at me. Colleagues say I haven't changed in years. A little more portly, it is true; but my increasing girth suggests success, not slovenliness. And yes, my hair is gray. But I try to keep myself up. I wear tailored suits. During faculty colloquia, I smile knowingly often enough that colleagues and students presume I remain intellectually alive. I chair convention programs and serve on university-wide ad hoc committees. I cultivate the characterization "distinguished."

Fagin, that ingrate, he's the one who's wearing me out. He keeps coming at me. All that computer printout. Tables, correlations, that damned italicized $p <$. He is relentless. And to think that it was I who brought him on board. It was I who raised him from an intern, a mere apprentice, to his current position of stature, made him a virtual equal.

Do I appear to rave, gentle reader? I apologize. I am prone to it these days. It's hard to maintain appearances when under attack. Fagin has me under siege! I may ghostwrite a denunciatory review of one of his articles. And I may make

227

sardonic comments about gray beards and young turks. But in my daily inter-course with him, I maintain an air of personal warmth and professional dis-interest. How I wish to have it out with him—in public! To his face! "Take your methodological sophistication and shove it!" There would be talk in the halls for weeks. I cannot do it. Really.

And still, he comes, lean and hungry, resolute, ready to match my every ex-pansive thought with a precise measure. Did I say "match"? No. He means to dismiss.

And so he comes. Arguing for more typewriters, upgraded computer capa-bility, more journal space. Occasionally, I rally. I publish a lamentation on the unfulfilled promise of the most recent methodological tool ("so-what measure-ment," as I call it under my breath) and then I make a new stand for productive conceptualizing. In my heart of hearts, though, I fear this is but a retrograde action. Fagin's getting the readers these days. He will devour me. Oh, so tired.

My office is like a medieval court. Here I sit, omnipotent, even if feudal. I sit at the far end of a great hall. My desk, like a throne, is raised up on a dais. Behind me are my books and journals, my trusted advisers and ministers. Ringed before me are 36 typewriters, courtiers who respond sharply to my bidding.

Change metaphors. I go at my work like a chess grandmaster giving a public exhibition of his prowess. I attack the first typewriter. Then the second, then the third. Over the years, I've developed some 30-odd opening moves. Then back to the first. I assay the development. Respond. Then on to the second. Round and round. In a good month, I can complete twenty articles, six book reviews, and ten convention papers. I'll admit it, competition with Fagin has increased my productivity.

There are no windows in my office. I do not look out on the world. I look before me, at my work in progress. And at the door at the far end of the hall. The door that leads to . . .

. . . to Fagin's office. Fagin's office is a mirror image of mine. A hall. Thirty-six typewriters. A dais. A desk. Behind Fagin, though, sits not a bookshelf with books but his enshrined adviser, a Univac 8000. (It wasn't always this way.)

I sense, gentle reader, that you are perhaps confused, perhaps amused. Do not patronize me! This business with Fagin is important, crucial even. Not just for me, but for the field. Don't you see the implications?

No, of course not. Of course not. You are, through no fault of your own, among the ignoranti. Let me enlighten you.

You see, dear reader, Fagin and I write the articles for *Administrative Science Quarterly*. All of them.

Don't be fooled by all those different authors' names. Fagin and I ghostwrite everything in *ASQ*. It's not really so implausible once you think about it. Haven't you ever noticed the unity of style? The fleshlessness and bloodlessness of authorial voice? Do you think that if one Shakespeare could write the immortal words of a Hamlet, a Lear, and an Antony, that Fagin and I could not write the admittedly perishable words of a March, a Lundberg, and a Weick? And consider further, if you will, when a March or Lundberg or Weick awakens some morning to find that an article has been published in *ASQ* with his name appended, which of them in this publish-or-perish world of academe will bother to deny their "authorship"? No, dear reader, in today's world, appearances are mere surfaces. The deep structure of academic publishing is not what it appears. You doubt me? Ha-ha. The innocence of modernity.

Why do we do it—Fagin and I? I can't speak for Fagin, although I confess that I suspect him of motives mean and low. Self-serving ambition. Compensation for lack of intellectual breadth. Some quirky response to a kind word bestowed on him by a high school math teacher.

Why do I do it? No, dear reader, I do not do it out of love. Nor is it just a "job." More compulsive than that. I have it in my blood to write articles, the way a spider has it in hers to spin a web.

Of course, that's the problem. I have tired blood.

Now I look back on those first 14 years without Fagin, when I did it all by myself. How easy it was then. Words were the masters. Oh, you might find a number or two here and there; I could tabulate with the best of them. But my voice was clear and unencumbered. I could write titles without colons or adjectivized nouns. Once I even started an article with so straightforward a sentence as "This is a study of how some 110 persons made a very important decision." How I long for those days again. But they are gone. Then it was a clean slate. Now there's too much history. We may erase the slate and banish the surface chalk, but Fagin and I have written the same way for so long now that the grooves are etched too deeply.

I can still remember that fateful day, back in '68, when Fagin came into my office and announced that he was about to become my son-in-law. His hair was short, his tie skinny, and he wore black plastic-rimmed glasses. He was so presumptuous and righteous, he never even realized how pathetic he looked. But he had "WAVE OF THE FUTURE" written all over him.

For his wedding present, I gave him two typewriters, 18 pages of journal space (all of which he devoted to tables), and, in a gesture of magnanimity that I rue to this day, I agreed to switch to the APA editorial style.

In my naïveté, I thought we could work together. Ha-ha. Here was my fantasy. I would continue to write thoughtfully, expansively. Fagin would cull the most promising of my ideas, and flesh them out with his own brand of precision.

And so it was, for a while. (I gave him more typewriters, gave him a computer account. He became fashionable. Let his hair grow stylishly long. Took to wearing wire-rims. People clustered around him at conventions.) But then, and this was the turning point, Fagin discovered that he had written his own critical mass of articles, and he no longer needed mine. He could "crank out" or "grind out" (those are his words, rightfully denotative) articles that were born not in the grandeur of past thought but in the inadequacy of past method.

We began to quarrel over resources, over status. He pointed to his own productivity and insisted on more typewriters. I struggled to maintain a suitable hierarchy. In 1972 I gave him fourteen more typewriters. In 1974 I gave him another dozen. In 1976 eight more, we were even then, so I started another journal with the editorial policy of not publishing empirical studies (no numbers, no Fagin—it was a transparent ploy). But he kept coming at me. No longer brash and aggressive, he is now insidiously persistent. No longer WAVE OF THE FUTURE, he now owns the present.

My son-in-law. So you see, dear reader, that while our relationship hasn't been exactly incestuous, it has been depressingly familial.

I know what you're thinking. And yes, it has dawned on me that I am a kind of Dr. Frankenstein who has created his own monster. Fagin's numbers, his precision, his production—all fit so well with my writings on efficiency, rationality, science.

Haven't you noticed, though? I am now sneaking in occasional articles on the side wisdom of waste, the logic of irrationality, the truth of art. Upsets the old apple cart, if you get my drift. At the least, these articles enrage and divert Fagin. They suit my present purposes.

Let me confess, dear reader, that there are times when in my heart of hearts I harbor the suspicion that I am not so much tired as I am bored. Perhaps what divides me from Fagin is neither so monumental nor of such consequence as I make it out to be. We both write with such certainty, with such an abstracted sense of topic, and with so muted an authorial voice. Neither of us has use for individuality or particularity, or for pleasure or pain. Still we magnify envies and petty jealousies. We stake out theoretical positions and glare across the line at one another, ignoring all the landscape to our sides and backs. We read each other's writings, and variously ignore, react, or elaborate, but we *read* each *other's* writings.

Sometimes I think that the problem is not that our conflicts are so major, but that we don't really mix it up enough.

Here comes Fagin again, waving his copy of the last issue of *Administrative Science Quarterly.* I can tell by his grin that he wants to negotiate again. What does he want now? How will he threaten our so perilously maintained parity?

Oh, gentle reader, when Fagin is my age, will he have grown tired? Bored?

* * *

How did the Grand Scrivener's plight arise? Why does he feel oppressively caught between the compulsion to publish continuously and the woeful enervation that such repetitive, formulaic publication engenders? What alternative, more satisfying approaches to the work of academic publication might he (and we) consider?

As we begin our task of analyzing organizational science journals, "The Grand Scrivener's" story gives us pause. Embedded within its hyperbolic humor are rich kernels of insight—distillations, if you will—of our more diffused and random intuitions about the estimable organizational science publication network. And so, we have chosen to use the Grand Scrivener's plaintive self-disclosure as our text, drawing from it certain interpretive hypotheses, highlighting and elaborating on the issues that it raises concerning the relationship between journal publications and modern academic professions.

Academic professions are linked to journal publications in mutually sustaining ways. In her book *The Rise of Professionalism* (1977) M. S. Larson contends that, despite manifest dissimilarities, all professions rely on a core of common strategies for establishing and maintaining their respective places within modern industrial society: the production of a distinctive exchange "commodity," standardization of professional services, and "the standardized and centralized [re]production of professional producers" (pp. 14-17). In exchange for the privileges of autonomy and prestige, academic professions produce knowledge as their principal "commodity," typically in such forms as research, scholarly inquiry, and expert opinion. Further, academic professions "standardize" the terms of their own knowledge claims by internally regulating what counts as valid research and, most critically, which discourses are to receive professional legitimation through scholarly publication. Finally, in the interest of disciplinary self-perpetuation, academic professions provide formal training and education in proper research techniques and forms of scholarly representation for future academic professional "[re]producers" (Larson, 1977, p. x). For the organizational sciences, as for modern academic professions generally, scholarly journals provide the primary discursive space or material setting where the crucial production and exchange of disciplinary "commodities" occur.

Viewed in these terms, our Grand Scrivener clearly exemplified a successful modern academician. His public status as a "distinguished" professional as well as his private feelings of insecurity and frustration are a direct outgrowth of his function within the academic "commodities" exchange. Notably, his career follows a trajectory that closely parallels shifting research emphases within the organizational sciences.

The Grand Scrivener recalls nostalgically the years before Fagin's arrival: "Words were the masters [then] . . . my voice was clear and unencumbered. I could write titles without colons or adjectivized nouns. Once I even started an article with so straightforward a sentence as 'This is a study of how some 110 persons made a very important decision.' " Similarly, during the first decade or so following World War II, organizational science publications featured individualized studies, the strength of which resided in the particular researcher's verbal skills and insight. With Fagin's emergence on the professional scene—an entrance at first heralded and nurtured by our Grand Scrivener as "the wave of the future" and a fitting complement to his own more expansive and rationalistic mode of inquiry—the Grand Scrivener was forced to compete furiously for journal space with the inexhaustible outpouring of Fagin's precise empirical measurements. Similarly, during the period from the late 1960s to the mid-1970s, positivistic or functionalistic research grew to dominate organizational science publications, claiming with hegemonic force the supremacy of logical empiricism and the authority of statistical methods. And now the Grand Scrivener reflects wearily on pointless intradisciplinary competitiveness with its proliferation of uninspired research as a condition that he himself has unwittingly invited: "It has dawned on me that I am a kind of Dr. Frankenstein who has created his own monster. Fagin's numbers, his precision, his production—all fit so well with my writings on efficiency, rationality, science." (He even admits that, as a desperate enlivening maneuver, he is "now sneaking in occasional articles on the wisdom of waste, the logic of irrationality, the truth of art.") Today, perhaps no other social study is more agonizingly self-reflexive or receptive to alternative, nontraditional methods of scholarship than are the organizational sciences.[1]

Increasing tolerance for a variable range of qualitative methodologies and the frequent appearance of such organizational metaphors as "tribes," "garbage cans," and "cultures" within recent journal publications have raised two questions of critical disciplinary concern: What types of nontraditional, interpretive studies should count as valid organizational science research? And how might these nontraditional approaches to organizational science be most appropriately represented in writing? (At this juncture, the vision of our Grand Scrivener and his number-wielding alter ego enthroned in their respective windowless offices, making deft unproblematic leaps from data—whether books or tables—to claims, fades into a shadowy blur.) If academic journals are to maintain their disciplinary gatekeeping function, some clear, if flexible, standards for assessing the quality of nontraditional scholarly discourses are essential (Weick, 1983).

The first question concerning what types of inquiry will count as valid organizational research has been expansively addressed by Ian Mitroff and Ralph Kilmann in *Methodological Approaches to Social Science* (1978). Using a Jungian framework, they propose a schema for charting four dominant types of scientific research based on the researcher's characteristic mode of appropriating the data and typical manner of decision making: the analytic scientist (sensing-feeling), the conceptual theorist (intuiting-thinking), the conceptual humanist (intuiting-feeling), and the particular humanist (sensing-feeling). Each of the four types entails a particular style and logic of inquiry as well as preferred research norms (ideology) that distinguishes it from the other three types. Thus the analytic scientist (Fagin in "The Grand Scrivener's" story) is the logical empiricist driven to embrace ever more sophisticated methodologies and, with scientific detachment, to let the normally quantified data "speak for themselves." The conceptual theorist (our Grand Scrivener himself) is concerned primarily with creating and rearranging schema, using data anecdotally and dispassionately to devise ever new and interesting category schemes, metaphors, and perspectives. The conceptual humanist, while not averse to conceptual theorizing, is motivated more by personal involvement and feeling, functioning as an engaged witness rather than as a passive observer during the research process. Finally, the particular humanist, relying principally on the authority of personal experience, aims for a detailed elaboration of the unique and singular through imaginative apprehension and empathic involvement in organizational life. Mitroff and Kilmann argue that a fully integrated science should accommodate and maximize the perspectives and insights of the less conventional conceptual humanist and particular humanist as well as the more traditional analytic scientist and conceptual theorist.

The second question concerning the selection of appropriate scholarly forms of discourse for representing interpretive research centers on the irreducible "gap" separating understanding and explanation in any interpretive endeavor. James Clifford (1983) describes this problem as it pertains to ethnographic field studies:

> If ethnography produces cultural interpretation through intense research experiences, how is unruly experience transformed into an authoritative account? How, precisely, is a garrulous, overdetermined, cross cultural encounter shot through with power relations and personal cross purposes circumscribed as an adequate version of a more or less discrete "other world" composed by an individual author? (p. 120)

Because, as Clifford compellingly argues, participant-observation research must always negotiate the continuous and subtle interplay between interpretive understanding and interpretive explanation, the form of discourse chosen to communicate research findings invariably becomes a matter of strategic choice. Notably, the form of discourse chosen is, as with professional writings in general, likely to be influenced as much by the professional audience for whom the researcher writes and by the constraints on professional publication as by the desire for accuracy in capturing interpretive understanding and insight (Clifford, 1983, p. 127; see also Culler, 1982, where a similar argument is applied to the process of literary interpretation).

Concentration on alternative ways of approaching organizational studies and on matters of strategic choice that shape professional journal publications brings us to our final, perhaps most important, observation drawn from "The Grand Scrivener's" story. The Grand Scrivener confides that his fundamental problem is boredom. The causes of his boredom are rooted deeply in the kind of professional reality that he inhabits, a reality that he and Fagin mutually and interactively sustain. We note that the dimensions of his professional world seem emotionally truncated, narrowly abstract. Feelings of personal involvement in the research and writing process have no apparent place within the Grand Scrivener's professional life. He acknowledges the absence of personal engagement, observing: "We [he and Fagin] both write with such certainty, with such an abstracted sense of topic, and with so muted an authorial voice. Neither of us has use for individuality or particularity, or for pleasure or pain." No doubt, personal reserve in styles of writing is in part attributable to the fact that he and Fagin are the principal, if hostile, audiences for which each other writes. The Grand Scrivener characterizes his own and Fagin's professional stances as baldly adversarial yet obsessively interdependent: "We stake out theoretical positions and glare across the line at one another, ignoring all the landscape to our sides and backs. We read each other's writings, and variously ignore, react, or elaborate, but we *read* each *other's* writings." However, despite the systemic infighting, professional rivalry, and overproduction of uncommitted research characteristic of the Grand Scrivener's professional world, his final musings "that the problem is not that our conflicts are so major, but that we don't mix it up enough" suggests that his professional life could be other than it is.

To grasp something of what "mixing it up" professionally might entail and to understand the significant difference that "mixing it up" as a mode of professional interaction might make for the work of academic research and publication, we refer to an evocative distinction between networks and communities depicted by Robert Bly in *The American Poetry Review* (1974). Bly grounds his discussion in the Jungian modalities of thinking, feeling, intuiting, and sensing as "four ways of grasping the world." Bly explains that whichever mode or way is weakest or least developed in a person serves as a channel linking that person to the rest of humanity. Failure to develop the weakest mode or allowing it to atrophy strains and, at times, severs that link, causing personal feelings of isolation and alienation. Networks exclusively comprise persons who share the same dominant mode or function. In modern industrial societies where weak modes are undervalued or ignored, networks flourish. Communities, on the other hand, unite persons of varying strengths and weaknesses, simultaneously providing nurturance for the development of weak modes and drawing back healing vitality from the dominant modes of community members. Persons in networks share similar freedoms. Persons in communities share similar duties and restraints that bind them together (Bly, 1974, p. 20).

Clearly, the Grand Scrivener's professional world and the modern academic professions generally are modeled on the network. Persons of like intellectual strengths and interests work together to advance and refine particular areas of knowledge, generating ever-new bodies of discourse in relative freedom from accountability to and interaction with the nonprofessional community. Professional journals mirror this discursive specialization and rarefaction. Our Grand Scrivener's enervation and boredom magnify some of the negative consequences of academic professional networking.

"Mixing it up" would require the adoption of a modified community model of professional life, one in which the research questions asked, the methods used in answering them, and the forms of scholarly discourse that research findings take would be fully informed by and interactive with larger community concerns. Academic professionals, such as our Grand Scrivener, if more directly answerable to community constraints, might also benefit from the personal enrichment that community affiliation provides. As Bly observes, communities are self-sustaining, while networks require nourishment from the outside (Bly, 1974, p. 20; see also Said, 1982).

NOTE

1. For a sampling of this self-conscious consideration of scholarly alternatives, see especially Weick (1979); the entire issue of *Administrative Science Quarterly* (December 1979), reprinted and updated as *Qualitative Methodology* (1983, edited by Van Maanen); and the entire issue of *Western Journal of Speech Communication* 46 (Spring 1982).

REFERENCES

Bly, R. (1974). The network and the community. *The American Poetry Review, 3*(1), 19-21.

Clifford, J. (1983, Spring). On ethnographic authority. *Representations, 1*(2), 120.

Culler, J. (1982). Stories of reading. In J. Culler, *On deconstruction* (pp. 64-83). Ithaca, NY: Cornell University Press.

Larson, M. S. (1977). *The rise of professionalism: A sociological analysis.* Berkeley: University of California Press.

Mitroff, I. I., & Kilmann, R. H. (1978). *Methodological approaches to social science.* San Francisco: Jossey-Bass.

Said, E. W. (1982, September). Opponents, audiences, constituencies, and community. *Critical Inquiry, 9,* 1-26.

Van Maanen, J. (Ed.). (1983). *Qualitative methodology.* Beverly Hills, CA: Sage.

Weick, K. E. (1979). *The social psychology of organizing* (2nd ed.). Reading, MA: Addison-Wesley.

Weick, K. E. (1983). Organizational communication: Toward a research agenda. In L. L. Putnam & M. E. Pacanowsky (Eds.), *Communication and organizations: An interpretive approach* (pp. 13-29). Beverly Hills, CA: Sage.

15

On Being Published
A Contemporary Preoccupation

VIVIAN M. RAKOFF

In the folklore of vampires, one of the ways in which the vampire state declares itself is the absence of an image in the mirror. Without reflection, the vampire is manifestly nonhuman, not present, not fully a creature of ordinary flesh and blood. It is as though there were a deep folk apprehension that being reflected is one of the characteristics of a fully realized humanity. Without such reflection, there is perhaps a fantasy that the very substance of which the creature is composed is not of the best kind. In the instance of the vampire, it is clearly close to the uncanny, but there are other examples in which the lack of reflection, the salute of recognition from the mirror, and the world, carries different social implications. It is, after all, a truism that most of humankind to this day (and in the industrial West it changed only recently) live with only the most fleeting physical reflection of themselves. People quite simply did not, and do not, know how they look. Most had to be content with a reflection in a pool of water or a naturally polished surface. But people have always seen themselves in the apparently haphazard and fleeting reflection one may have of one's face seen in the bright wet curve of the eye of someone close by: someone close enough physically so that one may be in the narrow focus of vision, and close enough psychologically so that one may pause long enough to see oneself in the small, distorting mirror of the eyeball. Other than these natural, nontechnically aided mirrors, only people of some power or wealth (and often both) were either important or rich enough to command the consistent affirmations of reflection—mirrors, polished surfaces, highly glazed ceramics, metal, and so on. Certainly only the very wealthy could command the permanent affirmation of presence, the portrait.

For the most part, the poor or the socially inferior appeared in paintings only as supporters of divinity or aristocracy. When they were depicted, they were generally representatives of a "genre" not present as individuals; they were not present in their own right. Visually they were mere adjuncts to a more central, denser, valuable species of mankind—those who are people of consequence, those whose actions had consequences, who left their mark on the world.

Those whose names signified a continuing reality had names tied to territory; names that echo power; the names of the nobility, the landed gentry. Most other people had their names recorded a few times in their lives in church registries, where their births, marriages, and deaths might have been recorded in the census-keeping Western world. In other places, the humble did not command even that minimal objective scratch signifying they had passed through. The long litanies of African praise singers were kept for chieftains and great warriors: The poor came onto the world tree like leaves; multitudinous, anonymous, transient, and replaceable.

Fortunately, we depend on affirming mirrors of ourselves, less on the domain of the public and technological than on the intimate, psychological signals of those close to us. Simply being human, we are constantly engaged in interactions with others who affirm, through their responses, the simple fact of our presence.

"We exist," and by the constant seamless quality of their reactions intimate others define our qualities. We learn how powerful, weak, malleable, attractive, loved, or unloved we are. But before we learn our qualities, we learn that we "are"; that we are not some fleeting autochthonous event saddled with experiences, many of which are simply painful or unbearable without the compensation of significance. We learn that we signify, that we matter and mean something, that we have (perhaps an illusory) place in the scheme of things. Winnicott, Lacan, Harry Stack Sullivan, and Kohut each, in their different ways, have described the necessity of mirroring experiences in human development. Winnicott (1971), echoing Lacan, puts it aphoristically: "In individual's emotional development the precursor of the mirror is the mother's face" (p. 111). The "mother's face" soon extends to the responding environment of family and, in ever extending circles, the whole of the physical, social, and mythological environment.

Descartes's great philosophical response to the question of human existence, its reality, is perennially preceded by the psychological conviction of most humankind that we are in the world as objective entities as well as psychological experiences, because we nuzzled against a breast, were fed in response to our hunger, were smiled at by particular personal others, and were indeed slapped by particular others, to whom we were of more importance than others like us. These events affirmed through unquestioned, prerational relationships our "being." Long before "cogito ergo sum," relationships of intimacy assuaged the terrible anxiety generated by the often unarticulated question: "Am I here? Do I exist?"

We know we exist through both internal and external affirmations of our reality, but purely self-validated existence does not seem to be possible for most human beings. At the most fundamental level, others are necessary for the maintenance of physical and moral integrity. From infancy to old age, affirming signals from others are necessary. Mere nutrition and protection from the weather are not enough to sustain babies. They require the constant presence of adults, who become not only representatives of the biological, intimate family but also, in most instances, the reference point for an elaborated sense of security in the world of public and historical structures. This is the way it is for the rest of life; although the forms of the socially validating network may change through the small "ecos" of the household, later to the street (however it may be defined in a given society), through the "polis" or public structures (however they may be defined in a particular society), through the mythic historical forms of religion, until all these finally coalesce in the reduced world of reference of the aged. At any of these stages, signals of individual significance derived from "out there" seem to be required.

Because we are addressing the question of publishing, it is clear that the longing for affirmation of significance is one of the functions served by the act of publishing. Setting aside the obvious question of professional and financial gain (perhaps the same thing), there are quite clearly other needs and satisfactions underlying the press to publish. In addition to, for instance, the universities' demand to "publish or perish," there is also clearly for some individuals a subjective demand to publish or fade in one's own estimation of oneself. Why else do well-established writers and scholars continue to torment themselves? Why do young people who are normally venal and lazy press themselves to write with promises reminiscent of the adolescent who vows daily that he or she "will never do it again"? In the adult it takes the form of "I promise myself I will write five hundred or a thousand words a day." The act of writing becomes an expression of control and willpower, and while it gives some satisfaction in itself, its explicit purpose is eventual publication. Apart from that rare literary hero, the careful and constant diarist, there are few who write for nonpublication. Even the most intimate form, the letter, is a publication involving one person at least—the recipient. If one were only addressing the problem of self-expression, one could ask: Why does the individual not simply tell a few people—immediate friends, the neighbor on the bus (if he or she will listen)—what's on his or her mind? At a more reduced level, why not simply express oneself in the privacy of the bathroom, or take a ride to an open place and call one's thoughts to the air? That would be self-expression. The paradox is that self-expression is rarely satisfying when it is confined only to expression to the self.

Why does the expression of the self in print, whether the product of scholarship or imagination, take on the particular value that it has in our civilization? How can a fundamental and serious human need for mirroring and validation be related to a relatively recent technological invention?

It would be easy to allow the technological question to confuse the issue. We do not have a cheap, three-dimensional equivalent of the statue. The portrait in bronze or marble is still infinitely rarer than the photographic portrait. The wish for an image of the self present in most human beings could not be democratically expressed until the invention of cheap available photography. Surely one of the principal reasons for the commercial success of the camera is that it satisfies a fundamental need to record and reflect the facts of existence. "One man, one vote," which was in Taney's terms the transformation of the theological equality of souls before God into the secular world of politics, acquired its aesthetic, iconic counterparts in the family snapshot. Now, not only is the surrender at Breda, or Napoleon's coronation, recorded forever in visual form, but so is "our wedding" and "bathing the dog." The transformation of a perennial need into a new form mediated by technology does not invalidate the notion that the need is indeed perennial.

Different societies at different times express the need for recognition of presence in ways peculiar to that society. The wish to have one's thoughts recorded permanently has a long history, although not as long as we may believe. There was a period when Greek literature began to flourish in the fifth century B.C. when written records of verse were thought to be inferior, somehow less worthy than the tradition of remembered poetry. Part of the education of a "civilized man," and certainly of a "literary man," was the capacity to recall thousands of lines of poetry. However, the Latin tag, "Words fly, the written remains," expressed for the Romans and for us, it seems, the superior value of print as opposed to speech. It is precisely the enduring quality of the printed and published that gives it its superior value. It transcends time and place. It may even move us beyond mortality—satisfying not only our need for affirmation but also a denial of death.

Historical fashion also gives to print a greater cachet than the other forms of communicating in public. Marshall McLuhan pointed out that a preceding technology somehow is more valued by society than the latest technology. He was making the point specifically with regard to the lesser value placed on television, compared with the stage and film, and the even greater prestige of books. The printed word has a particular magic for all of us. It is serious, seems permanent, and comes with a train of socially validating associations such as the law, the Bible, and newspapers. Through print, the ephemeral word can be trapped; time can be held in the hand.

It is not only a psychological need, however, that gives publication its particular magic. Academic departments and the general conventions of information exchange all demand a steady output of published material. In addition to the narcissistic needs of authors and would-be-authors, there are the realistic demands of the workplace. Again, it would be easy to lose sight of the particular subjective satisfactions of being published in the rational demands made upon the writer. Every writer (using the word in its loosest way) knows the satisfaction of seeing something published. Its crudest and simplest joy derives from seeing one's name in print—an event that still occurs only rarely for most people, even in the print-soaked Western world. Births, marriages, and deaths are still the only public printing of their names for most people; and the wedding invitation is still rarer. In addition to its qualities of objective presence and continuing reverberating feedback, print yields other satisfactions such as the subtle concretization of memory (who has not written and been surprised to see what was written, more or less coherent, on the page?). The surprise deriving from the difficulty of recalling exactly how it was when those exact words were written—the state of mind, the weather, the proprioceptive experience of being—like pain, the moments of composition are difficult to recall; they have about them an evanescent and fragile quality. The written word recalls our existence not only in the eyes of others but in our own experience of ourselves. We are rescued from evanescence. Elaborate publishing shares this characteristic with public graffiti: "Kilroy was here," or on the face of a sphinx, "Demetrios the traveler was here," which in turn is only a sophisticated derivative of scratching a mark on the clay or, at its most elaborate, the New York subway graffiti. The graffiti are signals of presence. Why do the subway painters not paint dogs and cats (or, because they are very much in the domain of the popular image, why not Superman—O Magical Superman)? Why is it that they write words—often no more than gang names, personal names, or obscure slogans that can have reverberation only in their culture—"Harlem Snakes" in red and green, a carriage wide? They are moving billboards: publications.

The word is not only a thing in itself. It contains a strong primary association with the human voice. Ultimately the word is the sound of a signaling individual. However abstract the writing, there is—behind it—someone's spoken voice. Even the anonymous words coming from voice-simulating computers are derived from a human source, so many decibels, such an accent, such a particular usage. While one is read in print, one is also, through no very elaborate or extended chain of association, being heard. In this sense the New York graffiti is a scream announcing little more than presence in the world.

Can vandalism also be seen as publication? Is the slashed and broken car seat also a kind of publication—to stretch the word horribly—is it not inexcusably but understandably an attempt by someone who is not affirmed by external mirrors, either subjective or objective, to signal back to the self and the world, "I exist and I can make an impression on my surroundings"?

Seeing one's writing on the page may be akin to Geza Roheim's notion that all language derives from the infant's cry in the night for the mother. Fanciful? It is not that fanciful when one considers the unique kind of hurt resulting from the rejection of one's submitted manuscript. All rejection and failure are painful, but the kind of wincing sadness in response to the rejection slip seems to be a special kind. It may be muted when the editor adds a few words "in his or her own hand," but the ultimate message is both rejection and exclusion on the basis of one's own efforts; exclusion from a group of those who have been accepted. Print always carries the implicit message that there are writers, and when one has not been accepted, the other writers are those whose work has been accepted. They are favored siblings in the great family of letters, who are considered to be more talented, wiser, more energetic, and (in the particular forum chosen to submit the work) better than the rejected writer. There are evocations of the smaller, intimate, unmoving family when a more primitive drama of sibling rivalries sketched the template for the later public contest between the loved and unloved, the heard and unheard, the embraced and the spurned.

The opposite side of the coin is the curious joy upon receiving the letter of acceptance. The dreary work of manuscript revision, the almost invariable irritation at the editor's picayune corrections, are muted by the great compensatory balm that the manuscript has been accepted; it will appear and others will read it.

Sometimes the sight of what was actually written, cold on the printed page, will make even the most well-defended narcissist cringe, but in general it is the rare author who will not turn first to his contribution to the journal or the magazine or pause in the bookstore anxiously searching for his or her book on display. This is surely not self-expression or communicating with others. This is communication with the self through others. Through the validation of acceptance and publication, the message to the self is one of worthiness, acceptance, and indeed existence.

Thomas Mann often returned to the theme of artists and their work. The work—to simplify his complex argument—is not so much an expression of the artist's life as it is a prosthetic adjunct to it. It is a form of compensation and redress for denied satisfactions. The product becomes the solution of problems and difficulties. This formulation does not address the nature of talent or the content of any particular work, but it helps to explain that peculiar blend of pain and compulsion that characterizes writing and publication. Tonio Kroger in his writing will create a satisfying outcome for a painful adolescent outcome. He will bring Ingeborg Holm to his side and restore himself to human centrality. He will overcome the marginality imposed on him by his romantic Italionate mother, who christened him Tonio in the Germanic world of Friedrich, Hans, Wilhelm, and so on. The Buddenbrooks scion, unable or unwilling to cope with commerce and politics, creates a domain of order and control for himself in music. The crippled, tyrannical magician, finally killed by the pragmatic, fully human Mario, is essentially a damaged soul. He compensates for his distorted, unlovable personality by malicious, public displays of control and dominance. The control he exercises over his audience is not based on the power of money or the state; it is an exercise of skill, literally of magic. He inspires uncomfortable involuntary awe in his audience because of capacities greater than theirs. He adds a further shade to the need for public acceptance of personal attributes. The message is extended from "If I am published (or listened to or watched), then I will feel accepted" to "If I am published, I am not only accepted, I am better than you. I compel the attention that has been denied. Look at me. Look at me. Look at me."

Trigorin in Chekov's *The Seagull*—a successful author, a moral narcissist— explains himself at one point, and perhaps also explains something about Chekov and most other authors. He is asked by the admiring young girl, Nina, about the joy he must experience being a writer:

NINA: Your life is beautiful.

TRIGORIN: What's so good about it? (Looks at his watch.) I must get to my writing directly. Excuse me, I haven't time to . . . (Laughs.) You've stepped on my pet corn, as they say, and here I am getting excited and rather cross. Well, then, let's talk. We'll talk about my beautiful, brilliant life . . . Where shall we begin? (After a moment's thought) There are such things as fixed ideas, when a man keeps thinking day and night, about the moon, for instance. I have just such a moon. Day and night I am haunted by one thought: I must write, I must write, I must . . . I have scarcely finished one novel when, for some reason, I have to write another, then a third, and after that a fourth . . . I write incessantly, at a furious rate, I can't work any other way. What is brilliant and beautiful about that, I ask you? Oh, what a preposterous life. Here I am talking to you, I'm excited, yet not for a moment do I forget that my unfinished novel is waiting for me. I see that cloud, it looks like a grand piano. There's a scent of heliotrope. I quickly make a mental note: cloying smell, widow's color, use when describing a summer evening. I catch up every word and phrase we utter, and lock them in my literary storeroom—they may be useful. When I finish work, I hurry off to the theater or go fishing, and there's where I ought to rest and forget, but—no, a great, heavy cannon ball begins rolling around in my head—a new subject for a story; and once more I am pulled back to my desk and have to rush to start writing and writing again. And it's always like that, always; I have no rest from myself, and I feel that I am consuming my own life. . . .

He is never free of the need to write. It is almost a kind of negative addiction. The act gives minimal pleasure in itself, but not doing it is an ineluctable torment. As both Dr. Johnson and Snoopy have said, writing is not a great pleasure: Dr. Johnson wrote, "No-one but a fool ever wrote for anything but money," and Snoopy, after he had written, "It was a dark and stormy night" many times— "Good writing is hard work."

People rarely leave a successful career in writing to become accountants, but the world is full of relatively successful accountants, physicians, and business people who yearn to be authors—not merely private diary keepers but published authors. For all the reasons referred to, writing and being published carry more satisfaction than the successful performance of designated professional or utilitarian work. The rewards of "a regular job" may be considerable in terms of prestige, power, and even, in Dr. Johnson's terms, money, but it is often reward for something external to the "core of the self." Publication, at its most essential, derives from a valued part of the essential person, mined out of the true nature of the writer, an evidence of his personal pure gold; him at his best. "See," says the written, published word, "the riches I have inside me." It declares, furthermore, "Others have seen what I have inside me, and they want it, and I have joined the elect on Parnassus."

Not all publication, of course, carries the full weight of personal validation external to the core of the self. Writing and publishing at their most essential seem to come from a subjective spring of authenticity; a great deal of writing and publication is hack work, mere duty, often anonymous and transient. Perhaps Auden gave the beginnings of a rank order of satisfaction in these matters when he wrote: "Encased in talent like a uniform, the poets have their ranks." Novelists and prose writers of other kinds may exercise will and labor to raise themselves up the slippery slopes of Parnassus, but the Muse's darlings, the truly gifted ones, are the lyric poets whose lifeblood turns to better-than-gold words, print, and publication. Other kinds of publication then derive their satisfaction from alloyed rewards in which the validation of self is augmented by utilitarian goals such as survival in the university, earning a living as the writer of advertising copy, reporting events in newspapers that disappear—all except archival records and the scrapbook of the author and his mother. But however anonymous or unattributed or unacknowledged, the published word reflects some quantity of the validating satisfaction of print; the whiff of love, dominance, and immortality clings to the discarded newspaper or, perhaps, even an advertisement for underwear.

REFERENCE

Winnicott, D. W. (1971). *Playing and reality.* London: Tavistock.

16

The Thrill of Victory and the Agony of Defeat
Reflections of a Psychiatrist

GERALD L. CLINTON

When A Human Soul draws its first furrow straight, the rest will surely follow. Hence-forth your existence becomes ceaseless activity. The universe belongs to him who wills, who knows, who prays, but he must will, he must know, he must pray. In a word, he must possess force, wisdom, and faith. Be conquerors on earth, your convictions will be changed to certainties.

Balzac

THE PROBLEM

Self-disclosure puts it on the line. Athletes, actors, and public servants live with this unique stress. Writers, especially poets and novelists, spill the essence of their souls into immutable black and white. All of us fear the consequences of self-disclosure and must develop adequate defensive tactics or withdraw from effective social involvement.

What is the risk? It is the issue of victory or defeat, affirmation or negation. Nature surrounds us with such polarities, from our subatomic structure, upward to high-order psychological and social organization: positive-negative, attract-repel, good-evil, Yin-Yang, success-failure, life-death, and being-nonbeing. Each of us, drawing from that deep programming of forgotten experiments, which we call intuition or emotion, feel the power of this positive-negative dyad and have learned from life that victory is a thrill and that defeat is agony.

Academicians have an additional problem; the processes of learning, mastery, and growth have special importance and remain an issue into the third, even the fourth, decade of life, long after peers have settled into secure self-acceptance.

How does growth come about? How can we actualize our potential? What are the steps toward maturity and success? To what extent can we shape our destinies? To what extent do we as teachers influence the growth process in others?

Alas, no one really knows; diverse disciplines are looking at these problems and a body of knowledge is forming. Like the blind men feeling the elephant, we are sharpening our perceptions, processing them, and communicating with others trying to sift ideas into a rational framework. In the meantime, I believe this victory and defeat dyad offers a useful perspective on the problem of growth; the purpose of this chapter is to explore that relationship and the problem of growth in general.

Defeat

Negation[1] is represented by destructiveness, alienation, rejection, denial of worth, and misanthropy. Physical expression brings bloody noses, wars, nuclear winter, and the like. More subtle expression, which we tend to label psychological, may bring equal suffering and death in addition to the numerous lesser problems of living. A potent form of negation is simply not supplying the essential psychological substrate for growth. In this context the absence of love is not hate but is apathy.

Psychiatry has generally looked for the source of our problems on this dark side, the seething cauldron of instinctive energies. More particularly, psychoanalysis has emphasized conflict as the source of repression, leading to various states of psychopathology. The model of deficiencies in the developmental process has been—I believe—somewhat neglected. A more complete picture of etiology is gradually emerging in which human needs, and deprivation of those needs, are considered.[2] Clearly our needs are different at different stages of life; varying degrees of deprivation occurring at different stages of emotional development, all in concert with inevitable repressions, situational factors, and genetic predispositions, create complex and infinite possibilities for psychological limitations.

An old proverb teaches: "Once burned, twice shy." The human infant, dependent and vulnerable for such a long time, may be shy for a lifetime if badly burned. For example, there is a syndrome called "marasmus" in which the very young infant, finding emotional needs unmet and life more pain than pleasure, fails to thrive and wastes away to death, in spite of prompt medical intervention. This is extreme deprivation and mercifully rare.

But none of us has found life totally satisfactory and in diverse ways we carry seeds of self-negation. Childhood and teenage suicide is epidemic—the third cause of death after trauma and cancer. Depression in the adult years, if survived, robs us of untold productivity. More subtle shadings of negation relate to psychophysiological illness, various neuroses in which we repeatedly find ways to snatch defeat from the jaws of victory or in other ways fail to be all that we potentially are. To some extent all of us are burn victims and end up fearfully looking at the world through the steel visor slits of a suit of armor[3] that we hope will protect us; as we design and wear that armor, we act out the essence of our psyche. I believe that this is what Thoreau meant when he said that most men live out their lives in quiet desperation.

Those of us who have had the ego strength and effectiveness to reach the level of graduate studies are perhaps psychologically blessed but not home free. We still may suffer from lack of emotional spontaneity, poor rapport with others, relationship failures, feelings of insecurity and uncertainty, indecisiveness, oversensitivity, an inordinate desire to please others, restrictive self-consciousness, feelings of intellectual incompetence, and lack of organization. All of these may be best understood as products of deficient nurturance at critical stages of life.

Victory

Affirmation has been the stuff of poets, religion, popular philosophers, motivational charismatics, and authors of countless salubrious paperback books. With a few exceptions, behavioral science has not looked at affirmation as an isolated phenomenon, and on the clinical level only scattered efforts have been made to modify behavior by systematic affirmative treatment.[4]

It is probably impossible to have too much affirmation, and truly well persons seem to have been blessed with an abundance. Egotism or other patterns of pride and conceit are clearly a desperate effort to gain some sense of worth. We remember vividly the all too rare moments in which someone touched us with the power of a timely, sensitive, and honest endorsement. That is when we grew.

Paradoxically, we hesitate or feel embarrassed to reach out in creative and healing nurturance. Equally strange, we close out the positive efforts of others toward ourselves and resist seeing ourselves as worthy persons. Such behavior seems to be a product of deficient affirmation.

Deficient modeling of effective adult behavior is a related problem. For example, it is easier to become a professor if one's mother or father is a professor. Teachers and professors become especially important sources of identity and must be selected with care.

Apparently it is true that if we can gain a mental image of a given action we learn more quickly. For example, suppose you have never observed the game of golf. The difficulties of learning the swing from written instructions may be insurmountable, but seeing a golf swing immediately creates a mental image to emulate.

In this way I sometimes ask clients to imagine themselves as winners, famous, successful, celebrated, admired, loved, whichever parameter may be to the point. The internal picture becomes a seed for growth.

I like to remember young Cassius Clay, irascible (read unaffirmed) but slowly mellowing into Mohammed Ali, secure and genuinely proud of his victories. In a similar way, young academicians change from shy uncertainty or brash compensatory aggressiveness to effective confidence through the learning (read success) process.

We do change; life is not static. To some extent we can shape that change.

Some Suggestions. Accept your uniqueness. No one else has your perspective or life experience. Share it. You may have a missing piece of the puzzle of life. Once accepting of ourselves, it becomes natural to be accepting of the uniqueness of others.

Thrash about, explore, do new things, dare to make errors; without them we do not learn.

Lean toward the fear.[5] We all fear what is new to us. Start slowly—detoxify the fear in small manageable steps, avoiding an early failure experience that may trigger retreat.

Some impediments we must live with; others are easy to remove. Get some counsel about which is which because few of us can be objective about ourselves. An interesting clinical example is that phobias and panic disorders are now treatable and relief is usually rapid and complete, despite genetic diathesis. Yet many people will go on living in their rut; it is tried and true, if not comfortable. "The good is the enemy of the best."

Hold hands with others. We need each other. Song birds raised in laboratory silence sing a rudimentary song of their family; released to the wild they learn marvelous embellishments from their peers.

We do not—perhaps cannot—learn without feedback. Some of it will hurt. But truly secure persons give affirmative, creative, enriching criticism; truly secure persons see destructive criticism for what it is and do not suffer damage to their self-image.

Learn to affirm yourself. At first this can feel like a futile exercise of the will—a bootstrap effort. But if we can turn the cognitive corner, the feelings, in due time, will follow and success will engender further success.

Especially to teachers, but to us all, affirmation must be congruent; that is, it must hit upon what is real. Without this, affirmation will feel like a Machiavellian manipulation.

Affirmation is not a technique or a method. To work it must be a way of being; targeted upon what is real it brings surprise, wonder, and change.

NOTES

1. Not to be confused with criticism that may be largely benevolent.
2. John Bowlby, Rene Spitz, Harry Harlow, Germaine Guex, Anna Terruwe, and others have focused on the question of early deprivations.
3. Wilheim Reich's apt metaphor.
4. Carl Rogers has taken a long, hard look at "positive regard" and has written about the necessary and sufficient conditions for growth; Russian psychiatry has derived healing methods from Pavlovian psychology. In the United States, psychiatry is evolving an eclectic and biopsychosocial model, enriched by neurophysiology, behavioral psychology, and so on, but is at risk of neglecting research of psychodynamic factors.
5. A contribution of Australian psychiatrist Claire Weekes.

SUGGESTED READINGS

Baars, C. W. (1972). *Healing the unaffirmed*. New York: Alba House.
Bowlby, J. (1960). Grief and mourning in infancy and early childhood. In *The psychoanalytic study of the child* (Vol. 15). New York: International Universities Press.
Guex, G. (1950). *La Nevrose d'abandon*. Paris: Presses Universitaires de France.
Harlow, H. F. (1958). The nature of love. *American Psychologist, 13*, 673-685.
Lidz, T. (1968). *The person, his development throughout the life cycle*. New York: Basic Books.
Rogers, C. R. (1961). *On becoming a person*. Boston: Houghton Mifflin.
Spitz, R. A. (1965). *The first year of life: A psychoanalytic study of normal and deviant development of object relations*. New York: International Universities Press.
Terruwe, A. A. (1962). *De Frustrstie neurose*. Roermond-Masseik: Romen and Zonen.

TWO

Realities in Publishing
Life in the Saddle

Reflections on Realities
Introduction

L. L. CUMMINGS
PETER J. FROST

I n this section, we present four perspectives on the realities of living in the editorial saddle. Professor Alan Meyer begins with an account of his "judgment calls" in well over 200 cases as a reviewer for two of the top-tier journals in our field. He traces his development from a self-description characterized by impersonal reviews, presented in an evaluative and critical style, using passive verbs to communicate "objectivity" and distance from the author. As he describes his maturing over 13 years of reviewing, the self-descriptions shift to "responding as a human reader to a human author," to offering feelings and hunches to authors, to inviting a participatory process of manuscript development to authors and to a self-consciousness about his own overreactions to reviewers' criticisms. What emerges is what Meyer refers to as the "activist" perspective on reviewing. This is reflected in reviews that are candid and lengthy, purposive to the author, coaching in style, pluralistic, and appropriate for the stage of the research and concepts being reported. That is, the activist attempts to fit his or her suggestions to the stage of paradigm and methodological development of the specific topic at hand. Meyer concludes his chapter with several clever hints concerning how authors can help reviewers become less like umpires and more like coaches as they work with authors.

Professor John Campbell continues with a published statement upon the occasion of his retirement from the editorship of the *Journal of Applied Psychology*. Professor Campbell's focus is on various prescriptions concerning not only the mechanisms for obtaining a publishable manuscript but also on some of the less obvious administrative and political issues involved in editing a journal. The remarks by Campbell are particularly important to place in a historical perspective. First of all, the *Journal of Applied Psychology* has a long history of representing important scientific, conceptual, theoretical, and empirical contributions within the various disciplines of applied psychology. Therefore, when Professor Campbell assumed the editorship of the *Journal of Applied Psychology*, he was inheriting a legacy of expectations built by previous editors and by previous policies and procedures of the sponsoring professional association, the American Psychological Association. As stated, the second important historical legacy to consider in interpreting Professor Campbell's remarks is that the *Journal of Applied Psychology* is sponsored by the American Psychological Association, which, in addition to the *Journal of Applied Psychology*, also sponsors and publishes a number of other scholarly journals. These facts are germane to the interpretation of Professor Campbell's remarks because both the history of the journal as well as the stature and wide scope of the American Psychological Association imply reasonably well-defined, and to some extent constrained, domains for the *Journal of Applied Psychology*. These in some sense institute constraints upon an editor's decision-making authority.

Professor Campbell's remarks, while essentially conservative in nature, offer a prescriptive account of what it takes to achieve publishable status in one of the front-running journals in the organizational sciences. The general domain of the *Journal of Applied Psychology* has probably been what one would refer to as within "the normal sciences," ranging across nearly all of the areas of applied psychology. Certainly the focus has been on industrial/organizational psychology with its emergence in the 1970s as a major outlet for work in organizational behavior.

Professor Campbell's prescriptions focus heavily upon what might be referred to as the craftsmanship of constructing publishable articles based upon good theory and/or well-designed and well-executed empirical research. He also offers prescriptions for good scientific writing.

Professor Campbell's editorial statement also testifies to the very large administrative apparatus and chores that are behind the scenes in a successfully edited journal. These range from the coordination of the various decision-making parties to managing interdependence between the editorial and administrative functions. In addition, as Professor Campbell notes, in a case such as the *Journal of Applied Psychology,* it is frequently important for the editor to keep in mind that the particular journal in question is part of a larger network of journals, professionally sponsored by the relevant professional organization. As noted earlier, this implies careful attention to the domains of the relevant interrelated journals and also implies certain constraints upon the editor as he or she carves out a niche for his or her editorship.

In contrast to the other three chapters in this section of this book, Professor Campbell's commentary is, of course, ex post; that is, he is commenting upon his reflections at the completion of an editorship. As we will note momentarily, the other three contributions in this section are, to varying degrees, commentaries upon other stages and other forms of the editorial function. It is noteworthy that Professor Campbell's considerable experience in the editorial function has led to prescriptions that are easily translatable into strategies for operating a journal as well as strategies for conducting and presenting research that is likely to make a significant contribution to the discipline. Because of his considerable experience, both as a theoretician and as a researcher in industrial/organization psychology, and his highly recognized status as a respected editor of the *Journal of Applied Psychology,* persons new to the disciplines might well want to note the explicit and implied prescriptions offered by Professor Campbell in his editorial statement.

Professor Weick offers rather direct suggestions for authors who wish to submit, and have positively reviewed, manuscripts that offer innovative theoretical content and/or methodological contributions. Most authors are inclined to think that their manuscripts would offer such characteristics. Sometimes the review process can be brutal and a source of great disappointment or even disillusionment, when one finds that one's colleagues, who are taking a more objective view, do not see the innovativeness that the author felt his or her manuscript projected. Professor Weick offers several direct prescriptions, which are interesting in their insightfulness as reflected not only by a scholar of considerable experience and an editor but a contributor of major innovations to the field of organizational studies. The prescriptions are interesting not only because of their source but because in many ways these represent the craftsmanship of innovation. In other places in this volume, particularly in the chapter offered by Professor Campbell, the craftsmanship of gatekeeping is well articulated. Professor Weick's prescriptions are offered at a similar level of detail as those prescriptions offered by Campbell. This counters the all too frequent assumption that the craftsmanship of innovation is somehow broader, more opaque, and less specific than is the craftsmanship associated with gatekeeping, particularly gatekeeping surrounding the review and assessment of more established, normal science positivistic contributions. Clearly the prescriptions offered by Professor Weick are different than the prescriptions by Professor Campbell, but their level of specificity is similar. There do appear to be reasonably well-established rules, at least rules derivable from an ex post analysis of one editor's extensive experience. Weick affirms that there are well-established guidelines for conceiving, writing, and publishing innovative contributions.

The reader might well ask him- or herself: How can the Weickian prescriptions be sustained over long periods of time and across many editors, associate editors, and extensive review panels without innovation and differentiation being replaced by more routinized, habituated patterns as disciplines begin to ask smaller and smaller questions in more and more refined ways? Professor Weick is quite encouraging in this regard: He projects an optimistic outcome of the process of applying the prescriptions that he advocates. There are implied answers to the above dilemma in Professor Weick's contribution. These include occasional special issues of a journal, a fairly fluid editorial board, and certainly a good deal of encouragement for controversy within the reviewing staff of a major journal such as the *Administrative Science Quarterly.* Of course the insightful reader will recognize that in this book there are several reflections of this controversy as it was revealed in the review processes associated with not only *Administrative Science Quarterly* but also the *Academy of Management Journal* and the *Journal of Applied Psychology.* These event histories, which are included in other parts of the book, represent actual manifestations of the process that Professor Weick is attempting to describe in his contribution. Those processes become manifest in the realities of the saddle when the person in the saddle is not only attempting to run an efficient, financially feasible and accountable journal but also to do that in a manner that allows the journal to become a self-regenerating and revitalizing enterprise.

Professors Thomas Cummings and Alan Glassman describe and interpret their exciting journey in establishing a new, innovative journal. They point to the importance of champions and institutions (The Western Academy of Management and Sage Publications) in persevering and succeeding. They also share several inside accounts of how naysayers and other sources of opposition were encountered and worked through in creating *The Journal of Management Inquiry.* It is noteworthy to compare the similarities between Professor Weick's account of attempting to build innovation into an established journal *(ASQ)* and Cummings and Glassman's account of establishing a *new,* innovative journal. Both are stories of notable success.

17

Balls, Strikes, and Collisions on the Base Path
Ruminations of a Veteran Reviewer

ALAN D. MEYER

The story goes that three umpires disagreed about the task of calling balls and strikes. The first one said, "I calls them as they is." The second one said, "I calls them as I sees them." The third and cleverest umpire said, "They ain't nothin 'till I calls them."
Simons (1976, quoted in Weick, 1979, p. 29)

The task of reviewing papers submitted for publication in scholarly journals has often been likened to the task of officiating in an athletic competition. Reviewers are termed *referees* and the leading academic journals that employ them are known colloquially as *refereed journals*. Publishing is the principal *game* played in academic circles, and analogies to baseball are especially popular. Editors and reviewers make *judgment calls* (McGrath, 1982). When authors submit their work, those fortunate enough to avoid *striking out* often talk about getting a journal *hit*.

In the big leagues of academic publication, the umpire squad consists of a journal's editorial board and ad hoc reviewers. While serving two terms on the boards of *ASQ* and *AMJ*, I have made well over 200 judgment calls about papers

AUTHOR'S NOTE: I thank Nancy Meyer and Jim Terborg for their helpful comments, and Jan Beyer, John Freeman, Mike Hitt, Rick Mowday, Bill Starbuck, and Karl Weick for teaching and supporting the practice of "activist" reviewing.

257

submitted for possible publication. I have learned that the editorial review process is largely a process of sense making (Weick, 1979) whose primary outputs
are suggestions about how papers might be improved and explanations about
why they cannot be published.

The three different approaches to sense making taken by Simons's apocryphal
umpires provide a useful framework for thinking about how a reviewer might
approach the task of evaluating manuscripts:

(1) Umpire 1 treats each ball pitched toward home plate as an unequivocal
event. A pitch lies either within or outside the strike zone when it passes the plate.
The umpire is an objective observer, and his or her task is limited to making the
appropriate call. The umpire has no part in creating the event; indeed, any capable umpire would have made the same call.

(2) Umpire 2 sees pitches as ambiguous events and umpiring as an exercise
in judgment. Pitches near the boundaries of the strike zone are sufficiently
equivocal that an umpire's eyesight, values, and idiosyncratic biases influence
the call. Umpire 2 understands that the role played by sensory perceptions makes
the umpire a participant in the event.

(3) Umpire 3 maintains that a pitch has no fixed ontological identity. It becomes a ball or a strike only through the pronouncement of the umpire—as
influenced by the ball's trajectory, the batter's behavior, and the umpire's beliefs.
Note that the umpire now has become a coproducer of the event.

"I CALLS THEM AS THEY IS"

When I was asked in 1981 to review my first manuscript for an academic
journal, I approached it somewhat like umpire 1 handles pitches. I set out to
determine whether the paper's arguments were logical enough and the methods
rigorous enough to justify publication. I saw the reviewer as a gatekeeper
charged with enforcing high standards, ensuring fairness, protecting readers
from fraud, and generally guarding the profession's status and the scholarly journal's reputation (Nord, 1985). The comments that I wrote to the author of that
first manuscript reflect three characteristics common to reviewers who follow in
umpire 1's footsteps:

(1) The tone of my commentary was highly impersonal. Although the feedback form instructed me to write "comments for the author(s)," I consistently

referred to him/her/them in the third person: "On page 6, the author claims that
. . ." In fact, in several passages I wrote as though the paper had no author: "This
manuscript argues that . . ."

(2) Most of my comments were evaluative and critical. I listed earlier studies
"with which the author is apparently unfamiliar," I identified "problems in how
this study was designed," and I characterized certain interpretations as "going
beyond the data."

(3) Most of my verbs were passive. Using passive phrasing in discussing the
manuscript suggests that, instead of seeing the paper as at an intermediate stage
in an ongoing process, I saw it as a final product. Passive verbs gave my commentary a static quality. (I may have adopted passive phrasing partly because I
was an assistant professor trying to emulate an academic writing style. But whatever the reason, the effect was to cast the research report under review as a fixed
product rather than an evolving process.)

For the next year or so, I continued reviewing papers using umpire 1's model.
I saw the peer review process as a cornerstone of the scientific process. Reviewing seemed a great honor and a grave responsibility. Gaining confidence in my
own judgment, I enlarged my focus from simply evaluating a paper's logical and
technical rigor to judging it's overall contribution to the field. I worked hard on
reviews, and when I ran into unfamiliar methods or incomprehensible concepts,
I had feelings of inadequacy and guilt. After reviewing about 20 manuscripts on
an ad hoc basis, I was invited to join the editorial boards of *ASQ* and *AMJ*.

"I CALLS THEM AS I SEES THEM"

As an editorial board member, my reviewing workload grew rapidly, and my
approach gravitated toward that of umpire 2. I changed my approach for several
reasons. One impetus was a growing interest in the philosophy and sociology of
social science. My faith in positivistic inquiry was shaken by reading Burrell and
Morgan (1979), Habermas (1971, 1973), Husserl (1931), and Schutz (1967); the
implications of their ideas for academic publication were spelled out in *The
Structure of Scientific Revolutions* (Kuhn, 1962) and *Publishing in the Organizational Sciences* (Cummings & Frost, 1985). Rather than serving exclusively as
forums for scientific communication, academic journals were apparently used
by some authors as vehicles for building their reputations, castigated by others
as bastions of elitism, and usurped by university personnel committees as tools
for evaluation.

Another impetus for change came from the direct feedback set up by journal editors' practices of mailing me copies of commentaries written by each of a manuscript's anonymous reviewers, along with a copy of the editor's decision letter to the author. I was surprised to see how often we reviewers disagreed, focused on entirely different issues, and offered inconsistent recommendations to authors. I found this feedback most enlightening, for as Pondy (1985) wrote: "The norms of reviewing are passed down from generation to generation in a subterranean exchange between author and reviewers, almost entirely hidden from public view" (p. 211).

I came to recognize that the review process in the social sciences is more subjective and political than in the physical sciences (Pfeffer, Leong, & Strehl, 1977) and that actors' positions in social networks play a far greater role. I saw that any differences between "enforcing high standards" and "screening out innovation" were subtle and ideological. I was unsettled by Morgan's (1985) suggestion that publication decisions may be "dominated by the interests and subjective decisions of editors and reviewers who are involved in an elaborate and sometimes unconscious game of control conducted under the guise of objectivity" (p. 63).

A third reason for changing my approach to reviewing is that I too was an aspiring author. Reviewers' overreactions to what I saw as insignificant errors in my own papers made me angry, and some of their criticisms stung bitterly. Sometimes I felt discouraged and disillusioned, and it was unsettling to realize that my reviews of others' work were no doubt evoking similar waves of doubt, anger, and disappointment.

As my perspective on reviewing moved toward umpire 2's approach to umpiring, I adopted different criteria in evaluating manuscripts, and I changed my approach in writing comments to authors.

(1) Instead of representing my comments as output of some mechanical metering device set to register ratings of a paper's rigor and significance, I decided to write like a human reader responding to a human author. To personalize my comments, I started writing exclusively in the first and second person: "On page 4 you say that resource scarcities motivate vertical integration . . ."

(2) To acknowledge my role in interpreting manuscripts, I began reporting my own feelings and reactions to the arguments offered: "I liked your explanation of prospect theory, but your discussion of commitment confused me." (Back when I made "objective" calls like umpire 1, I would have attributed any confusion experienced to a lack of clarity inherent in the manuscript.)

(3) I approached manuscripts as processes in which I participated. To one author I wrote, "In revising, you need to convince me that these two constructs are different." To another I said, "Before I can recommend your paper to my colleagues, you must . . ."

(4) Recalling my own overreactions to reviewers' criticisms, I tried to curtail authors' defensive reactions to my criticisms by invoking readers' needs instead of listing authors' shortcomings and failures: "ASQ readers have come to expect authors to ground their arguments in theory and tie them in to the current social science literature." To another author I wrote, "Readers who are unfamiliar with institutional theory may have trouble following this discussion."

Making minor adjustments of this sort probably made me a better reviewer. At least they let me feel that my behavior was reasonably consistent with my changing beliefs about social science research. But they didn't address a more basic problem. To this point, I had reviewed only a few manuscripts displaying careful scholarship, developing innovative methods, or offering creative interpretations. I was getting tired of plodding through turgid prose, illogical arguments, and poorly described methods. I tried not to think about how few of the manuscripts I was working on would be published, and not to dwell on authors' likely reactions to my recommendations. Reviewing was turning into a thankless, joyless task.

Nevertheless, I knew that the reviewing process sometimes takes a more positive turn. Two senior colleagues, Paul Nystrom and Bill Starbuck, were editing the *Handbook of Organizational Design,* and I found that they were using a more active, interventionist, and developmental approach than mine. Of course, editing invited chapters and reviewing blind submissions are different tasks. However, when I submitted a paper of my own to *ASQ,* it was assigned to Associate Editor Jerry Salancik, who also took an interventionist approach. Jerry saw in my paper a more ambitious article and a more important contribution than I did. With the reviewers' help, he pushed me to find that paper and write it (Meyer, 1982). The prospect of offering this sort of assistance to other authors revived my fading enthusiasm for reviewing.

"THEY AIN'T NOTHIN' 'TIL I CALLS THEM"

Umpire 3 was probably singled out as "the cleverest umpire" because only he or she fully appreciated an umpire's potentially pivotal role in controlling the flow of a ball game. The reviewer who sees a similar potential in the game of publishing can create opportunities to move beyond the gatekeeper role to become a coach, mentor, advocate, or even "defense attorney" representing an author's interests (Pondy, 1985). From my backstage vantage point as a board member, I started studying reviewers that I call "activists," hoping to learn how they go about helping authors flesh out promising insights, remediate seemingly "fatal" flaws, and exploit serendipitous findings.

My observations of activist reviewers suggest they enact a more humane, emotionally satisfying, and intellectually challenging role than reviewers who follow the approach of umpires 1 or 2. They enact this role by building a reputation with journal editors for doing constructive, developmental reviews. Editors often start sending activist reviewers papers that seem especially likely to benefit from their efforts. When this happens, activist reviewers find that they are working on papers that improve more during the review process, that these papers are more likely to be published, and that, irrespective of the ultimate publication decision, authors get more valuable feedback.

However, as a reviewer assumes an activist role, the time and energy he or she devotes to each manuscript are almost certain to increase. Working with authors, particularly less experienced ones, to develop their work into publishable papers is time consuming and emotionally involving. One must be careful to invest effort where it is most apt to yield a return. I would estimate that about one manuscript in ten has substantial unrealized potential for development. Manuscripts especially likely to benefit include those that try to build theory, combine different perspectives, open up new lines of inquiry, or develop innovative methodologies.

Even umpire 3 probably would acknowledge that not every pitch has the same chance of being called a strike—some go into the dirt and bounce across the plate. Likewise, not every submission has the same chance of being called a publishable paper. Some research questions just aren't worth asking, some data sets contain no useful information, and some papers are so far off the mark that no amount of developmental work can save them. Developmental reviewing is necessarily a joint venture between author, reviewer, and editor. However, some authors seem to be more interested in publishing than in what gets published. They see little value in developmental reviews and they are not responsive to them.

Activist reviewing also places additional demands on journal editors by requiring them to become more deeply involved in the evaluation of manuscripts. One reason is that activist reviewers can fall victim to escalating commitment (Staw, 1981). Advocacy often comes at the expense of objectivity, and the editor may need to intervene to sort things out. Some journal editors consciously assign beginning authors' manuscripts to developmentally inclined reviewers. In fact, certain manuscripts were identified in one editor's cover letters to activist reviewers as possible "diamonds in the rough."

Developmental reviewing is not widespread. Cummings, Frost, and Vakil (1985) identified two dimensions of reviewing style: the "coach" and the "critic." Coaches are reviewers who offer encouragement, identify strengths, instruct authors about how to improve, and explain reasons for their recommendations. Critics are reviewers who evaluate merits, identify flaws, and censure improper methods. Cummings and his colleagues (1985) content-analyzed 162 reviews of manuscripts sent to *AMJ* and found that "clearly, most reviewers score relatively high on the critic dimension while scoring relatively low on the coach dimension" (p. 479). Pondy (1985) explained the predominance of the critical approach like this: "Our present corps of reviewers have been trained and conditioned in a prosecution mentality, in large part through observing how their own manuscripts have been treated by an earlier generation of reviewers" (p. 211).

The activist reviewers that I admire are not afflicted with Pollyannaism. They are not uncritical optimists who invariably recommend inviting authors to revise and resubmit. Indeed, to be genuinely constructive, developmental comments must be based upon an incisive critique of the work. The best activist reviewers don't pull their punches. But after telling an author that they don't see his or her work as ready for publication, they go on to spell out specific changes that could close the gap. The feasibility of combining critical and developmental roles is supported by Cummings et al.'s (1985) finding that the coach and critic dimensions are not mutually exclusive. In fact, they reported that, in writing comments to authors, reviewers scoring highest on the sum of both dimensions were significantly more thorough, attentive to technical detail, methodologically oriented, and substantive.

My observations of activist reviewers' comments to authors point to several common characteristics:

(1) Activist reviewers' comments are candid and lengthy. They start with forthright criticism and proceed to recommend changes. Their stance is interventionist. Activist reviewers often refer authors to exemplars in the published literature. Sometimes alternative strategies for revision are proposed for authors to consider.

(2) Activist reviewers challenge authors to specify the purpose, outcome, and contribution of their research. "Why did you write this paper?" they ask. "What did you learn, and what does it mean?"

(3) Activist reviewers coach authors in expository writing. They think about how papers are structured, asking: "Does the argument unfold in a logical way?" and "Does it carry the naive reader along?" They often suggest consolidating related concepts, recommend resequencing of ideas, and offer specific plans for reorganizing arguments.

(4) Activist reviewers tend to be champions of theoretical and methodological pluralism. They can see value in different perspectives and often urge authors to combine methods.

(5) Activist reviewers are particularly sensitive to the alignment between stages in the research process. They ask, "Does the literature review adequately justify the hypotheses? Is the analytical model consistent with the conceptual model? Do the results as interpreted inform the underlying research question?"

I think my observations of activist reviewers have started to pay off. Some of my attempts to emulate this approach have had positive results. I hope I've helped a few authors express their ideas more clearly, educe more robust measures from their data, and see more interesting implications in their results. On several occasions, I have suggested a wholesale reorganization that authors then used to salvage an incoherent argument or to lay to rest another reviewer's seemingly insurmountable objections.

Now and then—out of the tedium of routinized, ritualized manuscript review cycles—a bona fide high-performing system emerges. On five occasions I have seen a seriously deficient or highly preliminary paper somehow pique the reviewers' interest—and trigger a set of especially thoughtful and constructive comments. Usually the reviewers' objections appear irreconcilable and their demands seem impossible, but instead of giving up the author rises to the occasion—perhaps by inventing a brilliant analytical strategy that answers a reviewer's concern or by laboriously collecting new data that remedy a fatal flaw. When the revision is resubmitted, the author's unexpected improvements delight and energize the reviewers, eliciting creative ideas for further sharpening the analyses, extending the argument, and enlarging the contribution.

It is an exhilarating and oddly aesthetic experience when a distributed network made up of blind reviewers linked to an anonymous author by a harried journal editor jells in this way. The review process becomes self-reinforcing and takes on the feel of a peak experience. I have noticed that the authors who elicit these unusually constructive review processes are generally young researchers. Among my personal sample of five "peak" reviewing processes, two were studies reporting the author's doctoral dissertation. Two others involved a recently hired assistant professor. The articles that resulted often won prizes and established their authors' reputations. Weick (1992) remarked that young ethnographers seem to get better data than older ones, and he speculated that this may be because they are less threatening to informants. My observations suggest that inexperience may also confer advantages in the review process. Perhaps new authors' manuscripts evoke constructive reviews by subtly signaling their naïveté.

HOW AUTHORS CAN TURN UMPIRES INTO COACHES

My ruminations on reviewing suggest that authors can take steps to encourage developmental reviews—and at the same time increase the odds that their work will be accepted for publication. I offer these recommendations to authors interested in doing so:

(1) Do not submit your paper prematurely. Use your colleagues as a sounding board. Volunteer to give a colloquium, listen to people's reactions, and use them to sharpen your thinking. When you finish a first draft, circulate it and invite criticism. Treat each and every misinterpretation of your writing as evidence that you've failed to communicate clearly. A good rule of thumb is to push your paper through at least two major revisions before submitting it. (When I've followed this rule, my publication "batting average" has been 1,000—when I haven't, I've been far less successful.)

(2) Make your paper user friendly. The introduction should answer a first-time reader's questions (What's the central research problem? Why is it important?). Foreshadow the paper's outcome and contribution (If I keep reading, what will I learn?). Provide enough information about your sample, measures, and instruments to enable the reviewer to understand exactly what you did and found. Having to guess irritates reviewers and distracts their attention from your argument.

(3) Be compulsive about craftsmanship. Your manuscript is the reviewer's only contact with your study. If it's not well crafted, attributions are likely to be made about the integrity of the whole research project. Typos, missing citations, and errors in calculations all suggest that you may not care about quality.

(4) No reviewer is ever wrong. Reviewers may be careless, bullheaded, or mean spirited, but not wrong. It is self-destructive to assume otherwise. Never go one-on-one with a reviewer. (I am amazed by how often authors defend their manuscripts by lashing out at reviewers.) Ben Schneider (1985) commented,

"Trying to publish in refereed journals is not a path to positive feedback" (p. 239). (If you want positive feedback, I recommend getting a dog—my golden retriever neutralized reviewers' unkind barbs for over 13 years, and he also forced me to get regular exercise.)

(5) The best way to appreciate the last recommendation is to become a reviewer yourself. The program chairs of the Academy of Management's national and regional meetings are constantly on the lookout for reviewers. Journal editors routinely use ad hoc reviewers. Write and volunteer to review, identifying your areas of expertise.

Journal editors also can help turn umpires into coaches. Editors can encourage developmental reviewing by recruiting activist reviewers, assigning them promising manuscripts, and monitoring the ensuing exchanges. Editorial policies can also help institutionalize development. For instance, *Organization Science* now requires authors submitting papers to include a 50-word statement justifying how and why the paper is appropriate for publication. This statement is forwarded to reviewers. Should the manuscript be published, the journal requires the editor who accepted it to *personally* introduce the paper to readers, explaining why he or she recommends it to them. These are small interventions, but they encourage authors, reviewers, and editors alike to focus their attention upon contributions of the research. This is an important cognitive shift, because the established norms of reviewing direct everyone's attention to shortcomings and flaws. Attending to what's right about a paper instead of what's wrong is an important first step toward development.

CONCLUSION

I have taken a controversial stance in this chapter by advocating an activist style of reviewing. Some editors discourage activism. Some reviewers see it as unseemly interference. Some authors regard it as high-handed meddling in their intellectual property. Some radicals may see activist reviewing as a means of exerting social and professional control.

Activist reviewing certainly carries risks. H. G. Wells once remarked, "No passion in the world is equal to the passion to alter someone else's draft." I once got carried away and offended a respected colleague. Envisioning a "far better paper" than the manuscript he had submitted, I suggested a complete recasting of the theory and data. I could hardly wait to see the revision. But my enthusiasm for the project was dashed when the author abruptly withdrew his paper from further consideration at that journal. My colleague later explained that, while he found my ideas for revising "insightful and most interesting," this was not the paper he had set out to write. He felt that I had tried to "hijack" his research.

Since then, I have taken pains to present any recommendations for significant changes as ideas offered for an author's consideration, not as conditions for a favorable recommendation. Authors invest their egos in their writing, and reviewers need to remember this. When an editor asked Henry James to cut just three lines from a 5,000-word article, he responded, "I have performed the necessary butchery. Here is the bleeding corpse."

Not every manuscript is a candidate for activist reviewing. In some cases, the potential contribution is well developed. In others, the potential is absent or minimal. But when the conditions are right, activist reviewing can catalyze significant advances in social scientific theory and research.

Peter Vail once said, "A .350 hitter isn't just a .350 hitter. Typically, he's a .350 hitter in *context*." Reviewers who know when to move beyond their roles as critics and gatekeepers to become coaches help create a context that can make the difference between a home run and just another long foul ball.

REFERENCES

Burrell, G., & Morgan, G. (1979). *Sociological paradigms and organizational analysis.* London: Heinemann.

Cummings, L. L., & Frost, P. J. (Eds.). (1985). *Publishing in the organizational sciences.* Homewood, IL: Irwin.

Cummings, L. L., Frost, P. J., & Vakil, T. F. (1985). The manuscript review process: A view from the inside on coaches, critics, and special cases. In L. L. Cummings & P. J. Frost (Eds.), *Publishing in the organizational sciences* (pp. 469-508). Homewood, IL: Irwin.

Habermas, J. (1971). *Knowledge and human interests.* Boston: Bacon.

Habermas, J. (1973). *Theory and practice.* Boston: Bacon.

Husserl, E. (1931). *Ideas: General introduction to pure phenomenology.* London: Allen and Unwin.

Kuhn, T. S. (1962). *The structure of scientific revolutions.* Chicago: University of Chicago Press.

McGrath, J. E. (1982). Introduction. In J. E. McGrath, J. Martin, & R. A. Kulka (Eds.), *Judgment calls in research.* Beverly Hills, CA: Sage.

Meyer, A. D. (1982). Adapting to environmental jolts. *Administrative Science Quarterly, 27,* 515-537.

Morgan, G. (1985). Journals and the control of knowledge: A critical perspective. In L. L. Cummings & P. J. Frost (Eds.), *Publishing in the organizational sciences* (pp. 63-75). Homewood, IL: Irwin.

Nord, W. R. (1985). Looking at ourselves as we look at others: An exploration of the publication system for organization research. In L. L. Cummings & P. J. Frost (Eds.), *Publishing in the organizational sciences* (pp. 76-88). Homewood, IL: Irwin.

Pfeffer, J., Leong, A., & Strehl, K. (1977). Paradigm development and particularism: Journal publication in three scientific disciplines. *Social Forces, 55,* 938-951.

Pondy, L. R. (1985). The reviewer as defense attorney. In L. L. Cummings & P. J. Frost (Eds.), *Publishing in the organizational sciences* (pp. 210-219). Homewood, IL: Irwin.

Schneider, B. (1985). Some propositions about getting research published. In L. L. Cummings & P. J. Frost (Eds.), *Publishing in the organizational sciences* (pp. 238-248). Homewood, IL: Irwin.

Schutz, A. (1967). *The phenomenology of the social world.* Evanston, IL: Northwestern University Press.

Simons, W. H. (1976). *Persuasion.* Reading, MA: Addison-Wesley.

Staw, B. M. (1981). Knee-deep in the Big Muddy: A study of escalating commitment to a chosen course of action. *Organizational Behavior and Human Performance, 16,* 27-45.

Weick, K. E. (1979). *The social psychology of organizing.* Reading, MA: Addison-Wesley.

Weick, K. E. (1992). Jolts as a synopsis of organizational studies. In P. J. Frost & R. Stablein (Eds.), *Doing exemplary organizational research* (pp. 99-104). Newbury Park, CA: Sage.

18

Editorial
Some Remarks From the Outgoing Editor

JOHN P. CAMPBELL

I served as editor of the *Journal of Applied Psychology* for 6 years, from 1976 to 1982, and as associate editor for approximately 2½ years. Including the year as editor-elect, this brings the grand total to over 9 years with the journal. Surely this entitles one to something. Consequently, I would like to take this opportunity to make a few outgoing comments. The topics I would like to touch

SOURCE: Journal of Applied Psychology. 1982, Vol. 67, No. 6, 691-700. Copyright 1982 by the American Psychological Association. Reprinted by permission of the publisher and author.

AUTHOR'S NOTE: Over the past 9 years I have come to owe a great deal to a great many people. Obviously the enterprise could not have functioned without a dedicated and expert editorial board and a large number of willing and highly competent special reviewers. Thank you all many times over. I also was fortunate to have as associate editors three of the finest colleagues one could ever know. Professors Bouchard, Goldstein, and Hulin served the journal in outstanding fashion and I will always value our associations. Special gratitude is due to Barbara Hamilton, who has been the person most responsible for holding the operation together during the past 6 years. But for her, editors, reviewers, and authors would have run amok, and some of you would still be waiting for a decision. Special assistance was provided for the preparation of this editorial by Loriann Roberson. Requests for reprints should be sent to John P. Campbell, Department of Psychology, Elliott Hall, University of Minnesota, 75 East River Road, Minneapolis, Minnesota 55455.

on are the organizational context of the journal, some opinions about the manuscript review process, and some general impressions about the current state of
the substantive literature. Surprisingly (to me at least), the views expressed are
more positive than those usually found in comments on the publication enterprise. Readers should keep in mind that this is the only article published during
the last 6 years that has not been subjected to editorial review.

During my 6-year term as Editor, the journal received 3,636 manuscripts.
Although we have done a certain amount of systematic categorizing and count-
ing, the bulk of the following remarks are based on opinions and biases that have
built up in the course of dealing with these several thousand manuscripts and
their authors. For example, I discovered that people change when they become
authors. They change again when they become reviewers. Mild-mannered colleagues become enraged adversaries almost by return mail.

JOURNAL PUBLICATION
AS A BUSINESS ENTERPRISE

Scholarly journals in the behavioral and social sciences vary widely in size,
form, and organizational structure. Compared to most, APA publications constitute a relatively large and well-organized operation. In fact, the association is
perceived as a leader in matters of policy, management, and production. It publishes 17 primary journals, a number of special separates, and one of the leading
scientific abstracts. It devotes resources to research and development and to
long-range planning; in my opinion, the publications operation faithfully tries to
carry out the mandate of the association, which is to publish a primary journal
in every major area of psychology. It is a well-run operation in which I think the
members of the association can take some pride. It is self-supporting and in fact
contributes revenue to the association.

However, because of the operation's size and complexity and the existence of
fixed production schedules that are the focal point of a budget of $7 million, the
editors are subject to a certain amount of management control. The enterprise
functions most smoothly when manuscript flow is at a constant level, no changes
are made after the printer gets the manuscript, no errors remain undiscovered,
and costs are minimized. Editors must periodically report things like number of
manuscripts received, rejection rates, editorial lag, and publication lag. Page al-
lotments and budgets are set 2 years in advance. Large fluctuations or departures
from targeted values raise eyebrows. Thus I have always felt a certain amount of
tension between the scientific enterprise, which tends to proceed by fits and

starts, and the business operation, which wants things to be smooth, predictable, error free, and efficient. However, during the past 9 years I have had no difficulty with the APA publication office or the APA Publications and Communications Board. They have been extraordinarily supportive and highly competent.

THE MANUSCRIPT REVIEW PROCESS: SOME OPINIONS

I began the job with a number of simplistic and naive notions about what the process of producing articles in a scientific journal would be like. Most of them have been shredded, and I am left with a different set of opinions about the review process.

The Editor as Gatekeeper

I previously thought that editors had a great deal to do with what got published in the journals, that they were "gatekeepers" in every sense of the word. In fact, there is a certain amount of literature on the subject of the editor as gatekeeper (e.g., Crane, 1967; Garcia, 1981), and the implication is that these powerful beings shape and mold the discipline to their liking, usually to the detriment of the field. My colleague Dunnette (1966) once said in an APA invited address called "Fads, Fashion, and Folderol in Psychology," which got a standing ovation, that one way out of our wilderness was to "get to the editors" (p. 642). I was eager to carry out such a mandate. Previous editors have told me they had similar expectations. The reality seems to be that there are few degrees of freedom within which to be a gatekeeper. The overall quality of the submissions was a bit lower than anticipated. In fact, it was a bit of a shock. With perhaps one or two exceptions there has been very little opportunity to exercise any professional biases (I think). One possible exception pertains to the use of a self-report questionnaire to measure *all* the variables in a study. If there is no evident construct validity for the questionnaire measure or no variables that are measured independently of the questionnaire, I am biased against the study and believe that it contributes very little. Many people share this bias. A second exception pertains to empirical studies of the characteristics that influence return rates for mailed surveys. Unless the studies were set in some larger theoretical context, we did not review them. There are other journals that do, and they are sufficient.

Publication "Policy"

A favorite exercise among authors, and that includes most of us at one time or another, is to try to capture the policies of the editorial staff so as to predict the accept/reject decision. Literally dozens of times during the past 9 years we have received letters from authors or prospective authors that began, "I know your policy is thus and so, *but* . . ." Almost without exception the basis for such statements has been a mystery. With the exception of the questionnaire policy just mentioned and the desire to publish no more atheoretical papers on what characteristics might influence mailed questionnaire return rates, we had no articulated policies about preferred and nonpreferred content beyond the APA mandate not to publish in the areas of clinical and counseling. The law of small numbers (Tversky & Kahneman, 1974) operates here with great force. Sometimes one decision on one manuscript was enough to suggest a policy.

Reasons for Rejection

It is also true that most people have definite opinions about why manuscripts are rejected. I certainly did. However, as a result of this experience my beliefs have changed. The most frequent reasons for not accepting manuscripts were the following:

(1) The procedure (not the statistical analysis) used in the study could not answer the question(s) that were asked. For example, there was every reason to believe that the measures used in a study had no reliability or validity or that alternative explanations for the results were much more likely.

(2) The question addressed was not a very meaningful one. That is, even if it was answered, no actual information would have accumulated. Nothing would have been added to the literature.

(3) It was simply not possible to understand what the author was trying to say. The biggest shock in the entire 9 years was the discovery of how many people cannot describe clearly and directly what they wanted to do, what they did, and what they found out. Clearly written manuscripts are in the minority.

(4) A much less frequent disqualifier was low statistical power. In some instances too small a sample was a reason for rejection.

(5) A still less frequent reason for rejecting was the judgment that the same thing had already been said enough times. This refers more to theoretical or conceptual papers than to empirical replications. We actually received very, very

few of the latter. However, the decision that a particular idea or theory has already been articulated well enough or that the conceptual paper under consideration does not go quite far enough beyond what is already available was a particularly tough and uncomfortable judgment to make.

(6) In my opinion, negative results were not a particularly important reason for rejection, although the recent study by Atkinson, Furlong, and Wampold (1982) suggests that when given a series of hypothetical examples, reviewers seem to be influenced by whether or not the results were statistically significant. Several thoughts come to mind. First, our own base rate for statistically non-significant results among the last 3,636 manuscripts was very low, something less than 10%. Nonsignificant findings just don't occur very often. I do not think that there are file drawers full of negative results. For example, a number of years ago Campbell, Dunnette, Lawler, and Weick (1970) used site visits and personal interviews to search dozens of file drawers in an exhaustive attempt to gather all available research information on management selection and development, and they could find very few negative studies. Instead I think most studies that get completed are designed well enough to yield a fairly high a priori probability of statistically significant results. Those that are not well designed tend to fall apart before being completed and are never written. Even if all the negative results submitted for publication were in fact rejected, they would account at most for only 10% to 15% of all rejections. That is, since the overall rejection rate runs about 80%, 85% to 90% of manuscripts rejected do in fact report statistically significant results. Finally, it is true that there is an evaluation asymmetry between significant and nonsignificant results. Besides the lack of any true relationship among the latent variables, the decision not to reject the null hypothesis can be a function of lack of power, lack of validity for the measures, unreliable measurement, lack of experiment control, and so on. Studies that wish to give a substantive interpretation to negative results must be reasonably well done.

The moral to be drawn from this recitation is that it is not the statistics, analytic methods, or even the particular subject matter that determine whether a paper is accepted or rejected. Subject-matter expertise, sound measurement, appropriate procedures, and clear exposition are the things that really matter.

Preferences for Short Articles

Believe it or not, it is a myth that editors prefer short manuscripts for the sake of shortness. This is a scurrilous and vilifying rumor that I emphatically and categorically deny. It just turns out that way. The basic objective has always been to turn the screws until blood is drawn and coerce authors into saying whatever they want to say in the clearest and most efficient manner possible.

I think there are far more important influences on article length than journal editors. Perhaps the most important is the way our research enterprise is structured. For the most part, it is composed of individual investigators working as individuals in academic settings. Relatively speaking, even a small project takes a lot of time, and because individuals judged as individuals cannot go for years and years with no visible output, the production of small discrete studies is encouraged. We frequently tried to get authors to combine two or more short papers into a longer manuscript. Such efforts always met with great resistance. Without getting into a chicken-and-egg argument, I think it is also true that most sources of research funding are set up to accommodate individual researchers working alone.

Publication Lag

Lots of people complain about publication lags. There is by necessity a relatively long interval between the time a manuscript is submitted and the time it is actually published. For APA journals a lag of 8-10 months begins to approach rock bottom. The average publication lag for the *Journal of Applied Psychology* over the past 6 years has been 10-11 months. About half of that is editorial time and about half is production time. The editorial time usually includes at least one revision of the manuscript by the author. Of the 3,636 manuscripts that were submitted during the past 6 years, *none* was accepted without revision. Bradley (1982) takes this as evidence that reviewers and editors are arrogant and incompetent. Although there may be some truth to this assertion, it could also be that there are few papers that cannot be improved by exposure to the comments of colleagues, if only to make them more appropriate for a broader audience.

During the past 6 years, publication backlogs have generally not been a problem for APA journals. If too large a backlog builds up, it has been the practice to budget additional pages to reduce it. Consequently, if the lag is longer than 10 to 11 months, it is because the manuscript fell through a crack in the editor's office, or the editor and author could not come to a meeting of the minds. Finally, even though a 10- or 11-month publication lag is a long time, it pales in comparison to the time that elapses between the completion of a project and the submission of a report for publication. Investigator lag can easily be 2 to 3 years. Thus the publication lag itself is usually not the cause of data being old. Sometimes it is the cause, but not usually.

Interreviewer Agreement

One of the most controversial and emotional issues in the editorial process concerns the competence and biases of reviewers. Much has been made of the unreliability or lack of agreement among reviewers. The question has been investigated a number of times for APA journals (e.g., Bowen, Perloff, & Jacoby, 1972; Cicchetti, 1980; Crandall, 1978; Gottfredson, 1978; McReynolds, 1971; Scarr & Weber, 1978; Scott, 1974). A variety of agreement indexes have been used (e.g., Pearson r, intraclass r, Cohen's kappa), and the results are reasonably consistent. Interreviewer agreement is low. In terms of correlations, most coefficients are between .20 and .50 (that is for one rater). Using the Spearman-Brown correlation to get the reliability for the average of two raters, the values are .33 and .67. We looked at this correlation twice, once for manuscripts submitted in 1976 and once for manuscripts submitted in 1981. Each time the correlation was computed on about 100 cases drawn at random. The first coefficient was .59 and the second was .23. For reasons I will explain, the first was a bit higher than expected and the second was a bit lower. The arithmetic mean of .41 is closer to expectations, and a .05 confidence interval placed around .41 would include both coefficients. However, a more fundamental consideration is that reviewers act as consultants and advisers but they do not make the decision. Consequently it is the reliability of the editor that should be an issue, not the reviewers. Further, reviewers are seldom, if ever, chosen to represent parallel measures. In fact, they are usually chosen to be deliberately nonparallel, as when one reviewer has substantive expertise and another has methodological expertise. As a result they focus on different things and may give very different evaluations. The important point is that there is no way a correlation between raters can be regarded as a reliability coefficient. The situation is deliberately set up to yield low correlations.

Publish or Perish

I think it is a fact that academic departments that evaluate faculty in terms of the number of pieces published hurt the publication system and the research enterprise. It was more than a bit uncomfortable for me to watch people carve a study into as many pieces as they could, send the same manuscript to several journals at the same time, and otherwise try to multiply titles. Most uncomfortable of all were the phone calls from authors who said that we simply had to publish their paper or they would not be promoted or granted tenure.

One cannot really blame individuals who must live under the publish or perish contingency. One can blame the academic departments who are apparently unwilling or unable to define and then assess individual contributions to the discipline.

The Process of Peer Review

Many of the above points pertain to the broader issue of peer review. No one needs convincing that the process of peer review is a fundamental ingredient in the scientific enterprise. It is a basic part of the allocation of research funds and the selection and promotion of academic staff. More important in terms of the present discussion is that peer review is the cornerstone of the editorial process for archival journals. Peer review has also come under periodic, sometimes vehement, attack as contributing to elitism, cronyism, the status quo, and various other ills. Manuscript referees for journals are often seen as ignorant, biased, and unreliable; the result is that lots of good work does not get published or that the wrong things get published (for a discussion on this issue, see, e.g., Brackbill & Korten, 1970; Einhorn, 1971; Newman, 1966).

Over the years a number of alternatives have been proposed, such as the following:

1. An "open" publication policy in which abstracts would be published for all manuscripts that met certain format standards. The full article would be available at reader expense.
2. An open publication policy followed by publication of solicited and/or unsolicited comments on the paper. The comments would serve the function of peer review but would not prevent the paper from seeing the light of day.
3. A fine tuning of the current procedure by using more referees per manuscript, more carefully training reviewers, keeping authors anonymous, or making reviewers identify themselves.
4. A systematic appraisal system for manuscripts with carefully developed scales describing the important characteristics to be evaluated and a carefully developed weighting system for combining information.

In general, I have come away from the last 9 years much more positive about the peer review system than before. By and large people who were asked to referee manuscripts tried to do an honest and thorough job, and I thank you all many times over for your assistance. Obviously there are a fair number of slip-ups and the reviewer or editor may miss something, insult the author, or be very late. The system cannot be perfect but it can be improved. The improvement will result largely from the editor and reviewer constantly striving to be thorough, knowledgeable, fair, and timely. Here is where the editor exacts great control: Reviewers need a certain amount of guidance as to what a review should contain; they must be carefully chosen for each manuscript; if they provide uninformative reviews, new reviews must be solicited; delinquent reviewers must be browbeaten into responding or else be bypassed; and sometimes their colorful language must be censored (authors tend to lose their sense of humor when their life's work is being evaluated). The editor *must* read the paper carefully (some do not), and either the editor's comments or the reviewers' comments must clearly support the decision that was made. My own test was to imagine that I had to justify the decision publicly in front of a jury of my peers. Did the file support the decision and would I feel comfortable defending it?

I do not think much will be gained by developing more formalized rating procedures for manuscripts. I also do not think it makes much difference whether reviewers and/or authors are anonymous or identified. The peer review system works if it is managed carefully; that is the editor's responsibility. One of my chief worries is that the system is too overloaded and people are being asked to do too much, with the result that manuscripts do not get as wide ranging an evaluation as they should. We must constantly try to increase the percentage of people who participate in the enterprise. One of my principal complaints is against the prima donna who believes (demands) that his or her work should receive quick and thorough attention but who is always too "busy" to contribute to the process.

THE SUBSTANCE OF APPLIED PSYCHOLOGY: SOME IMPRESSIONS

After dealing with so much material for so many years, one cannot help forming some rather definite opinions and impressions about the substance of applied psychology. The things that stand out most strongly are the following.

The Use of Theory

My strongest impression is of becoming much less positive about the way theory is used in research on behavior in organizations. The idealized deductive process of developing a theory, deriving hypotheses, and testing them to support or not support the theory is respected by almost everyone, but at the same time almost everyone realizes that the ideal seldom describes reality. Unfortunately, although most of us realize that the idealized process seldom occurs, I think too many people wish that it would. I believe that the field would progress much more rapidly if more research was in the nature of theory testing. It is this latter idea with which I want to take issue.

Lots of papers are submitted describing studies in which a theory or model (new or old) is proposed, the relevant variables are measured in some fashion, and data are then collected to test the theory. That is, the truth or falseness of the theory is to be established in some sense. This paradigm has not helped us much. Further, given the kinds of theories we have that pertain to motivation, leadership, attitudes, and the like, what would it mean if the theory or model was actually supported? Pick out your favorite theory and assume that everyone, from strong partisans to vocal critics, agreed that it has been strongly supported. What would happen next? What would we really know? Not much, I think. Most of our theories are collections of statements that are so general that asserting them to be true conveys very little information.

I argue that the problem is not with our theories (or theorists). Rather, the problem is that we do not use the theories to very good advantage. Perhaps we really were seduced a bit too easily by practices in the physical sciences. I used to think people were just expressing sour grapes when they complained that psychology was trying too hard to emulate physics and chemistry. I no longer think so. Almost all of us have read and respected the classic statement by the physicist Platt (1964) that a useful way for research to proceed is by formulating competing hypotheses that can be pitted against each other in an empirical study. I do not think this is very valuable advice for us. For example, I do not think it is possible to separate the effects of goal setting and reinforcement so as to pit them against one another, nor should we try.

Theories have great benefit as heuristics, and that is the role they should play. If a motivation theory says that expectancy is important, then questions about expectancy are what should be investigated, not whether $V \times I \times E$ correlates with something else. If a leadership theory suggests that leaders cannot be taught to change their behavior in certain ways, then that question should be investigated, not whether the theory's overall prediction of a certain pattern of correlations is supported.

In general I cannot disagree that we constantly need more and better theories. However, my strong feeling is that they should be used to identify particular questions that are especially crucial, to suggest interesting treatments or techniques that should be investigated and developed, or to identify the variables that are most in need of valid and reliable measurement. It is the accumulation of knowledge regarding crucial descriptive questions, important techniques, and valid measures that is important, not the generation of support or nonsupport for a theory as some singular end in itself.

The Form of the Research Question

Another strong impression I have is that there are certain forms of research questions that are best to avoid. They tend to lead to studies that are not very useful or that at least yield a very small return of information.

One such question is the tendency to pose a general question with the expectation that a general answer is possible. Examples would be: Is a training program effective? How should performance be measured? What makes organizations effective? Are the people in the organization motivated? If the investigator stays at this level too long, what tends to come out is a rather bland set of mixed results that at best suggest the need for further research.

Another kind of question that is worrisome is of the form: Is variable *A* or variable *B* a more important influence on variable *C?* Some examples would be: Is job satisfaction or job commitment a more important determinant of absenteeism or turnover? Is money or praise a more powerful reinforcer of a certain behavior? Is motivation or skill a more important determinant of performance? The answers to these questions depend in large part on the range of values for each variable that is included in the study. Unless the investigator has a reasonably good idea of the relevant population variances and can interpret the sample variances accordingly, the results can be misleading. Beware of two-factor designs with biased or haphazard selection of treatment level effects that are interpreted as if they were either fixed or random.

It is my strong impression that the most interesting and valuable research questions have come from the experience and/or strongly held convictions of the investigators. Although subject-matter expertise is a necessary condition for doing good research, the most useful research questions do not come from reading the literature. These points are developed at greater length in Campbell, Daft, and Hulin (1982).

The Null Hypothesis

One of the most frustrating aspects of the journal business is the null hypothesis. It just will not go away. Books (e.g., Morrison & Henkel, 1970) have been written to dissuade people from the notion that smaller p values mean more important results or that statistical significance has anything to do with substantive significance. It is almost impossible to drag authors away from their p values, and the more zeros after the decimal point, the harder people cling to them. It is almost as if all the statistics courses in the world stopped after introducing Type I error. It is not uncommon for over half the space in a results section to be composed of parentheses inside of which are test statistics, degrees of freedom, and p values. Perhaps p values are like mosquitos. They have an evolutionary niche somewhere and no amount of scratching, swatting, or spraying will dislodge them. Whereas it may be necessary to discount a sampling error explanation for results of a study, investigators must learn to argue for the significance of their results without reference to inferential statistics.

The Method, Not the Question

Another impression of mine is that too often research studies are still generated because the investigator has chanced upon a new method and wants to try it on something. That is, the method is chosen before the question. I say this primarily in the context of analytic methods (e.g., "I just learned about canonical correlation, where can I use it?"), but it also applies, perhaps with even more negative consequences, to substantive methods, as when the same management development technique is applied as a cure for every management problem. We still spend much too little time on needs analysis and problem definition. Some of the methods to worry about currently are structural equation modeling, latent trait theory, social interaction modeling, and reinforcement techniques. They all have considerable merit but they must fit the problem and they must be applied by someone who has mastered them.

Research That Does Not Get Submitted

It is also a fact that a lot of valuable research does not get submitted for publication. Most of it is done by military or government psychologists, people in contract research firms and large corporations, or gray-haired people with lots of tenure. For example, much of the research on police-officer and fire-fighter selection was not submitted for publication, and certainly much of the work in the military services on selection, training, promotion, and motivational issues goes unpublished in an archival journal. Because government or in-house technical reports are not as accessible as an archival journal and are not stored by libraries,

I think the field suffers accordingly. Any program of graduate education is certainly hurt by this phenomenon.

The Current State

To better understand the current state and any changes that have occurred over the past 6 years, we have content analyzed the manuscripts submitted during 1976 and 1981. I only wish to note a few things at this point. In spite of over-reliance on the self-report questionnaire, statistical hypothesis testing, and multivariate analytic methods at the expense of problem generation and sound measurement, the current state of affairs does argue that applied psychology is alive and well. For example, there has been considerable innovation over the last 6 years as reflected in the work (and argument) about validity generalization, performance rating as a cognitive process, and the accumulation of evidence on discrimination issues. There are lots of things to research, implement, and argue about, and lots of good people seem to be hard at it. It was also during this period that applied motivation came out of the closet (sorry, laboratory), and goal-setting and operant techniques were studied in a variety of real settings.

For better or worse (and I think for the better), cognitive psychology is beginning to have a greater and greater influence on organizational research. In addition to viewing performance appraisal as a cognitive process, the study of leadership, the study of the socialization processes that occur as an individual moves through an organization, and the development of training models are also benefiting from the cognitive perspective.

I am also encouraged that things like performance, turnover, and organizational effectiveness are more and more construed as constructs that have no single representation. It has led to more interesting question generation, more recognition of roles played by value judgments, and a more useful and practical view of these phenomena.

Finally, applied psychology continues to generate new research areas that have considerable practical importance. Two of them are lumped into the category we labeled *forensic psychology*. Such a category was not even around in 1976 but now includes considerable work on face-recognition methods as they are used in law enforcement agencies and on validity studies of the polygraph. It is gratifying that the analyses of polygraph accuracy data were significantly enhanced by the application of personnel-selection-type prediction models. Other new developments include the application of motivation models to energy conservation and specific productivity problems, and an increased emphasis on collective-bargaining phenomena.

282   REALITIES IN PUBLISHING

A FINAL COMMENT

In sum, I think it is true that applied psychology is in a viable state, particularly as it is applied to problems of employment and organizational life. This is in spite of the dismal state of research funding and an administration that thinks R&D grows on trees. One dominant characteristic of applied psychology is that we deal with a large number of very fundamental issues in our society, uncomfortable and controversial as that is at times. The research problems we face are anything but trivial or academic issues. They present challenges that incorporate considerable risk and much opportunity. We should make the most of it.

REFERENCES

Atkinson, D. R., Furlong, M. J., & Wampold, B. E. Statistical significance, reviewer evaluations, and the scientific process: Is there a (statistically) significant relationship? *Journal of Counseling Psychology,* 1982, *29,* 189-194.

Bowen, D. D., Perloff, R., & Jacoby, J. Improving manuscript evaluation procedures. *American Psychologist,* 1972, *27,* 221-225.

Brackbill, Y., & Korten, F. Journal reviewing practices: Authors' and APA members' suggestions for revision. *American Psychologist,* 1970, *25,* 937-940.

Bradley, J. V. Editorial overkill. *Bulletin of the Psychonomic Society,* 1982, *19,* 271-274.

Campbell, J., Daft, R., & Hulin, C. *What to study: Problem finding and question innovation in applied psychology.* Beverly Hills, Calif.: Sage, 1982.

Campbell, J. P., Dunnette, M. D., Lawler, E. E., & Weick, K. E. *Managerial behavior, performance, and effectiveness.* New York: McGraw-Hill, 1970.

Cicchetti, D. V. Reliability of reviews for the *American Psychologist:* A biostatistical assessment of the data. *American Psychologist,* 1980, *35,* 300-303.

Crandall, R. Interrater agreement on manuscripts is not so bad! *American Psychologist,* 1978, *33,* 623-624.

Crane, D. The gatekeepers of science: Some factors affecting the selection of articles for scientific journals. *American Sociologist,* 1967, *32,* 195-201.

Dunnette, M. D. Fads, fashions, and folderol in psychology. *American Psychologist,* 1966, *21,* 637-644.

Einhorn, H. J. Responsibility of journal editors and referees. *American Psychologist,* 1971, *26,* 600-601.

Garcia, J. Tilting at the paper mills of academe. *American Psychologist,* 1981, *36,* 149-158.

Gottfredson, S. D. Evaluating psychologist research reports: Dimensions, reliability, and correlates of quality judgments. *American Psychologist,* 1978, *33,* 920-934.

McReynolds, P. Reliability of ratings of research papers. *American Psychologist,* 1971, *26,* 400-401.

Morrison, D. E., & Henkel, R. E. (Eds.) *The significance test controversy: A reader.* Chicago: Aldine, 1970.

Newman, S. H. Improving the evaluation of submitted manuscripts. *American Psychologist,* 1966, *21,* 980-981.

Platt, J. R. Strong inference. *Science,* 1964, *146,* 347-353.

Scarr, S., & Weber, B. L. R. The reliability of reviews for the *American Psychologist. American Psychologist,* 1978, *33,* 935.

Scott, W. A. Interreferee agreement on some characteristics of manuscripts submitted to the *Journal of Personality and Social Psychology. American Psychologist,* 1974, *29,* 698-702.

Tversky, A., & Kahneman, D. Judgements under uncertainty: Heuristics and biases. *Science,* 1974, *185,* 1124-1131.

19

Editing Innovation Into
Administrative Science Quarterly

KARL E. WEICK

The journal *ASQ* is difficult to label. It contains diverse content from diverse disciplines described by diverse authors in manuscripts that are reviewed by a diverse board. Diversity alone, of course, is no virtue. But *ASQ* seeks diversity to help the field of organizational studies discover what it is about and what it wants to be about. The chance of discovering interesting answers to these questions is improved when the content being published is innovative, stimulating, and hard to categorize. Frost and Cummings have asked me to describe how we try to keep *ASQ* a differentiated source of innovation in organizational studies.

The tactics *ASQ* uses to keep from getting stale include the following:

1. Invited submissions
2. Special issues
3. Evidentiary review
4. Close copyediting

AUTHOR'S NOTE: This manuscript was completed while the author held the Thomas F. Gleed Chair of Business and Finance at Seattle University. This support is gratefully acknowledged, as is the editorial help provided by Nancy Wick, Linda Pike, Jerry Salancik, and Howard Aldrich.

These tactics often work, but they also often cause problems. To understand the fate of innovative ideas in journals is to see the problems these four tactics create. The way these problems are managed determines a journal's continuing treatment of papers that oppose current beliefs.

Before describing these four tactics, I want to describe the context of innovation, both as it exists in the field of organizational studies and as it exists at *ASQ*.

THE CONTEXT OF INNOVATION

The Field as Context

The context of innovation in organizational studies is summarized by at least eight characteristics:

(1) Ideas, concepts, labels, causal arrows, and typologies are a dime a dozen. They are the easiest thing in our field to produce and there are more of them than of anything else. These untested variations overload the selection system and that is a serious problem because the selection apparatus itself is now weaker. There are fewer federal funds to finance sorting, fewer personnel such as doctoral students to do the research that sorts, fewer qualified reviewers willing to spend time reading, less incentive to test someone else's idea, and more incentive to develop one's own. With more journals being published, there is less necessity to select anything, so everything gets preserved. The quality of innovation thus is uneven.

(2) There is virtually no such thing as a truly new idea. It has all been said before, even if authors do not know who said it or where it was said. Page through old journals if you do not believe this. To justify an innovation on the grounds of novelty alone is dangerous.

(3) The market for ideas is an efficient market. In the extreme form, it could be argued that there is no idea in our field right now that is getting less attention than it deserves, given our current stock of knowledge. Reviewers, people who read preprints or publications or proceedings, people who attend colloquia and meetings, all talk to one another and know much of what is available and how good it is. If these people hear an "innovative" proposal but it fails to reconnect any of their ideas, then that proposal has undergone an efficient, sufficient test of its worth. Most innovations do not survive a test like that.

(4) An innovation is assumption specific. The context within which an idea is original is usually the author's own initial assumptions that have been disconfirmed by some thought, reading, sentence, datum, insight, and so on. Thus the innovation is appreciated only by those who share the same initial assumptions.

(5) Brokering of concepts is not synonymous with innovation. Just because someone in some other field had an idea, coined a term, or adopted a metaphor that helped them, is no reason for organizational theorists to assume the same idea, term, or metaphor will help us. Concepts become valuable as they answer specific questions or resolve stubborn problems. If we do not work with the same questions and problems that other fields do, there is no reason to expect our thinking will improve if we graft their concepts onto our field, which was not asking the same questions in the first place, does not know enough to ask those questions, and might not be interested in the same answers even if it did ask the same questions.

(6) Innovation is meaningless in a field with an undeveloped paradigm. In the absence of paradigms, people have little agreement on criteria by which to judge innovation. When people work with an undeveloped paradigm, *all* work is innovative. The problem with an underdeveloped paradigm is not innovation, the problem is that there is little normal science.

(7) Innovation is ripe for effort justification. People work hard to develop the ideas they have. To justify the large effort invested, they may inflate the value of what is produced. Having inflated the value, they then are discouraged when reviewers raise questions about the work and are reluctant to revise it. Those who have more ideas often show less attachment to any one idea and are more receptive to suggestions about ways to improve specific ideas.

(8) The error-correction mechanism in journals may work against innovation. It is relatively easy for journals to learn when they have published something they should not but relatively hard for them to learn when they have not published something they should have. Errors of the first kind—things are published that should not be published—are discovered when authors stop sending manuscripts, readers cancel subscriptions, letters to the editor increase, the article is never cited or reprinted, board members complain, copy editors spend more time than usual on a manuscript, and no one feels any enthusiasm for the piece.

When journals fail to publish something they should have, they do not learn this with either swiftness or certainty. If errors of this kind occur, they probably occur disproportionately often with innovative pieces. The one optimistic note is that, if the time is ripe for an innovation, it will be submitted more than once by more than one person. Sooner or later, reviewers will get it right and the innovation will be published.

ASQ as Context

An innovation is an exercise in clarity. An innovation is basically a claim that readers will see organizations more clearly if they use fewer terms, different terms, or rearranged terms.

For example, innovations that claim that people will see more if they use fewer terms are found in Leblebici and Salancik's (1982) demonstration that responses to uncertainty can be dumped under changes in working rules, Bettman and Weitz's (1983) demonstration that explanations of corporate performance in annual reports resemble self-serving causal attributions, and Meyer's (1982) demonstration that ideology and strategy predict adaptation to abrupt changes more adequately than do structure and slack.

Innovations that claim that people will see more if they use different terms are illustrated by Useem's (1982) discussion of *classwide rationality* among corporate elites that cuts across and transcends corporate rationality; Ranson, Hinings, and Greenwood's (1980) suggestion that people treat structure as *structuring;* and McNeil and Miller's (1980) demonstration that *goodwill accounting systems* in the automotive industry may be related to warranty protection and consumer loyalty.

Innovations that claim that people will see more if they rearrange existing terms are illustrated by Gronn's (1983) demonstration that talk *is* the work of administrators rather than instrumental to administrative work, Anderson's (1983) demonstration that the subtasks in decision making occur in a different order than analysts presumed, and McCaffrey's (1982) argument that potential corporate domination of regulatory agencies is neutralized by problems of organization and information processing.

All of these innovations involve novel combinations that disconfirm existing formulations favored by editors and reviewers. The innovations represent a partial resistance to perpetuate past understandings and an implied promise that future understandings will be stronger if the innovations are substituted. However, a promise is still a promise. What an innovation can actually produce in the future can only be guessed at by people who are grounded in different innovations that have worked reasonably well in the past.

Given that innovations are virtually synonymous with clarity, to select and edit innovations is to be obsessed with issues of accessibility, coherence, vagueness, structure, and sequence—in short, with the quality of writing. The *ASQ* editorial process is built around the belief that "clear writing is not an adornment but a basic proof of grasp." Unclear writing is rejected; clearer writing is clarified. To understand how *ASQ* deals with innovation is to understand how *ASQ* deals with words.

THE EDITING OF INNOVATION

Invited Submissions

Innovative manuscripts are "invited" both by a journal's reputation and by enthusiastic reactions from editors and board members.

The *ASQ* culture may itself be instrumental in steering innovative authors toward or away from the journal. The rich mixture of strong editors, stronger managing editors, tight-fisted copyediting, unpredictable cover art, editors who model in their own work the degree of innovation they presumably would like to read in the journal, editorial board members who are strangers to readers and to each other, long articles that require a good night's sleep to penetrate (Warr, 1979, p. 237, calls them "discursive")—all of these combine to give *ASQ* character, distinctiveness, and visibility. These qualities may tempt authors to "give *ASQ* a try." As more authors send more things, editors have more input from which to select the more promising proposals of what the field should do next.

This is not to say that *ASQ* has a culture and other journals do not. Instead, it says that a journal's stance toward innovation is overdetermined. Clues to that stance are visible in a wider variety of trappings than people realize. Those clues pull or discourage innovative submissions.

At times I try to attract an innovative manuscript by letting authors know that *ASQ* would like to study their work more closely. When I do this, I usually get in trouble. Authors often describe their insights face to face with enthusiasm and subtlety, both of which seem to disappear when the insights are summarized in writing. As a result, my enthusiastic invitation—which made sense in the context of a face-to-face dialogue with the author—comes back to haunt me when a written version of the "same" idea is then reviewed and rejected without warning.

This scenario may be inevitable in innovative work. Enthusiasm and appreciation are scarce resources in fields built on criticism. To me, that means it is an editor's job to encourage people who try to solve problems of the past by creating a different set of problems for the future. But enthusiasm is simultaneously the friend of action and the enemy of wisdom. That dilemma becomes clear when invited work enters the review process and is judged factually less robust than it could be (or was heard to be by the editor). Rejection is straightforward, but the message that is heard by the author and the profession is that innovations are unwelcome.

Another way to attract new material is to publish special issues. During *ASQ*'s history, I have been the guest editor of a special issue on laboratory experimentation initiated by Bill Starbuck when he was editor (1969, Volume 14, Issue 2), and I have worked with guest editors on the topics of qualitative methods, utilization of organizational research, and organizational culture. Special issues are among the most controversial devices *ASQ* has used to introduce innovations.

My reasons for encouraging special issues include the following: Special issues call attention to a topic at a time when it seems useful to consolidate what is known so that the rate of improvement can be accelerated. Special issues introduce new reviewers into the normal review process. Special issues attract work that might have gone unnoticed. Special issues legitimize topics for investigation. They essentially say, "It's OK to do work of this kind." Special issues give editors a temporary reprieve when regular manuscripts are tied up in the revision process and it is difficult to fill an issue (a problem that is not shared by other journals that have less intensive review processes and that do not work as close to deadlines as *ASQ* does). Special issues provide a single source where people can get on top of a new field by reading original work rather than reviews. Special issues can also advertise that *ASQ* is interested in reading more work on topics that authors had not previously associated with the journal. It is hard for journals to break the stereotypes that are attached to them. One of the few ways to show that a stereotype is wrong is to publish work that people thought was alien to the editorial policy.

The darker side of special issues is summarized in Howard Aldrich's observation, "The probability that enough good authors are doing enough good work at the same time to really fill an issue is very small."

Frequent special issues may give the wrong signals to the field; namely, you should be involved in hot topics rather than pursue one area in depth until it is under control. Special issues can slow the progress of a field because they tempt people to drop what they are doing and draft something topical that might be accepted.

Reviewers worry that the threshold of acceptability is lower in special issues than in regular issues. It is argued that it is easier to get into a special issue than into a regular issue of *ASQ*. There is a disincentive to write for regular issues, where the chances of getting in (32 manuscripts accepted out of 300 submissions = 11% chance of acceptance) are less than for a special issue (9 manuscripts accepted out of 50 submissions = 18% chance of getting in): One chance in 5 of being accepted is considerably higher than 1 chance in 10.

Quality can be a problem in special issues for a quite different reason. If the best people in an area have not been recruited into the editing process itself, they are often too busy to write something that can be finished within the tight time deadlines associated with most special issues. Thus the best people either submit nothing or they submit something drafted in haste that is either rejected or published with reluctance.

Special issues make most sense if their publication is timely, meaning that the articles appear in print when interest in the topic is intense and building. Considerations of timeliness may conflict with considerations of quality. Initial submissions that are in good shape have a much better chance of being accepted than do those that contain the "germ" of a good idea but need an extensive rewrite. Although the "germ" might actually be more powerful than the polished submission, it tends to be swept aside in the interest of getting the issue out before people lose interest or before other journals stake out the topic. Special issues do draw attention to journals, even if some of that attention is critical, and any editor who wants to attract readers, authors, and income cannot ignore the value of having his or her special issue be a mandatory citation for anyone doing work in the area.

Aside from these reservations, regular authors often complain when their accepted articles are delayed while we insert a special issue into the publication schedule. One of the strongest inducements *ASQ* can offer authors is that, if they will continue to revise and improve their papers, we will publish the accepted paper within three to six months. The author who devotes full time to a revision gets both an improved manuscript and quicker publication than is possible with most other journals. But if regular publication schedules are disrupted by insertion of a special issue, editors cannot deliver on the promise of speed.

In an effort to signal that *ASQ* was interested in both regular topics and special topics, we split the special issue on utilization, publishing half of it in December 1982 and the other half in March 1983. The flow of regular articles was not disrupted, but some impact and continuity were lost when articles on the common theme of utilization were separated.

Evidentiary Reviews

The review process itself has a major effect on a journal's response to innovations. By definition, it is impossible to do peer review of groundbreaking pieces. Yet that is just what journals try to do.

The editor's job is to protect the authors of innovation from the review process, a process that usually makes visible the biases an author is working against. The review process is a conserving process in the sense that it asks innovators for more documentation, more evidence, and more literature to show why the proposal is better than what we have. Ideally, the editor guides the innovator to improve the argument so that it either incorporates the conserving forces or shows their irrelevance. The crucial priority is to preserve the innovation so that it does not get blurred, misstated, or assimilated while addressing the past history of a field.

The task of protecting innovations while they are simultaneously being evaluated, improved, and dismissed is made more difficult because of a peculiar property of the journal review system. Evaluations made by reviewers are often made in a private channel where they are not subject to the same standards of proof that are imposed on the public channels of publication. I have yet to return a review with the request that a reviewer revise and resubmit it. Reviewers are sometimes held to lower standards of evidence than are the authors whom they criticize. Science supposedly advances through a public forum where people improve each other's work by publicly criticizing it and demonstrating more valid ways to treat the issues. The private reviewing channel removes the public, contestable character of criticism and has the potential to insert idiosyncratic standards into the evaluation process.

The private reviewing channel can be especially hard on innovations because people who evaluate innovations often have vested interests in their own ideas and are not enthusiastic about ideas that refute or ignore them.

The private channel persists because it is difficult to contest reviews furnished by scarce experts whose participation is voluntary, time consuming, and unpaid. There are costs even to authors when editors override reviewers, because better reviewers leave the system and the remaining reviews are of poorer quality. Furthermore, the reviewing process itself takes longer because editors have to approach more people before they are able to compose a group that can provide credible input. The very thing that authors welcome, detailed prompt reviews, is made possible in part because editors do take reviewers seriously and go against their advice with reluctance.

There are several ways to make the private channel more accountable, and *ASQ* uses all of them. Editors evaluate manuscripts independently of reviewers and use these evaluations as a guide when they decide which reviewer comments the author should take most seriously. When editors do an independent evaluation, they treat reviewer comments as advisory, which can cause problems for both reviewers and authors.

Reviewers, believing that their evaluations are prescriptive rather than advisory, wonder why they should even bother to write reviews if editors seem to ignore them. What the reviewers do not realize is that their line of criticism often would not survive public scrutiny. Many reviewer comments that editors override say essentially, "This is bad because I say so."

Authors are often puzzled when an editor is highly critical of a manuscript that reviewers seem to like. Usually these discrepancies occur when the editors spend more time on the manuscript than the reviewers do, a division of labor that is not always evident to the author. The author is then in a bind as to whether he or she should respond to the editor or to the reviewers, who have said something quite different.

The private channel of evaluation undergoes some correction when reviewers read an editor's letter in which their reviews are either lauded or ignored, and when reviewers read how other referees evaluated the same manuscript. The self-correction, however, is slow and easy to defend against.

The private channel also undergoes correction when good reviewers are kept and poor reviewers replaced. However, replacement decisions are difficult to make. Thorough, thoughtful reviews take time to write and they tend to be written by people who are experts in their field. Experts tend to be overburdened. While they take their reviewing responsibilities seriously, they often are inundated by requests from many journals to review manuscripts. Editors have to wait longer for the better quality reviews, and therein lies the rub.

ASQ is committed to giving authors prompt, detailed feedback. When the demands of promptness and detail conflict, I have favored promptness over detail. I ask associate editors to make acceptance decisions using only two reviews if the third review is overdue and unlikely to materialize soon. I put pressure on the managing editor to tell authors to be patient and to tell reviewers that we are impatient. The pressured reviewer may then write a few hasty comments, which are basically useless because they say essentially, "I see nothing of merit here." When the editor ignores such a review, the late reviewer gets mad that he or she even bothered to write at all because people ignored the "review."

The question is this: Should slow experts be replaced? I have tried to keep them on, hassle them, and pay close attention to their graduate students as potential alternative reviewers. As a result, turnover on *ASQ* has been relatively slow. Against this background, when turnover does occur, it can leave some rough edges.

To manage the review process is to transform a particularistic, private evaluation system incrementally into a more universalistic, public system while retaining the relatively scarce, overworked voluntary participants who think the private channel is working just fine (until they submit work of their own).

Close Copyediting

Does editing improve or destroy innovations? Authors often complain that editing removes most of what is original in their papers, while editors complain that authors can neither write nor judge what is good and bad in their own work. *ASQ* has intensive contact with authors throughout the publication process. The question, "Just whose manuscript is this anyway?" often lies just below the surface in an author's mind, as reviewing, revising, and editing proceed.

To understand the complex relationship between editing and innovation is to understand the role of synonyms in organizational studies. One line of argument assumes that ideas inhere in specific sentences and that there is no such thing as a synonym. To change a word is to change an idea. Even though different words may seem equivalent, or substitute for one another, in fact different words mean different things. To use words synonymously when referring to a "singular" event is to introduce imprecision into thinking.

Under the assumption that there is no such thing as a synonym, authors resist changes of any kind in their written argument and copy editors *remove* synonyms rather than add them. The removal of synonyms may improve accuracy and precision, but often at the expense of generality in the explanation.

Those who feel that synonyms are a source of strength rather than weakness see things differently. Organizational events are viewed as overdetermined and oversimplified. Multiple descriptors are necessary to portray complex events accurately, and synonyms preserve multiple, related properties of a single event. Under the assumption that synonyms are a source of accuracy, authors state a single idea in several different ways, and copy editors add synonyms and rephrase the ideas they read.

When an author's grasp on an idea is tenuous, specific phrases or metaphors *are* crucial to preserve the modest understanding that has been won. Synonyms and editing *can* be dangerous at this formative stage. To describe the idea differently may be to lose the nuance that first caught attention. There is no question that innovations are shaky in their early stages.

The argument that editing improves innovation does not apply to the early stages of an innovation in which survival is problematic. The argument does imply that new ideas can be sent into the review process too soon. The editorial process is relatively heavy-handed and it is not organized to delicately handle delicate structures of argument. Delicate structures are best developed in very sympathetic, supportive company, which is not something most journals provide.

Thus editing works on synonyms. It removes them to make an idea more accurate. It adds them to make an idea more general. Either change is harmful if ideas inhere in specific sentences. Ideas are most likely to inhere in specific sentences when they are first developed. As they mature and become more general, their texture survives independently of specific expressions, and they are usually improved rather than worsened by synonym work.

(Note: The editors of this volume suggest that the reader see Chapter 13 for alternative perspectives on *ASQ*'s copyediting practices.)

THE EVALUATION OF INNOVATION

Despite the preceding problems, innovations still get evaluated carefully by thoughtful people who care about the substance and quality of organizational studies. This chapter concludes with a brief review of some of the questions referees ask when they examine an innovation and try to judge its value.

(1) How complete is the defense of the idea? A more fully developed defense has the following structure. The author starts by saying: "what I propose is an innovation because people have thought X all along. Here are some examples that show this; X, however, is wrong. Here is what should have been said instead. If you adopt this newer position, you can explain not only those original findings but also these additional findings that the old explanation can't handle. This position also implies what people should do next." In a full defense, the author shows how some display looks different before and after it is viewed using the innovation that is proposed.

(2) Relative to what is this an innovation? Innovations do not occur in a vacuum. Something is innovative relative to something else. When authors specify that something else, their innovation gets more attention. How authors handle a literature review is often a good clue to the adequacy with which they have handled this point, because most authors have it backward. We need more literature embedding around an innovation than around normal science. With normal science, everyone can fill in the relevant background because the work being done is so much like the work that has been done before. We need help, however, to

see where an innovative piece fits in, what people have done wrong before, and how the proposed innovation improves on related assertions made previously. Most authors give dense citations for normal science but cite almost nothing for innovations. That makes it tougher to assess how the innovation might be instrumental to improve theory.

(3) How much dirty work did the author leave? The easiest innovation to assess is the one where the author actually demonstrates the value of the idea through data, thought experiments, case analyses, or reinterpretation of old data. The hardest innovations to assess are those where an idea is proposed for someone else to test. Good ideas tend to be used. If people claim they are presenting a good idea, but haven't used it to further their own thinking, or if their own thinking does not look any better with the idea than it did without the idea, then there is reason to doubt the innovation.

(4) What signals will this manuscript give? If the work is innovative but flawed, reviewers worry about whether publication of the flawed piece will encourage other studies that are similarly flawed or other studies that are improvements. Innovations have drawing power. Unfortunately, they draw *both* imitations and improvements—and these two outcomes are not equally likely. People who are too busy doing their own research to read tend to be the better researchers and the people in the best position to improve upon innovative pieces. Those who have more time to read may be less active researchers and may be more likely to do simple extensions of published work that perpetuate flaws rather than correct them. There is no guarantee that poor work will attract better work. Poor work may simply legitimize other poor work.

REFERENCES

Anderson, P. A. (1983). Decision making by objection and the Cuban missile crisis. *Administrative Science Quarterly, 28,* 201-222.

Bettman, J. R., & Weitz, B. A. (1983). Attribution in the board room: Causal reasoning in corporate annual reports. *Administrative Science Quarterly, 28,* 165-183.

Gronn, P. C. (1983). Talk as the work: The accomplishment of school administration. *Administrative Science Quarterly, 28,* 1-21.

Leblebici, H., & Salancik, G. R. (1982). Stability in interorganizational exchanges: Rulemaking processes of the Chicago Board of Trade. *Administrative Science Quarterly, 27,* 227-242.

McCaffrey, D. P. (1982). Corporate resources and regulatory pressures: Toward explaining a discrepancy. *Administrative Science Quarterly, 27,* 398-419.

McNeil, K., & Miller, R. E. (1980). The profitability of consumer protection: Warranty policy in the auto industry. *Administrative Science Quarterly, 25,* 407-427.

Meyer, A. D. (1982). Adapting to environmental jolts. *Administrative Science Quarterly, 27,* 515-537.

Ranson, S., Hinings, B., & Greenwood, R. (1980). The structuring of organizational structures. *Administrative Science Quarterly, 25,* 1-17.

Useem, M. (1982). Classwide rationality in the politics of managers and directors of large corporations in the United States and Great Britain. *Administrative Science Quarterly, 27,* 199-226.

20

Breaking Frames
The Creation of JMI

THOMAS G. CUMMINGS

ALAN M. GLASSMAN

And the trouble is, if you don't risk anything, you risk even more.
Erica Jong

PROLOGUE

To understand the founding of the *Journal of Management Inquiry,* it is necessary to comment on the culture of its sponsoring organization, the Western Academy of Management. From our perspective, the Western Academy of Management (WAM) is guided by two primary, somewhat contradictory forces: (a) a pioneering verve associated with western folklore that encourages both informality/camaraderie among members and challenges to existing academic protocols and (b) a healthy fixation on the importance of nurturing newer members' interests while demonstrating respect for our heritage. As an outcome, it is not unusual for members to boast about the "creative tension" that exists within the organization and to perceive WAM as a leader in exploring new ideas for program development, member outreach, and personal growth. Moreover, at the annual WAM meetings, members often comment on how easy it is to differentiate WAM from the other "more traditional" regions of the Academy of Management.

As WAM entered the mid-1980s, a small, but increasing number of members raised questions around organizational complacency. Briefly summarized, they contended that, while they perceived the annual WAM program and ancillary activities as having good quality and/or value, there was a lack of freshness and an unwillingness to risk our limited resources to pursue new ventures. As stated at one business meeting, by an old-timer, "We're becoming too damn predictable!"

During the next several years, the desire to move into new arenas gained momentum. As a result, WAM initiated such activities as (a) a biannual international conference, seeking a one-third participation rate from other countries; (b) a doctoral/junior faculty workshop, emphasizing small group interactions with senior faculty and the questioning of traditional role expectations; and (c) reconfigured program designs, allocating more time to pursuit of a single theme and including more peripheral, controversial topics. It was in this receptive environment that *JMI* had its beginning.

The Last Session: Big Sky, Montana, 1988

The actual idea for *JMI* emerged at the final program session at the annual WAM meeting in Big Sky, Montana, in 1988. The last session features one or two distinguished western colleagues (e.g., Warren Bennis, Bob Tannenbaum, Warren Schmidt) who speak on a topic of personal choice. The only criterion is that they "provoke" thought/controversy among attenders.

The speakers at that session were Larry Greiner (University of Southern California) and Tony Raia (University of California, Los Angeles). Both, unbeknownst to the other, focused on dimensions of the academic socialization process, adopting the position that the "rules of the game" did a disservice to newer colleagues and that senior faculty (as guardians of the rules) were perpetuating an inappropriate and potentially psychologically damaging process. One presentation included an analogy to fraternity hazing.

Among their combined points (related to the eventual emergence of *JMI*) were the following:

- Junior faculty are compelled/coerced into focusing on narrow specializations and publishing in a few "A" journals to establish the reputation needed to obtain tenure; as a consequence, these faculty must often neglect longitudinal studies and set aside any eclectic interests until after they reach full professor (i.e., 12-14 years).

- Personnel committees, at all levels, value quantitative methodologies over qualitative approaches; this preference severely limits expressive thought as a means of exploring our field (of interest, we often seek the opposite for conference sessions).

- Both of the above are reinforced by the leading management journals, which seek "tight" quantitative studies whose methodology is beyond reproach; thought pieces do appear but seem to be the exclusive realm of the ensconced gurus of the subdivisions of the field.

Of course, the presentations encompassed many other dimensions of academic socialization, including assessments of Ph.D. training, mentoring systems, and instructional preparedness.

At the end of their presentations, Greiner and Raia received a spontaneous standing ovation—they had obviously touched a nerve among the attendees. The follow-up discussion uncovered many shared opinions and "war stories" from both nontenured and tenured faculty. Equally important, however, was the acceptance by the group of an alternative view (expressed by only a few) that, despite identifiable limitations, the existing academic order did achieve the needed rigor, depth, and quality expected by the profession. As the session concluded, nearly everyone agreed that the "intensity and richness" of the discussion exceeded expectations and probably would occur only at a WAM meeting.

FANTASYLAND

At nearly all professional conferences (including WAM), it is commonplace for most participants to abandon the meeting site immediately upon completion of the last session. Fortuitously, WAM was in Big Sky, Montana; many participants were staying for the skiing and many others had to wait several hours for a bus to the airport at Bozeman. This provided a singular opportunity for a large number of attendees to continue the passionate dialogue of the last session. As members sat around the main fireplace in the lodge exchanging thoughts, a number of "What if?" and "Why can't we?" questions emerged, several concerning research and publication (e.g., "What if there were a journal that published innovative ideas or work under development? Why can't we have high-quality alternatives in our field?"). Overall, the people were letting their collective imagination loose on academia with one wild idea followed by another; many of the most "radical" ideas came from newer faculty who were older and took exception to numerous institutional constraints that they insisted were designed for the younger doctoral recipient of another era.

It was during this time that Alan Glassman (the next year's WAM program chair and president-elect) and John Seybolt (the newly installed president) had a short chat over a glass of wine. John (who had recently started the initiative that would lead to WAM's first international conference in Shizuoka, Japan) believed that WAM needed to respond to the enthusiasm of the members by launching another new venture. Alan (who had recently coedited *Managerial Consultation* for Human Sciences Press and who unabashedly admits he enjoyed being an editor) suggested a WAM-sponsored journal. John agreed to support the initial exploration, which Alan could continue during the next year. The discussion lasted less than 15 minutes.

Flights of Imagination

The airplane that Alan took from Bozeman was crammed with colleagues who had to go through the Salt Lake City hub. This offered the first opportunity to "test" individual willingness to pursue the creation of a journal; the conversations were decidedly mixed. Briefly stated, advocates emphasized the need for an alternative journal for the often praised, but rarely published, nontraditional research and underground thought pieces, insisting that current journals were too restrictive. The skeptics, on the other hand, questioned whether such a narrow yet ill-defined purpose should be pursued, arguing that, although the journal made sense on an intellectual level, continuous high quality could not be sustained. Thus the first substantive one-to-one conversations suggested that a consensus to proceed with a WAM-sponsored journal would be difficult to obtain.

Yet the whimsical discussions from the end of the conference continued. Nearly everyone, regardless of opinion, liked the idea of a somewhat audacious professional journal as symbolic of WAM's self-image. In fact, some individuals seemed to exhibit the zeal of old-time missionaries, embarking on a new assignment to a newly discovered land—not knowing what they would find but confident in their rightness. Subsequently, emerging on this flight were several "champions" who agreed to gather ideas from others and begin the difficult process of conceptualizing the journal. Newt Margulies volunteered to develop a "working" proposal.

On the flight from Salt Lake City to Los Angeles, we (i.e., Alan and Tom) had our initial conversation regarding the journal, speculating on whether a niche really existed and on the difficulty of gaining credibility. We agreed that, if WAM undertook this venture, acceptance by the academic community needed to be the primary measure of success. We playfully ruminated on how we would appeal to officers of the Academy of Management; the challenge seemed formidable.

Tom also assumed the role that he would maintain throughout the developmental process—the friendly devil's advocate.

A Fairy Godmother and a Day to Remember

During the next six months, an effort was made to advance the developmental process by formulating a coherent vision. Alan maintained contact with the "champions," soliciting any innovative ideas for design and content differentiation, but he was disappointed by their lack of creativity; Newt prepared an initial proposal for a new journal, admitting that the document was not as persuasive/ powerful as desired and did not capture the excitement of Big Sky; Tom thrashed nearly all possibilities, noting the overall messiness of thought and the lack of any unifying academic themes. There were serious discussions on discontinuing the exploration. It was requiring more time and we did not seem to be making any noticeable progress in defining the journal.

During this period, the only truly encouraging remarks came from the conversations Alan and Newt held with Ann West, the editor for the management and communication fields at Sage Publications. Of the several publishers/editors contacted, only Ann expressed interest in pursuing an alternative journal—she described our array of ideas as nontraditional. She noted that, although Sage was a leading publisher of "mainstream" academic journals, the editors and executive staff had frequently discussed the need to revitalize existing journals and pursue new projects to capture the expansive thinking that was occurring in the field. She also reported that Sage had recently rejected several proposals as "lacking freshness." Without question, it was this external demonstration of support, during our most hesitant period, that provided the motivation to proceed.

With the impetus from the aforementioned discussions, Alan and Newt reverted to their belief in group process. With financial support from the executive committee of WAM, they invited a small group of colleagues to a one-day exploratory meeting in Los Angeles.[1] The meeting began with a critique of Newt's revised proposal—the group liked many of the ideas but was still stymied by the absence of a coherent theme. Then, feeling somewhat frustrated, the group turned to the well-established practice of generating a list of metaphors/expressions that encompassed their individual desires for the journal (see Table 20.1). As the list progressed, a sense of excitement emerged. Several hours later, the group had (a) agreed upon the name, *Journal of Management Inquiry,* (b) adopted the metaphor "the academics' *New Yorker*" to portray the theme of alternative forms of expression, and (c) identified the six primary sections, each (similar to some popular magazines) to have its own editor and editorial board

TABLE 20.1 *The Journal of Management Inquiry*

Self-Concept			
Unique	Provocative	Relevant	Readable
Inviting	Freeing	Citable	Groundbreaking
Scholarly	Exploratory	Impactful	Exciting
Catalytic	Eclectic	Integrative	Complementary
Current	Challenging	Broad viewed	Populist
Interesting	Irresistible	Varied	Authoritative
Good thinking	Learningful	Reputable	Subscribable

Excitingly written	Involvement enhancing
Learning from experience	Something that matters
Fast turnaround	A window for new approaches
Seminal	"Research," "preresearch," and "postresearch"

A way to think out loud professionally
Open to alternative modes of thinking and methods of inquiry
The academics' *New Yorker*
Multimodes of exposition—"all the modes that's fit to print"
Provokes innovative thinking and new ideas
Vehicle that stimulates, legitimizes, and normalizes creative reflective thinking
Contributes to the theoretical development of management practice
Expresses and enhances the consciousness of "the Westerns"
Not just another journal!!!

under the guidance/direction of a principal editor: essays, nontraditional research, reflections from experience, dialogue, meet the person, and reviews. In 1993 *JMI* added global voice.

It is impossible to capture on paper the ambience of the meeting. We all knew that we had cracked the traditional management journal paradigm—something special had taken place. As expressed by two group members, "this was an electrifying day" and "the best academic meeting I've attended in a decade."

ADVENTURELAND

During the next 18 months, we all relearned the time lag factor between idea conceptualization and actual execution. Among the more demanding events were the following:

- Outside reviews of the proposal (obtained by Sage) were split; reviewers either embraced or depreciated the focus on alternative modes of expression. This provided ammunition to the naysayers within Sage who argued that publishing the journal engendered too many risks, an issue that was decided by the president after several meetings.

- Negotiation of the contract between WAM and Sage Publications took several months and needed a vote of the WAM membership; this was a controversial issue given that most new journals lose money during the start-up years and WAM's investment could be substantial.

- Questions of fairness in the selection of the editors led to both an informal and a formal nomination and decision-making process; as expected, there was a fair amount of politicking and some hurt feelings.

In September 1990, more than two years after the Big Sky meeting, all the preliminary details were completed. We were appointed by WAM as the initial editor-in-chief and associate editor-in-chief. With the subsequent appointment of the section editors, we began the process of launching the journal. The goal was to publish the first issue in March 1992. Little did we expect that the adventure was just beginning and that we would need all that time.

Preparing for Launch

So far, conversations about the journal had been rather playful and metaphorical with limited time demands. This made it easier to obtain diverse inputs from participants, to build on each other's ideas, to gain broad commitment, and to agree on a general thrust. With the signing of the Sage contract and our appointment as editors, however, the venture rapidly shifted toward accomplishing specific tasks with demanding deadlines. Among the preliminary chores needing almost immediate resolution were (a) drafting an editorial statement and submission guidelines, (b) producing an initial call for papers and accompanying marketing materials, (c) selecting members for the editorial review boards for each of the six sections, (d) determining criteria for assessing submissions for each section, (e) deciding on the role responsibilities of the different editors (i.e., editor-in-chief, associate editor-in-chief, section editors) and their working relationship during the different stages of the review and publication process, and (f) establishing a working relationship with Sage's marketing and editorial personnel.

Thankfully, Sage assigned one of its most senior (and patient) editors, Harry Briggs, to work with us on these start-up tasks. From the beginning, Harry empathized with our struggle to define the unique niche for *JMI* and treated us as fellow explorers of new territory, both for Sage and for WAM. He genuinely liked the idea of a "nontraditional" journal and encouraged us throughout his tenure with the journal to "be different," to "be bold," and to "have fun." Not unrelated, Harry had a great sense of humor and delighted in tweaking the status quo. In some ways, he served as our conscience whenever we became comfortable. It also didn't hurt that Harry came across more like a disheveled scholar than a pinstriped book pusher.

During the next eight months, we held three organizational meetings, the first in Los Angeles in January and then at the WAM and Academy of Management annual meetings in March and August, respectively. The first two meetings involved the editors and Harry, while the third also included the newly appointed editorial boards for each section and the marketing manager for Sage. As preparation for the initial meeting, we proposed a policy statement, manuscript guidelines, call for papers, and publication timetable. The section editors developed preliminary descriptions for their respective sections and lists of prospective board members. At subsequent meetings, the editors and board members suggested nontraditional areas and methodologies that the journal might explore, individuals who might be invited to submit, and approaches to promoting the journal. This material served to guide our discussion and decision making. It provided an understanding of participants' perceptions and ideas; it offered a starting point for working through ambiguities and disagreements; perhaps most important, it accented areas where our thinking was decidedly traditional.

Taken together, these meetings provided an interpersonal forum for clarifying the purpose and thrust of the journal, for sharing and debating ideas on how to develop each section, and for making initial decisions on editorial process protocols and marketing. More important, however, the meetings enabled us to form strong personal ties with each other and to develop the requisite trust "demanded" by our structural design. Consequently, a set of behavioral norms and relationships emerged that have continued to serve us well. For instance, because none of the editors had experience with starting a journal, much less a nontraditional journal, we treated each other equally, with little role or hierarchial separation; there were no fiefdoms, and members felt free to offer each other ideas, express disagreements, and challenge perceived traditional thinking. The same practices applied to our interactions with Sage as we tried to pinpoint/promote our niche—at times we thought we were part of their creative staff. Throughout, the only sacred—and recurring—theme was the quest for high-quality, innovative forms of inquiry.

The shared fight to transcend traditional thinking served to bring us closer together as an editorial team. The irony was that this "common enemy" often resided within ourselves. After all, we had all progressed and prospered under the existing order. To counteract our personal tendencies toward the usual approaches to journal issues/administration, we adopted a useful norm: We would ask how a prominent traditional journal would most likely address the issue, then we would offer as many alternative suggestions as possible for doing it differently. At our annual meeting of editorial boards, for example, we eschewed such customary formalities as sitting in classroom format and distributing journal statistics. Instead, we sat in a large circle, ate and drank, and simply brainstormed ideas for enhancing/improving the journal. Over 80% of the discussion involved interactions (i.e., debates, explorations, discussions) among board members, while we sought to capture the ideas and determine their applicability. Two comments by different board members capture their sense of these meetings: "These are among the most stimulating sessions I attend . . ." and "You've made the meeting fun. . . . You are a little crazy." Of course, for us, in addition to having fun and developing stronger ties with colleagues, some of the best ideas for the journal come out of these informal sessions.

Some Technical Difficulties

During this period, we encountered a number of discomfiting obstacles that required prudent resolution. For example, several weeks after the first meeting, one of the section editors determined that the required time investment (due to the entrepreneurial nature of the venture) was unreasonable and withdrew. Finding an appropriate replacement was time consuming, while integrating another set of expectations tested our mediation abilities. Other problems/dilemmas included competition for board members (an individual could serve on only one board and a majority of each board needed to be from the western geographic area); subjecting invited papers by high visibility colleagues to the same review process as other submitters, resulting in some disputed rejections; and a contract interpretation misunderstanding between WAM and Sage.

The most serious start-up issue, however, was the quality of the initial manuscripts. As expected, we received many "bottom drawer" papers that were quickly rejected by our editorial board reviewers. Unfortunately, we did not receive many high-quality, nontraditional submissions. This seemed to reflect our difficulty in conveying in brief advertisements the thrust of the journal as well as the "wait and see" approach of potential contributors. Thus, for the first several issues, we struggled to maintain our standards for publication. In hindsight, we were favored with a few articles in each section that served as useful exemplars.

FRONTIERLAND

Although we made good progress on the start-up tasks at the early meetings, further clarification and choices on how to operate the journal and what to publish could only be made on-line as we reviewed manuscripts and made editorial decisions. In essence, we had to learn how to create the journal by actually doing it. This required constant discussions between us and the different section editors, ranging from whether a submission fit the nontraditional thrust of the journal (e.g., we rejected, often after heated debate, several high-quality articles that seemed more appropriate for already established journals), to determination of the appropriate section for a submission, to the acceptance boundaries for "radical" ideas. These conversations over specific editorial decisions helped us clarify our notions about the journal. They allowed us to co-reference on concrete choices and, through personal exchanges that were sometimes fuzzy, passionate, and conflictual, reach acceptable decisions. We felt comfortable with this "learn-as-you-go" process because we had expended considerable effort confronting and resolving differences during the initial meetings. From our perspective, there was also a great deal of mutual respect and caring.

Exploring the New Territories

The broad vision of the journal centered on offering alternative forms of expression for high-quality, innovative inquiry about management and organizations. As a point of departure, we used the original six sections proposed to Sage. These modes, although derived primarily from nonacademic sources, surfaced initially as potentially legitimate ways to express management knowledge. Because the modes were substantially different than those found in most academic journals in the field, we never envisioned ourselves as competing with existing journals. We always visualized ourselves as providing alternatives to the way we traditionally do and communicate about inquiry.

In the spirit of inquiry, we were not overly attached to our initial sections or expectations of appropriate material, agreeing that they would have to be modified as experience dictated. Over time, we discovered, for instance, that such forms of expression as "dialogue," "meet the person," and "reflections on experience" were more difficult to define, write for, and review than others. It appeared that, for many of us, these were uncomfortable forms of expression, usually ignored in the academic socialization process. In another example, we found ourselves pondering how to offer revision suggestions for an original dialogue.

In trying to define the different sections, we also found the potential for considerable overlap, especially among the "essays," "nontraditional research," and "reflections on experience" sections. Rather than enforce strict boundaries up front, we addressed territorial issues as they were encountered, sometimes talking to several editors before choosing the section to review the submission. One interesting case involved the submission of an "essay based on a personal reflection of nontraditional research." Feedback from our editorial boards and readers led to the addition of a seventh section after our second year of publication: "global voice."

Given these new forms of expression and conceding that the standards for judging manuscripts would be different across sections, we had to identify separate criteria for assessing "quality" and "innovativeness" for each section. This was developed by each section editor in conjunction with his or her editorial board and us. Like most activities with the journal, this required a reiterative learning process characterized by ongoing discussions and specific choices during the review process. Consequently, as a result of our own explorations, we took a great deal of care to assure that the early issues of the journal included a broad array of exemplars intended to show the kind and range of material that was appropriate.

Frontier Justice

Given our unique editorial arrangement (i.e., editor-in-chief, associate editor-in-chief, and section editors), we are often asked at professional meetings and by submitters to describe the review/publication process. Simply stated, after we determine the appropriate section for a submission, the review process is managed by the section editor, who essentially uses members of his or her editorial board as reviewers. Inherent in this autonomy is our mutual understanding of acceptance criteria for specific sections and, most important, our joint commitment to continuous discussions. Our goal is to maintain as much independence for our section editors as they are willing to assume. Thus, for the most part, each commands his or her own jurisdiction.

Our role focuses primarily on the global dimensions of the journal: (a) product mix and section coherence and (b) quality control. In "putting together" an issue, for instance, we are aware of the diversity of our readership. Recognizing the number of competing journals and the need to influence individual decision-making processes, we seek to include a wide variety of articles so that each subscriber will feel compelled to peruse at least two pieces. We also seek to include at least one article that challenges an established "way of thinking" or "pushes the boundaries" in the field. In pursuing these goals, we are overly concerned (paranoid, according to one of our editors) about the quality of the material. This reflects our personal belief that, for a nontraditional journal to succeed, it must obtain a "good quality" reputation for every issue for at least five years.

To ensure our standard of quality, we maintain the prerogative to reject or require a rewrite of any submission accepted by a section editor. At times, and after much discussion, we have rejected articles that we believed were too far from the mainstream and would be perceived as "flaky," or we have rejected articles that we believed belonged in a more traditional journal, or we have negotiated revisions with section editors, reviewers, and authors. As expected, these occurrences cause the most stress for us. Most often, we wind up playing "good cop/bad cop" as we work through the differences. We were once surprised when a section editor enlisted another section editor to intervene as a mediator. On another occasion, we sought out a section editor at a professional meeting to assure ourselves that our friendship had not been damaged by the volatile debate and our subsequent decision to reject. Overall, however, it is our perception that this arrangement helps to maintain the creative tension that has led to the early success of *JMI*.

MAIN STREET, U.S.A.—NOT

From the beginning, an important role for us has been the "selling" of the journal. At professional meetings, we have participated on journal panels and made presentations at business meetings. Similarly, we have spent considerable time each month returning telephone calls to potential submitters who are just discovering the journal. These interactions provide us with an opportunity to increase visibility for the journal and to further differentiate it from the more traditional quality journals. We also seek colleagues to submit, particularly when we become aware that they are pursuing a controversial or nontraditional topic.

The outcome of these entrepreneurial activities and the ongoing promotional campaign by Sage have resulted in a very successful beginning. According to Sage, *JMI* had the fastest growth rate (i.e., subscribers) of any journal in their history. The Western Academy of Management received royalties after only one year. Submissions continue to increase and our section editors are beginning to "fight" for space. And most important to us, nearly all the professional comments have been positive.

As we begin our third year, several colleagues have even suggested that the journal's future is secure. Paraphrasing one, "You've made it, you're part of the accepted journal community." We disagree! The journal is in the early stages of its life cycle and, as we noted above, we believe it will require five years to establish itself as a quality alternative for nontraditional, innovative work. We believe we have introduced a new frame to the world of management journals. We are a long way from Main Street—it is our goal to maintain the distance.

NOTE

1. This group deserves credit for the vision that became the *Journal of Management Inquiry:* Joan Dahl, André Delbecq, Roger Evered, Larry Greiner, Newt Margulies, Allan Mohrman, and Dennis Umstot. Tony Raia served as facilitator.

Epilogue

A s we close the book, we would like to offer our thoughts concerning three themes. These are intended as both summary and suggestion. They derive not only from our reading, rereading, and studying the work of the book's contributors but also from numerous private reflections by each of us. Of course, they have been embellished and refined by our hours of conversations as we absorbed what we and the others have done. As we have constructed, edited, and reviewed this second edition, we feel that the words we wrote on the epilogue of the first edition stand as the statement we want to have as the conclusion to the book. We think they are quite enduring.

WHERE HAVE WE BEEN?

What are the lessons that one might learn from the experiences, data, thoughts, and feelings presented here? We believe that the central learning is the importance and value of being conscious of the state and drama of the total publishing enterprise, including manuscript preparation, processes of submission, perspectives on reviewing, as well as the intellectual and emotional reactions associated with successes and failures. We believe this advanced consciousness provides a positive value of sensitizing new entrants and encouraging established scholars to frankly and openly articulate their perspectives, schemas, and biases. Sensitization and relevance alone were not our aims, however. We hope

310

that both can provide the basis for creativity, constructive self-reflection, and adaptability in our disciplines. All this, we believe, can be aimed at sustaining and enhancing the stimulation of our fields and the contributions to both scholarship and enjoyable intellectual growth.

What do we see, reflected in the contents of this book, as contributing to this central learning and hope? First, there do exist, and now they are documented through personally meaningful witnessings, multiple perspectives of position, of career stage, and of theoretical orientation toward the publishing enterprise. Persons clearly differ concerning most of the core issues, strategies, and questions in publishing. Furthermore, they differ systematically by their intellectual backgrounds, training, experiences, academic tenure, and positions of power and influence in our disciplines.

Second, the joys and, occasionally, euphoria of "becoming published," of authentication, of acknowledgment, and of making an intellectual contribution are not only real but are major sources of personal efficacy for many. Likewise, the pains, even occasionally the agony, of rejection, criticism, and unmet expectations are real. We believe that many of the testimonies offered here, by both the less and the more established, aptly document both sets of emotions.

Third, there is evident a certain sense of self-discovery within several of the contributions. In particular, we believe that Nord, Graham and Stablein, Schoorman, Daft, Pondy, Perrow, and certainly both of us experienced a certain sensation captured by the statement: "Now that I have committed to express my thoughts and feelings, and have actually articulated them, I better understand what I believe." Thus perhaps what we have seen here is partially the articulation of the implicit assumptions surrounding much of the publishing enterprise.

Fourth, many of the contributors have offered explicit prescriptions concerning several aspects of the publishing endeavor. As noted, and perhaps surprising to some of our readers, the prescriptions do not form a single, unified set of guidelines on "how to" and "how not to." These prescriptions are implicit in the perspectives of Frost and Taylor, Deetz, and Nord. Both of the chapters by the "entering" professionals offer hopes, fears, and prescriptions about how it "might be." Of course, each of our reviewer contributors offers prescriptions for reviewing, even though Rousseau might claim her contribution to be more descriptive than normative. Perrow and Schneider convert their years of "authoring" into guidelines and lessons. How to constructively handle the emotions elicited by successes and rejections is offered by the psychiatric perspective on experience, intellect, and emotion. Prescriptions are easily discovered just below the surface of the accounts of realities in the editorial saddle. Thus, while we did not set out to prepare a normative treatise, nor do we value our product primarily for its prescriptive contributions, the "how-tos," the "should bes," and the hopes and aspirations of our contributors do speak out.

WHAT WERE OUR (CUMMINGS'S AND FROST'S) DISCOVERIES AND SURPRISES ALONG THE PATH OF CONSTRUCTING THE BOOK?

Our insights and learnings were, most profoundly, as follows:

1. Our field is benefited by highly professional, concerned colleagues who are concerned about the following:
   (a) Being constructively prescriptive to colleagues about the issues surrounding publishing. The cynicism of the antagonist, of the rejectee, of the solely critical reviewer is not the only, perhaps not even the predominant, posture toward our enterprise. Perhaps we are seeing what we hope to see here. We think not. We believe that we have challenged others to express the latent desire to build a constructive, humane, highly professional, and high-quality platform for publishing and to reward those who contribute accordingly.
   (b) Leaving a meaningful, lively, self-regenerating, adapting legacy for others within our discipline.
   (c) Exploring how to effectively sustain, develop, and use multiple, even conflicting, minds (mostly between contributors but also within single personages in a few cases) about what is and what *should be*.
   (d) Articulating emotions, their anger, delight, depression, and mania about publishing as it relates to their and others' careers. The book is more emotive than we anticipated. We view that as an asset.

We interpret these concerns as having been latent within many of us, possibly for years in some cases. Perhaps the timing of this book was fortunate, both in the sense that our disciplines have reached a stage of maturity where self-reflection is instructive and in the sense that our contributors (and ourselves) had a *real* message to communicate, given the opportunity and the challenge.

2. The apparent magnitude of the changes in perspectives about one's work, one's importance, and the norms and strategies of publishing that occur across career stages are much larger than we initially anticipated. Both of us have experienced and are experiencing these. Their generality and commonness as articulated by many of our contributors was the surprising element. These shifts and their significance are seen particularly vividly in Perrow's longitudinal self-analysis and in a cross-sectional viewing of the "entering" contributors relative to the insights offered by the established researchers, authors, reviewers, and those in the editorial saddles. We believe that our field has clearly underestimated the magnitude and

importance of these shifts in perspective. It is also likely that their impact upon individuals' careers, feelings of efficacy, *and* the development of the disciplines (e.g., their paradigmatic nature, innovativeness, and potential for intellectual attraction and stimulation) have been underappreciated.

WHERE SHOULD WE HEAD?

What normative themes do we wish to advocate based upon our experiences in constructing this book? Our advocacies center on five concepts:

(1) Content or Substance. Strive for significance! A consistent theme throughout the book has been the emphasis from all perspectives on having something significant to say when attempting to publish. Significance seems to have at least three dimensions: intellectual stimulation of the scholar; contribution to the discipline's theoretical and substantive base; and, for some of our contributors, personal significance relative to ethical and/or social issues.

(2) Craftsmanship. Write well! Many of the chapters advocate and illustrate the centrality of high-quality craftsmanship in design, method, analysis, *and* writing. The commentaries by Perrow (Chapter 12), Pacanowsky and Strine (Chapter 14) are all well-articulated witnesses to the weight attached to craftsmanship in both self-evaluation of one's contributions and the evaluation of others' efforts.

(3) Courage. Have the courage to:

(a) write in the first place, to place one's work in the public domain;
(b) openly seek feedback about the quality of one's work;
(c) withstand criticism and to reflect upon that criticism cognitively, going beyond one's natural emotional reactions;
(d) provide honest, open, constructive feedback to others—both critical commentary and well-organized praise take courage.

(4) Tenacity. Be persistent! Upon occasion, dogged perseverance becomes an important ingredient in the pursuit of publishing. He or she is naive who comes to believe that the contribution of tenacity ends when the conceptualization and research are complete. Consistent, repeated pursuit of exposure to the scholarly

community can be central to receiving one's credits and recognitions and to exerting an impact on the disciplines.

(5) Emotion. Work with and through your (and others') emotions! Getting published, being published (even when it occurs serendipitously), being criticized, rejected, and even shamed generate deep-seated emotional reactions. Be prepared for the negatives; remember to celebrate the recognitions; support and join colleagues in both human conditions. Perhaps we do an incomplete job in anticipatory socialization of entrants to our disciplines. As noted upon several occasions in this volume, doctoral programs do not train reviewers and editors. Neither do they typically prepare us for the emotional content generated by our own behaviors and others' reactions to those behaviors. The point is, of course, not to remove the emotion. Rather, we believe the point is to use emotion toward constructive ends for ourselves, our colleagues, and our disciplines.

Index

Academy of Management, Western. *See*
    Western Academy of Management
Academy of Management Journal (AMJ)
    manuscript reviews by, 166-167
    relevance of, 103-104
Academy of Management Review (AMR)
    relevance of, 103-104
Acceptance/rejection rates, 193, 220-221, 273,
    289-290
Activist reviewing, 253, 261-267
Actors (authors, editors, and reviewers)
    power relationships among, 23-26
    rational model of, 36-39
    See also Authors; Editors; Reviewers
Adhocracies, 67, 69, 76
Administrative Science Quarterly (*ASQ*),
    284-296
    flexibility of, 212
    Grand Scrivener's, 228-231
    manuscript reviews by, 166-167
    relevance of, 102-104
Advocates
    editors as, 291
    reviewers as, 154, 162, 184-194, 262
Affirmation, self
    through publishing, 237-245, 248-250
Alienation
    from human networks, 235

from the publication process, 24-25, 76
    psychological nature of, 247-248
Allison, G. T., framework for decision making,
    14, 16
Alpha change (innovation), 154, 155
Alternative research. *See* Innovation
American Psychological Association (APA)
    journals of, 254, 270
    women editors in, 18
AMJ. See Academy of Management Journal
AMR. See Academy of Management Review
Analytic scientists, 233
APA. *See* American Psychological Association
ASQ. See Administrative Science Quarterly
Assumptions
    challenging of, 100-101
    for innovative ideas, 285-286
Authors
    advice from a psychiatrist, 249-250
    advice from newcomers, 119-121
    advice from other authors, 204-205,
        216-217
    advice from reviewers, 158-159, 177-181,
        265-266
    advice to, major themes, 313-314
    advocates for, 154, 162, 184-194, 262, 291
    authenticity of, xi, 54
    boredom of, 230, 234-235

Standard operating procedures (SOPs), for
 decision making, 30
Storytelling, 178
Surveys, 136-138

Talent for success, 204, 210-211
Teachers
  role of, 133
  self-affirmation by, 250
Teaching
  newcomers' questions about, 139-141
  research, balanced with, 139-141
  review process effects on, 157
Technical merit
  as a review criterion, 154
  as the ultimate criterion, 154
Temporal factors, for researchers, 109
Tenure. *See* Newcomers
Theory
  as difficult to master, 182
  as driver of research, 86
  data collection versus, 223-224
  extensions of, 101
  lack of, in manuscripts, 166-167, 174
  misaligned with research design, 167-168,
   174-176, 179
  organizational, 4, 30-35, 64-77
  qualities of, 153
  research versus, 207-208
  skills in building of, 176
  use of, 277-279
Time lag for publications, 274
Tone, writing. *See* Writing skills
Transitions in the publishing process
  development of authors, 203-214, 249-250
  development of reviewers, 195-202,
   261-265
  overview of, 108-110
Trigorin (fictional author), 243-244

Umpires, as reviewers, 257-267
Understanding, mutual, 45, 49-50, 60-62
University of Michigan, 207-209
University of Pittsburgh, 207-208
Unrefereed journals, 204, 205-207, 209-214

Values
  diversity of, 132-148
  effect on communication, 52-53
  effect on reviewers, 125-126
  in decision making, 16-17
  neutralization of, 53
  of journals, 143
  of newcomers, 115-116, 130-131, 132-148
Variables
  links between, 87-89
  moderating, 90-91
  overabundance of, 172
Voting strategies, for reviewers, 32-33

WAM. *See* Western Academy of Management
Weick, Karl, editorship of, 212-213
West, Anne, new journal launch, 300
Western Academy of Management (WAM),
 297-305, 308
Women
  as journal editors, 18, 19
  questions from, 122
Workplace setting, 204, 207-209
Writing skills, 254, 264, 272, 313
  amateurism of, 170-171
  as reasons for rejections, 176-177
  exaggeration in, 180-181
  for knowledge production, 55
  importance of, 182, 220
  practicing of, 224-225

Zeitlin, Maurice, controversial article by,
 210-211

About the Contributors

John P. Campbell is Professor of Psychology and Industrial Relations at the University of Minnesota. He received his B.S. (1959) and M.S. (1960) degrees from Iowa State University and his Ph.D. degree (1964) from the University of Minnesota. He is the author of *Managerial Behavior, Performance, and Effectiveness* (with M. Dunnette, E. Lawler, and K. Weick, 1970), *Measurement Theory for the Behavioral Sciences* (with E. Ghiselli and S. Zedeck, 1978), *What to Study: Generating and Developing Research Questions* (with R. Daft and C. Hulin, 1984), and *Productivity in Organizations* (with R. Campbell, 1988).

Gerald L. Clinton is a graduate of the University of Wisconsin (B.A., 1954) and the University of Wisconsin Medical School (M.D., 1957); Psychiatric Residence University Hospitals, Madison. He is a member of the American Psychiatric Association and Associate Clinical Professor in Psychiatry, University of Wisconsin. He practiced in Madison and taught psychiatry at the University of Wisconsin for 25 years and presently is practicing psychotherapy and psychopharmacology at the Jackson Psychiatric Center in Milwaukee.

L. L. Cummings is the Carlson Professor of Strategic Management and Organization at the University of Minnesota. Formerly, he served as the J. L. Kellogg Professor of Organizational Behavior at Northwestern University and as the Slichter Research Professor, H. I. Romnes Faculty Fellow, and Director of Business, University of Wisconsin—Madison. He has also served as Associate Dean of the graduate school there. He teaches and researches in the areas of organizational behavior, organizational theory, personnel, and management. He holds the A.B. (Summa Cum Laude) from Wabash College and the M.B.A. and Ph.D. from Indiana University. In addition, he held a Woodrow Wilson National Graduate Fellowship in Psychology at the University of California, Berkeley, in 1959-1960, a Ford Foundation Faculty Fellowship in organizational behavior at Carnegie-Mellon University in 1964, as well as Ford Foundation and R. D. Irwin Foundation Doctoral Fellowships. He also has taught at Columbia University, Indiana University, and the University of British Columbia. He is the author, coauthor, or editor of 24 books and has published more than 120 journal articles appearing in the *Academy of Management Journal, Administrative Science Quarterly, Journal of Applied Psychological Bulletin,* and other scholarly journals. He has served as a consultant for several national and international corporations. He teaches in several executive seminars and programs and has lectured widely in Europe, Japan, Thailand, Singapore, New Zealand, and South Africa. He is a Fellow of the American Psychological Association, a charter Fellow of the American Psychological Society, and a Fellow of the Decision Sciences Institute and has served as Dean (1990–1993) of the Fellows of the Academy of Management and as a founding member and past chair (1992) of the Society of Organizational Behavior.

Thomas G. Cummings is a leading international scholar on sociotechnical systems and organization development and change. He received B.S. and M.B.A. degrees from Cornell University and a Ph.D. from UCLA. He is currently Professor of Management and Organization at the Graduate School of Business Administration, University of Southern California. He has published more than 50 scholarly articles and 12 books, and is formerly President of the Western Academy of Management and Chair of the Organization Development and Change Division of the Academy of Management. Dr. Cummings is Associate Editor of the *Journal of Organizational Behavior* and Editor-in-chief of the *Journal of Management Inquiry.*

Richard L. Daft holds the Ralph Owen Chair in the Owen Graduate School of Management, Vanderbilt University, where he received his M.B.A and Ph.D. from the University of Chicago, is a Fellow of the Academy of Management, is Associate-Editor-in-chief of *Organization Science,* and served for 3 years as associate editor of *Administrative Science Quarterly.* He wrote *Organization Theory and*

Design, 5th ed. (1995) and *Management,* 3rd ed. (1994), and is currently writing *The Leader Within: Leadership Metamorphosis for Learning Organizations.*

Stanley A. Deetz, Ph.D., is President-Elect of the International Communication Association and Professor of Communication at Rutgers University, New Brunswick, New Jersey. He is author of *Transforming Communication, Transforming Business* (Hampton, 1995), *Democracy in an Age of Corporate Colonization* (SUNY, 1992), and editor or author of eight other books. He has published numerous essays in scholarly journals and books regarding decision making, human relations, and communication in corporate organizations and has lectured widely in the U.S. and Europe. In 1994, he was a Senior Fulbright Scholar in the Företagsekonomiska Institutionen, Göteborgs Universitet, Sweden, lecturing and conducting research on knowledge-intensive workplaces. Additionally, he has served as a consultant on culture, diversity, and decision making for several major corporations.

Peter J. Frost is the Edgar F. Kaiser Chair of Organizational Behaviour and Associate Dean in the Faculty of Commerce and Business Administration at the University of British Columbia. He has published several books and articles on organizational culture and leadership including *Reframing Organizational Culture.* He has published articles on the politics of innovation. He has recently coauthored a book on the research process titled *Doing Exemplary Research* and published the fourth edition of a practitioner-oriented book titled *Organizational Reality: Reports From the Firing Line.* With Bob Marx and Todd Jick, he published the first management textbook that fully integrates video and written material for students, *Management Live: The Video Book.* He is currently working on a book with Susan Taylor titled *Rhythms of Academic Life* and one with Rae Andre tentatively titled *The Teaching Experience.* He is a senior editor of *Organization Science.*

Alan M. Glassman is Professor of Management at California State University, Northridge. He received his doctorate in Labor Relations with minor areas in Social Psychology and Organizational Theory/Behavior from the State University of New York at Buffalo. He has been a mediator for the New York State Public Employment Relations Board and has been a Visiting Faculty member at the Graduate School of Business, University of Southern California. His research interests focus on the expanding role of organizational development in the public sector, privatization of government services, and the management of change. He has authored/coauthored or edited four books: *The Challenge of Management,*

Labor Relations: A Multidimensional View, Labor Relations: Reports From the Firing Line, and *Cases in Organizational Development.*

Jill W. Graham is Associate Professor of Management at Loyola University Chicago, where she teaches the capstone strategy course to both undergraduate and MBA students. Her research concerns various forms of virtue in organizational life, including principled dissent, organizational citizenship behavior, activist loyalty, servant leadership, and value-driven strategic management. She received her Ph.D. in organization behavior from Northwestern University in 1983, where she was an advisee of L. L. Cummings. As an assistant professor at the University of British Columbia from 1983-1986, she learned how to teach from Peter Frost. Graham has been part of the Loyola faculty since 1986.

Alan D. Meyer is the Edwin E. and June Woldt Cone Professor of Management in the Charles H. Lundquist College of Business at the University of Oregon. He received his doctorate in organizational behavior and industrial relations from the University of California, Berkeley. He is currently the Senior Editor of organization theory and design for *Organization Science,* and a former Consulting Editor for *Academy of Management Journal.* He likes using multiple research methods and collecting data by talking with informants on their own turf. He is interested in organizational behavior away from the equilibrium, and is currently studying the impacts of quantum changes in the structure and boundaries of health care, electric utility, and savings and loan industries. Before entering academia, he worked as an industrial engineer, a market researcher, and a ski instructor.

Walter Nord is currently Professor of Management at the University of South Florida. Previously, he was at Washington University–St. Louis (1967–1989). His current interests center on developing a critical political economics perspective of organizations, organizational innovation, and organizational conflict. He has published widely in scholarly journals and edited/authored a number of book. His recent books include *The Meanings of Occupational Work* (with A. Brief), *Implementing Routine and Radical Innovations* (with S. Tucker), *Organizational Reality: Reports From the Firing Line* (with P. Frost and V. Mitchell), and *Resistance and Power in Organizations* with J. Jermier and D. Knights). He is currently coeditor of *Employee Responsibilities and Rights Journal.*

Michael Pacanowsky is an Associate Professor in the Department of Communication at the University of Colorado. He was coeditor, with Linda L. Putnam, of

Communication and Organizations: An Interpretive Approach (1983). He has published fiction in *The Canadian Fiction Magazine* and *The Chicago Review.*

Charles Perrow (Ph.D., Sociology, University of California at Berkeley) is an organizational theorist with a decided bias toward "power" explanations encumbered by the vagaries of historical contingency and bounded rationality. Presently holding on at Yale, where they threatened to close the Sociology Department, he has had to leave several universities: Michigan, Pittsburgh, Wisconsin, and SUNY at Stony Brook. His current project, titled *A Society of Organizations,* is the history of industrialization in the United States conceived organizationally as a normal accident, a project much delayed as he reflects on recent accidents in occasional papers.

Louis R. Pondy received his Ph.D. in Industrial Administration from Carnegie-Mellon University in 1966. He began his academic career at the University of Pittsburgh, followed by a 5-year appointment at Duke University. He was hired as a full professor at the University of Illinois in 1973, where he remained until his death in 1986. As an academic scholar, he was a highly respected contributor to the field's understanding of organizational conflict, behavioral aspects of budgeting and resource allocation, health systems research, organizational structure and design, and phenomenological approaches to organizations.

Raymond L. Price is currently employed with Hewlett-Packard and has worked in the Management Training and Development Department, recently as manager of Management and Employee Development. In these positions, Ray has attempted to identify improved methods of management and use these methods to implement organizational changes. Ray received his Ph.D. in organizational behavior from Stanford's Graduate School of Business and his M.A. and B.S. from Brigham Young University.

Vivian M. Rakoff is Professor Emeritus of Psychiatry at the University of Toronto. He was born in South Africa and received his Master's degree in Psychology at the University of Cape Town. After completing his medical degree at the University of London, he trained in psychiatry at McGill University. His major interests include the family, addiction, and adolescence. In addition, he has written plays, talks, and book reviews for radio and television.

Elaine Romanelli is Associate Professor of Management at the Georgetown University School of Business. Her research focuses on entrepreneurship as a key dynamic in both the strategic development of organizations and the evolution of industry competitive structures. Her current research focuses on the international biotechnology industry and the U.S. motion picture production industry. Both studies are longitudinal using data going back to the inceptions of the industries. Professor Romanelli has published articles in *Administrative Science Quarterly, Academy of Management Journal, Organization Science,* and *Research in Organizational Behavior,* among other outlets. She received her Ph.D. in management from Columbia University.

Denise M. Rousseau is a Professor of Organization Behavior and Public Policy at Carnegie-Mellon University. She has been a faculty member at Northwestern University, the University of Michigan, and the Naval Postgraduate School (Monterey). Her research addresses the impact of work group processes on performance and the changing psychological contract at work. Rousseau is the author of more than 60 articles that have appeared in prominent academic journals, such as *Journal of Applied Psychology, Academy of Management Review,* and *Administrative Science Quarterly.* Her books include *Promises in Action: Contracts in Organizations, Trends in Organizational Behavior* with Cary Cooper, and *Developing an Interdisciplinary Science of Organizations* with Karlene Roberts and Charles Hulin.

Benjamin Schneider is Professor of Psychology and Business Management and Research Professor in the Center for Innovation at the University of Maryland, where he has been, off and on, since 1964. He received his Ph.D. there in 1967, then went to Yale to learn more, returning to College Park in 1971. He has consulted on long-term research projects with Citicorp, AT&T, JCPenney Co., and GEICO, and many of his publications have come about as a result of these relationships.

F. David Schoorman is an Associate Professor of Organizational Behavior and Human Resource Management and Director of the M.S. program in Human Resource Management at Purdue's Krannert Graduate School of Management. He received his M.S. in 1978 and Ph.D. in 1983 from Carnegie-Mellon University. His teaching interests include organizational behavior, organization theory, and research methods, and he is a regular instructor in Krannert's Executive Education programs. His current research interests include organizational effectiveness, decision making, work teams, and trust. He is coeditor of the book *Facilitating Work Effectiveness* and the author of numerous book chapters and journal articles. He currently serves on the editorial board of the *Journal of Applied Psychology.*

Ralph E. Stablein is Associate Professor on the Faculty of Commerce and Business Administration, Otago University, New Zealand. His research interests center on individual work motivation and related organizational systems. He earned his Ph.D. in organizational behavior from Northwestern University in 1984.

Barry M. Staw is a Professor of Organizational Behavior and Industrial Relations at the University of California, Berkeley. He has taught previously at Northwestern University, the University of Illinois, and the University of Iowa. His research has focused on issues of organizational commitment, decision making, and job attitudes.

Mary S. Strine, Associate Professor of Communication at the University of Utah, teaches in the area of interpretive and critical studies. She is the author of reviews and articles on modern critical theory, the rhetoric of cultural forms, and the relationship between American literature and culture, which have appeared in various national and regional journals.

Ronald N. Taylor holds the George R. Brown Professorship in the Jesse H. Jones Graduate School of Administration and is Professor of Psychology at Rice University. He received his Ph.D. in Psychology at the University of Minnesota in Industrial and Organizational Psychology. Prior to joining the faculty of Rice University in 1982, he taught for 13 years at the University of British Columbia, where he was a Professor in the Faculty of Commerce. In addition to professional positions at Northern Natural Gas Company, Deere and Company, and North Star Research Institute, he has consulted with a wide variety of firms. His research investigates behavioral aspects of managerial decision making and strategic planning.

Karl E. Weick, who is the Rensis Likert Collegiate Professor of Organizational Behavior and Psychology at the University of Michigan, is also the former editor of *Administrative Science Quarterly.* He was trained in Psychology at Ohio State University, where he received his Ph.D. in 1962. Since graduating from Ohio State, he has been with the faculties at Purdue University, The University of Minnesota, Cornell University, and the University of Texas. He studies topics such as how people make sense of confusing events, the social psychology of improvisation, high-reliability systems, the effects of stress on thinking and imagination, indeterminacy in social systems, social commitment, small wins as the embodiment of wisdom, and linkages between theory and practice.

Printed in the United Kingdom
by Lightning Source UK Ltd.
108028UKS00003B/76-93